Chronicles of Wasted Time

Part 1: The Green Stick

MALCOLM MUGGERIDGE

Chronicles of Wasted Time

1
The Green Stick

I used to believe that there was a green stick, buried on the edge of a ravine in the old Zakaz forest at Yasnaya Polyana, on which words were carved that would destroy all the evil in the hearts of men and bring them everything good.

– Leo Tolstoy

COLLINS

St James's Place, London

1972

William Collins Sons & Co Ltd
London · Glasgow · Sydney · Auckland
Toronto · Johannesburg

First published September 1972
Reprinted September 1972
© Malcolm Muggeridge 1972

ISBN 0 00 215119 7

Set in Monotype Imprint

Made and printed in Great Britain by
William Collins Sons & Co Ltd Glasgow

LONG AGO I copied out from a Life of the French sculptor, Rodin, a letter he addressed to his wife, Rose, dated 24 August, 1913. It occurs to me now that in it he says to her exactly what I should wish to say to my wife, Kitty, and that there could be no better place for saying it than here. So, transposing the names:

My dear Kitty,
   This letter is just to tell you that my mind is full of the greatness of God's gift to me when He put you at my side. Keep this thought of mine in your generous heart.

Your,
M.

Contents

1 A Part in Search of a Play   *page* 11

2 A Socialist Upbringing   23

3 Twilight of Empire   92

4 The Pursuit of Righteousness   131

5 Who Whom?   205

Index   277

1 *A Part in Search of a Play*

Nous ne vivons jamais, mais nous espérons de vivre; et, nous dis-
posant toujours à être heureux, il est inévitable que nous le soyons
jamais.

– Pascal

WE COMMUNICATORS – vendors of words, to use St Augustine's expression – tend to accumulate a lot of waste matter as we go along. I
mean press-cuttings, maybe pasted up in books, or just stuffed into
envelopes; old letters, whether of personal significance, recording some
moment of ostensible drama in one's life, or from unknown correspondents, flattering or abusive (television appearances bring in sackfuls
of these), in both cases ministering to one's self-esteem. Books once
considered to be of special interest, or just review copies for some reason
unsold to the knackers; for that matter, one's own books, still standing
in tattered dust-jackets on one's shelves. Photographs, souvenirs,
presentations, certificates; even – a mania of my own – all the different
passes, *laissez-passers*, visas and other such documents needed to make
one's way about this increasingly obstructed world. The rags and
tatters of a professionally exhibitionist ego. After half a century in the
business, I have a mountain of such junk.

The fact that I have allowed these, what the French police call
pièces justificatives, to accumulate at all, indicates, I suppose, that I
attach a certain value to them, and have an intention some day to sort
them out and arrange them chronologically with a view to their preservation, maybe at some American university, grateful for any pabulum
to fill its air-conditioned, dust-and-damp-proof vaults. I doubt, though,
whether I shall ever bring myself to undertake the task. The odds are I
shall die with it still undone, and I see no reason why anyone else should
bother with it. Unless my beloved Kitty, if she outlives me (as I pray
she may, rather than leaving me, desolate, behind), were for love of me
to cherish them, staple or sew them together, and stow them away in

boxes in her neat, methodical way. Then perhaps one of my children or grandchildren might subsequently have a look at them. Or flog them for what they would fetch – which would not, I fear, be much; apart from an occasional signature or letter from someone distinguished enough to be considered worthy of 'collecting' in the saleroom sense. My years of journalism have, in any case, inculcated in me a strong and, as I consider, on the whole salutory resistance to re-reading or re-considering anything done earlier than yesterday. With a few special exceptions, I have had no wish to renew acquaintance with my past writings, whether published or unpublished. Even when they have been re-issued, I have not cared to revise them, or, if the truth be told, read them. That mysterious saying *Let the dead bury their dead* applies, as far as I am concerned, with particular force to words, which exist like insects in the tropics, buzzing briefly round a hurricane lamp and then piling up in dead heaps on the ground.

Nonetheless, from the very beginning of my life I never doubted that words were my *métier*. There was nothing else I ever wanted to do except use them; no other accomplishment or achievement I ever had the slightest regard for, or desire to emulate. I have always loved words, and still love them, for their own sake. For the power and beauty of them; for the wonderful things that can be done with them. I had a memorable example of this once when I was in Darwin, Australia. A message came to me that a man in hospital there had expressed a wish to see me. It seemed he had heard something I said on the radio that had taken his fancy. So I went along. He turned out to be a wizened old fellow who had spent much of his life in the bush, and now was obviously soon going to die. Also, he was quite blind. At first, I just couldn't think of anything to say and felt the silent reproach of his dead eyes. Then, suddenly, there came into my mind what Gloucester says in *King Lear* when Edgar commiserates with him on his blindness – 'I stumbled when I saw.' Just five simple, ordinary words, but the effect was immediate and terrific. My man loved them, and kept saying them over and over. As I went out of the ward I could hear him still repeating them in a loud, joyous voice: 'I stumbled when I saw.'

So, as a child, a writer was in my eyes a kind of god; any writer, no matter how obscure, or even bogus, he might be. To compare a writer with some famous soldier or administrator or scientist or politician or actor was, in my estimation, quite ludicrous. There was no basis for comparison; any more than between, say, Francis of Assisi and Dr Spock. Perhaps more aware of this passion than I realised, when I was still a schoolboy my father took me to a dinner at a Soho restaurant at which G. K. Chesterton was being entertained. I remember that the proprietor of the restaurant presented me with a box of crystallised fruits which turned out to be bad. As far as I was concerned, it was an occasion of inconceivable glory. I observed with fascination the enormous bulk of the guest of honour, his great stomach and plump hands; how his pince-nez on a black ribbon were almost lost in the vast expanse of his face, and how when he delivered himself of what he considered to be a good remark he had a way of blowing into his moustache with a sound like an expiring balloon. His speech, if he made one, was lost on me, but I vividly recall how I persuaded my father to wait outside the restaurant while we watched the great man make his way down the street in a billowing black cloak and old-style bohemian hat with a large brim. I only saw him once again. That was years later, shortly before he died, when on a windy afternoon he was sitting outside the Ship Hotel at Brighton, and clutching to himself a thriller in a yellow jacket. It, too, like the pince-nez, seemed minute by comparison with his immensity. By that time, the glory of the earlier occasion had departed.

Long before I could read them, or even properly identify the letters, I used to turn over the pages of my father's books. Also, I regularly scrutinised our newspaper, the *Daily News*, more particularly because my father told me it had once been edited by Dickens, though its contents, too, were largely as mysterious to me as Egyptian hieroglyphics. I even remember the arrival of the first issue of the *New Statesman*, my father being an original subscriber. Its rather soggy paper – almost like blotting-paper – could, I discovered, be used to make ersatz cigarettes. I puffed at it before I began to read it, still less to write in it, deriving, I dare say, more solid satisfaction from it then than ever I did subsequently. On one of my early birthdays I was given a toy printing-set with whose large rubber letters I was able to print off my first composition. It was a story of a train going along very fast and, to the satisfaction of the passengers, racing through the small stations along the track without stopping. Their satisfaction, however, turned to dismay, and then to panic fury, as it dawned on them that it was not going to stop at *their* stations either when it came to them. They raged and shouted and shook their fists, but all to no avail. The train went roaring on. At the time I had no notion what, if anything, the story signified. It just came into my mind, and the rubber letters dropped into place of themselves. Yet, as I came to see, and see now more clearly than ever, it is the story I have been writing ever since; the story of our time. The imagination, at however rudimentary a level, reaches into the future. So its works have a prophetic quality. A Dostoevsky foresees just what a revolution will mean in Russia – in a sense, foresees the Soviet regime and Stalin; whereas a historian like Miliukov and his liberal-intellectual friends envisage the coming to pass of an amiable parliamentary democracy. Similarly, a Blake or a Herman Melville sees clearly through the imagination the dread consequences industrialism and technology must have for mankind, whereas, as envisaged in the mind of a Herbert Spencer or an H. G. Wells, they can bring only expanding wealth and lasting well-being. It was not until much later that I came to identify the passengers in my train as Lord Beveridge, Sidney and Beatrice Webb, Kingsley Martin, Eleanor Roosevelt, and any number of progressive prelates, mahatmas, millionaires, regius professors and other such eminent persons.

Words being my single pursuit, I have to accept my output of them as being, as it were, my gross personal product. And what an output! – millions and millions, on all manner of subjects and in all manner of contexts. Declamatory leading articles and little ridiculous gossip paragraphs; sonorous obituaries, news stories of all shapes and sizes; miscellaneous book reviews, feature articles, captions, commentaries and scripts. If, after aeons of time in hell or heaven or purgatory, I were to be asked what earthly life was like, I should still, I am sure, say it was a sheet of paper fixed in a typewriter and needing to be covered with words; not to-morrow, or next week, or next year, but *now*. I should say it was a clapper-board snapped to, followed by a peremptory voice pronouncing the word: 'Action!' A floor-manager's hand raised, then dramatically falling; a camera advancing with bloodshot eye. Voice, hand and camera equally demanding instant words.

Surveying now this monstrous Niagara of words so urgently called for and delivered, I confess they signify to me a lost life. Possibilities vaguely envisaged but never realised. A light glimpsed, only to disappear. Something vaguely caught, as it might be distant music or an elusive fragrance; something full of enchantment and the promise of ecstasy. Far, far away, and yet near; at the very farthermost rim of time and space, and in the palm of my hand. In any case, whether strained after in the remote distance, or reached for near at hand – unattained. No light seen more enduring than a match flickering out in a dark cave. No lasting ecstasy experienced, only a door closed, and footsteps echoing ever more faintly down stone stairs.

I am not for one moment suggesting, let me hasten to add, that this sense of a lost life is due to there being no *Times Literary Supplement*-certified or Leavis-sanctified *Oeuvre* among my remains. My grave is quiet; I have no regrets for masterpieces unwritten, for genius unfulfilled. It has long seemed abundantly clear to me that I was born into a dying, if not already dead, civilisation, whose literature was part of the general decomposition; a heap of rubble scavenged by scrawny Eng.Lit. vultures, and echoing with the hyena cries of Freudians looking for their Marx and Marxists looking for their Freud. This, despite adam's apples quivering over winged collars to extol it, and money, money, money, printed off and stuffed into briefcases to finance it. At the beginning of a civilisation, the role of the artist is priestly; at the end, harlequinade. From St Augustine to St Ezra Pound, from Plainsong to the Rolling Stones, from El Greco to Picasso, from Chartres to the Empire State Building, from Benvenuto Cellini to Henry Miller, from Pascal's *Pensées* to Robinson's *Honest to God*. A Gadarene descent down which we all must slide, finishing up in the same slough.

By the same token, a strange certainty has possessed me, almost since I can remember, that the Lord Mayor riding in his coach, the Lord Chancellor seated on his Woolsack, Honourable and Right Honourable Members facing one another across the floor of the House of Commons, were somehow the end of a line. That soon there would be no more Lord Mayors, Lord Chancellors, Honourable and Right Honourable Members, the Mother of Parliaments having reached her time of life or menopause, and become incapable of any further procreation. That figure in a velvet-trimmed gown with a floppy black hat on his head leading a procession of familiar celebrities similarly attired – he can't really be a Vice-Chancellor, can he? Any more than that red-tabbed one is a general. Or that braided one an admiral. Surely the old gentleman in the purple cassock so weirdly grimacing – surely he's an extra, hurriedly fitted out by the wardrobe mistress at the last moment and pushed on to the stage. Even the cash – yes, even the cash – so eagerly or earnestly accumulated and stowed away in the great bank-refrigerators, won't last; there's been a power-cut, the electric current has gone off, and it's melting away.

As for literature and the arts, as cherished by Jennie Lee, and nestling under Lord Goodman's downy wing, listen to the *Missa Solemnis* after the Beatles, and be thankful to Cage for his soundless concertos and symphonies. Likewise, render hearty thanks to Beckett for his wordless, actionless, mindless play after taking a look at *Oh Calcutta!* Corbusier's high-rises are sweet, but those unbuilt are sweeter. After Bacon's canvases, blessings on those empty ones trendy curators delight to buy for vast sums of money and hang in their galleries! Where are the Parnassians of yesteryear; the dear, drunken Americans gathering in Paris at the Shakespeare Bookshop with Sylvia Beach to care for them, Gertrude Stein or Alice B. Toklas to bore them? Or drying out their hangovers in the Riviera sun? Alas, poor Scott, and poorer Zelda, and Ernest with a self-made hole in his head; the only shot he ever fired that found its target! Whether back into the dark unconscious with Lawrence, or to the end of the night with Céline; whether forward with Marcuse, or sideways with McLuhan, or all over the place with Sartre – no matter. Existentialists of the world uniting, and old Shaw lighting the way to the Good Fabian, Stalin. Oh, Brecht, where is thy sting?

Doubtless other glories lie ahead. Bigger and better capsules carried to the moon; down in the test-tube something stirs; 'I think, therefore, you're not,' says the computer. We all know, though, in our hearts, that our old homestead is falling down; with death-watch beetles in the rafters, and dry rot in the cellar, and unruly tenants whose only concern is to pull the place to pieces. Thus placed, my own inclination has been to join in the buffoonery, but the more scholastically inclined may emulate T. S. Eliot and construct a Wasteland out of bits and pieces culled from Donne, Milton and many a metaphysical compilation. As the Romans, when they were no longer capable of constructing triumphal arches, would still erect one to celebrate some fraudulent hero's home-coming, using for their material bits and pieces taken from old fallen triumphal arches put up in the days of Rome's greatness.

Nor is my sense of a lost life due to repining over opportunities missed, hopes unrealised, happiness vainly pursued. There are no human causes I wish I had served better, no wonders I wish I had seen, no women I wish I had seduced – or, for that matter, wish I had not seduced; no books I wish I had read, languages I wish I had learnt; no events whose outcome I wish I could know. I have never greatly cared for the world, or felt particularly at home in it. Just walking along the road we lived in when I was a child I would find myself wondering, with a poignancy I find it difficult now to convey, who I was and how I came to be in that place. As though it were a foreign land and I a stranger, knowing no one and unable to speak the language. On occasions later, when I was in some sort of position of authority – say, in an editorial chair – I found myself likewise wondering how it could possibly have happened that decisions should be referred to, of all people, me. As it might be looking at dummies or roughs of drawings, finding things to say – I like it, I don't much care for it, it might be better thus and thus. Ultimately deciding to go with that and that rather than that and the other; but lacking any true conviction or involvement. Not truly participating, even though ostensibly deciding.

Again, in the ultimate fantasy of war, wondering: What's that on my shoulder? Pips? A crown? Hands raised to their caps to salute me, mine raised to salute others. Why? Or yet again, in the even more ultimate fantasy of sex – Whose is this body lying beside mine? To what end? How did it get here? How, for that matter, did I? Watching my own body making bizarre movements, emitting strange groans, in relation to this other body, as though I were in no way concerned. Like seeing oneself on television – a figure on a screen, a stranger, a speaking shadow whose words seem to come out of some immense cave; dry and remote and dead. In this sense, it is possible to look back on a life as so much footage. Or, better – a scene that has often come into my mind, both sleeping and waking – I am standing in the wings of a theatre waiting for my cue to go on stage. As I stand there I can hear the play proceeding, and suddenly it dawns on me that the lines I have learnt are not in this play at all, but belong to a quite different one. Panic seizes me; I wonder frenziedly what I should do. Then I get my cue. Stumbling, falling over the unfamiliar scenery, I make my way on to the stage, and there look for guidance to the prompter, whose head I can just see rising out of the floor-boards. Alas, he only signals helplessly to me, and I realise that of course his script is different from mine. I begin to speak my lines, but they are incomprehensible to the other actors and abhorrent to the audience, who begin to hiss and shout: 'Get off the stage!' 'Let the play go on!' 'You're interrupting!' I am paralysed and can think of nothing to do but to go on standing there and speaking my lines that don't fit. The only lines I know.

There are so many plays to have a part in. As it might be a great love scene; flesh to flesh, and eternity in your eyes. Nonsense! That comes from *Antony and Cleopatra*. Or a great drama of action; firing off-stage, alarums and excursions, a dashing salute. 'Sir, I caught the spy!' Nonsense, again! Leave that to Fleming. Or a political satire, Trollopian, Disraelian, with the part of an *eminence grise* for me. Or rather, *déclivité*. No, that will never do either; render unto Snow the things that are Snow's. Or a majestic voice on the telly – a voice, though, that is for ever Dimbleby. Or a typewriter mightier than the sword; meaning Don Quixote's, of course. So many and so varied plays, but never a one with my lines in it. Yet I remain ever more convinced that

C.W.T.—B

at last I shall find the play my lines belong to, and speak them. Like choristers waiting to sing; hearing unfamiliar music rumbling from the organ; poised ready, and then – the notes they are waiting for, the tune they know. Uplifted, their faces shining and glorious, they pour out their song, filling the air with confident, full-throated notes.

How can I ever explain to those who insist that we must believe in the world to love it that it is *because* I disbelieve in the world that I love every breath I take, look forward with ever-greater delight to the coming of each spring, rejoice ever more in the companionship of my fellow-humans, to no single one of whom – searching my heart – do I wish ill, and from no single one of whom do I wish to separate myself, in word or thought or deed, or in the prospect of some other existence beyond the ticking of the clocks, the vista of the hills, the bounds and dimensions of our earthly hopes and desires? To accept this world as a destination rather than a staging-post, and the experience of living in it as expressing life's full significance, would seem to me to reduce life to something too banal and trivial to be taken seriously or held in esteem. The only thing that could make me falter in taking a position of extreme, if not de-mented, optimism about our human condition and prospects would be if one of the prospectuses for an earthly paradise – whether Scandi-navian-Styled, British-Beveridge, old Stalin-Ware, Dollar-Reinforced, Mao-Special, Tito- or Castro-ised – looked like providing a satisfying or fulfilled way of life. On this score I see no cause for present anxiety. To attempt to expose and ridicule the fraudulence of such prospectuses is no more life-denying than exposing the fraudulence of one for building a housing estate on the slopes of Etna would be shelter-denying.

In other words, the Christian proposition that he that loves his life in this world shall lose it, and he that hates his life in this world shall see it projected and glorified into eternity, is for living, not for dying. After all, it was a St Francis who truly loved the world he so gaily abjured, as his enchanting prayers and canticles convey; not a Père Goriot who so cherished its commodities. It is misers and Don Juans who moan; spendthrifts and saints are always laughing. As the writer of Ecclesiastes so delightfully puts it: 'For to him that is joined to all the living there is hope; for a living dog is better than a dead lion.' All I can claim to have learnt from the years I have spent in this world is that the only happiness is love, which is attained by giving, not receiving; and that the world itself only becomes the dear and habitable dwelling place it is when we who inhabit it know we are migrants, due when the time comes to fly away to other more commodious skies.

I have never, I should add, learnt anything from any exhortation or homily; any political, ethical, theological or philosophical exposition; any presentation in any form of plans, programmes or blue-prints for happy living. Nor from any supernatural visitation or sudden Damascus Road prostration. Only from the experience of living itself, or – what is the same thing – the distillation of that experience in the visions of mystics and the productions of great writers and artists. Learning from experience means, in practice, learning from suffering; the only school-master. Everyone knows that this is so, even though they try to persuade themselves and their fellows otherwise. Only so is it possible to understand how it came about that, through all the Christian centuries, people have been prepared to accept the Cross, ostensibly a symbol of suffering, as the true image and guarantee of their creator's love and concern for them. To climb the highest, stoniest mountain to set it on its peak; to carry it to the remotest, darkest, most forbidding corners of the earth; to build great cathedrals to glorify it; to find in it the inspiration for the most sublime achievements and noblest lives over the last two thousand years.

'I desire to set before my fellows the likeness of a man in all truth of nature, and that man myself,' Rousseau begins his *Confessions*, and then proceeds to construct a vast, serpentine edifice of lies and fantasies. The hazards in the way of telling the truth are, indeed, very great. Seeking it, one can so easily become enmeshed in lies; 'A truth that's told with bad intent/Beats all the lies you can invent,' Blake wrote. Every man the centre of his own universe; insensibly, we sub-edit as we go along, to produce headlines, cross-heads, a story line most favourable to our egos. How indestructible, alas, is that ego! Thinking to have struck it down once and for all, I find its hissing cobra-head lifted again, deathless.

Yet even so, truth is very beautiful; more so, as I consider, than justice – to-day's pursuit – which easily puts on a false face. In the nearly seven decades I have lived through, the world has overflowed with bloodshed and explosions whose dust has never had time to settle before others have erupted; all in purportedly just causes. The quest for justice continues, and the weapons and the hatred pile up; but truth was an early casualty. The lies on behalf of which our wars have been fought and our peace treaties concluded! The lies of revolution and of counter-revolution! The lies of advertising, of news, of salesmanship, of politics! The lies of the priest in his pulpit, the professor at his podium, the journalist at his typewriter! The lie stuck like a fish-bone in the throat of the microphone, the hand-held lies of the prowling cameraman! Ignazio Silone told me once how, when he was a member of the old Comintern, some stratagem was under discussion, and a delegate, a newcomer who had never attended before, made the extraordinary observation that if such and such a statement were to be put out, it wouldn't be true. There was a moment of dazed silence,and then everyone began to laugh. They laughed and laughed until tears ran down their cheeks and the Kremlin walls seemed to shake. The same laughter echoes in every council chamber and cabinet room, wherever two or more are gathered together to exercise authority. It is truth that has died, not God.

I often wonder how, in such circumstances, it will ever be possible to know anything at all about the people and the happenings of our time. Such masses and masses of documentation! Statistics without end, data of every kind, eye-witness accounts, miles and miles of film, video abounding. Surely out of all this, posterity, if so desiring, will be able to reconstruct us and our lives. But will they? I think of Sidney and Beatrice Webb down at Passfield patiently collecting and collating every scrap of information they could lay hands on about the Soviet regime. Travelling about the USSR to the same end. As experienced investigators, so rigorous and careful. Checking every fact, testing every hypothesis. And the result? – a monumental folly, a volume of fantasy compared with which Casanova's Memoirs, Frank Harris's even, are sober and realistic. Or I think of the messages of Our Own Correspondent, here, there and everywhere, and of all the different factors which shape them and slant them and confection them. I remember the yellow ticker-tape piling up in my office in the Washington National Press Building, and delving into it to pull out a nugget to whisk off on my own account to New York and London. Will this be much help to posterity? I doubt it. Comment is free, but news is sacred, was C. P. Scott's great dictum for *The Guardian*. Yes, but whose news?

> This Life's dim Windows of the Soul
> Distorts the Heavens from Pole to Pole
> And leads you to Believe a Lie
> When you see with, not thro', the Eye.

There never have been such adepts at seeing with, rather than through, the eye, as the purveyors of Scott's sacred news; inducing their readers, all too willingly, to believe a multitude of lies.

Or, again, I think of a camera crew on the job. Sound recordist and

cameraman umbilically linked as they back away from their commentator, sedately walking and communing; their producer anxiously
hovering behind to prevent them from stumbling and falling. Moving
with a kind of *pas-de-deux* step, rather like a matador approaching his
bull. Are they holding a mirror up to nature? Cinema *verité* or *falsité*?
Where's the plastic grass? Or, as I once saw written on a can of film –
surely the perfect celluloid epitaph: 'Dawn for dusk.' The eye is the
window of the soul; film an iron-shutter, says Kafka. On the day that
Harold Wilson became Prime Minister for the first time, I happened to
be in Chicago, and stood in Michigan Avenue with a camera crew and
a microphone asking passers-by what they thought about him and our
change of government. To my great satisfaction, I was unable to find
anyone, old or young, black or white, smart or stupid, who had heard
of the event or cared anything about it. Behind where I was questioning
them, up above the *Tribune* Building, there was one of those devices
whereby news flashes by in fiery letters. Every minute or so it repeated:
DOUGLAS-HOME RESIGNS . . . HAROLD WILSON NEW BRITISH
PREMIER . . . A fine background to cut to! In Moscow when the great
purges were on, some moon-faced Intourist, trying in good liberal style
to be fair to both sides, asked one of the British newspaper correspondents there – A. T. Cholerton of the *Daily Telegraph* – whether the
accusations against the Old Bolsheviks standing trial were true. Yes,
Cholerton told him, everything was true, except the facts. It fits, not
just the purges and Moscow, but the whole mid-twentieth century
scene. Perhaps some astronaut, watching from afar the final incinera-
tion of our earth, may care to write it across the stratosphere: *Everything
true except the facts.*

Yet again, supposing a wish on the part of posterity to know what
some of our great ones were really like. John F. Kennedy, say. In the
archives, trainloads of material. Photographs and profiles without end;
abundance of tape, both video and sound. We can show you him smiling,
walking, talking. On stage and off, as it were; relaxing with his family,
addressing the nation, eating, dozing, praying. We have his jokes, we
know the books he read; you can see and hear him delivering his great
speeches, or fooling with his kids. You can pretty well see him being
assassinated; you *can* see his assassin being assassinated. What more do
you want? Isn't that the man, the whole man, and nothing but the man?
Well, not quite. It's like a nightmare I once had. I was calling on someone I loved dearly; the door open, the kettle boiling, a chair drawn up
to the fire, a book open, spectacles laid beside it. But no one there.

Maybe upstairs. With growing anxiety I climb the stairs. Not in the bedroom, though clothes are scattered about; not in the bathroom, though it's still moist and misty from a bath recently taken. Downstairs again; really terrified now. Maybe gone to post a letter. To exercise the dog. Listening for every footstep, starting at every sound, the tension becomes unbearable, and I wake up. In the same sort of way, our methods of representation include every detail, leaving out only the person to be represented. In a sense, they're too perfect. Simulation becomes what it simulates; the image becomes the man. In Kennedy's case, even his signature was done for him by a machine which so exactly reproduced the hand signing his name that experts cannot distinguish between his real signature and the mechanical ones. In the excitement and distress of the Dallas tragedy, no one remembered to turn the machine off. So the President went on signing genial, 'personalised' letters after he was dead.

In this Sargasso Sea of fantasy and fraud, how can I or anyone else hope to swim unencumbered? How see with, not through, the eye? How take off my own motley, wash away the make-up, raise the iron shutter, put out the studio lights, silence the sound effects and put the cameras to sleep? Watch the sun rise on Sunset Boulevard, and set over Forest Lawn? Find furniture among the studio props, silence in a discotheque, love in a strip-tease? Read truth off an autocue, catch it on a screen, chase it on the wings of *Muzak*? View it in living colour with the news, hear it in living sound along the motorways? Not in the wind that rent the mountains and broke in pieces the rocks; not in the earthquake that followed, nor in the fire that followed the earthquake. In a still small voice. Not in the screeching of tyres, either, or in the grinding of brakes; not in the roar of the jets or the whistle of sirens; not in the howl of trombones, the rattle of drums or the chanting of demo voices. Again, that still small voice – if only one could catch it.

2 *A Socialist Upbringing*

The world will become a heavenly commune to which men will bring the inmost treasures of their hearts, in which they will reserve for themselves not even a hope, not even the shadow of a joy, but will give up all for mankind. With one faith, with one desire, they will labour together in the sacred cause – the extinction of disease, the extinction of sin, the perfection of genius, the perfection of love, the invention of immortality, the exploration of the infinite, and the conquest of creation.

– The Martyrdom of Man, by Winwood Reade

MY LIFE BEGAN in a small semi-detached house in Sanderstead, part of the dormitory town of Croydon. This was in 1903, when there were still traces of its village past. A drinking-trough for horses, for instance, an ancient churchyard, and other such intimations of antiquity. But already the tidal wave of London was sweeping over the place, so that soon it would just be part of a single huge urban area, with no difference between one district and another save the postal address and the name of the railway station. In this urban conglomerate I was born and bred. My brothers and I – we were five boys – were brought up to look with distaste on the suburbia which was our native habitat. It was mean and foolish, like the Pooters in *The Diary of a Nobody*; and came under the general anathema of being *petit-bourgeois* which, in the vague Marxism which provided our theology, signified contemptible, despicable. We would say of someone we disliked that he was *petit-bourgeois* in precisely the same way that middle- or upper-class boys at that time would say he was under-bred. This attitude bred in us – or at least in me – a sort of social schizophrenia; we were snobs in relation to our neighbours, and anti-snobs in relation to those above and below us in the social scale. I know that I had a dream fantasy of a 'real worker' sitting in braces in front of a roaring fire and drinking cups of strong tea which his missus had just prepared for him. A Hoggartian figure straight out of *Sons and Lovers*; illiterate, maybe, but gloriously so, putting to shame the literate with the pungency and grace of his utterance and ways. The salt of the earth. Likewise, of a 'real gentleman', contemptuous of the paltry hopes and timidities of suburban gentility; a Steerforth figure, or Brushwood Boy, audacious, arrogant perhaps, and too conscious of his own superiority, but still someone worth emulating, even though, at the same time, packing him off in a tumbril.

Between these two dream fantasies lay the suburban no-man's-land in which we lived. Hateful, despicable, ridiculous; little houses with preposterous names like The Elms, Chez-Nous, The Nook; with tradesmen's entrances when there was scarcely room for a tolerable front door, and mock-Tudor beams and gables. I discovered in the Blitz, rather to my surprise, that my hatred of this environment of my childhood had survived, to the point that I found myself exulting in the minuteness of the deposit left behind after the bombs had fallen. No more than little heaps of dust and debris. Gone, just like that; lacking the solidity and dignity even to make a ruin. In most of the successful writers of our time (politicians, too, for that matter; not to mention the pundits of the air and campus), coming, as they do, from the same sort of environment, similar stigmata may be detected. H. G. Wells, for instance, and his Kipps and Mr Polly. D. H. Lawrence storming out of Nottingham with his Baroness on his arm. Lucky Jim, and the wilder fantasies of Brideshead. That fearful symmetry Blake writes about, inexorably discloses itself. I think with awe of the perfection of the demonstration in, for instance, Evelyn Waugh and George Orwell; the one in his country gentleman's outfit, loud checks, overcoat sweeping the ground, grey bowler perched on large head, ear-trumpet to hand; the other in corresponding proletarian fancy-dress, corduroy trousers, not actually tied up with string, but as near as can be, choker round the neck, ancient drooping coat, hand-rolled shag cigarette. Both taken from back numbers of *Punch*. Why bother to write when the Lord provides such pictures?

My father was a small man, with wide shoulders and a frame that seemed to belong to a bigger body than his. The reason for this dis-crepancy between the structure and substance of him was, he told me, that as a child he had been badly and poorly fed. At the same time, being very energetic by temperament, he had always kept on the move. He had a sense of himself as being physically grotesque. 'I'm an ugly man,' he said to me once with a kind of droll pathos. 'I've always been ugly.' It was true in a way, and yet not true. He had a quality of distinction about him; even a certain beauty, deriving from his energy and exuberance. I should explain that he often reminisced and ruminated about himself to me in a way that, in those days, certainly, was unusual. Thus I came to have an exceptionally vivid sense of him and his life. More so, in a way, than of my own. Of his moods of melancholy and self-depreciation; of his large-mouthed sensuality, his spongy pincushion nose, his gift of the gab, his ultimate sense of his own and everything else's intrinsic absurdity; of his abounding, irrepressible ego. Am I describing myself? As I only realised long afterwards, of all things, he wanted me to be different from him. To go to Cambridge and emerge like one of his heroes – Tawney, or Lowes Dickinson, or even Hugh Dalton. To speak down my nose as dons and Fabians did. To be as well informed as Sidney Webb, as rumbustious as Wells, as witty and rich as Shaw. Devastatingly amusing, splendidly eloquent on behalf of the down-trodden and oppressed; author, orator, statesman, seer. And all that emerged was another edition of him. So much effort and money expended just for that!

There was one terrible occasion, some dinner at the Greyhound Hotel in Croydon when I was the guest of honour. I've even got a photograph of it. Local notabilities in miscellaneous evening dress; white waistcoats showing under black coats, dubious bow ties. My father among them. Then the dreadful moment; pray silence for . . . I rose to my feet, knowing, as always, exactly what he was thinking and hoping. Witty remarks, audience convulsed; then punching home some profundities, memorable phrases reproduced in the local paper – the *Croydon Advertiser*, the *Croydon Times*. I could think of nothing to say except how I loved and respected him, what a wonderful human being he was, how much he had done for me, for Croydon, for the poor and ill-used everywhere. I plunged ever deeper into my fatal misconception, and as I went on saw he was stricken. At one point he actually ejaculated a strangled: No! I have always been touched by the way Dr Johnson went to Lichfield and stood in the market-place for a whole day as an act of penitence for lack of consideration for his bookseller father. I ought to do the same thing, in front of the Croydon Town Hall, a Betjeman-beloved neo-Gothic building of quite exceptional architectural confusion; stand there and recall that dreadful dinner, and the anguish and disappointment I inflicted on my father at it.

As he recounted his life to me, it sounded exactly like a Dickens

novel. Dickens was a great bond between us. He would read aloud bits
to me; like Silas Wegg declining and falling for the edification of Mr
Boffin. Doing the accents; I can hear him now – Wegg, having been told
by Mr Boffin that if anything took his fancy he was to mention it,
pausing majestically: 'I think I see a weal and ham pie!' How I laughed,
and, for that matter, cried over the sentimental passages like the death
of Dora Copperfield, which I also loved. Dickens is the true inspirer,
and remains to a great extent the embodiment, of English Radicalism
or Leftism; his stamp is still upon the Labour Party stalwarts, as it was
upon my father. How appropriate that in the USSR his strictures on
the Poor Law and other abuses of his time continue to be regarded as
valid! In a sort of way they are, too. His capacity for turning on a
passionate flood of righteous indignation at any time; his tears for the
poor, and love of money and success; his scorn for his social superiors,
and passion to be like them; the sentimentality in which all his emotions,
public and private, were drenched, and the corresponding humour
which so incomparably expressed what he really felt, how he really
saw his fellows and the world he lived in – is not this characteristic of
any of our leaders of the Left, from Lloyd George and Aneurin Bevan
to Harold Wilson?

I took Dickens's novels out of the Croydon Public Library one after
the other, and somehow managed to tear the pages of *Our Mutual Friend*
rather badly, which was noticed when I returned the book. I awaited
the awful consequences, which duly came when I noticed a letter from
the Chief Librarian in my father's morning mail. He read it, frowned,
taxed me with the offence, which I admitted. I had no choice. Then he
went off to catch his train, and all through the day I wondered what
dreadful fate would befall me. However, in the evening my father
seemed particularly cheerful, and read aloud to me the reply he had
sent to the Chief Librarian. It apologised on my behalf for my offence,
offered to make restitution for the damage done. Then came the beautiful sentence which put the letter, as far as I was concerned, in the same
class as Johnson's to Lord Chesterfield (a subsequent comparison,
naturally): 'I feel sure that the damage done to the book was due, not
to any spirit of wanton destructiveness on my son's part, nor even to
the natural carelessness of youth, but rather to his love of the book in
question, and impatience to get at its contents.' (Remembering it
from so long ago, I may not have got the words exactly right, but I am
sure approximately so.) He liked the words as much as I did; they came
rolling lusciously off his tongue. I knew my troubles were over. Nor,

as it turned out, did my father even have to pay the Librarian any compensation.

My father was the eldest of a large family; I think nine children, but there may have been more. Their father had an undertaker's business in Penge, and was, it seemed, weak and self-indulgent, though possessed of certain social graces. He abandoned his family when my father was twelve, but reappeared from time to time. At thirteen my father left school, as you could in those days, if you were clever and passed an exam. It was the exact opposite to now when you pass an exam to be able to stay on at school. Both arrangements seem rather silly. His mother, meanwhile – a woman of strong character – set up in a second-hand furniture business in Penge High Street. I have been up and down this street trying to imagine where the shop may have been. When I asked my father how she conducted the business, he tapped the side of his nose in a very Dickensian way, winked, and said: 'She bought cheap and sold dear.' Anyway, the business enabled her to support the family. On leaving school my father took a job as an office boy with a firm of shirt manufacturers, remaining with them for the rest of his working life. He became secretary to the company, and was at one point invited to join the board if he would agree to give up his political activities. This he declined to do, and so never became rich. He told me that his salary never reached a thousand a year, but he may be said to have thriven. We never lacked for anything essential.

He contributed to his mother's household from the few shillings a week he earned as an office boy. From that time on, he once wryly remarked, he always had people dependent on him. To economise, he took what was then called the Workmen's Train from Penge to London Bridge, which went very early, but was cheaper than the ones later in the day. (What would it be called now if it existed? The Health Train, maybe. Or, more whimsically, the Early Bird Train. Or, for the ideologically alert, the Workers' Train.) It meant that he arrived an hour or so before his office opened, which he spent roaming through the City. In those days, he told me, he used to run more often than walk. Strolling through the City, as I sometimes did on a Sunday afternoon when I was working in Fleet Street, I have often imagined him darting about those streets like an excited sparrow. Between his departure on the Workmen's Train and return to Penge round about seven was a long stretch, sustained, more often than not, by nothing more substantial than buns and meat pies. His office was in New Basinghall Street off Moorgate; it was totally destroyed in the Blitz. I visited him

there when I was little older than he had been when he first started
working, and can just remember, on what must have been that occasion,
riding with him in a horse-drawn omnibus. His office, as I recall it,
gave an impression of being dusty and murky. My father and his friend
and colleague Mr Button were seated on two high stools with ledgers
before them in the outer part of the office, from which doors opened
into the private sanctums of the partners in the firm. Did my father
ever graduate into one of these private sanctums? I rather doubt it.
He had very beautiful hand-writing; not exactly copperplate, but the
next best thing. Remarkably clear and regular and easy to read. I have,
of course, many examples – letters, and so on – but the one I cherish
most is the inscription in the first book I ever possessed. *A Pageant of
English Poetry*, published by the Clarendon Press, which he gave me
for Christmas 1914, when I was eleven; the year of doom.

As my father's circumstances improved, he acquired a house in
Penge – with a mortgage, it goes without saying. By this means, he
explained to me, he could protect his mother from the unwelcome visits
of her husband. In fact, he had occasion to order him out of the house;
something that afterwards he looked back on with a certain amount of
remorse. I know, not only from what he said to me, but from scraps of
writing that he left behind, that his attitude to his father distressed him.
He felt he had been priggish. Once, he told me, he had seen his father
on Victoria Station with his arm round a lady, and it had upset him
considerably. After his father's death (he did not go to the funeral), this
lady, or maybe another, came to see him, saying that she was his step-
mother and that there were a number of half-brothers and sisters he
might care to meet. He showed her the door rather harshly, saying that
he only knew of one wife his father had, and that was his mother. What
happened to the lady and her offspring history does not relate. With
his own five children and numerous other commitments, it was impossible for him to take on a new lot, especially on such dubious
credentials. All this gave me a great curiosity about my procreative
undertaker grandfather whom I never saw, but the only trace of him I
could ever find was an ancient dim photograph revealing a weak indeterminate face lurking behind a large blond moustache. From it I
could easily imagine how appropriate a figure he would be in a funeral
procession, as his profession required; top-hatted, frock-coated, sure
and soft of foot, expression grave, and eyes downcast. His wife, my
paternal grandmother, on the other hand – whom I also never saw –
was clearly a very tough lady indeed; as she needed to be. She success-

fully brought up her nine children, though losing some on the way from tuberculosis – a family complaint, of which I also had symptoms at one stage. When she lay dying in her late fifties, my father was with her, and described to me how he went to support her, but somehow messed it up, and she fell back among her pillows muttering: 'You always were clumsy!' Again, it was so exactly the sort of thing that might have happened to me. A photograph of her shows her in a bonnet, with resolute eyes, a large decisive nose and firm mouth.

It would be possible to portray my father – certainly, he was liable to see himself so – as a victim of social injustice. He was prone to self-pity, as I have also been, though admittedly with far more justification than I. Yet even I, despite almost inconceivable good fortune, could drum up a case. How much more he, with his genuine deprivations and hardships. Obviously, nowadays he would have a quite different life. Go to a grammar school and on to the university, where he would undoubtedly have distinguished himself. Get into Parliament young enough to have a ministerial career (he was already in his sixties when he got elected for Romford in 1931); certainly in the Cabinet, maybe an outside chance of being Prime Minister. If Attlee, then any Labour Party stalwart may be considered as in the running. In any case, he would have thriven in the lush pastures between the London School of Economics, Whitehall and Westminster. There are plenty of prototypes among existing socialist brass. He would have been spared all those years of City drudgery; all that laborious learning French by himself and learning to play the piano. That strumming away at the piano, pipe in mouth, and so intent that spittle used to run along the stem, forming a great gob for whose falling I watched, fascinated! *The Flying Dutchman* played with immense vigour and verve, and a song from *Faust* which my mother used to sing in a quavering voice – 'Oh Marguerita, Oh Marguerita, still on the bough is left a leaf of gold.' I was unfortunately not with him when he died, but away on war service on some tomfool Intelligence mission; but Kitty was, and described to me how he departed this life with a broad, joyous unforgettable wink. As a Rt. Hon., D.Lit., M.A., C.H., P.C., etc. etc., we shouldn't have had the wink. I cherish it.

Each age has its special pigeonholes for sorting out lives. In the nineteenth century my father would have been type-cast as the office boy who worked his way up to be boss; in our time, as an example of gifts and abilities wasted for lack of opportunity. Now all that has been put right; look at Roy Jenkins. Well, look at him!

I remember my father most vividly and characteristically at the top of Surrey Street on a Saturday evening, where in those days there used to be a street market, with gas flares by the booths, and plenty of hucksters coaxing passers-by to take advantage of a wonderful chance to buy a gold watch for next to nothing, or a salve that would cure anything from the pox to pink eye, or shaving soap so pure and luscious that you could eat it – which the huckster then proceeded to do to prove his point, stuffing the suds into his mouth as though they were turkish delight. Meanwhile, my father had set up his little frail platform, almost like a gallows against the evening sky, and climbed on to it. He was bearded by now, having grown his beard as a result of being afflicted with a skin complaint called barber's rash which, I imagine, has now disappeared along with the cut-throat razor. The beard gave an extra dimension of drama to the scene; making a prophet of him, a voice crying in the wilderness against the soap suds man. I led the applause and the laughter, such as they were. Even at ten I knew for the most part what he would say; as well as all his jokes. They did not lose their piquancy for me because of that. I waited for them, sensed that they were coming, exploded with mirth prematurely when he was still working up to the pay-off line. 'Now ladies and gentlemen,' he would begin, addressing some ten or a dozen casual passers-by, who had paused out of curiosity to listen to him; along with myself, a couple of Labour Party stalwarts who had turned out with him, and perhaps another urchin or two – 'Now ladies and gentlemen, can you tell me this? It's His Majesty's Government, His Majesty's Navy, His Majesty's Stationery Office. His Majesty's This and His Majesty's That. Every blooming thing seems to be His Majesty's. But it's the National Debt. Why isn't that His Majesty's? We'll gladly let His Majesty have that, won't we?'

It might raise an occasional smile, but mostly the point was lost, except on me and the two stalwarts who, of course, had also heard it many times before. Undeterred, my father slogged on, abolishing poverty, illiteracy, war, inequality, every conceivable ill and injustice, and ushering in the glorious era of everlasting peace, prosperity and happiness. His voice rose, his gestures grew more intense; against the night sky, he was a gesticulating enraged shadow calling on mankind to turn away from their follies and false leaders and realise their true destiny. What a sublime prospect it seemed! How relatively easy of attainment! And yet the people in Surrey Street seemed strangely in-different; their attention more easily held by the gold watch, the magic salve, the edible shaving soap than by this sure prospectus for living happily ever after. Defiantly, my father, the two stalwarts and I sang 'The Red Flag' together, my small tuneless voice mixing with their deep ones, folded up his platform and made off carrying it.

On these occasions I was always uplifted, never doubting that my father was right, and that all he promised could and would come to pass, despite the seeming indifference of those he addressed. In my copy of *The Pilgrim's Progress*, much thumbed, with its coloured illustrations, Surrey Street was Vanity Fair, which, though it scorned us, would in the end come to follow the way we sign-posted. Even then I preferred Bunyan's imagery to the statistical forecasts of our ultimate triumph, showing how we would capture the borough councils, Parliament, the Government, until we were able to take over everything and everyone. Meanwhile, the co-operative societies – we were ardent co-op supporters – must in due course, since they gave back their profits to the customer, get all retail trade into their hands. Already the Croydon trams were run by the Corporation. How virtuously they glided along compared with the roistering free-enterprise buses! I should no more have thought of setting foot on a bus in those days than a strict Methodist would have thought of going into a public house. When I was sent shopping, it was taken for granted that the co-op must be my first call. Though co-op shops also had counters, and men in white coats who patted the butter into shape, and arrays of packaged goods, they were not as other shops. The coins one paid dropped into the till rather like a church offertory than a payment made and received; the bills had a picture of a wheatsheaf on them, and texts from the sayings of the Rochdale founding fathers. I remember so well that little row of shops; after the co-op, the butcher; the chemist, maybe, who also pulled out teeth for a shilling a time; the baker, who would add an extra crusty sliver of bread to make up the weight of a loaf which I munched on the way home.

My mother came from Sheffield, where her father and some of her brothers worked in the cutlery industry. My father met her while on holiday in the Isle of Man. She was staying there with some relatives, the Gadsbys, who were relatively prosperous tradesmen. They had, my mother told me – she always spoke of them with a certain awe – several jewellery shops in seaside resorts, and, having taken a fancy to her, liked her to make long stays with them, which she cheerfully did. She greatly appreciated their superior affluent circumstances and the pretty dresses they bought her. It was an experience which much influenced her future tastes and aspirations. She told me once that her dream had been to go to church on Sunday mornings on my father's arm, he in a top hat, and we five children following behind in single file, in order of seniority, each wearing Eton collars and jackets. Alas, this dream remained unrealised; like my father's, as it would now be called, elitist one of my becoming a socialist toff, begotten by Keir Hardie out of Balliol with Toynbee Hall intervening.

How, precisely, she and my father met I never learnt, but I think it must have been some sort of a pick-up. She was extremely pretty, with very fair hair, and an expression of fathomless innocence which she retained to a considerable degree to the end of her days. Only, if you looked deep into it, far, far below the pellucid surface, you came upon something steely, tough, and even merciless, there. I imagine a Wellsian encounter, my father and the two office pals who were on holiday with him, in high spirits, and my mother flattered at being the object of the attentions of such sprightly young fellows. My father returned to Penge and New Basinghall Street in a state of extreme exaltation. Some of his early letters to my mother remain extant; they are couched in highly romantic terms, and bear unmistakable traces of his literary studies. I found them touching, and rather beautiful; to me preferable, in their implications, to contemporary arrangements which, in any case, had they prevailed then, might well have precluded my being born at all. No great catastrophe, it might be contended, and I agree; though for me, all the same, a deprivation of sorts.

My father went to Sheffield to be looked over, and gave satisfaction; my mother visited Penge, and though his mother, as appeared afterwards, had certain doubts, she kept them to herself, and gave her blessing to their union. A wedding photograph in a family album shows the bridal pair looking appropriately uplifted, though in my father's case I thought I detected just a flicker of a reservation. No mood with him was ever quite homogeneous – another trait I inherited. Their marriage lasted to the end of their days, with suitable silver and golden celebrations. When my father died my mother closed his eyes, with a certain irritation at their refusing to open again, but never accustomed herself to life without him. The bed in which they had slept side by side through so many nights had two hollows in it; with the other unoccupied, my mother lay disconsolately in hers.

Our Sheffield relations were a great source of interest and delight in our childhood. All of us at different times visited them for longer or shorter periods, which was considered a very special treat. (The family name, by the way, was Booler; I had to dredge it out of my memory years later when I applied to join a club in Washington D.C., and was required to give the name of my maternal grandmother in order to prove, presumably, that my blood was uncontaminated by Jewish or any other alien admixture.) They were particularly kind, warmhearted, cheerful people. Each Christmas they sent us a hamper of food containing parkin, home-made pork pies and other Yorkshire delicacies. Though my mother – as she certainly believed – might be considered to have improved her circumstances by moving south and marrying my father, we always thought of the Boolers as living more comfortably than we did. Their houses warmer and cosier, with a more ample table. At the same time, they were quite definitely working-class in their ways and outlook, as we were lower-middle-class. So, in the social categories of revolutionary mystique, they were downtrodden and oppressed, and we the running dogs of the exploiters.

Looking back now, I find it curious that I never saw any disparity between the Boolers as I knew them and my dream fantasy of the noble proletarian; between my actual feelings about them and their allotted role in the great drama of revolution which I hoped with all my heart soon to see enacted – with, of course, a star part for me. I did once, it is true, ask my father how he could be sure that if, as he proposed, the proletariat were subjected to the same sort of education and style of living as our neighbours in South Croydon, and given the same little suburban houses to live in, and gardens to tend, and schools to go to, they would not just turn into *petits bourgeois* themselves, with all the stuck-up attitudes and philistine tastes we found so abhorrent? I really believe this was the only occasion on which we got anywhere near a political disagreement up to the time I left Cambridge, and probably a good deal beyond that. My father assured me that, with the right sort of education, things would not work out so, and I had to accept his word for it, though with some inward doubts. I might have cited the Boolers as a case in point, but didn't. The truth is, of course, that the whole notion of a working class with a specific political or cultural, or even spiritual, role *qua* working class is a fantasy invented by guilt-stricken renegade proletarians like D. H. Lawrence, or by renegade bourgeoisie on the run like William Morris or, for that matter, Marx and Engels themselves, or just by sociologists looking for a subject and a job. It was serving in the ranks as an ageing private in my late thirties that clinched the matter for me. I discovered then that proletarians in a barrack- or

NAAFI-hut included all the familiar types (opinionated extrovert, shy introvert, artistic, homosexual, assertive, lecherous, etc. etc.) to be found among a similar collection of bourgeoisie. I might have been back at Cambridge, and in a very short while thought I was.

I often sat up with my mother waiting for my father's return from political meetings and municipal activities in which he was heavily engaged. Most evenings he was out. There was a certain tension in the air, a sense of impending drama. She resented, I knew, my father's absence night after night, and, as I dimly understood, suspected that he did not necessarily tell her precisely where and with whom he had been. She felt excluded from all this part of his life; in his eyes, far the most important and significant part. So she sat there bolt upright in a sort of folding chair she always chose, looking severe and censorious. Even if she dozed off, her features remained set and taut. We talked little on the whole; she was not much of a conversationalist, except when reminiscing about her childhood and staying with the Gadsbys – that golden time. There was not really much to talk about from my point of view. She had read little, and even when she did read, it was very slowly, with her lips visibly moving as she spelt out the words. Writing a letter was, for her, a heavy labour – a round hand, with no punctuation, and shaky spelling. Yet I have to record that when I was away she quite often wrote to me; letters, as I should have remembered, representing so much effort on her part and, oddly, signed 'Annie', not 'your affectionate mother', or anything like that. Once when she was seriously ill in a nursing home near Bournemouth, and I went to see her, she indicated that she had something particular to say to me. I bent down my head, and at last she got it out; someone I was very interested in had in the past once occupied that house . . . someone . . . but she couldn't quite manage the name. Then she managed it – Tolstoy. Afterwards I found out that she was quite right. Tolstoy had briefly stayed in the house during a visit to England. It was only afterwards that I remembered how touching it was of her to have stored up for me this particular piece of information which she knew I should cherish. One remembers such things too late.

My mother had a way of sometimes using unexpectedly lurid phrases. Thus, at one of our evening sessions she noticed that I was apparently reading an English translation of Rousseau's *Confessions* I'd picked up from among my father's books. In point of fact, the book was far too difficult for me at that stage, and it was mere pretence on my part to be reading it. I was given to this sort of affectation, and even much later in my life, if I was reading in public – say, in a bus or a train – I liked it to be something that would strike anyone who happened to notice as being abstruse and exotic. Later I came to love the *Confessions*, even their many lies, for some elusive quality of luminosity in them which comes out in their very style, so beautifully clear and supple. My mother, for reasons of her own, held Rousseau in the utmost abhorrence and, while indicating this to me, volunteered the information that he had been born with his blood boiling. It was an observation that greatly intrigued me, and, not understanding at all what my mother was getting at, I tried to imagine someone with his blood on the boil, bubbling and steaming like a saucepan of porridge. I was so preoccupied with this that I failed to follow my mother's subsequent remarks, and only picked up the thread when she was saying that she would rather see me, as she put it, dead at her feet than doing something or other – what I had no sort of an idea. It is a curious thing that though, as far as my reading was concerned, I was precocious, delving freely into my father's books, as far as I know, it had absolutely no effect in making me sexually precocious. My favourite book at this time, when I was about fourteen, was *The Three Musketeers*. I loved it passionately; it is the only book that, in the whole of my life, I have finished reading and then at once turned back to page one and begun again. In my edition there was a picture of d'Artagnan running away from a meeting with Milady. He is wearing only his shirt, but it did not occur to me to wonder why he should have taken off his trousers.

Even so, my mother's whole manner, and the lurid phrases she used, gave me the feeling that something unusual, frightening and in some way exciting was at issue. Without actually complaining about my father, I felt that somehow she was pointing an accusing finger at him. Once she said to me darkly that she hoped I would never know what she had had to put up with. On Sunday mornings, when my father was usually at home and, if the weather was suitable, working in the garden, this vaguely accusatory manner was liable to take a more concrete form. In a house at the back of ours, and overlooking our garden, there was a small attic window in which, my mother had managed to convince herself, a maid-servant would sit exposing herself or otherwise sending my father erotic signals. It was a preposterous notion, but so real to her that she would flit in a kind of frenzy from window to window in our house, peering out from behind the curtains and trying to catch a glimpse of the offending siren; my father, meanwhile, going on calmly planting his potatoes or hoeing between the rows of his spring onions.

My mother's expression on these occasions seemed to be quite horrifying; enflamed and enraged and somehow animal. It was my first glimpse of authentic evil, and – as always happens with evil – infected me, evil being the most infectious, and even contagious, of all sicknesses. I found myself likewise peering up at the attic window and imagining I saw there an obscenely smiling face, and two pendulous breasts hanging down like Christmas turkeys to attract my father's gaze. The only comparable incident that I have come across in contemporary fiction occurs in a novel by Iris Murdoch in which the heroine likewise mutely displays her breasts. If my mother had written a novel, it would, I fancy, have been in rather the same vein as Miss Murdoch's.

The undercurrent of suspicion running through my mother's mind frequently led to rows. My father would explode, shout with sarcastic rage: 'Take care, the servants are looking!' and go out, violently slamming the front door behind him. I dreaded these outbursts, and one of the reasons I would sit up with my mother waiting for my father's return was that I thought my presence would serve to mitigate any trouble that might arise. Even if I did go to bed, more often than not I lay awake waiting to hear his key in the lock, straining to catch the sound of their voices, to make sure they were not raised, infinitely relieved when I heard them putting out the lights and climbing upstairs to bed; one more day gone by. The precise nuances of feeling and sense of deprivation behind these rows I, of course, had no means of knowing, and should not have understood if I had known. Perhaps if my parents had been rich and more attuned to the moral dissolution of the times, they might have parted and sought other partners. I doubt if they would have gained thereby, and we children would certainly have lost. They stayed together for our sake; in any case, they were too conscientious about their financial responsibilities for others, to be in a position to do otherwise. Something for which I honour them. When I think of their companionship in old age, their interminable games of two-handed bridge, how utterly lost they would have been without one another when the Blitz made them homeless in their seventies, I marvel anew at the extraordinary strength of this bizarre institution of monogamous marriage, which goes on surviving despite the furious attacks directed against it and its own intrinsic disabilities.

Incidentally, to the best of my knowledge, my mother's suspicions about my father were quite without foundation. There was nothing he ever said to me (and we were at times exceedingly frank with one another; more so than our disparity in years might seem to permit) or in his papers to suggest the contrary. Also, as I had occasion to see for myself when I was still quite young, he was singularly naïve in sexual matters for a man of his years and experience. It happened that we found ourselves in the spring of 1927 in Paris together. I had just come back from India, he having met me in Naples. It was a wonderful thing to find my father standing there on the quay when my boat came into Naples Harbour – my first sight of it – at dawn; his bowler hat on his head, and that look about him that I knew and loved so well, of expectancy, a boyish conviction that something wonderful was going to happen. We travelled to Paris, stopping off at Rome for two or three days. In Paris we ran into someone my father knew – some sort of a progressive travel-agent, Welsh, I fancy, with a dark chin, who asked us out for an evening to see the sights. It involved going to various brothels and lewd or blasphemous spectacles arranged for tourists. I imagine they have all long ago shut down now that rather inferior versions of the same shows are to be seen in the West End, but then they were in full swing. At one of them, when we entered, girls with nothing on except diaphanous scarves and high-heeled shoes came and perched on our knees, ordered expensive drinks, and when we left tried to haggle over the tips we gave them. Here our progressive travel-agent was useful, and soon shut them up. What preoccupied my father afterwards as we strolled down the Champs Elysées under the stars on our way back to our hotel – the Francois 1er – was that when he gave his girl a pound she put it in her shoe, though, as I pointed out, actually she had nowhere else to put it. Nonetheless, he continued to mutter to himself: 'She put it in her shoe!' as though there were any number of possible alternatives. The next day, rather shamefacedly, he asked me whether it had been my first visit to places of that kind. I assured him – not quite truthfully – that I was, if not an *habitué*, at any rate quite accustomed to them, whereupon he cheered up. Whether or not our behaviour would have come into the category my mother had in mind when she said she would sooner see me dead at her feet than guilty of it, I never knew. Nothing would have induced me to breathe a word to her about our spree.

My father's unfamiliarity with the brothel scene was the more surprising because prostitutes and prostitution played a big part in our Leftist mythology, providing us with a classic case of exploitation; of the power of money in a capitalist society to override normal human feelings, and even animal instincts. *Resurrection* was one of our classics – among the very best; and again Blake gave us the *mots justes* in his lines about the harlot's cry from street to street weaving old England's winding sheet. They call them *filles de joies* in Paris, my father would say sarcastically, almost spitting out the words, and he liked telling a story about a man who was advised by his doctor to have a woman for health reasons. 'Then may I have your daughter?' the man says. When the doctor expostulates, he goes on: 'It has to be somebody's daughter, hasn't it?' My father delivered this pay-off line with great verve, in a tone of voice he reserved for famous retorts; for instance – also a great favourite – Voltaire's '*Je ne vois pas la nécessité.*' It is rather sad to reflect that the prostitute has gone the way of so much of our old Leftist mythology; driven out of circulation by ardent amateurs, as the armament manufacturer, or merchant of death – another great standby – has been superseded by ardent governments eager to flog their weapons, and the arrogant landowner by the arrogant bureaucrat.

What, I think, worried my mother more than any suspicion that my father was engaged in illicit amours was the notion of free love, then very current among Socialists, especially young middle-class ones. She disapproved of this strongly, and did not hesitate to say so when the subject came up, whereas my father and his friends, though most of them extremely respectable in their own lives, felt bound to accord the notion a faint gesture of sympathy. H. G. Wells in his autobiography describes making the discovery – almost with the excitement of an Archimedes – that it was possible to sleep with young progressive girls of good family without having to pay or, as was then the case, running any appreciable risk of catching venereal disease. Even the danger of pregnancy was reduced, in the sense that their families were perfectly capable of paying for an abortion, or, in the event of a baby being born, disposing of the bastard. For a time I belonged to the 1917 Club, founded to commemorate the Russian Revolution, and the scene, very appropriately, of Ramsay MacDonald's first public appearance as Labour Prime Minister in 1924, when he was greeted by a female of the locality as her Yorkshire Boy. In its somewhat dingy premises in Gerrard Street, well-spoken, good-looking girls up from the Home Counties or farther afield, who had become convinced by the *New Statesman*, or maybe some itinerant university extension lecturer, that they had nothing to lose but their virginity, were much in evidence. I once asked one of them who had fallen briefly into the hands of Wells how the first approach had been made. It was at a party, she told me, and after some preliminary conversation, Wells had whispered to her: 'Shall we go upstairs and do funny things with our bodies?' I asked her whether the things they did had turned out to be funny. 'Not particularly,' she said.

Anything like this was, of course, infinitely remote from our suburban milieu, but even so the notion was abroad, and my mother had picked up a tiny bat-squeak of it among the Socialist faithful in Croydon; sensing a menace in it, hanging primarily over my father, but also to a lesser extent over my brothers and myself. About the siren in the attic window I had heard her mutter splenetically: 'Man-mad!' How much more, then, some charming infants-school teacher, crammed full of Ann Veronica and Havelock Ellis, not to mention Marie Stopes. The whole thing was crystallised, as far as my mother was concerned, by the Colony, a Tolstoyan settlement in the Cotswolds started by Socialists from Croydon with whom we maintained connections. They made no bones about it, but lived openly with one another, unmarried, and, in principle at any rate, when they felt like it, changing their partners. They also, incidentally, eschewed private property and the use of money, held their goods in common, and otherwise detached themselves from contemporary usages – all points about which my mother's feelings were tepid compared with her attitude to their sexual *mores* which, she considered, put them in the class of Sodom and Gomorrah, if not well below it.

As it happened, I got to know the Colony rather well, having been boarded out near it when I developed vague T.B. symptoms and, on medical advice, was sent into the country for a spell. In view of his family history, my father was naturally hyper-sensitive about anything of the kind. I doubt if I was particularly ill, but I just remember coughing rather a lot and feeling inordinately tired, as I still do from time to time. As for the possibility that I might prove to be tubercular – something that I dimly understood – it both frightened and fascinated me. After all, Keats suffered from this complaint, which might be regarded as among the more interesting ones. At the same time, I had a vivid awareness, gathered from having seen relatives of my father in the last stages of T.B., of what it was like; the high colour concentrated round the cheek-bone, the abnormally lurid eyes, the sputum that had to be kept for subsequent examination, the transparent skin with fever just under the surface – like a furnace seen through a plate-glass window.

I loved my time in the country, from the moment Miss Lidiard met me with a pony and trap at Stroud Station, and we trotted along to the delightful old cottage in the village of Sheepscombe where she lived with her mother. The house made me think of David Copperfield's home before his father died, and I decided to be David there. Like, I suppose, most children, I often took the parts of characters I admired. I can remember going about for days on end as d'Artagnan, and then as Tom Sawyer – though, oddly enough, not as Huckleberry Finn, even though I admired him more than Tom. I suppose I just didn't want to *be* him. There was a large damson tree in Miss Lidiard's garden, loaded with fruit, and in the capacity of David, despite her protests below, I climbed to the very highest branches, and stripped them.

It was part of the arrangement at Sheepscombe that Miss Lidiard should give me some lessons. These went ill, and she occasionally chastised me with a cane, though I can't recall that it caused me more than passing discomfort, or any appreciable psychological distress. I was, I fear, an almost unteachable child, the reason being that I never had – or for that matter have – the slightest interest in the subjects taught at school and university, with the possible exception of scripture. Algebra, geography, physics, history even – I never wanted to learn about such subjects any more than to listen to some boring guide telling me about the Parthenon or the Sistine Chapel. As for English, the one subject I did care about – just because I so cared about it the maunderings of teachers, up to and including university ones, were somehow irrelevant. Poor Miss Lidiard! She tried her hand at arithmetic, spelling and the rivers and promontories of England without any appreciable success.

From time to time Miss Lidiard took me to visit the Colony, which was only a mile or so away. She was a gentle, reserved and rather severe lady who certainly did not approve of the Colony's ways and ideas. Her connection with it came about through Will Straughan, my father's closest friend, whom she subsequently married. Indeed, it was he who arranged for me to go to Sheepscombe. Various of his relatives had joined the Colony, and though he personally took a derisory view of everything to do with it, he continued to keep in touch with them. He was a truly enchanting human being; gentle, humorous, quixotically generous, original; somehow giving a vague impression of sadness, and yet indissolubly associated in my mind with laughter. I count such men among life's major blessings; as well as implying a strong hint of better things to come. If it is possible thus to live kindly and companionably and cheerfully in the world without any elevated mystical or philosophical insight to buoy one up; without fasting in the wilderness, or being nailed to a cross, or speaking with tongues; just as a mortal man with other mortal men – to use Falstaff's blessed expression; why, then, surely our poor benighted human race will never wholly succumb to the follies and brutalities to which we often appear to be inexorably given. However deep the darkness, these small steady lamps continue to shine, bringing great solace.

Will Straughan's marriage to Miss Lidiard was a great success, though childless, she being, I should suppose, too old to conceive. The occasion of their nuptials remains fixed in my mind because of a remark my mother made, and the sharp retort it brought her from her mother, who was staying with us at the time. She said something to the effect that Will, after his long bachelor years, might be somewhat at a loss on his bridal night. 'Don't be a fool, Annie!' her mother sharply retorted. This maternal grandmother, left a widow shortly after my parents married, used to come down from Sheffield – whence nothing would dislodge her permanently – to look after us when my father took my mother away on holiday, which he did every year, usually abroad. Jaunts that he loved, and refused to economise over. We enjoyed our grandmother's regime, though it was more severe than her daughter's. She was a tiny, energetic lady who still wore a cap indoors, and bustled about the house, washing, brushing, polishing, cooking. For her weekly bread-making session, she put on a pair of white sleeves, and pummelled the dough with great zest. We were allowed to take the crisp overflow of the baking pans. I occasionally ran into trouble, as I had with Miss Lidiard, over answering back; an offence which has brought me rebukes and chastisement, both public and private, all my life. Once, I remember, when I had been disparaging the story of Daniel in the Lions' Den, she shut me up by remarking with great emphasis: 'If Daniel isn't true, nothing is.' I revisited Sheepscombe some years ago for the first time since I had been there as a child. In the churchyard I found the graves of Will Straughan and his wife, but the damson tree seemed to have disappeared.

Whatever Miss Lidiard might feel about our visits to the Colony, I looked forward to them enormously. The place was not much to look at – just a group of wooden huts, with a larger one for communal gatherings; but I vaguely detected something exciting, stimulating, in the air. The Colony had been started in the first years of this century, largely in response to Tolstoy's ideas. A party set out from Croydon on their bicycles, with only very little money and no agricultural experience, with the idea of settling on the land, producing all their own necessities, and so being able to detach themselves wholly from the wicked ways and pursuits of the society around them. It was a truly heroic enterprise; the more so as most of the participants were clerks and schoolmasters and shop assistants, with absolutely no experience of fending for themselves under primitive conditions. Like Brigham Young when he first caught a glimpse of the Great Salt Lake in what is now Utah, they saw some fifty acres of rough land in the Cotswolds, and said: This is the place! The land was cheap in those days, and they acquired it by purchase; then, to demonstrate their abhorrence of the institution of property, ceremonially burnt the title deeds. It must have been a touching scene – the bonfire, the documents consigned to the flames, their exalted sentiments. Unfortunately a neighbouring farmer heard of their noble gesture and began to encroach on their land. To have resorted to the police, even if it had been practicable, was unthinkable. So, after much deliberation, they decided to use physical force to expel the intruder; which they did on the basis of a theory of detached action, whereby it is permissible to infringe a principle for the purpose of a single isolated act without thereby invalidating it. The intruding farmer was, in fact, thrown over the hedge in the presence of the assembled Colonists.

There were many such tragi-comic incidents in the years that followed; as well as quarrels, departures, jealousies, betrayals and domestic upsets. In the end, the Colonists found it necessary to reestablish their title to the land by means of squatters' rights, and then proceeded to bicker amongst themselves as to who should have which portion. Free love did not preclude the troubles of matrimony; men still tired of ageing mates and turned to younger ones. Nor did the deserted resent their abandonment any the less because they had not been shackled in the chains of matrimony. To-day, I suppose, the Colony would be called a Commune, but essentially the same hopes and desires are entertained, with the same disappointments and disillusionments lying ahead. It is a minor vexation of growing old that what seems novel and audacious to the young is stale and already discredited in the light of one's own experience.

I wandered about the Colony a year or so ago, noting how the roof of the communal meeting-place was leaking, and how weeds obscured its windows. How some of the huts were derelict and abandoned, and others that were occupied had an air of being poor and ill-tended. How the few Colonists who were still there seemed mostly old and dispirited. Back into remotest times, I reflected, this notion has existed of a Utopia, a kingdom of heaven on earth, or heavenly city; of a little perfect community existing within the larger imperfect one of human society; from time to time finding expression, always disastrously. History is littered with the debris of extinct Colonies and Communes. The early Christians were fortunate enough to be saved from taking any such disastrous course since they enjoyed the inestimable advantage of believing that the millennium was near, which precluded them from seeking to establish a beneficent regime in this world. In the time at their disposal it was just not worth while. Perhaps the best hope of reviving the Christian religion would be to convince the Pope, the Archbishop of Canterbury and other dignitaries likewise that the world will shortly be coming to an end. A difficult undertaking, I fear, notwithstanding much evidence pointing that way.

When Miss Lidiard and I visited the Colony it was still in reasonably good shape. The leading figure among the Colonists at the time was a Czech philosopher, Francis Sedlac, who had come to the Colony originally as a fugitive from Austrian military service, and was held in great respect. Few of the Colonists could understand his philosophy, but all were prepared to esteem it. He was a tall, bearded man of decidedly imposing appearance – so much so, the Colonists would tell one with great pride, that he had once been offered the part of Christ in a Hollywood production of the Gospel story. As they did not think much of the traditional Christ, and Hollywood represented everything they considered most abhorrent, the pride they took in this offer was a little difficult to understand. Sedlac, in any case, rejected the offer. I was allowed to peep in at the great man where he sat, as I thought, playing with coloured bricks. Actually, as it turned out, he was working at his philosophy, which was based on geometrical premises. His consort at that time was a certain Nelly Shaw, an old friend of my father who occasionally visited us in Croydon. Before his marriage, my father and Nelly, we were given to understand, had gone bicycling together, when she had scandalised the neighbourhood by being one of the first ladies to appear in public in bloomers. She might be regarded, I suppose, as a forerunner of the Women's Lib movement to-day; with a harsh, resonant voice, a plump, clumsy body, and a face full of irregularities: tufts of hair, moles, pits and protuberances, the whole impression not appreciably improved by a string of large red beads that she invariably wore tightly round her neck. If my mother nourished any suspicions about her, they were, I am confident, misplaced.

The Colonists were, of course, pacifists to a man and a woman, and

Sedlac, as one who had faced persecution and exile rather than take up arms, was a hero in their eyes. Rather in the same sort of way as their like to-day are concerned about money invested in South Africa, they were exercised as to whether or not the communal funds they had accumulated should be invested in government securities, which one of them – actually, Will Straughan's sister – said would be tantamount to 'dipping it in the blood'. Sedlac, too, as a dedicated anarchist, was strongly opposed to having any truck with Treasury bonds, which he regarded with abhorrence. Altogether, he looked with disfavour on the Colony's growing prosperity, though contributing to it in a sense, as being one of the sights of the place which brought coach-loads of curious visitors from the surrounding neighbourhood to stare and buy cakes and wholemeal bread at the Colony's bakery. I was interested to find that picture postcards are still on sale in Stroud of the Colony, one of them being of Sedlac as a typical Colonist. He appears as a kind of agnostic Ecce Homo; in the style of Edward Carpenter, Walt Whitman, and all the other prophets of wind on the heath, up to and including the most distracted of them all – D. H. Lawrence. The other attraction which brought in local sightseers was the reputed nude bathing which took place at the Colony. There was, in fact, a small pool fed by a spring in which on warm days the Colonists were liable to disport themselves. Most of them, male and female alike, seemed to my childhood eyes more curious than alluring in their state of nakedness, but there were two young girls with the first bloom of adolescence upon them who caught my attention with a stab of excitement. It was my first intimation of sex, and without conscious deliberation I decided to keep it to myself. The incident must have impressed me, since I remember the names, admittedly bizarre, of the two girls in question – Elfie and Doddles.

In the Colony's early days, when the prohibition of the use of money was rigorously observed, Sedlac decided that the only way he could be sure of the safe delivery of an article he had written for a learned philosophical magazine was to take it himself to London where the magazine was published. He might, it is true, have followed the practice of some of the Colonists and put the article in the post without a stamp in the expectation that the recipient would meet the postage due. This practice greatly exasperated my father when he was the victim of it, though, loudly protesting, he would always pay up and accept the letter or package. Sedlac was above such devices and, bare-footed, with his article in his knapsack, and no money in his pocket, he set out for

London. It was mid-winter, and soon he ran into a bad snowstorm.
By the time he had covered some thirty miles he was at the end of his
strength – which was considerable; he was a tall man, rather the build
of Bernard Shaw, whose appearance he perhaps copied more closely
than that of Christ. What to do? He had reached a small village and
decided to apply to the vicarage there for food and shelter. The vicar,
a kindly man, sympathising with Sedlac's situation, offered him some
money, which, however, Sedlac explained, he could not accept – not
because it would be charity, but because he would no more possess or
use money than he would heroin or any other destructive substance.
For years the notion of this dialogue fascinated me, and I tried several
times to reconstruct it, with Sedlac, like Lear, abandoned and alone
in a stormy world where his logic was unacceptable. I saw it as a
confrontation, like Dostoevsky's between the Grand Inquisitor and the
returned Saviour, between the vicar and the Colonist, between the
authoritarian and the anarchist; as the eternal dialogue that began when
Adam, hand in hand with Eve, walked out of Paradise, and, looking
back, saw the flaming sword barring his return. Likewise, mounted in
the desert two thousand years ago, when the Devil, with the kingdoms
of the earth in his gift, offered them to Christ, who rejected them,
leaving His followers to be displaced persons for ever. I was so interested
in the dialogue that I forgot to find out what happened to Sedlac, and
whether his article ever reached its destination. No doubt Nelly Shaw
arrived on the scene, reassuring in her red beads, and baled him out,
explaining matters to the vicar in terms that were comprehensible to
him.

Sedlac and Nelly are, of course, long since dead, as, I should suppose,
are all the first-generation Colonists. I found a number of them,
including Sedlac and Nelly, in the Minchinhampton churchyard,
where an area well apart from the other dead has been allotted to them.
Sedlac is described on his stone as an Hegelian, as though this might
somehow bring him more into line with the susceptibilities of the
Anglican authorities and the local worthies among whom he lies. It is a
strange last resting-place for them. In the early days of the Colony the
then Minchinhampton incumbent was particularly incensed against
the Colonists for their atheism, their curious attire (at one point, some
of them affected ancient Greek costume) and, above all, their attitude
to the marriage tie. Especially in England, time softens everything; I
have always thought that if Wilde had lived into his eighties he would
probably have been made an honorary Commissioner of Scouts. Will

the Californian Communards all likewise find their way at last to Forest Lawn? It would not surprise me.

When I returned home from Sheepscombe the family had moved into a new house in South Croydon, built in accordance with my father's specifications. It was semi-detached, the original intention being that Will Straughan should live in the other half. Alas, his financial circumstances took a turn for the worse at this time, and he had to remain in Sanderstead. As I learnt afterwards, he characteristically impoverished himself in order to keep a shipping business in Leadenhall Street going rather than sack the employees. Our house had one large combined sitting- and dining-room on the ground floor, with a study for my father in which he had a roll-top desk that I greatly admired. French windows looked out on the garden and, inevitably, were fated to play a role in my mother's operations against lickerish domestics in neighbouring houses. There was one new piece of furniture which dominated the sitting-room – a sort of old-fashioned divan with a narrow seat and tall back, covered in red damask. It had, in fact, been in the snuggery of a country pub, and became known to us all as the cosy corner. Nothing could have been less appropriate in our semi-detached suburban house, or more typical of my father. I always sat in it when I could, exchanged my first amorous kiss on it, and found it a perfect lurking-place to avoid being noticed or sent to bed when my father and his friends were plotting the overthrow of the capitalist system. My mother disliked it very much, and strongly protested when it first made its appearance. She was out of sympathy with these occasional romantic flights my father indulged in. Thus, on their silver wedding anniversary he proudly appeared with a huge silver fruit salver, called, according to him, an *épergne*, that he had bought in some second-hand shop. It was made in the shape of a naked boy – presumably Cupid – offering a plate of fruit; a majestic object, acquired, I imagine, from a restaurant when it went bankrupt. I saw my mother's face fall, and as it fell all the steam went out of my father. It was heartbreaking. I wanted to say how I admired the salver, how it was something needed in our household, but I knew it was no good. I just kept quiet. My father told me afterwards that in the night he had awakened to hear my mother quietly crying, and had thereupon opened a bottle of champagne procured for the silver wedding occasion, in which they had toasted one another. The next day my father turned in his *épergne* and, at my mother's request, got instead a cutlery chest.

My father's sessions with his friends took place on Saturday evenings. They would assemble after supper, Scotch and water was provided, and they would talk far into the night. My mother soon dozed off in her folding chair, and I, lying low in the cosy corner, with a bit of luck might survive until ten or ten-thirty. Even in my bed I still strained my ears to catch what they were saying, and shared in their laughter when it came rolling up to me. They were a bizarre company of conspirators; I doubt whether, if the Lord Chief Justice or the Home Secretary had been able to listen in to them, he would have been seriously perturbed. Yet, ostensibly at any rate, their conspiracy has succeeded sooner and more efficaciously than they would have dared to hope. They looked like, and indeed were, a collection of typical lower-middle-class clerks, decently dressed, obviously thriving, and, anyone would think just from looking at them, Tory voters to a man.

Will Straughan was a regular attender, bringing his wife with him, who also was a non-participant in the conversation, though she did not, like my mother, doze off. He was not nearly as politically inclined as my father, and but for him would probably not have bothered much with politics at all. I remember how once, when Northcliffe was mentioned, he tied a piece of string round one of his fingers and drew it tight, like a man being hanged. Then there was Mr Jordan, my father's tailor, and mine when I went to Cambridge. His suits were solid rather than stylish; and he got involved in an intrigue with the girl in his shop, all the details of which were familiar to me because I heard them being recounted in a dramatic whisper by Mrs Jordan to my mother. While he was measuring me up, and the girl was taking down the measurements, I eyed her appraisingly, but without detecting in her the qualities which had so enflamed Mr Jordan. Mr Patterson, another regular attender, was a Scotsman with a sandy moustache and a gold watch that he kept in a little leather bag, carefully taking it out when he wanted to know the time, and then as carefully putting it back into its bag. In the same methodical manner he filled and lit his pipe, blowing out the smoke in rhythmic gusts through his sandy moustache. He was an accountant who subsequently became a company director and rich. There were others who came occasionally, all of the same type – men of humble origins who were making their way in the world and wanted the world's ways to be changed. They were not in any real sense revolutionaries; rather, they planned to take over the existing social and economic system and run it better and more equitably. Their arguments seemed to me irrefutable, their hopes for the future impeccable. Instead of lots of milkcarts coming each day to each little street, there would be one; instead of money being squandered on battleships ('I'm interested in ships too,' was another of my father's open-air gambits: 'Hardships!'), it would be used for schools, hospitals, garden suburbs, and so on. Instead of railways, coalmines and industry generally being privately owned and enriching the few, they would be publicly owned and enrich us all. Listening to them in our little sitting-room seated on the cosy corner, I saw a rosy future before us if only my father and his henchmen would take over the country. Actually, I lived to see them – though not in their own persons – take over, but the rosy future continues to be elusive.

Though I did not notice it at the time, a notable absentee at these gatherings was the beneficiary of all our endeavour. I mean the worker, or, as we still called him, workman. (The change from 'workman' to 'worker' was as significant, semantically, as from 'master' to 'boss', or from 'the people' to 'the masses'.) It is true that among my father's growing number of visitors there would occasionally be one of whom my mother would say he was a workman, meaning by this, quite specifically, that he did not wear a bowler hat and a winged starched collar like my father, or polished boots, or cuff-links, or an overcoat with a velvet collar. He generally turned out, however, to be some special kind of worker, like a school caretaker or a road foreman. At Ruskin House, too, the headquarters of the local Labour Party, there were vaguely proletarian figures to be seen, but many more teachers and Quakers and ladies with private means who had been forcibly fed in suffragette days. Trotsky, in his History of the Russian Revolution, tells how a *mouzhik* was included in the Bolshevik delegation to Brest Litovsk. In his sheepskin coat and felt boots he was the admiration of all beholders, until one day, having taken a drop too much vodka, he actually started addressing the peace negotiators. Then he was speedily shut up. A worker is someone for whom everything is done as long as he keeps off stage; trade union leaders or shop stewards may have long speaking parts, but workers are for ever extras. Once, when I was conducting a television discussion on strikes, I asked for a worker to come on the programme. Our scouts searched far and wide, and at one point reported that they had found one in the neighbourhood of the Oval who would agree to appear. He turned out to be black and, in any case, failed to turn up. So we had to make do with the usual collection of notabilities from the nationalised industries and Transport House, topped up by a smattering of industrialists, civil servants, sociology dons, business efficiency experts, MPs, Hungarian economists, and a shop steward or two with King Street affiliations. Thus, in accordance with the BBC's Charter, all sides were represented.

Though we had little or no contact with workers, we were, as it happened, vouchsafed an occasional glimpse of the prospective Labour Party Front Bench. This was because when any of them came to Croydon to speak or lecture (which happened fairly often because of Croydon's nearness to London), my father usually took the chair and invited them home for hospitality. As a child, I saw both Ramsay MacDonald and Snowden; Hugh Dalton and J. R. Clynes came for a meal, and there were numerous other lesser Fabian lights who visited us in this way and cropped up subsequently as under-secretaries and ministers without portfolio. My mother treated these occasions as she might have done a visit from the Gadsbys; got out her best silver and crockery, and put us all into our best clothes. My father was inclined to be surly, and I, as usual, taking my cue from him, also affected to regard the fuss made as foolish and unnecessary. The thing that struck me about our visitors was their enormous condescension; they felt themselves already so near the seats of authority that they had begun cultivating the appropriate style.

This was particularly true of MacDonald, who shook hands by extending two fingers, made conversation by asking fatuous questions, and engaged in little playfulnesses almost like royalty. He was still relatively coherent, but the verbal circumlocution which was to make his last public utterances totally incomprehensible had already begun to gain on him. I can remember him holding forth about reading and taking country rambles – two activities to which, ostensibly, he was much given – and the words all getting mixed up into something like 'wandering and rambling to be alone in my library'. His picturesque appearance; the loosely tied coloured tie, the tweed suit, the carefully dishevelled grey hair, the sonorous Scottish voice with the R's rolling and rumbling like thunder – all produced what would be called nowadays a good image. My father in principle detested him, but in practice was rather proud of him as billed to be the first Labour Prime Minister, and at one time contributed a small sum weekly to his support, Members of Parliament in those days not being paid. Afterwards he considered it as money very ill-spent; worse than dipping it in the blood. In little more than a decade after MacDonald's appearance in our Croydon sitting-room, he was acting as co-host with Lady Londonderry at a Londonderry House reception – far less time than it took for the

Colonists to make their peace with the Vicar of Minchinhampton and qualify for admission to his churchyard. Though MacDonald was, on any showing, a derisory figure, I am inclined to think now that he was perfectly cast as the first Labour Prime Minister; with all the right attitudes and responses – the capacity at a moment's notice to break into a discourse about the peace of the worrrld; the reassurance he provided to the middle and upper classes that any fears they might have entertained that he seriously intended to take their money or dissolve their Empire were quite groundless; his translation from the poor boy in Lossiemouth to the Prime Minister in Downing Street. It all added up, I cannot help thinking, to what we actually wanted in Ruskin House, and we got it. The really terrible thing about life is not that our dreams are unrealised but that they come true.

Our Fabian visitors were more sympathetic to my father; careless, untidy, pipe-smoking men; ladies whose bosoms floated loose instead of being laced up like my mother's, and whose hair was piled upwards like an overcharged haystack instead of being tightly curled like hers. They were, in my father's sense, cultured; had been to the university, mostly Oxford or Cambridge; had contributed to the review columns of the *New Statesman* and the *Nation* (then still separate), and maybe written books; called Lytton Strachey 'Lytton', and Keynes 'Maynard', and Shaw 'G.B.S.' They represented everything my father most admired; had effortlessly acquired what he so desperately sought. They were what he wanted to be. Those hours at City libraries when he should have been eating or playing; the poring over French irregular verbs in order to be able to have a come-back if someone on the Croydon Council (an unlikely enough eventuality, I must say) quoted a Latin tag at him! – none of that for them. They were at ease in a world from which he felt he had been excluded, and which therefore seemed the more alluring – what he saw as the world of culture. How was he to know that this culture, for which he had an almost mystical veneration, was dying, if not already dead? That a neo-Stone Age rather than a neo-Fabian one lay ahead?

My father's working day lay between the 8.05 from Croydon East to London Bridge, and the 6.05 from London Bridge to Croydon East. The morning tide took him City-wards, the evening one brought him Croydon-wards. He boasted, justifiably, that he knew the track so well that he could tell from the sound of the train's wheels precisely where he was. I quite often accompanied him to the station; up the steep hill to the Recreation Ground, by the Water Tower (the tower that, for me, was the dark one Childe Roland came to); on past the little open-air stage and auditorium where the concert-party performed on summers' evenings (Kevin Billington in his magical way unearthed some survivors for a film he made about my childhood; creaking, groaning, a bit stiff on the lock-step, they were still able to give a suitably soulful rendering of 'I'm for ever blowing bubbles/Pretty bubbles in the air'); then the last stretch to the station with my father looking anxiously at his watch. Good-bye at the barrier, waving; he joining the throng down the slope to the platform, where I could just see him; then off to London Bridge. Over the Bridge, all of them stepping out; like a mighty army going as to work; most of them bowler-hatted, few girls in those days. Then dispersing, he to New Basinghall Street, and his high stool and his ledger. Quite often I was waiting at the barrier on his return. Train after train coming in, and a foolish dread seizing me that perhaps he never would come – anxiously scanning the faces as they came up the slope and went past the ticket collector. At last, there he was; always in the first batch, well to the fore, striding along. Only in the very last years of his time in the City did he allow himself the indulgence of a first-class season, and marched in a dignified way with the rear echelon. How delighted I was to see him! How overjoyed! Apart from one or two other rare occasions, there is no face except Kitty's I have ever picked out with such joyous relief as his, leading the field up the slope from the arrival platform at Croydon East.

From the station I quite often accompanied him to the Town Hall; down George Street and round past the fire station into Catherine Street. There was a time when I thought of the Croydon Town Hall as a kind of Duomo or Villa Borghese. Some grain of esteem for it must have survived, for I found myself vaguely regretful when I heard that there was a plan to demolish it and build a skyscraper on the site. As a special treat I was occasionally allowed to sit in the public gallery during a meeting of the Borough Council, where I followed the proceedings with breathless interest; especially, of course, when my father spoke, as he usually managed to do when I was present. For some years he was the only Labour councillor, which gave me a tremendous sense of the odds he was taking on in attacking the citadel of capitalism. I saw the Mayor in his red gown, the Town Clerk in his wig and black gown, the serried ranks of aldermen and councillors, as the hosts of the Philistines, and my father as David with his sling defying them. Politics for us consisted of this unequal combat, which nonetheless our side was destined to win. We licked down envelopes almost in our prams;

VOTE FOR MUGGERIDGE were almost the first three words we learnt to recognise. We wore red rosettes; when we were old enough we canvassed; we even appeared as a family group in my father's election address, having a family being regarded in those days, before anyone had heard of a population explosion, as a sign of civic virtue, especially in the case of a Labour candidate who might be associated by his opponents with dark reports of the nationalisation of women under the Bolsheviks in Russia.

Elections were for us like saints' days or festivals. The committee room in an empty shop, with trestle tables covered with leaflets; the windows darkened with posters; the lady helpers, mostly veterans in the cause, with grey untidy hair and cigarettes drooping from their mouths, vaguely partaking of the physical excitement which elections stir up. The endless cups of tea made on a gas-ring; the badinage with the candidate when he drops in; the interminable folding of paper and addressing of envelopes. Then the going from door to door as the evening comes on, and street lamps are lighted; Sir, Madam, I'm calling on behalf of the Labour candidate. Door slammed in your face, maybe; or some half-ribald, half-insulting remark of dismissal. Or a ding-dong argument – 'What I say is, they've got the money . . .' In any case, something a little furtive, shameful, in the way the steps come to the door in answer to one's knock; then the door opening a crack. Like making an indecent proposal – I want your vote, I want your body; love me! vote for me! Then the meetings in the school classrooms, with algebraic formulae, or other educational abracadabra still on the blackboard. Ladies and gentlemen, I'm here to-night . . .; the ladies and gentlemen not particularly responsive, apart from an occasional planted heckler. Finally, the climax: polling day, with hosts of Conservative cars, and our occasional Austin Seven. Lurking outside the polling stations with an impossible assignment to count the Labour voters; he looks like one, she looks like one – excuse me Sir, Madam. Not a seduction now, but rather the opposite; making off – Good-bye, it's been wonderful, I'll never forget, I'll call you, I'll . . . Forgetting even as the poll is declared. We're in, hurray! We're out, never mind, we'll try again.

This early grounding in electioneering has left me with an abiding interest in the pathology of universal suffrage democracy. In strange lands, where others might seek out ancient monuments, or folk music, or marriage customs, I seek out legislature, and spend enchanted hours listening to Honourable Members of all races, colours and creeds going through the weird and increasingly meaningless rigmarole which Westminster has imposed on the rest of the world. The Lok Sabha – what a version that is, with non-violent Swamis in their white *kadi*, their spinning-wheels left at home, shouting and shaking their fists at one another. Mejlis, Dail, Cortes, Senate and House of Representatives, and all through Black Africa, where majority rule prevails and oppositions languish in gaol. Dusky faces under judicial wigs; maces where studded clubs might be more appropriate; 'On a point of order,' and other such parliamentary plainsong, intoned in Orientalised English, with the words racing musically after one another, attributable, I have often thought, to the fact that the early teachers of English in these lands were often Welsh missionaries. Likewise in the USSR I have been fortunate enough to witness the gathering of what English newspapers like to call Soviet MPs; observed their rapture as Stalin addressed them; watched the supervisory policemen timing their applause when he had finished to make sure it reached the regulation seven and a half minutes; seen how when a resolution is put to them, each hand is raised in perfect unison. This surely the final and sublime apotheosis of majority rule, of government of the people for the people by the people, which we in our small, inadequate way were trying to operate in Croydon.

My father's political activities brought us into contact with two categories of local residents whom we should probably not otherwise have known: Quakers and clergymen. Now that the Labour Party has become so integrated with the political, economic and social *status quo*, it may seem strange that a family like ours should, because of our Socialist views, have been so isolated in a suburban residential district. In the ordinary way we should never have thought of so much as nodding to the local vicar, assuming unquestioningly that he must disapprove of us as much as we of him. The Quakers were rather different; for the most part, they were Liberals and Pacifists, readers of the *Manchester Guardian* with some sympathy for our position, and in any case, dedicated rather self-consciously to taking up an ostensibly brotherly attitude towards all men, whatever their views, ways and circumstances. What in the ordinary way would have separated us from the local Quakers would have been simply their affluence. Our ones all seemed – and I think were – decidedly rich; and riches are somehow more noticeable and forbidding when combined with a self-consciously abstemious way of life and awareness that love of money is the root of all evil. I think the rich young man who came to Jesus for guidance, and was told to sell all he had and give the proceeds to the poor, must have been a Quaker. My mother, I may add – much the most honest member of our family – liked Quakers *because* they were rich. She put them in the same category as the Gadsbys, and treated them accordingly. The rest of us took a somewhat more equivocal attitude. The Quakers were useful, certainly; they had motor-cars, for instance, and provided almost the only ones available to us at election time. They would ferry my father about from meeting to meeting, and help him out with his election expenses. At the same time, behind their backs, we used to make sly innuendos about the disparity between their wealth and their principles, and how they could scarcely be regarded as following out the precept not to lay up treasure on earth. I thought of them when I read in Wesley's Journal his cry of distress about how those he converted were made thereby industrious, abstemious and honest; virtues whose practice inevitably led to their becoming rich, and then, as he put it, all the work was to do again. My father was occasionally asked to speak at the local Friends' Meeting House, and I went with him. I noticed how his manner of speaking was slightly modified; less ranting and rumbustious, with no jokes about the National Debt or anything like that. When prayers were on he bowed his head with the others. Though he professed himself an atheist, I should not say that he was an irreligious man. In Penge he had attended a Baptist Church, though more for the ancillary activities like the Literary Society and the Mock Parliament than for the worship, I fancy.

I occasionally visited the Duncan Harrises, a Quaker household quite near us. She was a magistrate, a largish woman with a red face and faint moustache; full of good works and worthy purposes. He was appreciably smaller; a little wizened man with a limp, maybe from polio, who appeared rarely; I fancy, some sort of banker. They were obviously well off, and I observed with interest how this expressed itself even in the austerities of their way of life; the curtains in natural dyes, the bare unpolished wooden table, the oatmeal coverings of chairs and divan, the handwoven carpets and homespun dress Mrs Duncan Harris habitually wore. Wealth, like the kingdom of heaven, is within; one senses it, not so much in ostentation and luxury, as in a sort of inner gilded complacency. In Mrs Duncan Harris's case, this complacency extended to all her views and endeavour. She was a forerunner of what might be called the Good Panellist; a type as characteristic of our time as the Good Apprentice was of the Victorian age. As the Good Appprentice's virtue met with its reward in personal success, theirs does in public esteem. They hold all the right views and espouse all the right causes – family-planning clinics, legalisation of abortion, divorce reform, raising the school age, abolition of capital punishment, support for the United Nations. I could go on and on listing their virtuous attitudes, which call for a contemporary Samuel Smiles to celebrate them. It is a litany that many misspent years of participation in BBC and other panels had made excruciatingly familiar to me. Sometimes, sleepless, in the night I hear the Good Panellist holding forth; voice rather high and tremulous but with that ineffable sense of rectitude I first detected in Mrs Duncan Harris – 'What is needed is more and *better* education . . .'

Our relations with the clergy were rather different. The fact was, we made use of them. In view of the scurrilous stories circulating about our moral attitudes (in which the Colony figured), it suited us to have a clergyman on the platform, and if he wore his clerical regalia for the occasion so much the better. My father and his friends all called themselves atheists, and greatly enjoyed making what would then pass for being blasphemous jokes about, for instance, the Virgin Birth – much, I may add, to the distress of my mother. In view of their attitude, how was it possible for them to find common ground with a beneficed clergyman whose very livelihood – to put it no higher – depended on praying to God and promoting belief in Him; and who was under a statuatory obligation to recite a creed each Sunday which laid down specifically a whole series of beliefs about the deity, the incarnation, and the resurrection? Such questions may seem very naïve nowadays when we have grown used to clergymen adopting all sorts of positions, from glorifying *Playboy* magazine to detecting spiritual undertones in cults like Mau Mau. Then, however, we still had a vague notion that clergymen believed in Christianity, and upheld whatever particular version of it the denomination they belonged to based itself on. Subsequently, it has become clear that, far from this being the case, many clergymen are particularly drawn to any movement or position which denigrates the Christian religion and its founder. Having, perhaps, lost their faith, but being committed for one reason or another to their cloth, they derive great, if unconscious, satisfaction from anything that undermines the one and discredits the other.

The formula for peaceful co-existence between my father and his clerical supporters was 'making the world a better place'. Surely, one of our local clergy would say, puffing at his pipe and putting on an expression of almost excessive amiability, while seated, to my mother's great satisfaction, I may say, in her folding-chair – surely we can agree on a programme of social betterment. More money on education, slum clearance, welfare services, and so on. That's loving our neighbour, isn't it? As for loving God – we'll see about that in due course, ha! ha! ha! This, of course, is an over-simplification, but there *was* a sort of implicit pact whereby God was left out on the understanding that my father would accept the other's credentials as a progressive. On such a basis, they could co-operate; the clergyman taking the chair at Labour Party meetings, and even standing up for 'The Red Flag', and my father in his speech referring to his good friend the Rev. so and so, and even accepting a benediction at the end of the meeting if one was offered. In Croydon at that time such an arrangement was considered highly obnoxious by most church-going people, as well as by the Marxists and other extremists among my father's supporters, but it was the way the wind was blowing. Archbishop Temple would proclaim Christianity the most materialistic of religions (like saying that vegetarianism is the most carnivorous of all diets), and the episcopal contingent in the House of Lords, if they did not line up with the agnostics and atheists in matters like divorce and the legalisation of homosexuality, came in time to accept these 'reforms' as permissible, even desirable. One ought not to have been surprised. After all, only a few centuries after Christ had been crowned with a crown of thorns his alleged representative on earth was being crowned with a gold one. Human beings have the rather endearing trait, when they falsify the record, of doing it absolutely. Has not the Labour Party done exactly the same thing to William Blake, transforming his mystical New Jerusalem into a Welfare State, and using his exquisite verses on the subject at the obsequies of party worthies, even though Blake himself believed, as he wrote on one of his Dante designs (his last commission), that Dante had made the same mistake as Swedenborg in believing that 'in this world is the Ultimate of Heaven. This is the most damnable Falsehood of Satan & his Antichrist.'

I got to know one of our tame clergymen, and quite liked him. At the same time, I found him somehow too hearty and gross; his mouth seemed somehow too red and raw, his breath too noisy as he sucked at his pipe. With his shabby-genteel rectory, its large poorly tended garden, where his wife Dorothy, in gardening gloves, worked rather hopelessly at the beds; his plain daughter learning shorthand and hoping to study at RADA, his son at a minor public school who talked unconvincingly about backing horses and taking out girls – these were the poor whites of the bourgeoisie, and the first to leave the sinking ship. The Rev. Old Bill, looking for a better 'ole, found it, as he supposed, in the Labour Party. (Not a bad guess, as a matter of fact; Labour Prime Ministers, like any others, were prone to reward their sympathisers with preferment.) It was in such households that the crack-up of the bourgeoisie first showed; daughters turning up at the Windmill Theatre; sons among the delinquents, nature's double-agents, in the dock surprising the magistrate – 'After all the advantages you've had; a good home, a good education!' I should have expected some sociological Kinsey to work on the subject. Indeed, I might have tackled it myself, having been interested all my life in priests, clergy, monks, nuns, evangelists; any sort of professional religious or *exalté*. Perhaps I should have been one; I like to think a monk notable for his austerities, the voice of one crying in the wilderness; but more probably a tiresome Unitarian in Walsall who writes incessantly to the local paper. Anyway, the genus Intelligentsia may generally be considered as consisting of priests and religious *manqués*. The Rev. Stephen Spender, Fr Connolly, Rabbi Levin, Dom Graham Greene, Sister Brigid Brophy. It sounds right.

At week-ends and on bank holidays my father marshalled us for country walks or bicycle rides, the countryside being then easily accessible. Bicycling, and what was later called hiking, was another item in the early progressive package. There were Clarion Clubs and specially organised rambles; a love of nature was proclaimed as an enlightened alternative to religious worship, especially by healthy white-haired ladies with pink cheeks, and their weather-beaten consorts. The cult no doubt went back to Wordsworth and the Lake poets, but more immediate inspirers were Walt Whitman and Edward Carpenter, both celebrants of health and exuberance and the body beautiful, and both, as it happened, homosexual. Our copy of Whitman's *Leaves of Grass* had a splendid frontispiece of him, bearded, looking strikingly like Hemingway, and with a butterfly perched on his finger. Later, I learnt that among his effects was found a preserved butterfly with a specially fitted ring attached for fastening on his finger.

As we rode along on our bicycles with my father in the lead, he would shout back at us rapturously about the beauties of the surrounding landscape. Just look at those trees! What a view across the valley! Have you ever seen anything like the colours in the distance! His enthusiasm never flagged. My mother had given up bicycling long ago, and so did not accompany us. She had only enjoyed it when the two of them rode a tandem together, and she could occupy the rear seat; on her own, she found riding or pushing her bicycle uphill too arduous, and free-wheeling downhill too scaring. I assented eagerly to my father's exuberant appreciation of nature, but only to please him; without truly meaning or feeling it. Then, on a particular occasion, I found I really did mean it. I can remember the occasion perfectly; it was near Chipstead, going along a lane that ran past the church, on a June evening at about seven o'clock. I expect the lane now is in the middle of a housing estate. The light of the setting sun slashed the trunks of the trees, so that they were half gilded and half in shadow. Suddenly I realised with a tremendous feeling of exultation that this golden light of the sun, this fragrance of a June evening and light rustle of leaves – the whole golden, glorious scene had some special significance in which I participated. That in its all-embracing beauty it conveyed a oneness, and that to identify oneself with this oneness, and with the spirit animating it and giving it meaning, contained the promise of ecstasy. It was a moment of great illumination. Ever afterwards I have felt lost and imprisoned when only concrete lay around me for long. Like waking up in New York, and looking out of a hotel window before the day begins. Seeing the tall grey buildings as impenetrable prison walls; the narrow streets as for monotonous, aimless prison exercise; the tops of the buildings intersecting against the remote sky as prison bars. Thus imprisoned, what is there to do but live as prisoners do on fantasies of eroticism and violence; stupefied with drugs or their own despair? I owe to, of all people, Ilya Ehrenburg, an image that I invariably turn to for deliverance from such nightmares. Speaking of Pasternak's writings during the darkest days of Stalin's oppression, Ehrenburg said he saw in them the promise that, however high and thick the concrete might be piled, however widely spread, even though it covered the whole earth, there would always be a crack, and in that crack – greenness, life.

I will not pretend that, bicycling with my father and my brothers by Chipstead Church, all, or any, of this came into my mind. At the same time, it marked a sort of turning point; thenceforth, wherever I have been, and however dismal my situation or prospect, there has been the never-failing solace of feeling earth below my feet and seeing sky above my head. Aldous Huxley in one of his essays makes the rather silly, but characteristic, point that such solace is available only because nature has been tamed, and that we hug our urban sanctuaries if the alternatives are wild jungle or parched desert or roaring tornado. Actually, jungle and desert and tornado, no less than meadow and stream and gentle breezes, express what concrete hides – our own true habitat, the creation of which we are part and the creator responsible for it. It is in his inexorable separation from this habitat, in all its aspects, that the present alienation of technological man consists. The lost connection can be made in a desert or a jungle just as surely – perhaps more so – than in a landscaped garden or olive grove cultivated for centuries. Poor Huxley! – he was always looking for mystical truth in a scientific theorem; searching for a Holy Grail which turned out to be a retort; climbing up St Simon Stylites's pillar only to find himself when he got to the top in the Cavendish Laboratory. How fitting that he should end his days with Dr Timothy Leary as his *guru*, muttering drug-induced psychedelic banalities, and provide a name for one of the San Francisco junkies' favourite haunts – Brave New World. His Huxley heritage could not have been more appropriately expiated.

On Sunday evenings my father read aloud to us from the plays of Shakespeare. He had a large three-volume edition illustrated with engravings. There was a companion volume of Dante's 'Inferno' with illustrations by Doré whose pages I often turned over, shivering at the plates of poor souls roasting in Hell even though I was brought up to believe that no such place existed. My father read all the parts in the Shakespeare plays, modifying his voice for the clowns and minor characters, and giving everything he'd got to Othello, Lady Macbeth or Hamlet. I doubt if he was a particularly good reader; I, anyway, found the blank verse difficult to follow, and derived little benefit from the readings, though in a way I enjoyed them; I think, again, because of the enormous zest my father put into them. My first appreciation of Shakespeare came a little later when I attended a series of special matinees for school children at the Old Vic, at which we saw most of his better-known plays. We paid sixpence for our seats, and fourpence for the journey by tram from Croydon to Waterloo; swaying and screeching our way through Streatham and Brixton on those old double-decker LCC trams whose connections with overhead electric cables on frosty days gave off clouds of sparks. I dare say the Old Vic productions were pretty rough, and the scenery scanty – I seem to recall mostly curtains – but I loved every minute of them. The star was Sybil Thorndike, who seemed to take almost every part, male and female, though she can't have played Lear; I remember her brother Russell in the role, memorable because at one of the most dramatic moments his beard came off. No doubt there have been greater actresses, but to me she has a unique glory, because of those Old Vic performances. I was glad the other day to have an opportunity to tell her so.

My father's books consisted of six or seven shelves-full in a case with glass doors. I got to know them intimately. A stranger could have deduced from them everything my father hoped for and believed in. I, who was no stranger, saw them as the bricks out of which he had constructed his Heavenly City, to whose coming to pass his life was dedicated, and as I thought then, mine, too. Quite a number of the books are now forgotten, or remembered only for their period interest, but at the time similar collections must have existed in many a progressive household. In a way it was an odd assortment. I have mentioned Rousseau's *Confessions* and Whitman's *Leaves of Grass*, which represented the wilder flights of freedom – ostensibly, along with justice, our ultimate objective. With them, a volume of Kropotkin's *Reminiscences*. He was greatly revered among us, and always punctiliously given his title of Prince. Just about when I first turned over the pages of his *Reminiscences* he was returning to his native land in triumph; to die there shortly afterwards, and to be accorded a State funeral. As the cortège passed the Leningrad prison, his followers, incarcerated in it, shook their fists through the bars – the last anarchist demonstration ever to take place in the USSR.

Beside Kropotkin, there was the Everyman edition of *Das Kapital*. Did my father ever read it? I doubt it; I certainly didn't, and haven't. Then a collected edition of Carlyle in five brown volumes which I still possess. I felt I had a right to them because, my father told me, I was given my second name, Thomas, after Carlyle. It is a little difficult now to see how Carlyle fitted in with the others, given his loathing and contempt for representative government, his adulation of leadership as exemplified by a Frederick the Great and a Cromwell, his wild vituperative outbursts against reformers, and – as they would now be called – do-gooders. Somehow, however, the trick was done, and Carlyle given a place in the pantheon of the Left. To-day he would be seen as displaying early intimations of Fascism. I myself, whether out of satisfaction at being his namesake, or from a natural affinity, find the crusty old fellow very much to my taste; especially his curious wry humour; for instance, his account of going out to see Coleridge at Highgate – a comic masterpiece – in his Life of his friend Sterling. Standing alongside Carlyle was Ruskin's *Unto This Last*; the book that Gandhi said, along with the New Testament and Tolstoy's *Confessions*, had most influenced him. Ruskin's socialism was, from my father's point of view, suspect, but he was held in affection for his denunciation of the sheer ugliness capitalism had created everywhere, especially in the industrial north – what we now call pollution.

In a similar vein, William Morris's *News from Nowhere* and *Earthly Paradise* (from which also Sunday evening readings were given), with their nostalgia for medieval guilds, knights in armour, and Pre-Raphaelite ladies with long white necks; aspects of socialism which figured little in our Croydon Labour Party. The Webbs' *History of Trade Unionism*, two weighty tomes; Tawney's *Acquisitive Society*, *The Ragged Trousered Philanthropists*, Edward Bellamy's *Looking Backward*; socialist classics all, stood together in a solid phalanx. The last I never persevered with; on the wall of my bedroom there was a picture of a man in a field bending over a furrow which purported to illustrate it, but I never understood that either. Rather apart from the others, a Schopenhauer volume, in the Home University Library, and Heine's Autobiography, from which my father loved to quote what he regarded as sparkling *mots*, a particular favourite being a remark that the Venus di Milo had beautiful hands. This brought out with great archness and, to make sure I got the point (which I didn't), an aside explaining that the Venus di Milo had no arms. Then the famous first collection of Fabian Essays, Shaw's *Plays Pleasant and Unpleasant*, and Ibsen's Plays. Shaw was, of course, to my father the incomparable hero of our time; he treasured his acquaintance with him, and proudly displayed the correspondence they exchanged over the Boer War (including a postcard on the top of which Shaw had drawn a Union Jack), in which Shaw, ever on the side of the big battalions, supported Chamberlain, whereas my father was a pro-Boer. My own reading of his plays and their prefaces was decidedly desultory, but somehow I picked up a reference in them to Maria Bashkirtsef, who had created a sensation by disclosing in her published diary that she was prone to sexual desire – something no lady had ever before publicly admitted. This was a discovery I did not pass on to my mother, but brooded upon it, without coming to any clear conclusions as to its significance. Recently I noticed walking along the Promenade des Anglais at Nice, that the plaque to Maria on a house there where she had stayed had recently been enlarged. This seemed appropriate.

This diverse pabulum constituted my father's sacred texts, showing him the way to salvation. First, the existing structure had to be overthrown; not with bloodshed and violence, but through persuasion and the ballot box. It was a kind of revivalism without tears; sinful men were to be washed, but not in the blood of the Lamb; in, as it were, municipal water, with carbolic soap purveyed by the co-op. Having captured the machinery of government by means of a parliamentary majority, it would be possible to take over industry, the banks, the land etc., and operate them, not for profit, but in the public interest. So, State, producer and consumer – a new version of the Trinity; three in one and one in three – would be harmoniously related, and all impediments to the enduring health, wealth and happiness of mankind removed or, like the State in the Marxist version, allowed to wither away. All this was only, in my father's estimation, a means; the end was the Earthly Paradise, the translation of William Morris's *News from Nowhere* into *News from Somewhere*. Then Whitman's sense of abounding joy in his own and all creation's sensuality would sweep away the paltry backwaters of bourgeois morality; the horrors of industrial ugliness which Ruskin so eloquently denounced would dissolve, and die forgotten as a dream (phrases from hymns still washed about in my father's mind) as slums were transformed into garden cities, and the belching smoke of hateful furnaces into the cool elegance of electric power. As for the ferocious ravings of my namesake, Carlyle, about the pettifogging nature of modern industrial man's pursuits and expectations – all that would be corrected as he was induced to spend ever more of his increasing leisure in cultural and craft activities; in the enjoyment of music, literature and art.

It was perfectly true – a point that Will Straughan was liable to bring up at the Saturday evening gatherings – that on the present form the new citizenry might be expected to have a marked preference for dog-racing over chamber music or readings from *Paradise Lost*, but, my father would loftily point out, education would change all that. Education was, in fact, the lynchpin of the whole operation; the means whereby the Old Adam of the Saturday night booze-up, and fondness for Marie Lloyd in preference to Beatrice Webb, would be cast off, and the New Man be born as potential fodder for Third Programmes yet to come.

Very properly and logically, my father sent my brothers and me to the local elementary and secondary schools, in this differing from many Socialists of his sort who, like Lord Snow, praise the State system while preferring Eton or some lesser establishment of the same kind for their own progeny. It is something for which I personally am profoundly grateful. If I had gone even to the local grammar school – which rated as a public school of sorts – I feel sure that vanity, and a congenital and rather lamentable passion to be liked, would have induced me to fit into the system, and I should have gone on to Cambridge, not as an outsider, but already with the requisite preliminary conditioning, emerging fully brain-washed to take my place with the new Socialist elite, the Hendersons and Greenwoods and Noel-Bakers, corresponding to the Cecils and Percys and Cavendishes in the Tory Party. From this abysmal destiny I was saved by the happy accident of going to an elementary school when, to all intents and purposes, such schools were considered to be only for the children of parents too poor and un-ambitious to look for anything better. Later, of course, this changed, with the coming to pass of comprehensive Etons like Holland Park School, specially earmarked for the progressive elite. As for my second-ary school – it had just opened and, in the conditions of the 1914–18 war, was largely staffed with a bizarre collection of aged and incompetent teachers who for one reason or another had been rejected for national service. Neither type of school was likely to make any very strong impression on the boys who went through them, and I emerged un-scathed and largely unlettered. Some years ago I returned to my old secondary school and found that it had now become a grammar school, with all the usual appurtenances in the shape of houses, prefects, blazers, a school song, and so on, and is no doubt turning out as good a crop of long-haired, pot-smoking, discotheque-frequenting youths as any other establishment of the kind. Alas, my father's vision of the intellectual, moral and aesthetic transformation this kind of education was going to bring about seemed as far from realisation as ever, if not farther.

My elementary school was in one of those stark bare buildings which successive Education Acts spawned over the country; wherever children liable under the Act were gathered together. It stood in an asphalt playground; inside, the classrooms were divided by partitions which could be pulled back to provide an assembly hall. Here we gathered in the morning for prayers and a hymn, and on Friday afternoons to sing 'Now the Day is Over' – which we did with enthusiasm since it signified two clear days of freedom ahead. This somewhat lugubrious hymn, if I happen to hear it, still awakens in me an instinctive response of delight. The headmaster presided; a grey, distinguished-looking man who spoke with great distinctness, as elementary teachers did in those days. He sounded us off with his tuning-fork. Never having been able to sing in tune, I developed a faculty for appearing to be joining in eagerly, but actually making little or no sound; a faculty that has proved useful in all sorts of ways subsequently. For instance, in listening to long anecdotes, or expositions on how the monetary crisis can be solved. Once the late Professor Namier read me a whole front article he had written in *The Times Literary Supplement* – some three to four thousand words – in a slow deliberate voice. It was a searching test, but as he droned on, I was back in my elementary school, ostensibly singing away at the top of my voice but actually thinking of other things. After the singing, the Headmaster offered prayers; we had some difficulty with the aspirate in 'hallowed be thy name', and were sometimes required to repeat it several times before we said it to his satisfaction. I asked afterwards in class whether God was as particular about aspirates as the headmaster, and was rebuked – alas, the first of many similar occasions.

My first teacher was Miss Corke, a young girl straight from college; earnest and pretty. I did not then, of course, know, but she had become friendly with another elementary school teacher in Croydon – D. H. Lawrence – with whom she spent much of her spare time. While she was taking me through my alphabet, Lawrence was taking her through his dark unconscious. Her reminiscences of Lawrence, when I came to read them, seemed to me to give a clearer and more sympathetic picture of what he was really like than the rest of the regiment of women who ravened round him and subsequently produced their testaments. Some of his poems are addressed to her, and one of his novels – *The Trespasser* – deals with a tragic incident in her life, about which she also wrote a novel, *Neutral Ground*. Thus, an Eng. Lit. scout who wanted to could make a comparison between the incident itself, Lawrence's treatment of it and her own. I was able to persuade her to come and talk to me about Lawrence in my garden under the camera's eye. This is one of the things that television can do uniquely well – recording an experience or a relationship in the very words, and with the very gestures and expression, of the person concerned. Meeting again in such circumstances after so many years was a strange and pleasant experience; she a small white-haired lady in her eighties, but as sharp and clear as a bird, and I the person I am, in my late sixties. The June weather happened to be perfect, the garden at its best, the flowers at their brightest. Lawrence's uneasy ghost seemed to be hovering round. I still felt as I had all those years before, that I was in the presence of my teacher, whose rebukes must at all costs be avoided, and whose praise was infinitely desirable.

When the cameras had gone, and as the evening wore on, a difference of view, if not a dispute, arose between us. This concerned what human life is about, and where we who are involved so mysteriously in this experience of living are being led. Miss Corke still took the view that mankind have their destiny in their own hands, and are passing on to new heights of understanding and achievement, with the prospect of ultimately being themselves the masters of their own universe. She even read me a passage – I must say, little to my taste – in this sense from Wells's earlier writings. I did not unkindly remind her of how totally, in *Mind at the End of its Tether*, his last work, he retreated from this position, groaning and beating his breast over, of all things, atomic fission, which, in the light of all his previous utterances and prophesies, should have been for him an occasion for great rejoicing. It was as though, on the last day, a Salvation Army band paraded with its colours flying, only to turn tail and run when the earth began to shake and the heavens to unroll like a scroll. I did, however, try and explain that this whole notion of Man climbing a mountain peak at the top of which he finds his total and definitive fulfilment is, to me, not merely absurd, but highly depressing. That, rather, as it seems to me, he is as Bunyan saw him, a pilgrim making his way through all the perils that his own appetites and wickedness create, to an ultimate enlightenment. The pilgrimage is endlessly made, from generation to generation, and from age to age, and the way is always the same way; more likely to be found by the lowly and the pure of heart than by the strong and the proud. I could see that my words impressed Miss Corke as little as her reading had me. Her preference for Darwin over Bunyan was marked.

After Miss Corke had retired to bed, I stayed awake a long time thinking of the chasm which divides those who believe in a mortal destiny, however glorious, and those who cannot find the heart to live at all, to go on from day to day, except on the basis of an immortal one. Belonging, as I do, so strongly to the latter category, the former seem to me fated, either to suppose themselves to be gods and, like Icarus, fly into the sun, there to perish, or to fall back upon their animal natures, and the Sisyphus task of maintaining a condition of permanent rut. Miss Corke's friend and would-be lover, Lawrence, straddled the two positions. With one side of him he saw with true imaginative clarity the ruinous course the world was set on – 'as if a whole social form were breaking down, and the human element swarmed within the disintegration, like maggots in cheese . . . so that it seems as though we had created a steel framework, and the whole body of society were crumbling and rotting in between'. But all he had to offer in the way of a solution were the sick phallic fantasies and perversities of quasi-impotence, carried in his last novel, *Lady Chatterley's Lover*, to a pitch of absurdity seldom, if ever before, equalled.

He was one of those men, tragic and gifted, who work out in themselves the conflicts and dilemmas of their time; who are themselves our own fever and pain. In Lawrence's case, his sickness became the cult of succeeding generations; Lady Chatterley, sponsored by a motley collection of writers, clerics and miscellaneous intelligentsia, was the progenitor of a torrent of porno-eroticism which her creator would have found deeply abhorrent, and incidentally so enriched her publisher in the process that his shares were quoted on the Stock Exchange as Chatterleys. It only remained for the Warden of All Souls to exercise his considerable, but dormant, scholarship in demonstrating conclusively that Mellors's own sexual fancies were distinctly abnormal, to round off a superb exercise in contemporary fatuity. When, in 1930, I heard of Lawrence's death – actually, at a cocktail party in Cairo; a quasi-literary affair of the sort that used to take place there in those pre-British Council days, in which a very little literature was served up with a lot of Levantine dressing – I found myself crying, though even then I was beginning to realise how shallow was the soil in which his thought and talent had grown and developed. It is the only occasion I can recall in which I cried over the death of a public figure unknown to me. I suppose I was unconsciously aware of how in some sense Lawrence was the prototype of us all – weaving a phallic cult out of his impotence, turning his shrill rage against the inexorable doomsday march of our time, howling down the corridors of time to produce a thin delphic echo. With his ribald seraglio of Baroness, Hon. Brett and Mabel Dodge; with Middleton Murry for John the Baptist and a sometime Bishop of Woolwich for posthumous advocate, he surely deserved my Cairene tears.

The first event in the outside world that I remember as something actually happening and involving me was the outbreak of the 1914–18 war. My father came home with a newspaper and told us. His face was grave, but what I most vividly recall is the tremendous excitement of everybody. The crowds in the streets shouting and cheering; the sense of terrific events about to happen. Contrary to what pacifists and other humane persons would like to believe, wars, when they break out, tend to be popular. They offer the illusion of an escape from the boredom which is the lot of, particularly, technological man. He will be able to make off, not shamefacedly or furtively, but as a hero; the routine of his daily life and domestic relationships will be broken, and the sameness of his days give place to uncertainty and drama. In August 1914 they shouted: 'Hurrah for war!'; in September 1939 they did not dare to do that after the Peace Ballot and all the talk about another war being the end of civilisation, but a lot of people may well have felt the same without letting on. How it would be in the event of yet another war fought with atomic weapons is difficult to say. It is true that the Vietnam war has been unpopular, but mainly among students, who have no routine or domestic relationships to escape from. If recruitment, instead of being among the young, had been restricted to married men of forty and upwards, I doubt whether there would have been much trouble.

Many accounts have been written of this undoubtedly momentous occasion, which will probably appear in the history books as marking the final decline of Western European dominance in the world. There was Grey with his 'They are putting out the lights . . .' (which apparently he didn't say or, if he did, meant something quite different), and Kitchener sitting behind his big moustache, and estimating, to everyone else's total incredulity, that the war would last at least five years. Leonard Woolf told me that he and the Bloomsburyites saw in the outbreak of the war the end of all their hopes, reasonable in the pre-1914 context, as he considered, for moving forward into a kindlier and better civilisation. One imagines them wailing together over those lost hopes. My father's face was grave, but he had doubtless just read in the paper that people reading the paper had grave faces. As for me, I was soon calculating that if only the war would go on for another five years I should be called up. I even, when the war had been going for two years, went with great trepidation into a recruiting office near the Town Hall and said I was seventeen, though I knew I looked, if anything, younger than my years, and my voice still had not properly broken. The recruiting sergeant, a kindly old regular with a rosette in his service hat, told me to come back with a birth certificate. My two elder brothers were soon both in the services – my eldest brother a subaltern in polished riding-boots, and the next one in the newly formed Royal Flying Corps with a tunic fastening on his shoulder like a fencing jacket and a fore-and-aft cap – and I envied them inordinately. Recruits, still in civilian clothes, were marched with a band to the railway station, and I sometimes trailed along behind them. Our school cadet corps had been revivified, and we occasionally marched through the streets to the sound of kettle drums, led by our headmaster, an unsoldierly figure who habitually wore his Sam Browne over the wrong shoulder. I myself rose to be CSM, having developed an unexpected gift for bellowing out orders.

The outbreak of the 1914–18 war, among many other things, confronted my father and his friends with a delicate situation. They had all been pro-Boers in the Boer War, and were more or less committed to a pacifist position. One of my father's strongest points in Surrey Street was always to draw attention to what might be achieved in the way of schools and hospitals with the cost of just one dreadnought. Again, he frequently denounced war scares as a device of cunning armament manufacturers to increase the demand for their wares. General Roberts, who went about the country calling for rearmament in face of German aggression, was, if not as abhorrent as Northcliffe, a decidedly unsympathetic figure. Armament manufacturers – commonly known among us as merchants of death – were a godsend in the way of providing us with an identifiable villain; one of the great needs of the political Left being to be able to point an accusing finger at someone, or some corporate body, as being responsible for public and private wrongs and misfortunes. We spoke darkly about Vickers, Krupp, the *Comité des Forges*, above all about a certain mysterious Sir Basil Zaharoff, as being allied together to keep us all spending our money on useless armaments, to their consequent enrichment. It was one of our arguments that, if only private trading in arms were stopped, wars and war-scares would likewise automatically come to an end. How surprised we should have been to know that governments flogging arms to all and sundry would far outdo private operators, and that actually a future Labour Government would employ a representative at a very high salary to go about the world for that very purpose.

Then there was the question of Germany, greatly preferred in those days in progressive circles to France. Carlyle may have had something to do with this, and even the Prince Consort, reputed to be a progressive sort of man. Above all, there were the German Social-Democrats, respectable, God-fearing, beer- rather than wine-drinkers, who could surely be relied on to curb the sabre-rattling policies of the Kaiser and the Prussians. When in the Reichstag they voted for war credits, the bottom fell out of this whole position. At the next Saturday evening gathering, the talk went on longer, and more whisky and water was drunk than at any previous one. In the end it was decided, rather along the same lines as the Colonists when they ejected the farmer who had started nibbling away at their land, that the war must for the time being be supported in the hope that, once won, it would be possible to take steps to prevent anything of the kind occurring again. I, listening in the cosy corner, agreed, and when, on Monday morning, on my way to school, I saw some boys throwing mud at a drawing of Kaiser Bill which had been chalked on the wall, I joined in. Being a hopelessly bad marksman, I failed to reach the target.

It was at this time that I started going to the cinema. One had opened in South Croydon. On Saturday afternoons one could get in for three-pence, and stay there till the early evening, reeling out, blinking, into the sunshine or the dusk. There was a long serial that I followed assiduously, starring Pearl White; the early Charlie Chaplin comedies were shown, and once a production of *Macbeth* by Beerbohm Tree, with Sarah Bernhardt playing Lady Macbeth. A flickering, incomprehensible film which yet stuck in my mind because of this extraordinary old woman appearing in it, by this time incapable of even standing up. In those days the cinema was in almost total darkness, broken only by the torches of the usherettes flickering like glow-worms as they showed people in and out. Every now and again, to relieve the musty, stuffy smell of the place, perfume was squirted along the rows and over our heads. A pianist tinkled away, and there was usually a singing item in which a figure on the screen appeared to be singing a song that was actually played on a gramophone. The sync frequently went awry, with the words of the song and the movements of the singer's lips not tallying. What fabulous development this presentation of moving pictures on film was to undergo! Picture palaces as fanciful as Kubla Khan's, stars whose blown-up, long-drawn-out embraces would provide erotic fantasies and dream bed-fellows for all mankind; organists, seated at their jewelled instruments, rising out of the floor; then the shadows on the screen speaking, changing from black-and-white into colour, acquiring three dimensions, to be at last piped via aerials, or dreaming spires, into private homes; a nightly spectacle effortlessly watched, with every sitting-room a Caliban's magic island, filled with sounds and sweet airs which give delight and hurt not, so that when the viewers wake – if they ever do – they cry to sleep again. The reign of the camera had begun. I cannot pretend that I was aware of the implications of my protracted Saturday afternoon communings with shadows flickering across a screen, but it is certainly true that, increasingly, when I emerged, what was outside took on the character of the pictures I had been looking at, rather than the other way round. All the world in a picture palace.

When the zeppelins, those great silver fish, came to bomb us, we strained our eyes looking for them in the sky, heard the explosions as they dropped their bombs, then with one accord made our way to where the bombs had fallen – in this case, Brixton. Many others who had the same notion, were milling about there, looking for souvenirs; bits of bomb or shrapnel, frenziedly digging out of the wooden blocks of the roadway any fragments of metal they could find – actually, more often than not, the metal studs of motor tyres which had got embedded there. Somehow it recalled scenes I had read of in historical novels of massacres or martyrdoms in which the spectators bathed their handkerchiefs in the blood of the victims.

Or, again, Armistice Day, when with a school friend I took a bus to Woolwich, staying on at the terminus and returning in the same bus to Croydon. From the open upper-deck we watched the crowds singing, shouting, dancing, embracing, vomiting, climbing on to the tops of taxis, grabbing one another and making off to the parks. It was, to me, an eerie and disturbing, rather than a joyful, scene – those flushed animal faces, dishevelled women, hoarse voices. Perhaps at fifteen – which I then was – I should have liked to join in; at the same time, in the light of my father's hopes, I had to consider that it boded ill. Were these the future citizens of his Socialist Commonwealth? Was this what freedom meant? I found myself, as I so often have, in the position of a reluctant and indecisive prig. Then, I was too young to decide the matter one way or the other; when the next Armistice Day came round, some twenty-seven years later, too old.

At home my father attached a small Union Jack to the porch of our house. There were, of course, many other flags flying that day, but that my father should put one out was stupefying in its implications. It would scarcely have been less surprising if he had suddenly announced that he had been appointed a Governor of the Bank of England, or that he was contemplating taking Holy Orders. Union Jacks were for Conservative rallies on Empire Day, or to drape over the table at Conservative election meetings; not for us. When the National Anthem was played, we stood up as a matter of form, but in a languid way, with a deprecatory expression on our faces, indicating that the tune and the ceremonial had nothing to do with us, but belonged to the world of bearded King George V and enamelled Queen Alexandra; of prelates and judges and peers, of Lloyd George with his white locks falsely floating in the wind, and Lord Kitchener with his pointing finger; of admirals and generals and air-marshals in their glittering regalia. My father realised that the flag on our porch was something that required an explanation, and so went on to deliver what amounted to a little formal apologia for it, with an eye cast, especially, in my direction.

In the first place, he said, he felt immeasurable relief at the ending of the war's senseless slaughter and destruction, and at the survival of my two older brothers. Then he looked forward to a new and better world. If he did not actually say one fit for heroes to live in, he might well have. We like to think that we saw through the fraudulence of the past, but actually the same false money jingles in every pocket. Furthermore, he went on, however dubious had been the purported causes of the war, and however monstrously unscrupulous its conduct, it had, willy nilly, turned into a war to end war. There must, there could, never be another; mankind would not stand for it. Already the phrase League of Nations had entered into my father's vocabulary, and thence into mine; already the Fourteen Points, and President Woodrow Wilson who propounded them, belonged to our kingdom of light. The turgid discourses of this Princeton professor were, to us, golden words, and he a knight in shining armour who could be relied on to champion righteousness. As it happened, I saw the President in the newsreel at one of my Saturday afternoon cinema visitations. He moved across the screen from his motor car to the Palace of Versailles with the quick step and in the silver rain of early movies; tall black hat jerkily raised, spectacles shining, lantern jaws opening and shutting, but no sound coming. I suppose I had expected something quite different; someone Garibaldi-like, Byronic, with shining eyes and floating hair, rather than this sober-looking professorial figure who might easily have been one of my undertaker-grandfather's men. At that moment of history he was the centre of all attention, the focus of the hopes of millions of people. It was reported that Eastern European peasants made wooden models of him before which they lit candles and prostrated themselves. If so, I hope very much that one or two exemplars remain, to be discovered by future anthropologists, if there are any. Their observations on the cult would be interesting.

Looking back, it strikes me as curious that the Russian Revolution, to the best of my recollection, made so small an impact at the Saturday evening gatherings. I should have expected it to be an occasion for great celebration, especially as my father made a sea trip to Russia shortly before the outbreak of the 1914–18 war to recover from a minor operation, and had numerous anecdotes of the police surveillance to which he was subjected there. The reason, perhaps, is that, in the wartime Press, news of the Revolution, and of the Kerensky regime which followed, was played down, and by the time the war was over the Bolsheviks were in control. About them, Fabian Socialists like my father were extremely dubious, and with an election coming along they did not want to be identified with men who were systematically represented as murderous, anti-Christian and cynically untrustworthy. In the posters and cartoons of the time, the Bolsheviks are usually shown as bearded, piratical figures, with their hands dripping blood – visibly, if the picture happened to be in colour. Very much, in fact, as capitalists are shown in *Krokodil* to-day. Shaw, the Webbs and the other leading Fabians were likewise strongly opposed to the USSR in its early struggling days; they only began to admire it when it had hardened into an authoritarian terrorist regime. Their admiration turned to besotted adulation when Stalin took on the role, and very much the style, of the deposed Czar; only more brutally, efficiently and vaingloriously.

It should be remembered, too, that up to the outbreak of the 1914–18 war, the early Socialists assumed a continuance of the international status quo as far as Western Europe was concerned, and so took little interest in foreign affairs. In the famous first collection of Fabian Essays, not one deals with this subject. It is assumed that England will continue to be strong, rich and stable, disposing of the requisite means to introduce, constitutionally and by consent, practical socialist measures. In the shambles that followed the Versailles settlement, this assumption was rudely shattered; thenceforth the Polish Corridor, the Sudetenland, the Anschluss, the re-militarisation of the Rhineland, the Saar Plebiscite, became part of daily life; salt cellars and cutlery were arranged on the table to show that whoever controlled so-and-so dominated somewhere else. Clausewitz came to be quoted rather than Heine or Schopenhauer, and my poor father, who had put out a flag on 11th November, 1918, found himself constrained in the years that followed to pore over atlases in search of new and old frontiers. At the end of his life he ruefully reflected that, when the means to install Socialism were available, there were not enough Socialists, and when there were, if anything, too many Socialists, the means were lacking.

To me, when I got to hear more about it, the Russian Revolution seemed a glorious episode. I related it to the taking of the Bastille and all the events that followed as I had read of them in Carlyle and *A Tale of Two Cities*. The fact that both Carlyle and Dickens present, on the whole, unfavourable pictures of the French revolutionary regime did not detract from its essential glamour in my eyes; nor prevent me from believing that the October Revolution and its outcome were similarly glamorous. A love of revolution for its own sake, quite apart from its circumstances and consequences, is part of the romantic out-look; then, as the young do now, we shouted for revolution without thinking of how, in France, it had resulted in Napoleon, the prototype for every power- and notoriety-seeking villain who has afflicted mankind subsequently; nor, of course, knowing that in Russia it would result in Stalin, one of the most blood-thirsty and obscurantist tyrants of all time. We called the Metropolitan Mounted Police Cossacks, rejoiced over early Soviet films like *Mother* and *The Battleship Potemkin*, spoke of workers' control and cadres and agitprop, and I personally decided inwardly that sooner or later I would go to Russia and throw in my lot with the new and better way of life that, I was confident, was coming to pass there. It may be that this cult of revolution for its own sake is now coming to an end, despite the vociferousness of its student prac-titioners. The fact that one of its most unsavoury devotees – Byron – has recently been honoured by being accorded a place in Westminster Abbey, suggests as much. What the Dean and Chapter approve to-day history will have abolished yesterday.

Now I fell in love for the first time. I happened to see Dora, a girl of about my own age, whose brother I vaguely knew, playing tennis on a public court, and instantaneously the whole of existence for me was concentrated on that one face, uniquely beautiful, as it seemed, and distinct from all other faces. At the same time, the scene itself in which I saw her was glorified and became angelic; as though the wire-netting of the court were golden mesh, the grass greener and softer than any grass ever before seen, the sound of the tennis ball against the racquets, and the laughter and shouts of the players, joyous and most wonderful. Whatever bodily stirrings accompanied these transports were merged and lost in this larger ecstasy, and I should have been outraged to think that what I felt could be reduced to the dimensions of schoolboy eroticism, with which, inevitably, I had become familiar. I was reminded quite recently of how deep-seated these feelings were when I happened by chance to see a schoolgirl wearing in her hat the same badge – an ivy leaf – as Dora had done, and found myself suddenly alerted, as though I were still constantly on the watch for it, just as I had been more than half a century before.

After our first casual encounter we spent nearly all our spare time together; often in the evening at her home. I grew very fond of her father particularly; a delightful character who called his wife 'Peach

Blossom' and was given to playing 'The Lost Chord' on his cornet. It sometimes happened that, to stay with Dora a little longer, I missed the last tram and had to walk the three miles or so home along the empty track; somehow borne up on my way; not quite fixed by gravity on the tarmac, or governed by the regular chiming of the Town Hall clock. I suppose there are few routes more intrinsically remote from Blake's notion of piping through the valley wild than from Thornton Heath, where Dora lived, to South Croydon, where I did, following the tram lines. Yet, for some reason, of all my memories of her, this one, of trudging homeward after the last tram had gone, has a special glow about it. There were, of course, quarrels and angry partings; we exasperated one another with the sexual urges we mutually aroused, and then only partially and inadequately, or not at all, satisfied. We went for country walks together, picked blackberries, talked about books and writers, and what we were going to do in the world. I even bashfully read out verses I had written addressed to her, most of which are now, mercifully, lost. I recall with shame one thing I did, which was to use some of these verses in a satirical sense in a play I wrote – *Three Flats* – that was put on by the Stage Society in 1931, and subsequently published. From time to time throughout my life, without deliberate intent, I have done such cruel things, directed often against those I cared for most.

Our youthful love belonged to the suburban setting in which we lived; to the rows of small identical houses; to the Crescents, and Rises and Avenues; to the gravel of unadopted roads, and the parks and recreation grounds and surrounding countryside into which new housing was constantly seeping, like ink on blotting-paper. In cinema darkness we sat clasped together, caught up ourselves in the silent swollen embraces and grimaces and posturings on the screen. Emerging into the lights and crowds outside, I felt vaguely uneasy and shamefaced. In the Blitz, by a strange accident, I found myself alone with Dora in a cellar after we had not seen each other for years. She by this time had been twice married, and I, too, had fully experienced what are still called in our weird jargon the facts of life. Yet we stayed side by side like grizzled adolescents, while outside the world in which we had been youthful lovers crashed and shook and burnt about us.

My going to Cambridge seems to have been almost accidental. Like most lovers of mankind, my father was inclined to be casual in making arrangements for his own family. Though my academic attainments were decidedly meagre, I somehow got myself accepted. It necessitated passing an examination in Latin, a language I had never studied, and now know nothing of. So there must have been some sleight-of-hand. I seem to remember learning off by heart the translation of a Latin comedy which seemed to me abysmally unfunny – a premonition, maybe, of becoming editor of *Punch*. There was also, in those days, a compulsory divinity exam which I somehow managed to get through. This involved mastering Paley's *Evidences*, a long-forgotten work which purports to prove the existence of God. I cannot now remember any of the arguments, but I know they failed to convince me at the time; something I did not confide to the examiners. Finally, to go to Selwyn, an Anglican foundation, it was necessary for me to be baptised and confirmed, which none of us had been; my father as a convinced agnostic would have blushed to subject us to such a practice, though my mother would have quite liked it. I forget exactly how, but I got myself done by a bishop along with a number of others who, like myself, came into the Prayerbook category of riper years. The only thing I remember about the ceremony is that somehow at some point in it I got out of step, and that, noting this, the officiating Bishop wore a look of great irritation and ill-temper.

So, when I was seventeen, I went into residence at Selwyn College – then, officially, a public hostel, not a college at all – with the intention of reading a Natural Science Tripos. The subjects I was to take – chemistry, physics and zoology – were the only ones available at my secondary school for post-matriculation study. Thus, my choice of them was more or less unavoidable, despite the fact that I had no interest in them, and only the scantiest knowledge of them; in the case of zoology, none at all. Four years at Cambridge did little to alter this situation. I managed to scrape up a pass degree, but have never opened a book or thought about any of my three subjects from that day to this. I looked round curiously at my fellow-undergraduates. Even at Selwyn, most of them were from public or grammar schools; I must have been one of the very few secondary school specimens in my year. This was my first acquaintance, in their own native habitat, with the English middle and upper classes, whose characteristics were, I think, more noticeable at Selwyn than at more fashionable and famous establishments like King's and Trinity; in the same sort of way that a virus fighting for its existence is easier to detect and isolate than one in a lush, favourable environment. The only gentry I had known previously were the aforementioned clergy, Quakers and Fabians, all of whom might be regarded as, in a manner of speaking, class Quislings, and so not typical. The first elucidation I had was when the Dean, in the course of an address to freshmen in the college chapel, remarked, as an aside, that none of us were likely ever to be in want, or to lack for the essential requirements for a bourgeois way of life. (He did not put it in precisely those words, but that was what he meant.) I had absorbed sufficient of my father's sense of economic insecurity, as well as of my Booler relatives' attitude to unemployment as a kind of natural catastrophe always hanging over their heads, to find this remark completely novel. It had never occurred to me that, in coming to Cambridge, I was moving into a world in which the economic hazards I had hitherto assumed to be as natural to our human condition as illness, or even death itself, just did not arise.

In South Croydon our notion of the upper classes was expressed by a notice outside a large house standing opposite ours which read: 'Oxford House School for the Sons of Gentlemen'. Now, when education has replaced institutional religion as a fount of hypocrisy and sanctimoniousness, the very naiveté and simplicity of the notice gives it a certain charm, and even dignity. At the time, it was a constant source of derision to us, especially when we saw the Oxford House boys in their splendid caps and blazers mustered for an outing, or, in singlet and shorts, on a cross-country run. As I came to realise after the Dean's address, it was more or less true then that a boy who had been to a public school and taken a degree at Cambridge could assume that his livelihood was assured; especially as we still had an Empire on which the sun never set, as distinct from a Commonwealth on which it never rises, offering him all sorts of openings, from governorships and colonial bishoprics to affluence and a good chance of a knighthood on the banks of the Hooghly. Hence the self-assurance, and in the more ill-mannered among them arrogance, which so struck me among my fellow-undergraduates.

The converse face of this self-assurance or arrogance was the highly developed system of sycophancy which prevailed; fags required to be sycophantic to their masters, players to the captain of games, boys to prefects, prefects to their housemasters, housemaster to headmaster, and so on. I found the undiscriminating application of this sycophantic attitude of mind to anyone of note or in authority quite surprising until I got used to it. Even then I was sometimes astonished; for instance, to hear quite senior figures in the Foreign Office – regarded as an upper-class pasture – speak with almost breathless admiration of an Anthony Eden or an Ernest Bevin; even more absurdly, a heavily moustached Head of Chancery in an Embassy refer to Ramsay Mac-

Donald in terms which might well have seemed excessive if applied to Bismarck. In the army, again, I marvelled at the adroitness with which public-school-reared junior officers helped their brigadiers on with their overcoats compared with the clumsy efforts of us socially inferior officers to ingratiate ourselves with them. Even in the Labour Party the unlikely emergence of figures like Hugh Gaitskell, R. H. S. Crossman and Wedgwood Benn may well have been fostered by their sycophantic skills. Bertrand Russell's elder brother, when he was a member of a Labour Government, told me that he had never before been so conscious of the advantages of being an earl. I doubt, however, whether the built-in sycophancy of the upper classes can be regarded as a social asset, precisely because it is so undiscriminating. A Khrushchev attracts it as readily as a Curzon. As the Nazi régime, particularly, showed, anyone who gets into power may count upon being adulated in the upper social echelons; it is the poor whose support is difficult to attract.

The great difference I observe when I visit Cambridge nowadays is that, compared with my own time there, they are all – dons and undergraduates alike – on the run, and, as is the way with fugitives, tend to discard more than they need to make a getaway. Whereas in my time poor boys like myself were induced to copy the others – their clothes, their ways, their speech – now it is the other way round. The upper-class boys copy the poor ones, decking themselves out in a weird kind of proletarian fancy dress, and speaking in an accent which sounds like a badly rehearsed number in a satire show. They are social descenders, who display, in reverse, all the absurdities, and more, of social climbers. The most comical part of the whole thing is that when, to clinch the transformation, they adopt what they consider an appropriate ideology, it usually turns out to be a half-baked regurgitation of the Marxism and associated revolutionary notions which were fashionable at the time of the Spanish Civil War. Again, the parallel with the situation in reverse as I knew it is strikingly close. The social climber in my day felt it necessary to go to the extremes of Kiplingesque patriotic loyalty to King and Country, in precisely the same way that the social descender nowadays goes to the extremes of revolutionary disruption. It is difficult to decide which of the two attitudes is the more ludicrous; but on the whole, the latter seems to me to be the more deleterious. A ruling class may gain strength from its apes, but the forces of necessary change are weakened and discredited by jackals.

As a secondary schoolboy, I was, of course, an outsider. Public schoolboys, whatever their particular school – from the most famous like Eton, to the most obscure – had a language of their own which I scarcely understood, games they played which I could neither play nor interest myself in, ways and attitudes which they took for granted but which were foreign to me. For instance, their acceptance of sodomy as more or less normal behaviour. When I went to Cambridge I scarcely knew what this was apart from vague references in the Bible. It was not, at any rate, in those days, a proletarian or lower-middle-class vice. The university, when I was there, was very largely a projection of public school life and *mores*, and a similar atmosphere of homosexuality tended to prevail. There was also a hangover from Wildean decadence, with aesthetes who dressed in velvet, painted their rooms in strange colours, hung Aubrey Beardsley prints on their walls, and read *Les Fleurs du Mal*. The nearest I came to being personally involved with these was when a High-Church ordinand after dinner read to me from Swinburne's *Songs Before Sunrise* in a darkened room faintly smelling of incense. I emerged unscathed.

There were also a lot of ex-service undergraduates, men some years older than the rest of us, who wore British warms and scarves, and who had served in the war. I remember them as being all, in their different ways, versions of the war books which were later to be so popular. Minor Robert Graveses, Richard Aldingtons, Ernest Hemingways, Siegfried Sassoons born to blush unseen. University ways and regulations understandably irritated them, and many of them seemed always on the point of exploding; a consequence, no doubt, of the appalling strain of their experiences in Flanders and other theatres of war, about which they were ready enough to talk on occasion, with mounting hysteria. In a way, they were tragic figures. At Selwyn a good number of them were ordinands, mostly in the Woodbine Willie, or padre, style; a version of Christianity which emerged from the 1914–18 war, enormously sincere, ardent, and at the time seemingly vital, but which subsequently, for the most part, ran into the sand. This invariably happens when it is attempted to relate a transcendental faith to an earthly hope – in this case, pacifism. Like bringing back an alpine plant from some arduous rock climb and bedding it out in a window-box. Among ordinands generally, especially at Selwyn, the ultra High-Church or Anglo-Catholic Movement was still in full swing. There was a great deal of talk about the Reserved Sacrament, Popeing (which meant going over to the Roman Church), vestments and other liturgical and ceremonial embellishments. I was taken on one occasion to breakfast with an aged Anglican priest called Father Tooth (the 'Father' was stressed in such circles) who had once been stoned when celebrating Holy Communion in gear that was considered Romish for an Anglican service. The vestment in question, along with one of the stones heaved at him, was preserved in a glass case in his living-room. It seemed a mini-martyrdom.

Cambridge, to me, was a place of infinite tedium; of afternoon walks in a damp, misty countryside; of idle days, and foolish vanities, and spurious enthusiasms. Even now when I go there, as my train steams into the station or my car reaches the outskirts, a sense of physical and mental inertia afflicts me. It was my father who tingled with excitement at the thought of my being at Cambridge; not me. I suspect that the prestige of a university education is almost entirely due to the yearnings of those who feel they have been deprived of one, and that the present decline in its prestige comes of there being fewer and fewer who feel so deprived. Perhaps, when there are none to feel deprived, its prestige will sink to nil – one of the few benefits to be expected from the institution of free university education. It was my father who used expressions like 'my Alma Mater', or 'sporting my oak'; when he came to visit me at Cambridge he was thrilled by my rooms, the Union, dinner in hall, boating on the river; everything. If only he had gone to Cambridge instead of me! How hard he would have worked to get a first, whereas I did nothing and just managed to get a pass degree; how assiduous he would have been at the Union debates, whereas, though he paid for me to have a life subscription, I scarcely ever attended, and never once spoke. For me, the years at Cambridge were the most futile and dismal of my whole life. I look back on the self I then was with the utmost distaste – the showing off when I came to Croydon in the vacations; the getting into debt (which my father always paid with little complaining, though he could ill afford it) through buying clothes and other unnecessary things out of vanity; the fatuous imitation of a sort of person I could never be, nor ever wanted to be.

How somehow second-rate it all was! The clock at Grantchester and honey still for tea. Rupert *en beauté* to-night, as glimpsed by Lytton Strachey at Covent Garden; to be smothered in his beard, or deafened by Hugh Dalton's boom, or just transfixed by Maynard Keynes's frosty lechery. Rupert the dead poet-hero of our time. The Prince of Wales, another hero, likewise magnificently unprepared for the long littleness of life in the Boulevard Suchet. Or the even more macabre one, Lawrence of Arabia, with many a scruffy acolyte sitting cross-

legged and elfin among the unwashed-up crockery; his seemingly indestructible legend surviving every exposure of fraudulence and
depravity. Lectures by Quiller-Couch, notes shaking in shaky hands.
The sea! The sea! Wide checks and massive coloured tie to offset the
gown and mortar-board. Or Old McTaggart muttering philosophically,
and scattering anecdotes about himself with a lavish hand. In the labs,
where I was supposed to attend for long sessions, dogfish needing to be
cut up; something boiling in a retort. High up in the lecture theatre
(like, I used to think, trying to comfort myself, the Mountain in the
French Revolution) hopelessly making notes; the single piece of information acquired there which has stayed with me being a silver-haired
professor's complaint that, having hit upon some chemical drying agent,
he patented it for making bricks out of sand, whereas someone else
used it to manufacture Cerebos Salt, and made a fortune. Poor silver
head!

On the river – Give her ten! Or watching games and yelling. Or the
university rag; requiring so little modification to become the university
demo. Or just trudging to and fro on desolate afternoons. Then in the
evening the chapel bell intruding into buttered toast, and sounding
across the darkening court. The porter in his bowler pricking the names
of those who attended evensong. Wearing a surplice; 'Dearly beloved
brethren,' spoken down the nose with a sniff at the end of each sentence,
'I pray and beseech you, as many as are here present . . .' Perhaps the
only good thing I got out of Cambridge was a certain familiarity with
the incomparable Book of Common Prayer. Then into hall for dinner.
That smell always hanging about there of stale bread and old cheese!
It must have got into the wood of the benches and tables. The clattering
plates, the passing food, the Latin grace. Perhaps it all had a meaning
once, but not for me. I found it as moribund as El Azhar, where the
Mullahs chant monotonously and unintelligibly to a little circle of
students dozing round them.

In my last year at Cambridge, through my friendship with Alec
Vidler – a friendship that has lasted all my life – I went to live at the
Oratory House. It was the headquarters of an Anglican religious order,
the Oratory of the Good Shepherd, to which Alec belonged, consisting
mostly of priests and ordinands of the Anglo-Catholic persuasion. The
offices were said during the day, periods of silence were enforced; in the
afternoons I often worked in the garden with Wilfred Knox, a rare,
sweet human being of whom I became very fond, and for whom I
sometimes acted as server when he celebrated Holy Communion. I

fell into this way of life with great contentment, enjoying its remoteness from the University, and its relative austerity as far as food and domestic comforts were concerned. Austerity has always made me happy, and its opposite, miserable. I find it strange that, knowing this, I should so often have inflicted upon myself the nausea of over-indulgence, and had to fight off the black dogs of satiety. Human beings, as Pascal points out, are peculiar in that they avidly pursue ends they know will bring them no satisfaction; gorge themselves with food which cannot nourish and with pleasures which cannot please. I am a prize example.

Living so contentedly at the Oratory House did not make me the more inclined to throw in my lot with friends like Alec and Wilfred Knox; *Lord, I disbelieve, help thou my belief* was more my cry. Despite the agnosticism of my home and upbringing, I cannot recall a time when the notion of Christ and Christianity was not enormously appealing to me, though where Peter only heard the cock crow thrice on that one tragic occasion, for me it has been over long years matutinal. I knew from a very early age – how I cannot tell – that the New Testament contained the key to how to live. I somehow knew it to be our only light in a dark world. Not just in my father's sense that Jesus himself was a good man, and his moral precepts greatly to be admired, even though his ostensible followers in the various churches ignored and perverted them. I soon saw through this, understanding that Jesus could not be turned into just a finer version of Wilberforce or William Morris or Robert Owen, into a paid-up member of the Labour Party, and potential Life Peer, without diminishing him to the point that Christianity became too trivial to be taken seriously. He was God or he was nothing.

No, what appealed to me were the wild extravagances of faith; the phrases about God's wisdom being men's foolishness, St Francis of Assisi rejoicing at being naked on the naked earth, the sublime paradoxes of *The Marriage of Heaven and Hell*. Surveying the abysmal chasm between my certainty that everything human beings tried to achieve was inadequate to the point of being farcical, that mortality itself was a kind of gargoyle joke, and my equal certainty that every moment of every day was full of enchantment and infinitely precious; that human love was the image vouchsafed us of God's love irradiating the whole universe; that, indeed, embedded in each grain of sand was eternity, to be found and explored, as geologists explored the antiquity of fossils through their markings – surveying this chasm, yawning in its vastness to the point of inducing total insanity, tearing us into schizophrenic pieces, I grasped that over it lay, as it were, a cable-bridge, frail, swaying, but passable. And this bridge, this reconciliation between the black despair of lying bound and gagged in the tiny dungeon of the ego, and soaring upwards into the white radiance of God's universal love – this bridge was the Incarnation, whose truth expresses that of the desperate need it meets. Because of our physical hunger we know there is bread; because of our spiritual hunger we know there is Christ.

I will not pretend, of course, that I saw all this then, just as I have written it down, or for that matter that I see it now as I should love to see it – as a child sees in the dawn the sure prospect of a joyous day, or reaches up for its father's hand in the sure knowledge of its loving support and guidance. Yet, then as now, I knew it, and knew it more confidently than I knew anything else; in the confusion of a wilful, opinionated and ill-trained mind, it alone was steady and luminous. Where I faltered was in establishing a connection between what I knew and the practice and dogmas of the Christian religion, even as exemplified by someone as noble and profound as Alec, or with as delicate and whimsical a spiritual perception as Wilfred. The churches altogether seemed to me part of the whole decaying social structure, the stench of whose decomposition was so strongly in my nostrils. Passing Wilfred the wine to transform into blood, the wafers to become the body of Christ, in the little Oratory House chapel, I felt perfectly at peace. As I did, saying the offices. Or ringing the Angelus for the others. Equally at peace, in the knowledge I have always had, and never wholly lost, that we are pilgrims here, with a dwelling-place elsewhere. (Never wholly lost – but sometimes the darkness falls, impenetrable, seemingly for ever!) Yet how to connect the two – the worship and the knowledge of God? This I have never solved.

Once, sweeping up dead leaves with Wilfred, he spoke of the priestly vocation. What use would I be? I asked him. His answer I found curious – that I could persuade people to do things. What things? I asked. But he left the matter there. He had this way of dropping out half sentences, fragments of jokes and innuendo, scraps of speech and thought. His brother Evoe, my predecessor but one as editor of *Punch*, though utterly different in every respect and, to me, less sympathetic, had the same way with him; so resembling his brother in this that I sometimes thought he must be there with us. Likewise, another brother, Ronnie, who, after he had become a Roman Catholic convert, was given the task of re-translating the Bible; a Via Dolorosa indeed for him, since, as the son of a Protestant Evangelical Bishop, he knew the Authorised

Version by heart. It was like asking a veteran of many Burns dinners to devise a new setting for Auld Lang Syne.

Round about the same time that I fell in love, I became acquainted with the other great fact of our earthly existence. I mean, death. Something that cannot be hidden however hard we try to persuade ourselves that we are immortal; able to replace our spare parts as they wear out, and so be kept on the road indefinitely like vintage cars; to go on having orgasms even when our flesh is dry and wizened, and our bones creak abysmally. In the end, nothing can hide the fact that this hand now tapping out these words will in a matter of at most a few years fall inert, and this mind framing the words likewise cease to function; while the words themselves over which I struggle and torment myself, be they as sublime as the sunflower weary of time, or as banal as a feature article in a travel supplement, or, more probably, something in between, matter no more to me than the *Bonjour, madame* I said this morning to an unknown lady exercising her dog.

The experience of death came suddenly, its herald being a policeman, who appeared at the door while my father was crunching his last mouthful of toast washed down with his last gulp of tea preparatory to racing for his train. When my mother opened the door to him, the policeman entered and took off his helmet, thereby at a stroke transforming himself from a portentous figure of authority into a rather appealing pink-and-white face jutting out of a blue uniform. From a whispered colloquy with my father, it appeared that my brother Stanley – the one next to me in age who served with the RFC – had met with a serious accident on his motor bicycle, which he rode daily to work, and was now in the Croydon General Hospital in a grave condition. It was decided that my mother should stay at home with her tears and fears, and my father and I made our way as quickly as possible to the hospital, passing on the way the crossroads where the accident had occurred; a place well known to me because of a crossing-sweeper there. I should suppose he was one of the last of his kind; a man with a dragging leg (I imagine he had suffered some kind of a stroke) who, while he swept his crossing, babbled away incomprehensibly to himself; something that naturally appealed to schoolboys. On this particular morning he was babbling away, as it seemed to me, more furiously than ever, which I attributed to the accident whose debris still lay about the road, including, as I thought, some traces of blood. Whether the blood was really there or not, I cannot now be sure, but whenever, afterwards, I conjured up the scene, I saw it there.

At the hospital we were shown at once to where my brother was, though we did not see him because of a screen round his bed. From behind the screen there came a curious spasmodic gurgling noise, due, as I learned afterwards, to a tube which had been inserted into his throat through which he was breathing. While I was listening to the sound with fascinated intensity, as it might be to a count-down, it became more spasmodic, and began to falter, like a top running down. Then it stopped, and I understood that my brother was dead. This was death – a gurgling noise faltering, and then stopping. I caught a glimpse of a white dead face, already drained and shrunken, and beginning to look like a skull, but with a strong resemblance to my mother which I had not noticed before. I had been intending to play tennis with Dora that morning, and so was in flannels, with a white boating blazer (to which I was only dubiously entitled), which added a touch of grotesqueness to the occasion.

On the way home my father remarked in a ruminative tone of voice: 'I'm very resilient.' It was so utterly characteristic of him that it brought tears to my eyes for the first time that morning. I knew exactly what he meant – that though he would be as grief-stricken as any other father, he would not allow this grief to prevent him from attending the next meeting of the Croydon Borough Council. After my father's remark about being resilient, we fell silent, and there came insistently into my mind the memory of an incident concerning my brother's fiancée, a luscious, bold, rather beautiful girl whom I found very appealing. Once she had come up to the little room at the top of the house where I kept my books and was supposed to study during the vacations. I must have made some sort of amorous gesture, for she looked down complacently at her legs (skirts were almost as short in those early post-war years as to-day's mini-skirts) and said: 'They're already booked,' or words to that effect. I had brooded over these words at the time, finding them crude and inelegant, but in a way exciting. Now, returning from seeing my brother die, they repeated themselves over and over as though they had some special point or significance.

At home, my father tried to comfort my mother, and I felt it necessary to go through the motions of relieving my feelings, which I did on the ample bosom of Mrs Milne, a lady who lived next door in the house that was to have been Will Straughan's. Round her mouth, as I had noticed before, were some sparse tough hairs on which particles of food were liable to get skewered – something that must have struck me forcibly, for I notice these hairs recurring several times in some sketches for short stories that I scribbled down round about this time. The Milnes had the first motor-car I ever rode in, an Overland whose hood was put up and down with great difficulty. Its fixtures included some holes in the sides of the car into which they would put wine glasses with the stems broken off when they wanted to refresh themselves, which was rather often. It was a device which gave them great satisfaction. I never saw my dead brother's fiancée again.

I spent my last long vacation in Belgium working for Lunn's Tours. This came about through my friendship at Cambridge with Leonard Dobbs, with whom I shared rooms after I left the Oratory House. His father was a director of Lunn's, and responsible for operations on the Belgian coast. As a result of this interlude I subsequently married Leonard's sister, Kitty, and got to know Hugh Kingsmill Lunn, who became a close friend; two of the greatest blessings of my life that I owe to Leonard. He was an unusual, rather sombre man, very gifted; a brilliant skier, a scientist of exceptional promise, curious about many things, enormously argumentative, and with a propensity for carrying every thought and notion to the extremes of fantasy. At the end of his life, when he was living with Kitty and me, he devoted himself to making an enormous gramophone horn, so huge that it could not be moved from the room in which he was working on it. At one point he married a Mlle. Cantaloupe, but their union was not a success. He died in the early part of the 1939–45 war, I think with relief. Hugh Kingsmill said of him – and I am inclined to agree – that he was more lovable than likeable.

On the Belgian coast I was one of the shepherds of the Lunn flock. We met them at Ostend where they arrived, saw them to their hotels, arranged tours for them, and generally watched over their welfare. It was an occupation which, more than I realised at the time, had great bearing on things to come. In taking parties to Bruges, for instance, and addressing them on the town, its history and its art treasures, I acquired a facility for talking convincingly on a basis of very little, if any, knowledge; an accomplishment equally useful in education, journalism and television. I also learnt at an early age the great truth that the twentieth century is an age of almost inconceivable credulity, in which critical faculties are stifled by a plethora of public persuasion and information, so that, literally, anyone will believe anything. It is on this basis that our great newspapers, television and radio networks, universities and schools, churches and, above all, our great advertising agencies and all their ancillary activities in the field of public relations, are conducted.

The lesson was brought home to me by a figure of Chaste Susannah in Bruges, which, I used to say, following another Lunn's man, Louis Wilkinson, was fittingly fashioned in white alabaster. At the end of the season I was disconcerted to learn that she was in black ebony. In any case, no one ever raised the point. In later years, whenever I was troubled about some hideous misconception which had slipped into print or on to the air, I always turned for comfort to this white alabaster Chaste Susannah, never in vain. Louis Wilkinson was a writer – a novelist and literary critic – and so held in great admiration and respect by me. He had flowing auburn hair and a spade beard to match; knew the Powys family, and spoke much about them, every word of which I treasured, and as a schoolboy at Repton had written fan letters to Oscar Wilde, enclosing a photograph. Despite this daring gesture, a subsequent meeting with Wilde in Paris proved disappointing to both of them. Dining with Louis and his wife, Nan, as I sometimes did, at Blankenberg where they were staying, he always made a great fuss about the wine, praising particularly some Volnay which, he implied, was a useful aphrodisiac. Though I never liked wine or had the slightest interest in it, I used for years afterwards to repeat this panegyric of Volnay as though it was a precious piece of wine lore of my own.

After we left the Belgian coast I went to stay for a week-end with Louis and Nan at their flat in Christchurch Road, in one of the remoter regions of London. It was a fairly modest dwelling with, however, many literary trophies which held my attention – Louis's own books in their jackets, letters from Maugham, J. C. Squire and other writers, photographs of the Powys brothers. His voice was slow and ponderous, very like a clergyman's (he was, in fact, a clergyman's son), and became in time tedious. His jokes likewise palled; as when he would say that though he himself had taken no part in the war, he had given two of his boys to fight for King and Country. Nonetheless, I continued to hang on his words, though later I ridiculed him in various fictional guises. Nan was a minute creature, also a novelist, and suffering from tuberculosis. While Louis was away for some reason or other, we went for a walk together in the neighbourhood of Christchurch Road. Because of her illness she was not allowed to talk while walking, so we went along hand in hand in silence, every now and again pausing while she coughed, and then spat out the sputum into a blue bottle she had with her for the purpose. The following morning she climbed into my bed, but I was unable to appreciate this gesture owing to the looming presence of Louis who could be heard singing in his bath. A few years later I heard that Nan had died. Long afterwards I met Louis again. He looked exactly the same except that his skin was drier and his hair more carefully combed and spread over his head. He repeated his joke about giving two of his boys to fight for King and Country, even though, by that time, another war had intervened.

Lunn's Tours, of whose operations on the Belgian coast I had this brief experience, were pioneers in what was to become an enormous industry – holidays and travel, which not only kept the Press going with its advertisements, but also provided the world of the mid-twentieth century with one of its few elements of stability. International *Wagon-Lits*, it seemed, rather than the 'Internationale', united the human race. The founder and head of the firm, Sir Henry Lunn, made the discovery on which his flourishing business was based when, as a young missionary returned from India, he was given the task of organising a conference at Grindelwald for the reunion of the churches; an early essay in ecumenicalism. He found that, if a hotelier was offered an assured consignment of clients, he would reduce his charges, thus leaving a comfortable margin of profit for the entrepreneur. Applying this principle, he established, first, the Church Travellers' Club, then, at a slightly lower social level, the Free Church Touring Guild, and might have gone on to complete the social spectrum with a Workers' Travel Association. This, however, was left to other hands. He did mount higher with his Hellenic Travellers' Club and Public Schools' Alpine Sports Club, both of which catered specifically for the upper classes, and to make sure that this not only happened but was seen to happen, a number of free places were provided for peers, dons and other certified gentry. It was in the too lavish provision of these free places that the good man came to grief, his snobbishness, very creditably, proving greater than his cupidity.

I got to know him later on through Hugh Kingsmill, one of his three sons, the other two being Brian and Arnold. Hugh so disliked everything about his father that he dropped the 'Lunn' from his name. Sir Henry was, admittedly, a somewhat Pecksniffian figure, but with some redeeming traits of naïveté and absurdity. Once, going up on the train to London from Hastings, he told me that when he had persuaded some bishops to attend his Grindelwald Conference, W. T. Stead – the famous editor of the *Pall Mall Gazette* whose series, 'The Maiden Tribute of Babylon', made straight the way for many another moralistic campaigner fulminating against wickedness, and thereby advertising it – admonished him that he should now never go back to curates. When I said that this was as though, after the conversion of St Luke, Jesus should have been instructed never to go back to fishermen, his face fell. His knighthood was a great solace, but his hopes for a peerage were disappointed. The nearest he got was to be on the list Asquith prepared of the names of those who would be recommended for peerages if their elevation proved necessary to force the passage of the Parliament Bill through the Upper House. How exasperating for them, good Radicals all, that standing up to the House of Lords did not involve their going there. I am occasionally reminded of Sir Henry when I catch a glimpse of some beach where bodies lie packed side by side roasting in the sun, or on one of the more lurid prospectuses for a fortnight at the Costa Brava, and wonder how, as a good Methodist, he would react to this outcome of his first faltering steps in the tourist business. Was it for this that he made his discovery about getting advantageous terms from the Grindelwald hoteliers when he brought together those earnest would-be reuniters of the churches – precursors of the World Council of Churches and the Vatican Council. Perhaps, after all, it was.

Mr Dobbs, Leonard's father, and my future father-in-law, was a genial Protestant Irishman who by chance had joined the crew of this Methodist brig Sir Henry sailed with such panache in the triple winds of piety, snobbishness and cash. It was he who first mentioned Kitty to me as having returned from a stay in Switzerland. The things that really happen to one, I have found, have all happened already; the other happenings – like wars, and seductions, and prizes, and going to the moon – are theatre merely. Thus, I heard of Kitty's return as I might hear of the weather forecast for a day already lived through; as something that did not need to be said because it was so obvious, and yet in its very obviousness good to hear. It is this sense, in all the true – as distinct from the theatrical – drama of our lives, that it is pre-ordained, that it not only has been and will be, but *is*, that makes us know we are immortal, and, within the smaller dimensions of imaginative literature, supports the action of coincidence – something for which a novelist like Anthony Powell is sometimes criticised, in my opinion unjustly, since coincidence is not only plausible, something that undoubtedly happens, but part of the very fabric of life itself. All our true living has already happened, and will go on happening for ever; all our true relationships already exist when we make them, and can never be broken. So, you take someone's hand, and use a name, perhaps embrace, before a hand has even been offered, or a name been given, before you have even looked in one another's faces, because that hand, that name, that embrace are part of both; part, as Donne puts it, of the atomies of which we grow – souls whom no change can invade. There are only a few occasions on which I have felt so, and this was one of them. I saw Kitty afterwards at the villa where her family were staying, and all of us went bathing and walking over the sand-dunes. All I remember about her then is that she was wearing some sort of a red knitted jumper with patterns on it, and that she was tanned from her stay in Switzerland. During the next – and my last – term at Cambridge, she visited Leonard, and we went for a walk by the Cam. I helped her over a stile.

Somehow – I forget the precise circumstances – I had tea with Mrs Dobbs, Kitty's mother, at a café in Heyst before Kitty returned from Switzerland. She was sitting waiting for me, and I had no difficulty in spotting her. A hat decorated with artificial fruit was perched on top of her noticeably small head; she wore, as she almost invariably did, a shirt with a stiff high collar and tie of sorts; her boots were dusty, and made for comfort rather than elegance; her battered suit was cut in the style of the early part of the century, with a long coat and flowing skirt. By her side was a bag containing her painting materials, a small stool, and – though of course I did not know this at the time – some provisions of uncertain age. A large nose jutted out of a weather-beaten face; her hands were bony, with long fingers, and covered in paint; her voice, when she addressed me, was gruff and impossible to place in any of the social categories of accent and pronunciation. She might have been a gipsy beggar-woman or a duchess, or anything in between; there was no means of knowing. I greeted her, and ordered tea and cakes, which, when they came, she consumed with great zest. There was nothing she liked better than free hospitality. As I came to know later, she was a woman of almost inconceivable generosity, who would, literally, starve to give her children something they wanted. At the same time, economising was a passion with her, and she carried it to inordinate lengths; like serving horse-meat for sirloin, watering marmalade, and eschewing butter in favour of margarine, which, she said, was indistinguishable from butter, and anyway she liked it better. Her abounding hospitality led her to invite many guests to the villas and chalets and rented houses between which her family moved; her parsimony led her to provide only the same amount of food however many there might be to consume it. I suppose it could be said of her that she was one of the most maddening of human beings; certainly the most maddening I have ever known. Yet she was also, as I vaguely grasped at this first meeting with her, a kind of angel, in Blake's sense, that she belonged directly and wholly to the great fount of life and energy, with no involvement in the systems of thought and morality and aesthetics which men create with their minds to evade living as angels in their imaginations. She had no mind; only a being. I think of her as I have often seen her, painting away to catch the last rays of the sun, immune to heat and cold, to buzzing insects as to curious spectators, utterly intent on what she saw around her, herself a part of the scene; as it might be, a bit of old creeper, or a weather-stained rock, or a tree shaken and tossed and still precariously standing on a cliff-face.

'You are a friend of my son, Leonard,' she said, and I nodded. 'I hear you have very Left-wing views.' I nodded again. 'I take my political views,' she went on, 'from my sister Beatrice Webb and the *New Statesman.*' I proceeded to try and demolish both, citing the Russian Revolution, which the Webbs at that time held in great abhorrence. She replied with 'Beatrice says . . . Sidney says . . .' It was impossible to argue with her, then, or ever. She had a way of dropping out wildly controversial statements, often chosen with great cunning to produce the maximum irritation in the person to whom they were addressed, and then, when the storm broke, of placidly repeating her original statement. We moved on to the subject of personal immortality, in which she had a passionate and abiding interest; desperately wanting there to be an after-life, but only if it were here, on the earth, with sunsets and dawns and high waves breaking against wild rocks. Dreading that there might be no immortality at all, only darkness and obliteration; or, if there were, that it would be heavenly instead of earthly, with a judgment at which she would fare ill. We went to and fro, with this subject, until it was dark. Then she abruptly got up to go, and made off, carrying her bag, with those loose-fitting boots of hers scraping the pavement as she went along.

I had no particular idea what I should do after Cambridge, except that I was committed to teach in one capacity or another. In addition to my poor pass degree, I had taken a diploma in education; yet another course of instruction of which I can remember nothing except turning over the pages of some sort of treatise on child psychology and of another volume called significantly *The Play Way*, as well as participating in various teaching demonstrations. These included a music lesson, at which, being unable to produce or recognise any musical sounds, I was at a heavy disadvantage, and giving a demonstration lesson myself, under the eye of a supervisor, on some distasteful verses by Walter de la Mare beginning: 'Three jolly gentlemen dressed in red,/Rode their horses up to bed.' My impression was, and is, that, happily, the children had not the faintest idea of what I was talking about. Then, by chance, I heard an Anglican missionary, the Rev. W. E. S. Holland, appealing for staff for an Indian Christian college in South India, and on an impulse offered my services. I was accepted, and found myself in possession of a steamship ticket to Colombo, with general instructions to go on from there to Alwaye, in what was then Travancore, and present myself at the Union Christian College.

3 *Twilight of Empire*

The world's too little for thy tent,
A grave too big for me.

– George Herbert

SAILING DOWN THE THAMES on a P & O liner – the SS *Morea* – on my way to the open sea and India, I felt well content. I have always had a great weakness for making off. Shutting a door behind me never to open it again; disengaging myself from a sleeping figure, and tiptoeing away, downstairs and out into the street and the grey anonymous dawn of another day. Now I was making off, leaving everyone and everything behind me; unpaid bills and overdrafts, actual and emotional. I had seen little of Dora of late. We had drifted apart, largely through my fault. The self I had become as a result of my idle, conceited years at Cambridge was a very unalluring one. I recall with shame the falsity and pretentiousness of letters I wrote to Dora after we became estranged. They were even worse than Keats's to Fanny Brawne; a relationship which greatly interested me. I was always trying to be some literary figure or other. In the case of Keats, there were two major deficiencies in my impersonation; I wasn't a poet and I didn't die.

My father came to see me off. He never had an engagement important enough to stop him from being with me on any special occasion. We walked up and down the deck together, neither of us being easy sitters, and talked about politics. Ramsay MacDonald's first Labour Government had taken office without a majority in the House of Commons, and so was dependent on Liberal support. Suddenly, MacDonald, a much hated man, especially in the 1914–18 war years, had become a popular folk hero, with pictures of him in the papers; at Chequers wearing his tweed knickerbocker suit, his grey curls awry in the wind, and a faraway look in his eyes. My father's esteem for him, never very marked, was diminishing rapidly. He feared, all too justifiably as it turned out, that

MacDonald was succumbing to what sour critics of his social ways called the aristocratic embrace. The assimilative power of the English upper classes was still formidable, enabling them to absorb into themselves alien elements; Jewish, Asian, Levantine, Negro even, not to mention a distracted Scot from Lossiemouth who went down as smoothly as an oyster. Later, as their fortunes declined at an accelerating rate, it was the other way round; the aliens absorbed them. No reference was made to where I was going, or to what conditions would be like when I got there, for the very simple reason that neither of us had looked the place up on the map, or had more than the sketchiest notion of what I should be expected to do, how I should live, or even what I was going to be paid. This was not disinterestedness, but just an engrained improvidence, to which both my father and I were prone; uncorrected, in his case, by hardships and responsibilities, and in my easier circumstances, quite unchecked. When the bell rang for visitors to leave the ship we shook hands. I cannot remember ever kissing my father, though I must have done so as a small child. As I watched him leave the ship and walk away, I was surprised, and rather disgusted with myself, to find that I felt a kind of relief at leaving him too.

The fallacy about making off, as I soon discovered, was, of course, that I remained myself; whether travelling round the Inner Circle or out to India. In this particular case, too, the SS *Morea* proved to be just a little bit of Croydon sailing over the high seas. Once again the suburban style of living proved to be the master-print of the age. I was sharing my second-class cabin with an Indian clergyman, the Rev. C. K. Jacob, who afterwards became a bishop, and in that capacity visited me when I was editor of *Punch*. I noticed that, as a bishop, he cracked his finger-joints in exactly the same way as he had when he was just a simple clergyman. After we had been at sea for some days, I became aware that my sharing a cabin with an Indian, even though he was a clergyman, aroused comment. I actually overheard one of the passengers – a man who put on white shorts after Marseilles and worked in the Army Ordnance Department – saying with considerable moral fervour that it wasn't right. Even though I knew that at Cambridge the question of Indians and Africans becoming captains of games had aroused controversy, I had not hitherto run into the Ordnance man's attitude, whereby for an Englishman to mix on intimate terms with an Indian (other than on the most intimate terms of all: viz., to sleep with Indian women, which practically all Englishmen in India did at one time or another) was morally reprehensible. There was already a large and growing literature on the subject, I know, but for some reason I have always instinctively shied away from books about racialism, with titles like *The Clash of Colour*. Kipling I had read and enjoyed, though reading him in my home was comparable, I should suppose, with reading pornography in a Methodist one. I must, I think, have got hold of *Kim* and *The Jungle Book* at school.

Kipling has come to signify an extreme racialist attitude, but, in point of fact, the hero of *Kim* – the book of his I enjoyed most – is a little half-caste boy whose affections and loyalties are more Indian than English. Again, his brilliant short story, *Without Benefit of Clergy*, is a beautifully touching account of a love-affair between an Englishman and an Indian girl; so touching that I have always thought that it must have been partly autobiographical and may account for the curious fact that, after he left India in his twenties, Kipling never once went back there, though he was an inordinate traveller all his life. As will assuredly come in due course to be seen, he represents the only truly artistic yield of the years of the British Raj; not excepting New Delhi and *A Passage to India*. Curiously enough, it is Indians to-day who are more aware of this than Kipling's fellow-countrymen, whose judgment is twisted and distorted by excessive guilt feelings about ever having ruled over India at all, and who, in the present climate of opinion, would sooner appear as rapists than as racialists. On the recent centenary of Kipling's birth I gave a televised lecture on him to the Kipling Society. A man in the audience astonished and delighted me by claiming that Kipling was a Marxist. I have long been expecting an ecumenical pilgrimage to Marx's grave at Highgate Cemetery, led by a Salvation Army band, with the Archbishop of Canterbury well to the fore, and the Atheist International (there must be one; at any rate there's a branch at the BBC) bringing up the rear. Even in that delectable gathering, though, I had not anticipated the presence of a representative from the Kipling Society.

The effect on me of the Ordnance man's attitude was to make me spend more time in Jacob's company than I should otherwise have done. He was, truth to tell, a bit of a bore, and, had he been white, I should have seen little of him outside our cabin. As it was, I felt bound to walk up and down the deck with him, to ensure that we sat at the same table in the dining saloon, and generally to make him my bosom companion. This may well have been as tedious for him as for me, but it was imposed on us by the attitude of most of our fellow-passengers.

An exception was a piano-tuner on his way to Singapore, who also sat at our table and who behaved impeccably. I marvelled that there were sufficient pianists in Singapore to provide a livelihood for a piano-tuner, but I heard afterwards that he opened a music shop there, throve, and during the Japanese occupation behaved with great courage and charity. A weakness for the bottle, and a forlorn, lost expression I noted in his right eye, were due, it seems, to personal troubles he had been experiencing. I cannot say that anyone actually insulted Jacob; it was just an awkward atmosphere created by my sharing a cabin with him ever having been raised as an issue at all. Race is something that, like love, should never be told; never seek to tell thy race, race that never told should be . . . The Race Relations Board to-day, and the racially conscious English in India in the days of the Raj, are alike offenders in this respect.

As the voyage proceeded, I noticed a strange transformation in my fellow-passengers. They had come aboard as more or less ordinary middle- or lower-middle-class English, with perhaps, in the second class, the latter preponderating. Now they were changing, the men becoming more assertive, the ladies more la-di-da; as it were, moving farther and farther away from Bournemouth and Bexhill and nearer and nearer to Memsahib status and invitations to Government House. Luncheon was tiffin, a whisky and soda a chota peg, and instead of calling for a steward, the cry was: 'Boy!' By Port Said the change was complete; those who had topees brought them out, and those of us who hadn't went ashore and bought one at a shop called Simon Artz. I acquired an enormous white one, very heavy, such as the Marines wear, that needed to be cleaned with pipe-clay from time to time. It was a preposterous headgear, which I carried about with me but rarely put on my head, though the direst warnings were given me of what would happen if I neglected to protect my European pate from the Asian sun. This mystique of the topee was universally accepted during the Raj; it was the badge of the Sahib, and cultivated by all his imitators and aspirants, whether Anglo-Indians or westernised Indians. Among Europeans in India the belief was almost universally held that to expose their heads to the sun even for a few minutes would have disastrous consequences; I have known them, when a group photograph was being taken, keep their topees on till just before the camera was going to click, then put them under their seats, pulling them out and putting them back on their heads the moment the picture was taken. Now that the Raj is over, practically no one wears a topee, with no ill consequences. It is an interesting example of how medical lore, like trade, follows the flag.

Wherever our ship put in now, we were met by a launch flying the Union Jack, with British officers aboard. This, of course, fitted in well with the changed personas of the passengers who, it seemed to me, almost visibly swelled with pride. For the first time I became aware of the British Empire, not just as a lot of red on the map, nor as a mystique to enthuse over or deride on Empire Day, but as a geographical and political entity. In this part of the world, it was clear, we were the lords of creation – a role which the great majority of my fellow-countrymen, from private soldiers to captains and kings with no intention of departing, found highly acceptable. The whole imperial set-up has disappeared so quickly and completely that one looks back on it now with a kind of wonder that it should ever have existed, but at the time it seemed very solidly based and durable. In the dining saloon one evening I was severely rebuked by the Ordnance man – who had blossomed more than most of them into a Burra Sahib – for saying that the British Empire, like any other, would have its day, and that its end might well be nearer than many now supposed. There was no one except the piano-tuner – who came out rather equivocally on my side – who found this proposition acceptable, on however long a view. They were one and all certain that the Empire would go on for ever; its bounds being set wider still and wider, and God who had made us mighty going on making us mightier yet, indefinitely. A view that was held at that time, I should suppose, pretty well universally on P & O boats ferrying to and fro between the Mother Country and her colonies, dependencies and dominions.

My own reaction was as predictable as that of Bunyan's Pilgrim to Vanity Fair. To my father and his friends, the Empire was a bare-faced system of exploitation, and the imperial idea additional opium of the people to supplement the dwindling soporific effect induced by religion. Though my father did once say to me that he had happened to see a British battleship come into Gibraltar Harbour, and that the sight had given him emotions of pride rather than reminding him of the old familiar equation of how many hospitals, schools and lidos the money it cost would have provided. I might easily have reacted in the same sort of way when confronted with the pomp and circumstance of imperial power, except that I was vaguely aware that its glory was already passing. There was something unconvincing about the Ordnance man as a custodian of Empire; even about the little launches as they shot out from the shore. I sensed – or thought I did – a process of decomposition at work behind the façade of unity and strength that the Empire still presented to the world. Though ostensibly bigger and stronger than it had ever been as a result of the acquisitions of territory in the Versailles peace settlement, it was somehow shaky about the knees; a little breathless going uphill, a little trembly about the hands. Like Pavlova, when I saw her dance in *Swan Lake* in Cairo shortly before she died as magnificently turned out as ever, as accomplished as ever, but just a little tremulous when she was up on her toes and about to be whirled around by her partner.

Of course, at the time, it was no more than a vague feeling that, despite a crescendo of imperial sentiments, ranging between high-minded *Round Table* prospectuses for English-speaking orchestration, Rhodes Scholarship pieties, and Kipling doggerel; with General Smuts devising his holier than thou philosophy of Holism, and Geoffrey Dawson, alias Robinson, or vice versa, in and out of *The Times*, and Lord Beaverbrook throwing his own gilded spanner into the works – despite all this, the Empire itself was running down. As is now clear, Imperialism only arose as a doctrine when the Empire was already in decline; as it is the sick who are obsessed with their bodies, the impotent with their virility, and the faithless with their faith. In any case, whatever gloss may be attempted, the glories of imperial power are threadbare and tawdry. Hence, the pomp and circumstance. As Pascal says, judges need their wigs and robes, priests their vestments, scholars their gowns – for that matter, hippies their long hair and fancy dress; otherwise, the fraudulence of their pretentions would be all too apparent. Similarly, the British Raj needed majestic titles, and silver thrones, and ceremonial durbars. In my years of journalism – a sort of *voyeur* role – I have never seen authority that did not give off a whiff of decay, or power that was not sawdust-stuffed, or glamour without grease-paint. That White House smile! That Kremlin glower! That Downing Street you-know-you-can-trust-me look! In the immortal words of the producer to the floor-manager when one of the Nixon commercials was being recorded in the Presidential Election of 1968: 'Keep the witch-hazel handy; we can't do the sincerity bit if he's sweating.'

On those long voyages one came to accept liner life as normal. Waking in the morning to the ship's sway, watching its silver wake at night before going to bed; the stars so very near, and enveloped in darkness like velvet. Bells punctuating the day, calling one to meals; the engines endlessly chugging and churning, like time inexorably ticking away.

The walks up and down the deck, an eye perhaps alert for one of the prettier young wives on her way to join her husband; or a fiancée going to get married, with golden dreams set to the music of the Indian Love Lyrics – 'Pale hands I love, beside the Shalimar' – tinkled out on a thousand upright pianos in a thousand sitting-rooms. Matins in the first-class dining saloon, to which we second-class passengers were admitted for the occasion, and Jacob permitted to officiate in a minor capacity, surplice and hood prudently stowed in Wanted-on-Voyage luggage. Passengers getting to know one another, chatting, gossiping, amorous or quarrelsome together; and the sea all round us always, like eternity, with our little ship-encompassed world cruising through it as our little atmosphere-encompassed earth cruises through space. The past written on water by our stern, our prow nosing into the future, and no present at all.

I hate to think how many hundreds of thousands of miles this ridiculous carcass of mine has been carted about the world for one reason and another. As the years have passed, the carriers have grown faster and faster. Five weeks from Tilbury to Colombo; then five days from Delhi to London, with night-stops along the way, sometimes at mysterious desert stockades. Then flying boats following the African coast, hovering over jungle, and slithering down on to great stretches of muddy river water. Wartime flying fortresses, lying racked among the kit-bags in the fuselage. Then the stratocruisers, then the jets; faster than sound, faster than light, until our whole earth, and all its beauties and its wonders, can be encompassed in one piercing supersonic shriek. Distance annihilated, and the world with it. Bull-dozed away by the runway- and road-makers; jet-deafened, oil-drenched, smog-smothered; its inside gouged out like Prometheus's entrails. Trampled to death by stampeding travellers, consumed by curiosity's ravening eye, stung by cameras click-clicking and flashing like dragonflies. Where the rainbow ends; where the runway disappears and the motorways intersect. I cannot say that I myself derived any evident benefit from participating in this dance of death. Taj Mahal unvisited, Madura Temple with golden dome unseen, sphinx and pyramids barely noticed, Arctic splendours briefly glimpsed through a crack in a Boeing's shutter. 'We're now flying over Samarkand at a height of ... at a speed of ...' Where are you, Samarkand? What memories I must have of Peking, Celestial City! Of Katmandu where the junkies roam! Bring me my home Kine of burnished gold; bring me my transparencies of desire! Where are we now, air-hostess? Laying an extra coat of red on lips tired with smiling, she looks at her watch. 'We'll be landing at La Guardia in . . . minutes' time.' Travel narrows the mind.

So we chugged on, through the Suez Canal, where I noticed on the left bank a train arriving at a station, and the passengers getting out to cross to the other side of the Canal to catch another train that was waiting for them there; as it might be Clapham Junction. A weird enough little group to be discovered in the desert, consisting mostly of men in suits and trilby hats, carrying briefcases, some of them with umbrellas as well. Nothing, it seemed, could stop men with briefcases making their way about the world. So far, it must be admitted, nothing has. Then on into the Red Sea, where we celebrated Christmas Day. After we had finished our Christmas dinner, the Ordnance man – a shade more portentous than usual after a bottle of champagne – made a speech in which he spoke of the various services and professions represented in our second-class saloon, finishing up with: 'Not forgetting the education corps,' meaning me. The piano-tuner, who had also drunk a lot of champagne, applauded rapturously, and shortly afterwards fell asleep. It was a relief to arrive at Colombo, say good-bye to the passengers, and go ashore.

In Colombo I stayed with some kindly missionaries, and spent most of my time wandering aimlessly about the streets; as I nearly always do when I find myself at a loose end in a strange town. Just drifting along and watching faces as they pass, one of them myself; enjoying a kind of anonymous intimacy with all the others, yet separate from them, inviolate. Such a variety of faces and expressions! Whiskers and beards sprouting, eyes hooded or smiling; faces taut or withdrawn, or – as so many are in India – full of fathomless patience which is very beautiful and touching. Sometimes a face of rare serenity, so that you want to stop and offer thanks for it there and then. Or a face stamped with a lustrous beauty; momentarily glimpsed, then gone for ever. Or a beggar's face whining and cringing, mutely exposing sores or deformities, or holding up for inspection a wizened stunted child. Then, in passing rickshaws, with bells tinkling and the pat, pat of human feet sounding, some massive bearded merchant lost in his own thoughts and stratagems. Or a topee'd clerk or official. Or a minor Memsahib on her way to the Club. The unforgettable smell of spices, cow-dung, sweating flesh; the flies, the confused shouts; the little shops like opera boxes, exuding their own smells and tinkling sounds. A shoe-maker gravely intent on his work, with wrinkled brow and meditative face, like a philosopher. A pastry-cook, shining with the heat of his oven, arranging the delicacies he has made. A grain merchant dozing, with open sacks of rice, a shovel and scales ready to hand. A jeweller sitting, inscrutable, among his bracelets and trinkets and necklaces; as it might be some Maharajah's vizier or treasurer. A cloth-merchant with silks and brocades under his eye, quietly observant of any who come to look at them. And, as one passes, the whispered persuasion to come and buy, however seemingly hopeless the proposition. As though I should want a tortoise-shell comb to put in black silken hair! Or a little silver box for holding betel and lime!

From the moment of landing in Colombo, I was made conscious of my status as a Sahib. It was like suddenly inheriting a peerage and being addressed as My Lord. Just by virtue of being English and white, if you went to buy a ticket at a railway station, people made way for you. Similarly, in a shop. It was very insidious. At first I found it embarrassing and distasteful; then, though I continued to ridicule it, I came to count upon receiving special treatment. Finally, when for some reason it was not accorded, there was an impulse to become sulky and irritated. From that it is but a small step to shouting and insisting, as, in the days of the Raj, I saw happen often enough. Our position in India as a ruling race corrupted all concerned; soldiers – and other ranks just as much as officers, if not more so – missionaries, government officials, planters, business men, wives and children; everyone. It also corrupted the Indians, whether they kissed the rod and accepted a position of subservience, or whether they rebelled against it. Though alien rule can sometimes be more efficient and honest than self-government, it is bound ultimately to become deleterious to rulers and ruled alike. We accept bad government – we have to – but find it more bearable from our own kith and kin than from foreigners. The absurdity is to suppose that self-government, as such, is otherwise beneficent; that replacing a buffoonish colonial governor with a feathered hat by an equally buffoonish Jomo Kenyatta with a fly-switch, or white bully-boys by black ones, represents any moral or – as the World Council of Churches, that *pons asinorum* of all Christian endeavour, appears to suppose – spiritual advance. India without the Raj is, in this respect, in no way a better, or worse, place. The only essential difference is that the Sahibs are now brown instead of white.

There remained nonetheless the moral dilemmas with which life in India constantly confronted a reluctant Sahib in my time there. Take, for instance, the rickshaw. This horrible conveyance, invented, I believe, by a missionary in Japan, was often the only sort available; as I found

when I went on from Colombo to Kandy to visit Trinity College, a
boys' school. When I arrived at the railway station, the rickshaw coolies
surged forward; I chose one of them who seemed a shade more muscular
than the others, and got gingerly, with my luggage, into his rickshaw.
As he hauled me along, I watched with fascination a patch of sweat on
his shirt steadily expanding, until it occupied almost the whole of his
back. At the same time, I could hear him panting more and more
heavily, especially as we began to climb up to Trinity College, which
stands on a hill. Finally I could stand it no longer, and shouted to him
to stop. He took this to mean that I was dissatisfied with the speed we
were making, and quickened his pace. Thereupon I shouted louder,
and managed at last to make him understand that I wanted to get down.
Thenceforth, he pulled the rickshaw with my luggage in it and my white
topee perched rather absurdly on top of the luggage, while I trailed
along behind on foot, feeling self-consciously virtuous but also aware
that a patch of sweat was forming and growing now on *my* shirt where
the hot sun beat down on my back. In this way we arrived at the college,
where a row immediately broke out as to how much I should pay. This
was settled when my host, the acting-Principal, took the matter in hand.
Thenceforth, except *in extremis*, I never took a rickshaw, which greatly
annoyed the rickshaw coolies, who relied on an occasional Sahib's
inflated fare to augment their meagre earnings. In Simla the situation
was particularly difficult because motor-cars were forbidden there
except for the Viceroy and the Commander-in-Chief (they still are
restricted to two or three very senior officials), while the roads were so
steep that, notoriously, the rickshaw coolies all died young of heart
failure.

Once, when I was crossing the Perriar River by the ferry at Alwaye,
there was a rickshaw on it, accommodating a very large Indian, with a
very meagre one at the pulling end. A colleague from the College who
was with me overheard someone on the ferry remark: 'Look, there's
one man pulling another along. And they say there's a God!' Such remarks stay in my mind more tenaciously than speeches at the Royal
Empire (now Commonwealth) Society, or fulminations against injustice
and inequality, including my own, in progressive publications. I wish
they didn't. My inadequacy as a sightseer is illustrated by the fact that
every detail of the Kandy rickshaw ride is indelibly imprinted on my
mind, to the point that now, forty-eight years later, I could draw the
shape of the patch of sweat on the rickshaw coolie's back; whereas,
when I visited the famous Buddhist Temple of the Tooth in Kandy, it

made so little impression on me that now I cannot remember any single thing about it.

Trinity College proved to be one of those transplanted public schools which were instituted in most parts of the Empire when it was flourishing. The boys wore blazers, played rugger, sang English songs and hymns heartily, though in fairly cracked tones because of the different scale in their own Indian music; took cold showers, and were taught to be manly and speak the truth. The idea was that thereby an elite would be produced capable of leading their countrymen in the paths of righteousness while being loyal to the Raj. Actually, such institutions tended to turn out what were known then as subversives, and subsequently as national heroes. Despite – or perhaps because of – Trinity College, Ceylon was one of the first Commonwealth countries to have a quasi-Communist government; Achimoto in Ghana, an offshoot of Trinity College, incubated Nkrumah, as Harrow did Nehru. Worthy endeavour with an interested motive nearly always results in the exact opposite of what was intended. Thus, education aimed at producing literates for industry produces illiterates for anarchy. The more motorways the more accidents, the more psychiatrists the more lunacy; hypochondria burgeons with the health service, and delinquency with remedial prisons. Evensong in Trinity College Chapel, I found, was an exact reproduction of the same service in any English public school or college. I was to live to see the situation in reverse, with white hippies in saffron robes and with shaven heads chanting *mantras* along Fifth Avenue, and Allan Ginsberg giving a rendering of 'Hare Krishna' to the accompaniment of his hand harmonium in a Chicago law court.

I had vaguely assumed that, to get to Alwaye, all I should have to do would be to go to the railway station and buy a ticket there. It turned out to be a complicated journey by boat, bus and train. A Sahib travelling third class was something of a rarity in those days, unless he belonged to the Salvation Army or some other lesser Christian sect without the law. It was pretty uncomfortable and harassing, but also oddly gay and exhilarating. The carriage packed to suffocation; everyone chattering away, and spitting on the floor; from time to time partaking of highly spiced and highly smelling refreshments, of which I was offered a taste. As a Sahib in a suit, with luggage that, by Indian standards, was munificent, I was a subject of curiosity. Where was I going? What was I doing? How much money did I earn? How many children did I have? – such questions, put in broken fragmentary English. At a venture, I said I earned one hundred rupees a month (which turned out to be just about what I did earn at the Union Christian College, plus free accommodation); in European terms, a minuscule salary, but in Indian terms quite substantial. When I said I had no children because I was not married, they looked sympathetic. One of the difficulties of the missionaries of contraception who go about India preaching the gospel of birth-control, and distributing their coils and pessaries and pills as the early traders in Africa did coloured beads, sometimes even offering transistor radio sets in return for voluntary sterilisation, is precisely this attitude, obstinately maintained by village Indians, that children are a great blessing, and that to be sterile is to be accursed. No doubt they will learn in time as computers, television, supersonic bangs, James Bond and other intimations of civilisation reach them.

When I think of India, as I often do, it is such scenes as travelling in a third-class railway carriage that come into my mind. Or sailing with the fishermen at Cape Comorin, in a boat made just of two logs fastened together. 'Look what a strange white fish I've caught!' my boatman shouts to the others. Or going to bathe in the evenings. So many other bodies standing in the shallow river water, just letting the water lap over them; then bending down to cup it in the hands to pour it over themselves. All this to the thud, thud of clothes being beaten clean. Or waiting before dawn for a bus. Along it comes, with flickering lights, and all the passengers asleep; but still a place for me beside the driver. Off we go again, roaring and rattling along, through dark, silent villages, raising clouds of dust, barked at by dogs, driving stray cows out of our way. I sit watching for the dawn, for the first grey streaks of light in the sky. As the grey light spreads, the shapes of houses become discernible, figures stretching and yawning, the kindling of lights. And in the sky now a fabulous brightness breaking; like the beginning of the world – *Fiat Lux!* Such a golden, luminous glory! Such a beautiful coolness, faintly misty, preparing us for the leaden heat to come! Our passengers are beginning to wake up, rubbing their eyes, looking around them. Where are they? Who are they? The driver and I have a mild altercation – his lips red with betel, his eyes clouded and bloodshot from fatigue. He wants to charge me twice the normal fare; I protest, but he insists, explaining that I am sitting in the first class. Then where's the second class? I ask. Wherever you sit is first class, he counters. At this sally we both begin to laugh, and I pay up. At the next stop he brings me a glass of tea and a banana, which I gratefully accept.

They were all so poor; they all had so very little. Anyone from the

West was a sort of millionaire by comparison; even nuns and monks and vagrants. When floods came, and they had to leave their homes, they could comfortably carry all they possessed on their heads; a tin box, a mat, some cooking vessels; no more. Yet this very penury provided a kind of protection against the plastic world of the twentieth century. They had no sales potential; the siren voices recommending eating this, wearing that, urging them to consume, consume, would be wasted on their air. Their poverty immunised them against the chief sickness of the age. Perhaps it is in this that the blessedness of the poor – the least appreciated of the Beatitudes to-day – resides. In the first- and second-class railway carriages, on the other hand, in which Sahibs normally travelled, one met the other India. Indians in khaki shorts, smoking pipes and carrying briefcases stuffed with papers to read along their way; topees that sat rather low on their heads; their speech so loaded with English words and phrases ('coefficient', 'percentage', 'overall', 'output' etc. etc.) that it was possible to follow much of their conversation even when they were speaking in Malayalam or Tamil. Already proficient at the new international language of administration and business – computer-speech-to-be. They were executive material; budding survey-men, sociology-fodder. In short, men of our time.

The most convenient mode of travel in Travancore itself was by boat through the salt backwaters which, like Norwegian fjords, intersect the country. In this way I arrived at Allepey in the evening, the solitary Sahib aboard. As the Indian passengers surged ashore, and I struggled with my bags, I wondered where I should go for the night before continuing to Alwaye by train the next day. The noise, the darkness, the general air of excitement, of people arriving and being met, made it seem a rather wild and alien scene; the more so because the rickshaw coolies, when they saw me, all shouted with one accord: 'T.B.! T.B.!' At first I thought that perhaps they considered I looked tubercular, and their cry was a warning, like a leper's bell. Then I somehow understood that what they were suggesting was that they should take me to the Traveller's Bungalow which in those days was available for Europeans in places where there was no suitable local hotel. So there I was taken, and passed a comfortable night under a mosquito-net, having first been served an evening meal of curried chicken, rice and crème caramel; the almost invariable diet offered to Sahibs all over India. Subsequently, I grew very fond of sailing through the backwaters; preferably not on the regularly plying paddle-steamers, but on a hand-propelled boat, long and graceful, with coconut matting for protection against the sun. As the boatmen poled it along, walking up and down its length, they would chant with a weird haunting rhythm which fitted their movements. It was somehow very beautiful, with coconut palms along the banks, and houses on stilts, and little villages appearing and disappearing, and children racing along and shouting. Then, at night, lying in the bottom of the boat, lulled to sleep by its motion, peeping out occasionally at the bright stars and the moon-drenched water, the night settling round one like velvet. Conscious then of being an atom of life among innumerable other atoms. Momentarily separate, like drops of spray caught in sunlight; existing separately for an instant or two, then falling back into the sea whence they came.

Alwaye, when I arrived there, turned out to be a smallish place, little more than a village, though with a large Roman Catholic college dominating the view from the railway station. Now it has become quite a centre of new industries. I was met and taken to the Union Christian College some three miles away. To get there we had to cross over the Perriar River by ferry. The College was on top of a stony hill, the stone reddish in colour, looking over the river; a cluster of buildings barely finished, in one of which, a students' hostel, I had a room furnished with a bed and a table and chair and an oil lamp. There was also a primitive shower and a lavatory of sorts. Though the term had not yet begun, some of the students were already in residence, and gathered round in a semi-circle to watch me unpack. Their steady gaze was a little unnerving, and in their white *mundus*, with their dark faces and, in the case of the Brahmins, weird hair-dos, they had a strange air, especially as they maintained total silence, only smiling when I addressed them. This, as I found out afterwards, was because they could not understand my way of speaking English, having learnt the language – in so far as they could be said to have learnt it – from Indian teachers. It turned out that I had turned up sooner than expected; Holland, who, with his newly married second wife, occupied a mission house in Alwaye, had not yet returned from his Christmas holiday; Lester Hooper, another Englishman who was joining the staff, was due to arrive in a few days' time. Thus, no arrangements in the way of setting up meals and so on for me had been made. I suppose my situation in this remote place, where, of course, it was very hot and humid, with no one I could turn to for advice as to how to settle myself in, might be regarded as somewhat disconcerting. I cannot recall that I felt it so.

My life at Alwaye soon got into a sort of routine. I had a servant, or
bearer, named Kuruvella, who brought me tea early, about six o'clock.
Then I would go for a swim in the river. It was rather muddy, though
sometimes a strong current was flowing. Already the students would be
washing and squatting about the hillside. After breakfast, classes began.
My subject was English, and my sheet-anchor was a book known as
Little Dowden, a brief history of English Literature by a Victorian
clergyman of that name. There is, I believe, a Big Dowden, but I am
happy to say I have never even had it in my hands. From Little Dowden
I was able to hold forth about, say, the Lake Poets, or Milton, or
Restoration comedy; indeed, on almost any theme in the Eng.Lit.
rubric. Little Dowden provided not only the information but often the
actual phrases I used. Thus I would say, as though it had just occurred
to me: 'Dryden found English brick and left it marble.' The students
would copy this down, and no doubt find some means of bringing it in,
whatever the question, when they came to sit their examinations. They
copied down pretty well everything I said, and afterwards learnt it by
heart, so that one could actually hear them chanting it like some weird
liturgy as they walked up and down – 'Dryden found English brick
and left it marble . . . found English marble . . . left it brick . . .'

There were also set texts that had to be fought through, sentence by
sentence, and sometimes word by word. On this basis, I went through
Ruskin's *Sesame and Lilies*, *Macbeth* and *Wuthering Heights*, the last
being the most painful because totally incomprehensible to the students.
The sides of the classroom were open, as is the way with buildings in
South India; as we droned on together, we could see the bright green
paddy fields, and watch people working in them, treading round
bamboo irrigation wheels which made them look like inflated daddy-
long-legs, or bending in rows over the earth, singing as they worked.
Looking at them from our classroom, I felt at times an almost physical
anguish at being so preposterously engaged; at spending the daylight
hours in so derisory a way. ' "There's nothing serious in mortality" –
that means, in our mortal or earthly existence.' The students' solemn
faces were staring at me, drinking in the words; then bent to write
them down. ' "All is but toys: renown and grace is dead" – Macbeth is
saying that, after the murder of Duncan, everything seems trivial, like
playthings.' Again the dark eyes look up uncomprehendingly, the pencils
scratch. ' "The wine of life is drawn, and the mere lees/Is left this
vault to brag of",' I declaim: then lamely add: 'The image is taken from
a cask of wine, stored in a vault, the wine being, as we say, drawn,

leaving behind the lees.' Nothing serious in mortality – I waited for them to finish their scribbling, and then continued.

Examinations, for the students, represented the climax of their studies, the point of the whole operation; having once procured the requisite qualification, they could forget for ever the sorry, tedious business of learning, whose purpose would then have been achieved. They studied past questions with feverish intensity, making use of what were called 'Made Easies'; poorly printed, paper-backed volumes on sale wherever there were institutions of higher education, which purported to contain all possible permutations and combinations in a particular subject, with a guarantee that, if thoroughly mastered, they made a pass certain. There were Made Easies to be absorbed over a three months' period before taking the examination; even, in desperate cases, over a two weeks' period. The students addressed themselves to these Made Easies as the fateful day approached, tackling them in the only way they knew – by committing them to memory. I almost got to know them myself from hearing them said over and over late into the night. Mastering the three-months' version, still more the two-weeks' one, required a prodigious effort, and there was the danger that at the examination itself the information acquired might be in too concentrated a form to be readily disgorged. Wild-eyed and desperate with the effort, unshaven, distracted, the students might have been engaged in some strange obsessive cult or debauch.

In the case of other subjects some genuine interest may have been aroused, but in mine – the study of an alien literature in an alien tongue – there was none that I was able to discern. About the worst thing the British did to India, apart from introducing a totally unsuitable and farcically inefficient Westminster-style system of universal suffrage parliamentary government, was the educational system they foisted on the country; which still, incidentally, goes on, though now the English used has departed so drastically from the original as to be almost totally incomprehensible. That may, in a way, represent an improvement, in that it precludes any possible deviation into sense. I like to think that when the Raj at last ended, among the articles hurled after the departing Sahibs were at least a few Little Dowdens, as well as an occasional copy of *Sesame and Lilies*, *The Mill on the Floss* and the *Oxford Book of English Verse*.

Most of the students were Syrian Christians, for whom the College primarily existed. The records of their Church go back to the fourth century, and they claim that it was founded by St Thomas at the beginning of the Christian era. In the succeeding centuries it went through all the same sort of ups and downs and schisms as the Western churches, producing a similar crop of contending prelates – in its case, Archimandrites and Patriarchs – and for some sixty years, during the period of Portuguese domination, was forcibly incorporated in the Church of Rome. This fragmentation was made worse by Christian missionaries from many denominations in Europe and America who found the Syrian Christians a happier hunting-ground than the Hindus and the Moslems in other parts of India. The chief inspirer of the Union Christian College, K. C. Chacko, hoped that it would bring together all Syrian Christians, enabling them to find a basis for co-operation, if not for unity. There was a single chapel at the College for all to worship in, and under Chacko's aegis the different sectarians managed to establish harmonious relations. He was a man of great spiritual perception, with a high forehead, and a voice with a soft rich timbre, a sort of glow at the heart of it. I got in the way of often sitting with him on the balcony outside his room while he ate his evening meal, consisting, usually, of two huge bananas. Being a sufferer from tuberculosis – a common complaint in that humid, sultry climate – he had to live a semi-invalid life, though a very austere one. He always worked at a desk standing up to concentrate his attention the better. Alas, the cause he devoted himself to so fervently remains unrealised; the College has flourished, certainly, in the sense that it has steadily grown bigger, and more reputable academically, but the divisions and factions among the Syrian Christians still persist; the rival Patriarchs and Archimandrites bicker and contend, and, as is happening to all religions and denominations everywhere, the congregations grow smaller, and the faith of those who still belong to them, weaker.

The students themselves, apart from a few notably pious ones, were not much interested in Chacko's vision of Syrian Christian unity; their primary concern being to take a degree and get into Government employment, which at that time offered pretty well the only openings for graduates. Before long, there were many more graduates than openings, but still the passion for higher education continued unabated, with the result that unemployed graduates multiplied, constituting a natural field of recruitment for the Independence, or Swaraj, Movement. Thus, the higher education facilities which the Government of India provided, in the early days of the Raj with a view to procuring a ready supply of cheap clerical labour (Government clerks were known in those days as 'writers'), in practice produced the shock troops who played so important a role in bringing the Raj to an end.

I did everything in my power to stimulate the nationalist fervour of the students, seeing myself as a Garibaldi or Byron come among them to help them recover the freedom that was their birthright, and that British rule had taken from them. The cheers of students, anyway, are sweet in the ear, and easily procured, as many an aspiring politician and demagogic don has discovered. As I learnt subsequently, I was not much older than the students myself (though some of them were older than they seemed, prudent mothers, with an eye to future examinations, having quite often faked the date of birth of their offspring to give them a year or so in hand), and well primed with a romantic adulation of rebels and rebellion. I adopted Indian dress, wore *kadi* – the homespun cloth which Gandhi advocated – tortured myself by sitting cross-legged on the ground and sleeping without a mattress; risked catching hookworm by walking barefoot, and ate Indian food off a plantain leaf with my hands, acquiring some facility at moulding rice into little balls and aiming them neatly into my mouth. I even managed to simulate certain characteristic Indian gestures; as spreading out my hands with a look of profound disgust to indicate that I did not want another helping, or shaking my head from side to side instead of nodding up and down, to signify agreement.

A visit to the College by Gandhi in the course of a tour of Travancore gave a great impetus to Swarajist sentiment among the students and staff. I went down to the railway station to see him arrive; a vast crowd, at least ten thousand strong, had already assembled there. They had trudged in on foot from surrounding villages, nearly all of them peasants; in some cases, whole families. I wondered what had drawn them, what exactly they expected to see. Their faces provided no clue; from their expressions they might just have been waiting for a train for themselves rather than for a Mahatma. Waiting, as Indians do, having no timetables, with the utmost patience, sometimes all through the night, in the certainty that sooner or later a train would come in and take them to wherever they wanted to go. When Gandhi's train came, there was a stir; but mostly among students from the College, while a little group of local notables who had brought garlands with them took up action stations. The others remained largely impassive. Gandhi was sitting cross-legged in a third-class compartment, his curious gargoyle face showing no special awareness of the crowd and the notables and the cheers of the students. When he stepped down on to the platform there was a concerted movement to take the dust of his feet. All those thousands of people surging forward to get near enough to him just for that, to take his dust; then tramping back the miles they had come, padding silently along the dusty village tracks. Certainly, they were not Swarajist zealots; there was little enough of that in an Indian State like Travancore, where they had scarcely heard of the British Raj by the time it was over. Nor were they uplifted by Gandhi's championship of cottage industries and hand-woven cloth; in their primitive economy, a spinning-wheel such as Gandhi recommended would have been as unattainable as a Rolls-Royce car. He drew them to him, I decided, because he gave them a feeling that they mattered; that they, too, existed in the scheme of things, and were not just helots, extras in a drama which did not concern them. This was why they saw him as a Mahatma, and took the dust of his feet.

When Gandhi caught sight of some untouchables in a sort of roped-off enclosure, he went and joined them, and started singing with them what sounded like a rather lugubrious hymn, to the obvious conster-nation of the notables with the garlands. Later he addressed the students in the classroom where I took them through Little Dowden. But how different a scene! He spoke very quietly, in English, of which he had a subtle and discriminating command, but the effect on the students was terrific. They jumped up and down shouting '*Mahatma Gandhi Ki Jai! Mahatma Gandhi Ki Jai!*', their eyes glowing and the dreadful inertia of our excursion through *Sesame and Lilies*, our mournful celebration of Dryden finding English brick and leaving it marble, all obliterated and forgotten. I would scarcely have known them; they were trans-formed. In this case, of course, it *was* nationalism that enthused them. Millions of editorial words, including my own little bucketfuls, thou-sands of columns of Hansard, scores of White Papers, Royal Com-mission Reports, Blue Books and other State documents later, their objective would be attained. The peasants who trudged in and out of Alwaye to take the dust of Gandhi's feet would be trudging in and out of polling booths to vote for yoked oxen, a lotus flower or an umbrella; the Raj would be over, the Mahatma murdered, and India free, with a national anthem, a flag, an airline, a hydro-electric project, a seat at the UN, and other appurtenances of sovereignty.

After Gandhi's visit to the College I wrote him what was, I fear, an extremely impertinent letter, in which I argued that he would be better employed in promoting the socialisation of India's economy rather than in trying to persuade his countrymen to prefer a hand-spinning wheel to a mechanical loom. Industrialism had come to stay, and it was futile to take a Canute attitude, and try to hold it back in India; what the Indian worker needed was better living conditions and contraceptives to keep down the size of his family. Standard claptrap at the time, and still more so to-day. Gandhi replied courteously and at some length, though I thought evasively, and published the correspondence in the weekly magazine *Young India* he brought out in Ahmedabad. He also published an address I delivered in the College chapel calling on the students to rise up against the Raj, since nothing could go well for them culturally, economically or politically until they had ceased to be a subject people. Afterwards, a fellow-member of the staff whispered to me that men had served terms of imprisonment for saying less. Rather to my disappointment, the authorities either never heard of my vapourings or, if they did, decided, quite rightly, that they were of no importance, requiring no response on their part.

Gandhi's views, of course, were based on some of the same basic texts as my father's – Ruskin, Tolstoy, and the New Testament considered as a statement of ethics rather than of faith. He left out Marx, it is true, and included the *Bhagavad Gita*; but the resultant mixture was not so very different, and likewise appealed to Quakers who, when he was in England, formed a sort of non-violent bodyguard round him. At the time of the Round Table Conference I saw him in a nest of them at Friends' House. His face had changed from how I remembered it at Alwaye; it now somehow looked crafty and calculating. By this time he had become one of the *gurus* of the age, along with figures like Albert Schweitzer and Bertrand Russell (later to be joined by Che Guevara, Martin Luther King and Malcolm X) for all of whose plastic busts there was a ready sale. His bizarre turn-out – the loin-cloth, the spectacles, the watch with a large face pinned to his person – had become as familiar as Charlie Chaplin's big boots, baggy trousers and tiny bowler. Through his dominance of the Swaraj Movement he was able to impose on it, as an actual programme, the notions he had derived from Tolstoy and Ruskin and the New Testament, so that leading Swarajist desperadoes felt bound to sit at their spinning-wheels for a daily stint, wear *kadi* and profess non-violence – very unconvincingly, it must be admitted. I have myself heard Gandhi leading some of them in a barely intelligible version of 'Lead Kindly Light', his favourite hymn. Despite their ostensible adherence to similar notions, the farthest the Labour Party bosses went in this direction was to sing Blake's 'New Jerusalem' on particular occasions, and drop occasional asides to the effect that if

Christ came back to earth he'd assuredly be crucified again. One of the more bizarre consequences of the association of India and England through the Raj was that, not only Gandhi's homespun, Quakerish predilections, but the whole ideology of the British Left, came to be adopted by the Swarajists, so that when their cause triumphed this ideology automatically became the conventional wisdom of the new Indian Government and ruling class. It is true that during the struggle for independence, the example of Ireland was preponderant; I have a precious memory of a cracked rendering of 'The Wearing o' the Green' under the relentless glare of the Cawnpore sun – a companion piece to Gandhi's 'Lead Kindly Light'. When independence was achieved, however, and Nehru became the first Indian Prime Minister, it was editorials he had read in progressive publications like the *New Statesman* and the *Manchester Guardian* which provided the basis for his domestic and foreign policy. By a weird accident of history, some four hundred million Asians were thus harnessed to the confused thoughts and fluctuating loyalties of old-style English Leftists like Kingsley Martin, Harold Laski and Pethick-Lawrence. What on its home ground was regarded as being, at best, an acceptable irritant, to be pushed aside the moment a government of the Left took office, became in India the only evident alternative to the Thoughts of Chairman Mao.

In the evenings, when it was a little cooler, I usually went for a walk. The road I took, up beyond the College and in between the paddy fields, was nearly always crowded. There were cattle being driven home and a particular man I always looked for driving along a flock of geese, waving a thin, supple stick over them very delicately to keep them together; like the conductor of an orchestra. Bullock carts with sleepy drivers flicking at the bullocks, often a whole family huddled inside; solitary nondescript pedestrians, a file of women coming in from the fields moving with great grace in their coloured saris. Strange old hags with withered breasts and lined faces; an occasional bus loaded to the gills and stirring up a mighty dust; beggars, of course, dragging along elephantiasis-swollen limbs, or with bits chipped off them by leprosy, and children, and wandering cows. And a man I once saw proceeding in the most extraordinary way by falling down, reaching out his arm, marking the place, and then from there falling down again, and so on. He had, it seems, taken a vow to make his way in this manner, measuring his length in the dust, from Cape Comerin to the Himalayas. The estimated time it would take was ten years. At Alwaye he had barely started.

Everyone stared curiously at me, a Sahib walking instead of riding; especially when the monsoon rain was falling, and I took off my shirt to let it fall coolly over my bare flesh. Indian roads were like rivers, always full and always in movement; all India flowed down them, bare feet endlessly falling and stirring up dust, golden in the setting sun. My particular road delighted me, particularly as darkness suddenly fell, going oddly silent, so that you could hear somewhere or other tiny bells ringing, and voices singing; then see lights coming out one after the other. Families gathering, work over, the day done; shadowy figures squatting, very still and meditative. Later, when the full darkness had fallen, pedestrians with hurricane lamps, looking like glow-worms, sometimes carrying a lighted faggot which they swung to and fro to keep it alight, so that one saw it rhythmically flaring up and dying down as they went along. Then, quite soon, sleeping figures stretched out on mats or bare bedsteads, or just on the ground. Sleeping with a curious abandonment peculiar to Indians; utterly still, so that they can sleep tranquilly through the night on a narrow ledge, scarcely wider than themselves, with no risk of falling off.

When I got back from my walk I usually took another river bathe. There, too, stillness came with the evening; ablutions silently performed; the water silky or, if there was a moon, holding the moonlight like tangible sheets of luminosity on which one could lie like a raft. Beautiful Perriar River. This was an India I sensed, and even touched; utterly remote from Made Easies and Little Dowden; the splendid relic, as I felt, of a departed glory. Felt this with a kind of sadness, as though I knew that the vulgar destructive twentieth century was ravening near. Bulldozers on their way to bite into the ancient earth, dredgers and concrete-mixers to utilise the meandering rivers, diesel oil to belch out its exhaust over the shining backwaters, conveyor belts to disgorge plastic elegancies, replacing ancient heirloom vessels burnished and kept over the years. Wandering cows, creaky and bony and ready to chew at anything, even paper, all rounded up for extermination. Likewise, the thick-necked oxen, the sinewy fowl, the imperturbable goats. On the way, too, the family planners bringing the precious gift of fornication without tears; others bearing in their hands such delicacies as Tomato Ketchup, *Peyton Place* and after-shave lotion. Pill- and potion-makers with specifics for all ills, including political ones – in this field, remedies concocted afar; one-man-one-vote, majority rule, government of the people by the people for the people. Advertisers to unfold the secret of everlasting youth and beauty; of happiness without end, amen.

It was all beginning even then, and somehow I sensed that this India I knew, which had miraculously survived Macaulay, Curzon and Rabindranath Tagore, was nearing its end. I felt a profound thankfulness at having known it.

I spent a lot of my time at Alwaye in the staffroom which, like the classrooms, had no sides to it. Outside, one could see the sun beating down, and if there was a breeze it blew pleasantly in. When the rains came, falling like sheets of metal, it was cooler; almost at times chilly. There would usually be one or two other staff members likewise loafing between classes, ready to gossip or chat or argue. We often took our midday meal together. Apart from teaching, I found I had plenty of leisure. Little Dowden was soon mastered, and I felt no inclination to pursue matters further. Most professional employment, in my experience, leaves one similarly unstretched, containing, as it does, a large element of camouflaged parasitism. Those lavish luncheons on someone's expense account, extending from preliminary drinks to a dreamlike return to one's desk in the late afternoon; breath brandy-laden, and flakes of smoked salmon drooping from the corners of one's mouth! That picking over of the lavish offerings of news-agency services; like walking with a plate round a well-stocked buffet, and choosing, now a slice of tasty paté, now potato salad and eggs-in-aspic! Those army headquarters in some requisitioned palace or hotel, with majors dozing before in-trays, and colonels wrestling with their claims for field-allowance! Not really, properly speaking, work; though liable to be enervating. At Alwaye there were long empty spaces of time, which passed laggardly, stretched out on a bed, or staring uncomprehendingly at a printed page, or just staring out of a window – something to which I have always been prone.

My out-of-class activities, such as they were, consisted of bringing out each term a college magazine and producing an occasional play. The magazine (I still have an issue or two) was all too typical of such publications; feebly facetious, with reports of games and other activities. Exactly in the style of any English school magazine. The plays I remember producing were James Elroy Flecker's *Hassan* and Congreve's *The Way of the World*. Looking back on these productions, the former seems the more abhorrent precisely because it was supposed to be 'Oriental' in theme and diction; the latter merely absurd – Indian students in home-made wigs trying to be Restoration gallants. I felt a kind of inner shame and rage about all this. As I dimly realised, a people can be laid waste culturally as well as physically; not their lands but their inner life, as it were, sown with salt. This is what happened to India. An alien culture, itself exhausted, become trivial and shallow, was imposed upon them; when we went, we left behind railways, schools and universities, statues of Queen Victoria and other of our worthies, industries, an administration, a legal system; all that and much more, but set in a spiritual wasteland. We had drained the country of its true life and creativity, making of it a place of echoes and mimicry. Some four decades after these lamentable Alwaye productions, in Delhi I recorded a television interview with Nehru, and found myself irresistibly recalling them. He, too, I felt, partook of the same hollowness. A man of echoes and mimicry; the last Viceroy rather than the first leader of a liberated India. While our conversation was being recorded, one of the attendant guards fell noisily asleep, so that his snores punctuated our words as we spoke them. It seemed an appropriate accompaniment. A few months later I heard that Nehru had died.

In the evenings at Alwaye I sat with a pen in my hand and paper before me. Moisture from one's fingers was liable to smudge the ink; the lamp, no Alexandrian pharos, gave a meagre light, and buzzed with flying insects. Trying to coax out of the encircling sultry darkness, words. Oh, words! I have a folder, dim to read now in every sense, of these early efforts. They resulted in my very first earnings – fifteen rupees from the *Madras Mail* – which I sent home to signalise the occasion. My mother bought with the money a sort of tall white-metal ashtray, which she kept by her to the end, though she had long given up her very occasional cigarette. Later, to my father's great delight, I had a short sketch published in the *New Statesman*. It was in the vein of pastiche-Chekhov, very popular at that time, what with Katherine Mansfield and the Master himself appearing in the World's Classics series. The theme – an elderly elementary schoolmaster who had lost heart, felt himself a failure, etc. etc. My father wrote that, opening his *New Statesman* and finding my piece there, had kept him going.

I shared my servant, Kuruvella, with Lester Hooper. We usually took our evening meal together. He was a Harrovian; tall and thin and pale, with silky flaxen hair and, when he neglected to shave, a similarly silken beard; a meek and saintly person, with a passionate dedication to evangelical Christianity. His father was a pencil manufacturer, very comfortably off, and I imagine what is called self-made. He visited us in Alwaye, well loaded with all varieties of his commodity; large and small, hard and soft, delible and indelible, some of which I acquired. His mother, whom I also met in England, was one of those frail powdery ladies who sit well wrapped up in chauffeur-driven limousines; so completely belonging there that one is quite surprised to see them indoors without a fur coat, or walking about in the open air. Lester and I did not have a great deal to talk about; he disapproved of my political views, and I teased him about his complaisant attitude to what is now called the Establishment. I also, I regret to say, mocked at his pieties, and tried to shock him whenever I could. I can only now remember one single remark he made to me; *à propos* Jesus chasing the money-changers out of the Temple (a favourite episode, for obvious reasons, in my father's circle), Lester said with great earnestness and, for him, emphasis, that he was quite sure that the rope Jesus took up never touched anyone. He could not bear the idea of the Son of God, like any prefect, falling back on personal chastisement to enforce obedience. After I left Alwaye, Lester stayed on, devoting himself, along with some of the students, to missionary and welfare work among the un-touchables. Some years later, I heard he had died, and when I revisited Alwaye I sought out and stood contritely by his grave in the little Christian cemetery near the mission bungalow where Holland had lived, envious in a way of his quiet resting-place.

Occasional hospitality from the Hollands made an agreeable change. It was a well-run household; Mrs Holland belonged to an affluent Bristol family with strong Tory affiliations, and injected into her hus-band's austere missionary ways and vaguely progressive attitudes some of the certainties and amenities which still prevailed in English middle-class life in those days – certainties and amenities which, for some reason, were always symbolised for me by a little methylated spirits burner set under a silver tea-pot to keep it hot. I think I must have seen this particular device in use at a Quaker table, or perhaps at one of our tame clergymen's, but ever afterwards thought of it as being the imprimatur of bourgeois status. Mrs Holland used such a burner and silver tea-pot. Holland himself belonged to the old evangelical tradition. His face had a sort of granitic amiability; virtue was carved into it with – given the toughness of the material – surprising delicacy and subtlety, and, of course, guaranteed durability. When he prayed, he closed his eyes tightly and spoke to God as a head-boy might to his housemaster; in strong, steady and utterly straightforward accents. This second marriage fairly late in life took him into another milieu, socially, politically, and even spiritually (Mrs Holland was inclined to be high-church); but his splendid physical and moral constitution enabled him to withstand the shock, though leaving him beneath the surface, as I thought, a little shaken. After he retired from India he was given a City Church, once, as he proudly told me, attended by William Wilberforce. I visited him there, and was happy to find him little changed.

I sometimes went from the College to Alwaye by the river, in a little boat that I had acquired; a hollowed-out tree-trunk made into a rather primitive canoe, which I paddled along. It quite often overturned, which I didn't mind much. Once I took the Bishop of Colombo, an elegant man named Carpenter-Garnier, in it when we were both dining with the Hollands. He had got himself up in a splendid purple cassock, and I was sorely tempted to overturn the boat deliberately just to see whether the colour would run. However, I resisted the temptation, and we arrived safe and dry. Both Holland and the Bishop would have considered themselves missionaries; missionary enterprise, in those last years of the Raj, being still in full swing, with the object of actually converting the heathen and inducing them to be baptised. Nowadays, of course, this is no longer so; almost any missionary will preface any remarks he may make about his work with a statement to the effect that he by no means considers Christianity better than other faiths, and that he has learnt much from the heathen through his association with them.

In my time, apart from Holland – who was veering towards the new attitude – there were still plenty of the old-style missionaries around. One such I stayed with in Tinevelly, in South India. Besides being an evangelist, he was a doctor, and took me with him to a nearby village stricken with cholera. At first it looked as though the village was quite deserted; no one seemed to be stirring, all the huts were quiet, until my companion stationed himself by the well, and rang a bell he had with him. At its sound a few villagers dragged themselves out and gathered round him. He told them in Tamil that God had visited this misfortune upon them because of their sins; at the same time, it was also due to contaminated water, and he put some permanganate in the well to correct this. Then he went round injecting the sick with saline solution. His fearlessness and the simplicity of his faith were impressive, even though I considered it reprehensible to use the epidemic to, as it were, advertise the Christian God's power to punish. He told me how, at his dispensary, when he asked an out-patient whether his bowels had moved, the man replied, with the savage irony of the very poor, that as he had not eaten, it was scarcely to be expected that he would have anything to excrete. A similar example of this bitter wisdom in those who live on the very edge of total destitution was provided by an official in the Punjab who told me that once he had asked a small farmer there whether he hated the Government or the money-lender more. After some thought the farmer replied that he hated the Government more, because, whereas it was to the money-lender's interest to keep him just alive so that he could go on paying off his debt, the Government didn't care whether he lived or died.

In an Indian State like Travancore the British Raj seemed very far away. The only Sahibs living in Alwaye were Holland, Lester Hooper and myself; Mrs Holland was the solitary Memsahib. There were, it is true, also two Spanish Roman Catholic priests, bearded, and invariably in their cassocks, but somehow they did not qualify. Anyway, we never had anything to do with them. At Cochin, a few miles away, there was a small cluster of Sahibs – a bank manager, some business men, or box-wallahs as they were then called, with equivalent Memsahibs, a Club and other amenities. I only once spent an evening with them, at the Club. Like every other such establishment, existing wherever two or more exiled English were gathered together east of Suez, there was a dimly lit dining-room, a bar and lounge, old tattered copies of the *Illustrated London News* and the *Tatler* lying about, lots of servants in white and red sashes and turbans, and a flavour of stale booze and vestiges of old hangovers in the air. Outside, an elaborately watered garden and tennis courts. Brooding over it all, the sense of infinite tedium which characterised all these haunts of the expatriate English in India; more especially the ones frequented by the Memsahibs, who grew pale and randy and ill-at-ease with nothing to do under the tropical sun. My evening at the Cochin Club, I gloomily recall, ended with some rather macabre drunken festivities, which involved dragging a cart through the streets and pretending it was a tumbril.

I once or twice had occasion to go to Trivandrum, the capital of Travancore, where the Maharajah had his Palace and the State Government its seat. As the ruling family were Nairs, a matriarchal community, inheritance was through the female line and, the Maharajah being a minor, effective power was exercised through the Junior Maharanee; actually, a somewhat disreputable character. The Diwan, or Prime Minister, needed to be on good terms with her; a later incumbent whom I knew, Sir C. P. Ramaswamy Iyer, achieved this in the same sort of way that Disraeli ingratiated himself with Queen Victoria – by inordinate flattery and amorous protestations. When he was in Simla seeing the Viceroy, the stability of his situation was judged by the regularity with which the mangoes the Junior Maharanee sent him arrived. As long as they were duly dispatched it was assumed that all was well. He managed to keep in favour, with mangoes regularly arriving when he was away, right up to the transfer of power in 1949 which, considering he was well into his seventies by then, was no mean feat. He died full of years and honours in Ootacumund some years later. Incidentally, the Nairs should provide a perfect milieu for Women's Lib zealots. My memory is that the males always seemed unusually carefree and happy.

The local representative of the Raj was the British Resident; a man named Cotton, who lived in an old Dutch house with splendid wide verandas on an island in Cochin harbour. It was a delectable spot, and Cotton made the most of it. He maintained a stylish household, with a smart launch to take him to and from the mainland, and a brass band to play 'Colonel Bogey' and 'Lillibullero' on gala occasions. When he travelled to Trivandrum, all the ferries along the way were held to wait for him so that he should not have to suffer the smallest delay. On special occasions like the King-Emperor's birthday, he gave a garden-party to which even Anglo-Indians, if they were not too dark, and missionaries, if they were not too out-of-the-way, were invited. He was a man, I should have said, of considerable capacity, but indolent by nature, who preferred the remoteness from his bosses in the Political Department of the Government of India, the leisured life and the ceremonial status his post as British Resident in Cochin and Travancore provided, to more ambitious appointments which would probably have been within his reach. Two rather ravaged ladies who wore a lot of make-up and seemed always to be fatigued, to the point that they rarely managed to finish a sentence, and even long words tended to peter out before they got to the last syllable, were usually staying in the house. It was generally assumed that the younger of the two was his mistress.

It was a Somerset Maugham set-up, as I recognised subsequently; at the time I had never read any Maugham, whose works, like P. G. Wodehouse's, were considered improper in a socialist household like ours. Maugham, of course, would have made Cotton a more emphatic figure, who saved up his sea-borne copies of *The Times* to read at breakfast, and punctiliously dressed for dinner in all circumstances. The mistress would have been younger and slimmer, and have lost her heart to the Residency chauffeur, a Sikh with a black curly beard in a hair-net. The other lady would have been older, and have saved the situation by her worldly sagacity, and a discreet gift to the Sikh on the understanding that he sought other employment. The dénouement would have been a letter to Cotton from the Viceroy's secretary informing him that he had been awarded a KBE in the Birthday Honours. When I visited Maugham at Cap Ferrat, as I sometimes did towards the end of his life, I used to think of Cotton and his household, reflecting that it was the fate of this aged pederast with his parchment face and somehow Chinese features to catch, in the portrayal of characters like Cotton, the last afterglow of Victorian romanticism. Hence the popularity of his novels and stories. He and Galsworthy, in their writings, and later on the television screen, notably celebrated a lost bourgeoisie in the century of the common man, to the delectation of one and all; especially in the USSR and its satellite countries, where the bourgeoisie, abolished in a revolution and replaced by party cadres, was particularly mourned over.

I got to know Cotton quite well. He told me that his motive in the first place for seeing me was to consider whether I might not be a suitable person to be tutor to the young Travancore Maharajah, but that after only ten minutes' conversation he realised that I would never do for the post. It gave me a momentary regret that I had not been more guarded in talking with him. All my life I have teetered between wanting to be successful and despising what constitutes success. It is a rather ridiculous posture; like making ardent advances to a woman, and then, when at last she surrenders, feeling disinclined to take advantage of her accessibility. Perhaps such a temperament, applied to public affairs, is particularly suitable for the communications business. A Thersites role. Even now, I regret to say, something of this attitude remains; like the dregs of an old passion. I still find myself avidly reading gossip paragraphs about people I have never even heard of, and following public controversies whose outcome is a matter of indifference to me. It is Dr Johnson's splendid sentences which roll one most kindly in the dust of such fatuities; for instance, his account in *Rasselas* of the old man who endeavours 'to abstract my thoughts from hopes and cares which, though reason knows them to be vain, still try to keep their old possession of the heart'.

Of course the Maharajah's court in Trivandrum was a pretty tin-pot and unimpressive affair; but then so was the Governor of Madras when I watched him come clattering into church at Ootacamund, the hill station where I spent the summer vacation, followed by his ladies and ADCs, to occupy the front pew reserved for him, Indian worshippers

being restricted to the back pews. His grey frock-coat and topper somehow failed to suggest majesty, reminding me more of a Worshipful
Mayor than an Excellency. The Indian Princes at least had better props
and costumes; Highnesses all, and sometimes Serene ones, with their
jewels and elephants and dancing girls and dusky soft self-indulgent
faces, they belonged to the Indian scene, whereas the Governor seemed
to have strayed out of Croydon Town Hall. Both the Princes and the
Governor, had they but known it, were playing out their last act; the
one to be replaced by an Indian equivalent, though without the grey
topper; the others to linger on in their courts, the velvet upholstery
growing ever dingier and dustier, the dinner table display tattier, the
servants scruffier, the evening hours longer and the daytime ones
emptier. Cut off from their States, from India, finally from life itself;
vestigial figures, reaching back to Great Moguls, then to parchment
treaties signed, witnessed and delivered; suppliants at Durbars before
a bearded King-Emperor, a stately Queen-Empress, coming from afar;
resplendent in a Chamber of Princes, at Viceregal levees, with appropriate gun salutes to match their eminence. Finally discarded in consequence of dishevelled MPs striding or lurching through parliamentary
lobbies, some in winged collars, with waistcoats and hanging watch-
chains, their footsteps resounding on Westminster stone under grey
Westminster skies by the grey Thames. Kingdoms all lost to shouts of
'Division! Division!'; to them an alien and incomprehensible cry; yet
full of doom. At last deprived of their only remaining prop – their
Privy Purses. So finally bereft of all authority; little lost pools
of sovereignty left behind on a barren shore by a receding tide of
history.

When, years later, we were filming in Alwaye, by a curious chance
we stayed in Cotton's Residency, now become a Kerala Government
Rest House. The fine structure of the house remained intact, and a few
pieces of furniture and old faded photographs survived from its past
glory. It was the same launch which ferried us across, but, of course,
grown shabby with the years, and lacking the smart sailors and ensign.
The grounds too were sorely neglected; though on Sundays the few
Sahibs still remaining in Cochin came over to play golf, bringing with
them their Memsahibs and their own supplies of chilled beer. Hearing
their shouted badinage, it was almost as though a ghostly garden-party
was being re-enacted; I strained my ears to catch 'Colonel Bogey' and
'Lillibullero'; and half expected Cotton's portly but elegant form (it
was thought he might perhaps wear stays) to loom into view, exuding

the absent-minded geniality, the distant joviality, the unrecognising recognition of the ceremonially great.

In Ootacamund I stayed in a house named 'Farley' which belonged to Miss Hopwood, a zealous evangelical lady of some wealth who maintained the house to accommodate missionaries on furlough. It was, for her, a labour of love, not for profit; she charged very little, and looked after us all most kindly and generously. I grew to love her, and was very happy under her roof. To me she was consistently kind, if not over-indulgent, and even sent me baskets of fruit and fresh vegetables to Alwaye, thinking that my diet was inadequate there – which I daresay it was. We knew little of her own family circumstances, but she spoke sometimes of travelling about Europe with her mother, and attending musical festivals. Music was her only 'worldly' interest; otherwise, she considered all forms of entertainment as belonging to the Devil's domain. Hymn-singing was a permissible indulgence of her taste for music, and whenever possible she threw herself into it with tremendous zest, often, in her own house, providing the accompaniment as well on a small harmonium she had. She must have been rather pretty when she was young, and even in late middle age, when I knew her, she had still a grace and charm and gaiety about her, despite her severe, if not Calvinist, religious outlook. She insisted that German theologians were responsible for the erosion of Biblical faith, and set them as a heavy debit against her love for Mozart and Beethoven and even Wagner. Her household ran smoothly under her direction; she treated the servants well, and they stayed with her. I can see her now, with her energetic step, going about the garden and in and out of the house; the chains and bracelets she was given to wearing jingling and tinkling with her movements. Always busy, always breathless, always smiling. I regret to say that I sometimes said things intended to shock her, but she invariably forgave me.

After breakfast each morning, the 'Farley' residents would get down from their chairs and kneel at them for prayers; offered by any minister or clergyman who happened to be present, or, failing one, by Miss Hopwood herself. Kneeling there amidst the relics of a hearty meal was a bizarre experience; with the fat barely congealed on the plate off which one had just scoffed bacon and egg, and one's teeth still gritted with fragments of toast and shreds of marmalade. The prayers themselves, in the evangelical style, were likewise mundane; Father, we ask thee to help so and so in his studies for an external BA degree. Or someone else to get the wherewithal to build a greatly needed extension to his Mission

Hall. Once I heard an elderly Methodist minister, attired in an old-fashioned down-turned collar and white tie, pray: Lord, we offer unto thee Miss Ogilvie's leg. Miss Ogilvie, who was present, had broken her leg; in any case rather ample of size, it seemed enormous in a plaster cast, and not, I reflected, a particularly appetising offering. It was easy to deride these simple requests, and yet there was something very touching about their particularity, which I dare say made them as acceptable in heaven as intoned pleas for peace in our time, or for the well-being of those set in authority over us. They were a sort of prosaic plainsong; heavenly actualities. If God, as we are told, has indeed counted the hairs of each head, and cannot see a sparrow fall to the ground without distress, then the particular concerns of His servants must be of concern to Him, whatever they may be.

Under Miss Hopwood's roof I met a great variety of missionaries. There were Anglican bishops who, though they might call themselves Bernard Madras or Reginald Cawnpore, were still more redolent of a cathedral close than a bathing ghat; wild American evangelists ready at the drop of a hat to show lantern slides of their work among head-hunters on the Burmese frontier; tough maiden ladies who had travelled prodigious distances in bullock carts, and lived in remote places among ferocious tribesmen; stubborn fundamentalists who had acquired immense erudition through translating the Bible into obscure vernaculars. One of these last told me that, in the case of a vernacular which had never hitherto been written, the nearest equivalent he could get to everlasting crown was a hat that will never wear out. I found them on the whole interesting and sympathetic company; much more so than other foreign residents in India who were considered, and considered themselves, intellectually and socially superior. Somehow I have always had an inner and unaccountable conviction that any religious expression of truth, however bizarre or uncouth, is more sufficing than any secular one, however elegant and intellectually brilliant. Animistic savages prostrating themselves before a painted stone have always seemed to me to be nearer the truth than any Einstein or Bertrand Russell. As it might be pigs in a crowded sty, jostling and shoving to bury their snouts in the trough; until one of them momentarily lifts his snout upwards in the air, in so doing expressing the hope of all enlightenment to come; breaking off from his guzzling to point with his lifted snout to where the angels and archangels gather round God's throne.

The Nilgiri Hills, where Ootacamund is situated, looked very beautiful from the window of my room. Miss Hopwood, who loved them and, as I heard long afterwards, died within sight of them, gave them names from *The Pilgrim's Progress* and the Bible. As, the Delectable Mountains and Beulah. I went off with a pony and a tent to explore them; sometimes sleeping in my tent, and sometimes staying with a tea-planter glad to receive any visitor in his loneliness. They were generally rather hard-bitten men, with that aloofness which comes from being alone a great deal without any recourse like reading or listening to music by way of mitigation. A truly lonely loneliness. The coolies who worked for them, nearby in their godowns, were scarcely fellow-mortals, though they were fond of them usually, and treated them kindly; but not quite as considerately as they treated their dogs or horses, to whom they became deeply attached. If they had a native girl in to share their bed, as most of them did from time to time, it was still in the great majority of cases a purely physical, impersonal relationship. A release of sperm and sexual tensions. There would be the inevitable Club some miles away, which they would go to perhaps once a week, to play bridge or snooker, or look at the papers, or enjoy the company of the one or two Memsahibs who came in, with or without their husbands, from neighbouring estates. An evening with them at home was largely silent, with a lot of Scotch diluted with water in large tumblers consumed; faces getting redder, speech slower in the process. In one planter's house, when I was packing up to go, my host remarked how surprised he had been to notice how large a proportion of my baggage was books. The remark delighted me, though I affected to receive it deprecatingly. Actually, I have always been a great carrier of books; more, however, for show, as a kind of totem, than to read. There are books like Burton's *Anatomy of Melancholy* and Montaigne's *Essays* which I have carried about the world for years on end without ever reading a single word to this day. Johnson said he would sooner praise the novels of Congreve than read them (the reviewer's charter); similarly, there are a lot of books I'd sooner carry than read.

On my wanderings in the Nilgiris I often caught a glimpse of the plains below; yellow and sizzling, and so far, far away. It gave one a tremendous feeling of being cut off, utterly remote, from India with its noises and flies and smells and teeming population. In this aloofness and remoteness, up there among the fir trees, dark green against a piercingly blue sky, breathing the fresh mountain air, drinking the cool mountain water, bathed in the clear bright mountain sunshine, I had an overwhelming sense of being engaged in a quest. What for? I didn't know; I still don't know. Only that one has to stumble on, as I did with my pony, aware that each corner reveals another, as each horizon opens up another. So it was borne in upon me that there never would be an arrival; there never would be a home-coming. Only, at best, a transit camp, and something seen through a glass darkly – the lineaments of a face dimly picked out, the sound of a voice whose words with much straining could just be caught, a presence towards which one could reach. No more than that. On my way back to Ootacamund I saw Miss Hopwood and some of the 'Farley' residents coming to meet me. She had brought one of her incomparable picnics, to which we sat down cheerfully together, looking across at the Delectable Mountains, clear in the bright sunlight. Before beginning to eat and drink we sang one of her favourite hymns.

Mulling over this solitary journey afterwards, I had a notion that somehow, besides questing, I was being pursued. Footsteps padding behind me; a following shadow, a Hound of Heaven, so near that I could feel the warm breath on my neck. I knew I was making for somewhere, some place of light; seeking some ultimate fulfilment in which another reborn me would extricate itself from the existing husk of a fleshly egotistic me, like a butterfly from a chrysalis. I was also in flight. Chasing and being chased; the pursuing and the pursuit, the quest and the flight, merging at last into one single immanence or luminosity. Some scribbled pencil notes that have survived finish up with the barely decipherable question: Is this God? No answer is offered.

My last months at Alwaye were marred by illness. I developed Delhi boils; little Etnas in my flesh, which went on persistently erupting. Also, I was afflicted with two kinds of worms. Unfortunately, what destroyed the one nourished the other, and vice versa. At one point in these misfortunes a local physician was brought in; a wild-looking man with heavily oiled hair and sandalwood pasted on his forehead. Rather ominously he brought with him a jam-jar of leeches which, however, to my considerable relief, he did not propose using. I cannot say that his ministrations were effective, but I did somehow manage to get well enough to resume taking my classes. Conditions at the College were, it must be admitted, rather severe for a European, and if I had stayed on, as Lester Hooper did, I should probably, like him, have died there. It might have been the better course, but I was impatient for the end of the three years I had contracted to stay; not for any reason except that, once again, I wanted to make off. In all my life I have never stayed in any job much more than three years – five at the most. It has been a kind of Bedouin existence, feeding off one oasis after another. The things one is paid a salary for doing are never, in my experience, *serious*; never seem in the long run of any particular use to anyone. Thus I have come to think of financial rewards as purely arbitrary; like army pay which no one can foresee or understand. It is this arbitrariness, or – in the religious sense – mystery, of earnings which leads to the generally prevailing dissatisfaction with them; in the same sort of way that everyone is dissatisfied with what he pulls out of a lucky dip, irrespective of whether he has been fortunate or unfortunate.

My final departure was spoilt by an article of mine that appeared just before I left severely criticising Indian university education in general and, by implication, Alwaye in particular. The Principal, A. M. Varkey, an extremely nice man, was deeply upset, and told me that, whereas he had been looking forward to giving me a great send-off, now he had no heart for it. I was duly abashed. The curious thing is that I had no thought of the consequences of the article's appearance as I threw myself into writing it, struggling to give expression with the greatest possible emphasis to the cultural and spiritual emptiness, the intellectual and aesthetic shoddiness, of the kind of education Indian college students were getting. The same sort of thing has happened to me on numerous other occasions; I can only record, but cannot fully explain, still less justify, a propensity I recognise in myself to kick in the teeth institutions or enterprises I have served, as well as the individuals concerned in running them, at the moment of departure. This might seem to be, and has often been taken as being, deliberate treachery. If so, not consciously; rather, perhaps, a fatality arising out of an inability to follow Blake's dictum, and be a cut worm that loves the plough.

The fact that my departure from Alwaye *was* rather desultory and low-keyed did not prevent me from feeling greatly exhilarated when I found myself on my way home. The first part of the journey was by small boat on the backwaters, and I had with me Venketramen, a colleague at the Union Christian College who had become a close friend, and Mathail, a Christian sadhu or holy man, wearing the saffron robe and wandering without money or possessions from place to place, to whom I was also devoted. Their original purpose had been only to see me off at Alwaye, but then they very sweetly decided they would come with me as far as Alleppey. They needed no luggage, and felt under no necessity to inform anyone of their change of plan. I half hoped I might be able to persuade them to come on to Colombo, and even beyond, as I hated the idea of parting from them. I still had with me some examination papers to mark, which I proceeded to do in a desultory way, throwing them away in the backwater as soon as I had finished marking them and recording the marks awarded. It seemed a satisfyingly symbolic gesture. In my ebullient mood, the candidates fared well; I believe I scarcely failed a single one.

Venketramen was a Madras Brahmin; I greatly admired the strict austerity of his way of life. He had never tasted meat or alcohol or tobacco; I never saw him in a suit, but only in a spotlessly white *mundu* and shirt. Though I often visited his house, I only once or twice caught a distant glimpse of his wife. As a strict Brahmin, he wore the holy thread, but his hair was cropped, not kept in a bun. His features were sharp, his eyes bright, and he spoke with great precision and lucidity. His subject was mathematics, but he was widely read and introduced me to the *Upanishads* and the *Bhagavad Gita*. I was utterly fascinated to get to know this completely different kind of man from any I had encountered hitherto; a product of quite a different kind of civilisation. Christianity interested him little, and the evangelistic activities at the College, such as they were, touched him not at all. I will not say that he looked down on the Syrian Christians, who were his students and colleagues, but he held aloof from them with, as it seemed to me, a touch of aristocratic disdain. In the West the association between distinction of any kind and, if not affluence, then material ease and comfort, is so close that it is difficult to imagine it in any other terms. Yet I doubt whether Venketramen spent more than a minute proportion of his in any case modest salary on himself. He had no chairs or table, only a mat; no wardrobe, no motor-car, only a very few books. I remember once saying to him, *à propos* this austerity, that Indians had no interest in preserving trophies of the past; like manuscripts, inscriptions, monuments. That they were as spartan about the past as about their own present; reducing it to the same sort of simplicities. How long can the manuscripts or monuments be preserved? he asked. A thousand years? A hundred-thousand years? A thousand-thousand years? In the end, they are dust. So what's the point? He spread out his elegant hands in a way he had.

I am temperamentally incapable of understanding anything abstractly stated. When, for instance, I read (G. E. Moore): '*When we infer that a thing did happen in the past we are in fact doing that simply on an inductive ground from the fact that we remember it . . .*'; or (Wittgenstein): '*I have two different ideas, one of ceasing to exist after death, the other of being a disembodied spirit. What's it like to have two different ideas? What is the*

criterion for one man having one idea, another man having another idea . . .',
my mind shuts up; as it did when my father, as he was prone to, got
on to the subject of the Categorical Imperative. Thus, I have never been
able to get through any work on Hindu philosophy; I sat with the
Maharishi noting how supple were his legs folded beneath him, how
well tended his curly beard, how freshly and fragrantly groomed he was,
but as for the discourse he treated me to – why, it might have been
Professor Namier reading aloud to me that front he had written in the
Times Literary Supplement. From my association with Venketramen,
however, the times I spent with him, observing him washing and
gargling his mouth, as he did punctiliously, delicately picking his rice
from a plantain leaf with his quick fingers, dipping it, maybe, in curds,
taking his evening bath in the river, composing himself so precisely to
sleep on a narrow ledge outside his house – from all this I got a notion
of Hinduism. Something, in its top flights, very beautiful; all embracing,
subtle, gentle, static – above all, static. Making few demands, but few
concessions too; circular, not angular; going on and on, without any
drama to break the even flow. No darkening of the sun or rending of a
curtain; no finishing to begin and dying to be born. No voice crying
in the wilderness; rather the converse – the wilderness crying in a voice
    Superficially, at any rate, no one could have been more different
from Venketramen than Mathail was. He seemed to be composed of
bones only, without any flesh covering them; just skin. It was rare to
see him eat at all, and when he did he only pecked like a bird. He would
turn up suddenly, stay a little while, and then disappear; never going
anywhere in particular, or coming from anywhere in particular. I was
so fond of him that I always seemed to be on the watch for him. If,
when he came, you put an arm round him, it was like clutching a
bundle of sticks. When I first saw an El Greco portrait, I realised how
like one he was; the head shaved, the face gaunt, but with a great
beauty in it. His face somehow shining, in the El Greco style, with that
indomitable, inexorable Christian love; absurd, inane, if not insane, in
its total refusal to exclude anyone or anything from the range of its
radiance. All-inclusive to the point of idiocy; sweeping like a great
searchlight across the universe, from the tiniest midge buzzing round a
cow-pat to the burnished splendour of God's very throne. A sort of
beatific half-wittedness in it; a fantastic strength derived from an
equally fantastic weakness, an invulnerability born of being so very
vulnerable. A face pared down to nothing, but that nothing, everything;

the lowliest of faces, conveying the greatest heights ever aspired to. Truly a countenance divine; eternal in time, and timely in eternity. I felt very content in the company of these two; the happiness of our journey together glows still across the years that have passed. The sparkling water, the bright sunshine, the warm breeze; the sense of being detached from duties, responsibilities, affections even; yesterday gone, and tomorrow not yet come, and our boat propelled smoothly along; to give an extra point to my contentment, each examination paper discarded representing a defiant and final rejection of Little Dowden. We watched delightedly as the papers bobbed away on the surface of the water. Happiness is the most difficult of all things to convey. Tolstoy, I should say, comes nearest; for instance, in his description in *War and Peace* of Natasha's visit to the huntsman's house; how she and the others listened to stories, then danced, then rode back in their sledge through the frosty starlit night. With my two oddly assorted companions, gliding into the golden light of an Indian evening on my way back to Europe and home, I likewise was happy.

In Alleppey the three of us slept on the floor of a room in some sort of Christian institution with which Mathail was associated. After bathing, Venketramen sat cross-legged, still and silent, looking out at the night. Mathail's devotions were more fidgety; bowing down his head, grimacing and muttering, cracking his finger joints. The one passive, letting the Cloud of Unknowing settle about his head; the other restlessly seeking to pierce it. In either case, the Cloud remains unpierced, for 'there was never yet creature in this life, nor never yet shall be, so high ravished in contemplation and love of the Godhead, that there is not evermore a high and wonderful Cloud of Unknowing betwixt him and his God'.

As for me – I made no meditations or devotions at all, but was full of thoughts of becoming a famous author, holding audiences spellbound, seducing women. I felt like a Stendhal hero, avid for the world and what it had to offer; a true child of our time, worldly and sensual. Perhaps sensing this, Venketramen, very uncharacteristically in view of his habitual reserve, spoke to me about women and the danger they represented to someone like myself; they were ravening, he said, destructive, a coarsening and ultimately fatal addiction. His own temperament, and even physique, were so remote from anything of the kind, that his words scarcely registered; as when, his features reflecting the deep disgust he felt, he spoke of meat-eating. Mathail gave no indication of having heard what was said, but looking across at him I

C.W.T.—I

noticed a sort of half smile playing over his face. The next day I said good-bye to them affectionately, and left for Colombo. There I took a ship to Naples, where, as I have already mentioned, my father was waiting for me on the quay, his bowler firmly on his head. I was not to see India again for a decade, returning in very different circumstances; to live as a Sahib in Calcutta and Simla, never once recapturing the delight of those first magical years.

4 *The Pursuit of Righteousness*

> The reigning Error of his Life was, that he mistook the Love for the Practice of Virtue, and was indeed not so much a Good Man as the Friend of Goodness.
>
> – Johnson's *Life of Savage*

BACK IN ENGLAND, I went to stay in Birmingham with Alec Vidler, who was by this time a curate there in a parish in Small Heath. He and the other clergy, all celibates, lived in a clergy house, where I also stayed. Unmarried clerics, whatever their denomination, living together, create their own characteristic domestic interior. Austere, and, at the same time, careless; with tobacco smoke hanging about the curtains and upholstery, as well as in the lavatory, which gives an impression of being in constant use; like the crockery in a busy station buffet. No carpets, so footsteps echo up the wooden stairs and along the wooden corridors; the rustle of cassocks, and the fumes of plain cooking seeping through the service hatch; tea set ready for all and sundry in a large metal pot standing amidst an array of cups and saucers. A lot of joking, while standing in front of the fire, hands under black leather belt and black skirts billowing; in the early morning, celebrants coming and going, their faces severe and withdrawn, sometimes holding their gear; in the afternoons, a heaviness, and in the evenings an ebullience, at night vaguely heard groans and mutterings and twistings and turnings of uneasy sleepers.

The adjoining church was, of course, very high, with the little red light of the reserved Sacrament always aglow, the pungency of incense always in the air, Holy Water in good supply, and confessionals available like telephone kiosks as and when required. All this led to an acrimonious controversy with the then Bishop of Birmingham, Dr Barnes, who regarded the Eucharist as a distasteful form of magic. A sometime *Daily News* columnist, he was one of Ramsay MacDonald's clerical appointments, another being Dr Hewlett Johnson, Dean of Canterbury, who over the years preached Stalin and him sanctified from the pulpit of the Anglican Church's senior cathedral. Thus MacDonald, least revolutionary of Socialists, all unconsciously delivered a body blow at institutional Christianity far more destructive in its consequences than all the efforts of overtly anti-Christian crusades. The best demolition work is done by such unlikely agents; bourgeois society being a Prometheus fated to gorge its own entrails. Was it not two bourgeois Jews – a typical Viennese general practitioner, and a British Museum Reading Room *enragé* – Freud and Marx – who undermined the whole basis of Western European civilisation as no avowedly insurrectionary movement ever has or could, by promoting the notion of determinism, in the one case in morals, in the other in history, thereby relieving individual men and women of all responsibility for their personal and collective behaviour?

When I was working on the *Manchester Guardian*, I met Dr Barnes, a friend of C. P. Scott. He turned out to be a rather holy-looking man. Clergymen, in my experience, tend to get holier and holier-looking as they move farther and farther away from their faith; rather in the same way that a certain type of womaniser gets more ethereal looking the more women he seduces. It must be some kind of inner adjustment mechanics, like a thermostat. There never was a more deaconal dean than Dr Hewlett Johnson when, in his gaiters and with a large cross adorning his waistcoat, he sat beaming beatifically among his church's foremost enemies. Dr Barnes's rig was also elegantly clerical, and he had a gentle, purring, exaggeratedly meek manner of addressing one. At the time I met him he was much exercised about a new telescope which had just been developed. Telescopes, he seemed to imply, were getting so powerful that before long they'd be looking into heaven itself. Then all doubts would be set at rest, and science and faith come together in one blessed consummation. When Scott died, Barnes conducted his funeral service in Manchester Cathedral. In the course of his address on that occasion he remarked that some might consider it strange that he, an Anglican bishop, should be presiding over the obsequies of a distinguished Unitarian in an Anglican cathedral; but to him it seemed the most natural thing in the world, since Scott, like himself, had been a puzzled theist. This appeared in *The Times* report as 'puzzled atheist'. It confirmed my feeling that misprints, like the foolishness of men, are the wisdom of God.

Alec, though mixed up in the controversy with his Bishop, to the point that he stayed on in Small Heath much longer than he intended or wished in order not to give Dr Barnes the opportunity of appointing someone in his place with different theological views, was still, I felt, essentially uninvolved. He has an enviable capacity for being able thus to withdraw into some deep inward serenity of his own, and in that sanctuary, totally private and impregnable; there able to meet his God and work out the relationship between them. Without understanding precisely how this happens, or the terms arrived at, a third person can still draw strength from the resultant serenity. I regard Alec as one of the great Christians of our time, even though – perhaps because – I should have the greatest difficulty in defining just where he stands in the different theological disputes which have accompanied the steady erosion of Christian faith. To me he has been like a rock where there is always shelter, however fierce the hurricane. A lifelong comfort.

I worked in Birmingham as a supply teacher. This meant moving from school to school to replace masters on sick leave or otherwise absent. One seldom stayed long enough to get to know the staff or children in any particular school; as soon as one began to feel settled, it was time to move on. Some of the classes were enormous; I remember teaching one of sixty, with ages ranging between nine and fourteen (the then school-leaving age), and abilities ranging between average intelligence and what would now be regarded as sub-normal. It was impossible to do anything much except keep order, and that was difficult enough. No paddy fields to look out on as at Alwaye; only the asphalt playground. It was extraordinarily like a prison; an effect enhanced by the antics of the headmaster, a malignant-looking figure with a high colour, thin dark hair and a straggly moustache, who had a way of peering in at the classrooms. One would suddenly catch sight of him through the glass of the upper part of the door, or know of his presence by a sudden hush which descended on the class. His malignancy was in no way abated when he took prayers; if anything it was intensified, especially when he read some passage from the New Testament like the thirteenth chapter of Corinthians. He seemed almost to be grinding his teeth over 'faith, hope and charity', and working to a crescendo of fury when he came to: 'And the greatest of these is charity.' Even more than at my own elementary school, I found 'Now the day is over' on Friday afternoons quite magical in its promise of two days' release. I think I must have suffered more than I now remember, because even to-day, if I happen to hear that weird animal noise children make at their morning recess in a walled asphalt playground, my heart is liable to lose a beat, particularly if I then hear a bell ringing, followed by silence, which means that soon they will be back in the classrooms. At the – as they were then unashamedly called – better class schools, my difficulty was more with the teaching itself. In a number of subjects, geography and mental arithmetic, for instance, the children were well ahead of me, as was liable to emerge all too clearly. When I got into difficulties of this kind, my usual recourse was to switch to dictation, which gave one time to collect one's thoughts, and which anyway has a kind of drama about it; first a breathless silence, and then one's voice bringing out the words to be written down, like a judge delivering a death sentence.

The post-war spirit of ebullience had now spent itself, and the depression was beginning to loom; the economists who were going to squeeze Germany till the pips squeaked were in disarray, and John Maynard Keynes, straddling King's College, Cambridge, and the Treasury, collecting modernist pictures and directorships with equal avidity, pursuing at one and the same time a passion for Duncan Grant and for inflationary economics, was coming to the fore. Lloyd George, the man of destiny of 1918, had become a ribald figure whose venerable white locks and black cloak enclosed a goatish disposition, and whose claims to be able to conquer unemployment were as dubious as had been the previous ones to make a land fit for heroes to live in. His only asset was a political fund acquired by the sale of honours during his premiership, on a tariff – according to one of the entrepreneurs in the trade, Maundy Gregory – ranging between £15,000 for a knighthood and £40,000 for a peerage. The other men of the wartime coalition were likewise in abeyance, though Churchill, with his readiness to serve in any government at any time on any terms, had, to everyone's surprise, been made Chancellor of the Exchequer by the new Conservative leader, Stanley Baldwin. At the Treasury he did all the things he afterwards denounced; returning to the Gold Standard, cutting armaments to the bone, raiding the Road Fund, etc., etc. His only point of serious difference with the new leadership proved to be the extension of self-government in India, the single item in their programme which history was to justify.

Commentators on the political scene tend in retrospect to regard the figures who emerge into prominence as totally derisory. Understandably so. It is extremely difficult, as I know from personal experience, to spend time with one or other of them without reaching the conclusion that some accomplished clown like Peter Sellers has substituted for him. Yet, in fact, those set in authority over us, whatever the means they may have used to attain the position, whether force or fraudulence or bribery, do in some degree represent the governed. This applies to a Stalin or Hitler just as much as to a Roosevelt or Ramsay MacDonald, a Ted Heath or Nixon. It certainly applied to Baldwin, even though, at the time, I affected to regard him as a mere cardboard figure wheeled on by the bankers, industrialists and landowners whose interests he represented. His stance as a simple fellow smoking a pipe who loved England and sought to bring together hostile elements in our society, like capital and labour, went down very well. His style of oratory, seemingly artless but actually carefully concocted, was just what was wanted after a surfeit of heroics during and after the war years. He appeared as a prosaic, down-to-earth, nice man, with a prosaic, down-to-earth, nice wife, standing solidly for all the dull, serviceable virtues which seemed in the pleasure-seeking early twenties to have fallen into disrepute. Obviously, this picture of him was not true; it was what nowadays would be called his image. He was by no means the stolid, middle-of-the-road Tory and countryman he purported to be, but neurotic, treacherous and wily; temperamentally, more like his cousin Rudyard Kipling than the John Bull role assigned to him in cartoons. Yet the fact that his public image should have worked so effectively (and not only among Conservatives; my father, when he was an MP in the 1929 Parliament, thought the world of him) is itself significant, showing, as it does, the degree to which the British ruling class was already on the run, and so in need of subterfuges.

It was a relief when the summer holidays came. On an impulse I decided to go over to the Belgian coast again and see Kitty, who was, I knew, staying there with her family. I have always found that in the case of the rare things in one's life that really matter, that are truly serious, there is no deciding after weighing up the pros and cons. An inner momentum carries one along; each step seems, at the same time, both adventitious and inevitable. It is a kind of sleep-walking; or playing of a part so perfectly known that there is no conscious remembering of the lines or waiting for cues. So it happened now. I stayed with Kitty's family in their villa; one of a number recently built close to the sand-dunes. It was the same disorderly, ramshackle household I remembered from the previous occasion. Mrs Dobbs prepared the meals, such as they were; in the process getting herself covered with flour, caked with fat, sticky with sugar and burning her long leathery fingers – sores which she ignored. If the conversation was raging – which it usually was – she would emerge from her kitchen, steaming saucepan in one hand, a ladle in the other, and join in. Her intellectual interests took precedence over all other; there were no circumstances in which she would refrain from participating in a discussion on immortality or the extent of space. Dead or alive, she was there for the kill. Over the explosive sound of a brew boiling over, in the lurid light of a roast catching fire, one would hear her proclaiming her views on the ego which affirms and the ego which denies. When at last her tumultuous chores were over, the last mouthful of horse-meat washed down by the last gulp of vinegarish *vin ordinaire*, she was off to catch the final light of the setting sun, working away with her paints and brushes as long as she could see, and even after. She did not really need to see; what she painted was the notion of a sunset, rather than anything she saw in the sky, built up from many sunsets, seen, enthused over, and painted over the years. She could do it in her sleep. When she died, she left behind her trunkfuls of paintings, all equally good, or bad, and mostly of the same subjects. The only thing she liked better than painting was having rows, of which, when the family were in residence, there were endless possibilities. Once, when I was walking with her along the *digue* at Knocke, she noticed a crowd that had gathered, all looking out to sea. Excitedly, she rushed up to one of them and asked in her nasal French: '*Qu'est ce qu'on regarde?*' When she heard it was just a passing ship, her face fell: 'I thought it was a row,' she said to me, so disappointedly.

Mr Dobbs did not stay in the villa, making the excuse that his work required him to reside at one of the hotels to which the Lunn tourists came. He was a neat, particular man, well turned out, trim and gallant. It was a strange chance which had yoked him with so wild and wayward a spouse, and I daresay he pined at times for someone more amenable and more salubrious. Yet in some ways he admired his wife, to the point of almost being awed by her; he was like, I used to think, an Irish coachman driving a particularly wild pony in a jaunting car. Tugging at the reins, cracking his whip – 'Whoa, there!' but aware that his horse, however difficult to manage, was a spirited animal, comparing favourably with more mediocre ones even though they might offer greater ease, and perhaps even pleasure, to their masters.

They had met when Mrs Dobbs was a comfortably-off widow travelling about on her own in Europe. Her first husband, by whom she had one son who was killed in the 1914–18 war, died of syphilis, contracted as a young man. She once described to me his howls for morphia in the last stages of the illness, and other horrors, with the same objectivity as she did any other experience, good or bad. Her total absence of jealousy arose out of the same impersonality. On one occasion, she told me, her first husband, when he was away, had telegraphed to her to meet him at the railway station on his return because something terrible had happened during his absence. Greatly concerned, she met him, only to learn with relief that what was troubling him was that he had been unfaithful. 'I thought it was serious,' she blandly remarked. In worldly terms, she was totally innocent; Eve before the Fall, with no knowledge of good and evil. She made one realise how necessary the Fall was; without it, there would have been no human drama, and so no literature, no art, no suffering, no religion, no laughter, no joy, no sin and no redemption. Only camera work (towards which Mrs Dobbs's painting was reaching) and sociology (which her sister, Beatrice Webb, may be said to have invented).

The point was well illustrated by one small incident at the villa. Somehow, there had come into the house an artificial chocolate eclair, which, when you bit into it, emitted a squeak. This was tried on various visitors, with resultant hilarity, in which, however, I noticed that Mrs Dobbs did not join. When the humorous possibilities of the eclair were exhausted, she took possession of it with a view to trying it on a Belgian woman who worked for her, and who, having a large family, no husband and very little money, and being normally rather hungry herself, might be expected to bite into the eclair with genuine zest, thus, in Mrs Dobbs's estimation, giving a real point to the joke. In the Garden of Eden before the Fall, only such joking would have been permissible. Likewise, in the New Garden of Eden now taking shape, in which the twin curses of work and procreation laid on the erring Adam and Eve will be lifted – banished to computers and laboratories, and the knowledge of Good and Evil they illicitly acquired, abolished, thus restoring the innocence our first progenitors lost, and making the earth a paradise again – of a sort.

Mrs Dobbs's account of her adventures after her first husband's death, written down in a journal she kept in her nearly illegible spidery hand, meandering on and on like her speech, is full of repetitive descriptions of sunsets and mountain peaks, and banal moralising, with occasional flashes where she describes some human encounter luridly lit by that monstrous innocence of hers. Thus, in Rome she made the acquaintance of George Gissing, the dreary late-Victorian novelist, author of *New Grub Street* and *The Private Papers of Henry Ryecroft*, so beloved of Orwell, who was, he told me shortly before he died, projecting a book on him. Gissing at that time was staying in Rome, and, in the estimation of his friend H. G. Wells, being starved to death by a French woman with whom he was co-habiting. Mrs Dobbs, whom Wells knew, seemed the heaven-sent answer to the dilemma; as a good-looking, reasonably well-off, unattached widow, she was just the person to carry Gissing off, and give him three square meals a day. Every age has its own special buffoon; as honourable a role as any of Shakespeare's Fools. My choice for this comic *Ombudsman* of our time has always been Wells. I realised that he stood alone when I read his account of a conversation he had with Stalin in the Kremlin, in the course of which, as he put it, he tried to interest him in the PEN Club; but Stalin, he observes sadly, failed to kindle, which one can well believe. Gissing, it seems, responded favourably to Wells's proposal, and made what Mrs Dobbs used to refer to as an offer. After due consideration, she turned it down, less dazzled by Gissing's literary distinction than appalled by his meagre physique and melancholy disposition. Shortly after, she met Dobbs who, though no literary figure, had none of Gissing's other disabilities. She bore him five children, of whom Kitty was the middle one, and the only girl.

Remarriage provided Mrs Dobbs with ample opportunities for indulging her taste for having rows. It was virtually impossible to contract out, since the rows were not about anything. Thus, it was no use avoiding a particular subject, or refusing to respond to a particular inflammatory observation. The row existed apart from its occasion; it was in the air like lightning, and bound to strike. A row might be ostensibly about stoking the fire, the circumference of the earth, the date of the last General Election but one, or the coastline of Alaska, but after exhausting oneself on one or other of these themes, one realised that they were as irrelevant to the fury unleashed as Lear's 'Blow, winds, and crack your cheeks! rage! blow!' to the storm that raged about his head on the Blasted Heath.

Dobbs himself was, of course, a leading belligerent, though, not being in residence, he was able to make strategic withdrawals, as it were, into neutral territory to rest and re-equip. Kitty, too, was actively engaged. She felt passionately, as I understood later, that she had to defend herself against her mother's predatory innocence, which would otherwise destroy her. Thus, on one occasion her mother told her that if she wished to have a baby without getting married, there would be no difficulty about the cost and making suitable arrangements. I had a similar breath of Eden air – only in my case, being an outsider, it was just funny rather than suffocating – when Mrs Dobbs told me that, as a young girl, when she went out in London by herself she was followed at a respectable distance by a footman in case she needed protection. The family lived then in Kensington Palace Gardens, and her father – Richard Potter, a business man and speculator – was very rich. The arrangement, Mrs Dobbs remarked, struck her as quite derisory, since the footman was usually far more sexually attractive than anyone of her own class or acquaintance she was likely to encounter. I can quite see that, from Adam's point of view, the apple came as a blessed deliverance; the Fall was mankind's first step to heaven, and it is interesting that all the Devil's advocates, from Epicurus to Rousseau, Walt Whitman, Marx and D. H. Lawrence, want to abolish it and regain an earthly paradise.

An episode which Kitty described to me seemed to convey with particular clarity the character of her long wrestling match with her mother. The two of them had climbed Mont Salève, a hill overlooking the Lake of Geneva. Mrs Dobbs had been sketching, seated on her camp-stool, her easel set up, dipping and sometimes sucking her brushes, her unseeing eyes fixed on the Dent du Midi, whose outline she knew as perfectly as a Presbyterian minister his extempore prayers, or a television comedian his autocued patter. Overcome by the heat of the day, she lay down her brushes, and threw herself on the bare earth for a short rest. Kitty was reading, her face wearing an expression of rebellious resignation very familiar to me, and very characteristic of her. The quiet between them was broken when Mrs Dobbs let out a shriek, and said she had been bitten by an adder in her neck. Kitty made a move to kill the snake, but Mrs Dobbs told her not to hurt the innocent little creature since it had intended no harm. They were a long way from anywhere, and the only thing Kitty could think of doing was to suck the poison from her mother's neck, which she did, afterwards spitting it out. On the way home, down the steep and rough mountain track, she supported Mrs Dobbs, who occasionally passed out as the venom took effect. When they reached the bottom of the hill, Kitty wanted to take a taxi, but Mrs Dobbs would not hear of it. So they went by tram; a macabre journey, the two of them drawing many stares from the other passengers, of which Mrs Dobbs took no notice. She was always completely unconscious of other people, and what they thought; lying down, getting up, walking or eating or sleeping just when she felt inclined. I once, when we were living in Sussex, found her stretched out fast asleep on a tombstone in Battle churchyard; nor was she in the least abashed when she came to, and found me standing there and staring at her.

It somehow became understood that Kitty and I would get married. and quite soon. I cannot recall ever 'proposing' to her – something we should both have regarded as very bourgeois and conventional; terms of abuse in our vocabulary. Nor can I remember any moment of decision; or, for that matter, of indecision. Free will, in my experience, is tactical rather than strategic; in all the larger shaping of a life, there is a plan already, into which one has no choice but to fit, or contract out of living altogether. So, it was borne in upon me that Kitty and I belonged together; that somehow, to me, the shape and sense and sound of her existence in the universe would always be appreciable in every corner of it, and through all eternity. To this essential proposition all sorts of other hopes, desires, appetites, egotistic aspirations, corporeal needs and mental strivings, were attached, like subordinate clauses; sex being one of these.

Mr Dobbs was far from pleased; he considered me – and who shall blame him? – as socially and financially an undesirable match for his daughter. Mrs Dobbs, on the other hand, was delighted. I overheard her once, when the subject was under discussion, observe that I was a genius; a word which even then I regarded as derisory (still more so now), and that, as I well knew, signified, as far as she was concerned, something between Virginia Woolf and Verlaine, with Oscar Wilde hovering about in the distance. A Bloomsburyite figure with Montparnasse affiliations; boozy Augustus Johnian, bearded Laurentian, squeaky Wellsian; with broad-brimmed black hat, large floppy tie, Café Royal frequenting, Stein-Toklas admiring, James Joyce reading. A compendium of all horrors. All the same, I have to admit that, even on Mrs Dobbs's lips, the word, applied to me, gave me a secret *frisson* of demonic joy, such as, perhaps, Joan of Arc might have felt if she had overheard the Master of the King's Bedchamber remark that she bore a passing resemblance to Cleopatra.

Our union was duly registered at the Birmingham Register Office; a drab little scene in a dreary sort of place, where numerous couples were waiting about, though whether to be married or divorced or judicially separated their demeanour did not make clear. The Registrar himself made a forlorn attempt to introduce a festive note into the proceedings, and wore, I noticed, a rather better suit and a rather more colourful tie than might be expected in a civil servant of his grade. Did he, I wondered, receive a special allowance to cover this? Kitty's father, and a friend of hers named Elsie, were the only others present, and acted as witnesses. We affected to regard the occasion as of no particular importance; a mere legal formality, like signing a contract for a job or a lease of a house. It was not our intention, we insisted, to put one another under any sort of obligation; we were free to do what we liked, and would only stay together as long as both of us wanted to; not a moment longer. Even so, I bought Kitty a wedding ring; a very cheap one, admittedly, made of rolled, not real, gold, but it has lasted. She wears it still. I did not have a new suit; only a grey flannel one from my Cambridge days. Kitty wore a green velveteen jacket with an accordion pleated skirt. We had very little money – certainly not more than £100, and no furniture or possessions apart from clothes and a few books. I was a little dashed, if not alarmed, when, on receiving a cheque for fifteen guineas from Sir Henry Lunn as a wedding present, Kitty at once tore it up on the ground that he was a despicable figure. This happened at St Aidan's Clergy House in the presence of the clergy, who, after we had gone, piously gathered the pieces together and managed to reconstruct the cheque. It was never, however, paid into the bank.

It was very unkind, as I now realise, not to have asked my parents, especially my father, who, as I afterwards learnt, was deeply hurt. Incredible as it seems, I just didn't think of it; though there may have been some unconscious reluctance to have him there, some sense that his presence would be awkward. Mrs Dobbs showed me a letter from her sister, Beatrice Webb, in which she wrote that she knew my father as 'a Fabian and a very worthy person, though of modest means'. Truly, there is no snobbishness like that of professing equalitarians. My father bridled at Mrs Webb's attitude: 'And to think,' he wrote in a letter to me about it, 'that I gave up a directorship!' It was indeed ironical that she, a champion of Socialist fair shares, should look down on him for the very thing – his modest means – he owed to his espousal of the same cause. All this escaped me at the time; or rather, perhaps, I deliberately averted my eyes. I was well content to be marrying into so, in Socialist terms, patrician a family; like a young Tory marrying into the Cecils or Cavendishes, though admittedly a junior branch. I think my father was well pleased, too, despite Mrs Webb's patronising attitude, the Webbs having so honoured a place among his idols.

Mr Dobbs just turned up for our wedding without being asked; looking, as always, very trim; everything about him neat and shipshape, brown shoes shining, grey moustache like a well trimmed hedge, smartly cut suit, jaunty hat. He was devoted to Kitty, and felt that, if she should change her mind at the last moment, or events took an unexpected turn, he ought to be there to look after her interests and arrange a getaway if required. When, in the course of the ceremony, the Registrar put the crucial question, he intervened sharply, telling her in a loud voice that there was still time for her to withdraw. She just took no notice, and our union was legally sealed. It made as little impression on me as the baptism and confirmation service to get into Selwyn College. Once the matter was finally settled, Mr Dobbs put a good face on it, and gave us all luncheon with a bottle of champagne. Then he and Elsie left for London, and Kitty and I returned to our two furnished rooms and began our life together.

Marriage (whether registered or not) begins, not with setting up house, counting wedding presents, blowing kisses, looking at wedding groups, but with two bodies confronting one another like two wrestlers. To clinch and struggle and contend with one another. Rolling about, now one on top, now another; grunting, coaxing, sweating, murmuring, yelling. So the world began, with vast turbulence in the genitalia of space. Each bodily union is a microcosm of the same process; a continuation of creation, a reaching after creativity through the fusion of two beings – the flesh first; then the soul, the totality, to make a third. This achieved, peace follows; the work done, we may sleep, letting an arm grow numb rather than wake a sleeping head cushioned there. So serenely asleep after the battle, and maybe already ovum and sperm seizing the interlude to enact their own drama; the expense of passion quickening in its peaceful aftermath. We exist to continue existence; unite to be united; love in order to go on loving.

Kitty and I, after all, were children of our time. How could we be otherwise? We looked to our bodies for gratification, which we felt they owed us, and that we now owed one another. 'To our bodies turn we then, that so Weak men on love revealed may look.' It was inevitable that this pursuit should become the prevailing preoccupation, the obsessive quest, of our restless and confused generation. Sex is the only mysticism offered by materialism, whose other toys – like motor-cars and aeroplanes and moving pictures and swimming-pools and flights to the moon – soon pall. Sex pure and undefiled; without the burden of procreation, or even, ultimately, of love or identity. Just sex; jointly attained, or solitary – derived from visions, drug-infused; from spectacles, on film or glossy paper. Up and down moving stairways, with, just out of reach, legs and busts and mouths and crotches; ascending to no heights, descending to no depths, only movement upwards and downwards, interminably, with the trivial images of desire for ever in view, and for ever inaccessible. As enlightened readers of D. H. Lawrence and Havelock Ellis, with even a peep at Kraft-Ebbing, we looked for rarer pleasures than these. Our moving stairway, as we hoped, climbed into a paradise where ecstasy was attainable through sensation pure and undefiled. The Blessed Orgasm itself leaned out from the gold bar of heaven; and, rubber-stoppered against any adverse consequence like birth, sealed and sterilised and secured for *coitus non interruptus* that is guaranteed *non fecundus*, we pursued happiness in true twentieth-century style.

Kitty's family seemed to be bristling with lords and, if not million-aires, people who on Croydon standards were decidedly affluent. Mrs Webb told me once with quiet satisfaction that none of her brothers-in-law (except Mr Dobbs) had less than £20,000 a year, which seemed a lot. I had never made the acquaintance of a lord before, and though at the Saturday evening gatherings of my father and his friends the mere notion of titles was a subject of loud derision, they still had a certain glamour in my eyes. I found myself going out of my way to bring references to Kitty's titled relatives into my conversation, but hoped to counteract any sycophantic undertones by making the references scorn-ful rather than respectful. In this connection, I used to enjoy repeating one of my father's favourite anecdotes about how he had been mys-teriously approached as to whether one of his directors would care to have a knighthood for £10,000 – a very substantial sum in those days. After agonised consideration by the director in question, the offer was turned down. My father never found out for certain who was behind it, but had reason to suppose that the then monarch, Edward VII, who was notoriously impecunious, may have been concerned in the transaction. After all, if politicians were to enrich themselves, as, for instance, Lloyd George did, by the sale of honours, why not the sovereign, who bestowed them? I found my father's account of this affair among his papers.

The Potter clan, to which Mrs Dobbs belonged, like other plutocratic families whose wealth derived from business, tended to drift Leftwards politically; towards Radicalism, Socialism and the Labour Party, picking up peerages and knighthoods on the way. Richard Potter, the founding father, was a timber merchant who provided army huts in the Crimean War to any government that would pay for them, thereby making a fortune which he later increased by audacious speculation. As a rich man with a difficult, if not demented, wife, and a large family of spirited daughters, he took his philosophical notions from Herbert Spencer and his moral ones from Carlyle, whom he held in the highest esteem. So much so that, according to Mrs Dobbs, when the ferocious old Sage of Chelsea went exercising along the Embankment, muttering and grimacing over his gnarled stick, her father and one or two other rich and distinguished citizens often followed at a respectful distance behind him. The scene, as she described it, took my fancy as an early example of what Tom Wolfe has so felicitously called Radical Chic, though, of course, they have subsequently found other gurus, including Stalin. As for Spencer, largely forgotten now, but famous in his day as the exponent of Creative Evolution – he was a frequent house guest. Mrs Dobbs remembered him as a little frightening in the way he playfully tumbled little girls when he took them for nature walks in the woods. According to a theory plausibly worked out by Kitty, he may well have been the original of the Mad Hatter in *Alice in Wonderland*.

The first of Kitty's titled relatives whose acquaintance I made was Lady Courtney, her Aunt Kate, who asked us to lunch in her house in Cheyne Walk. Her husband, Leonard Courtney, by this time dead, had been a Liberal stalwart, a Member of Parliament and Chairman of Committees, and a *Times* leader-writer who was raised to the Peerage after the Liberal victory of 1906. One of those men of whom everyone speaks well, and who surprise everyone by leaving rather more money when they die than might have been expected. He actively promoted a whole string of good causes – bimetallism, proportional representation, anti-imperialism, disarmament – with which I was to become all too familiar on the *Manchester Guardian*. He was fanatically devoted to the poems of Robert Browning, which he was fond of reciting to his nieces on Beachy Head, sometimes in a howling gale. Kitty recalls embroidering bedroom slippers for him as a child. I never saw him, nor even a picture of him, though there must have been many in the Cheyne Walk house, but I had a very clear impression of him as bearded, sedate, immensely solid and deliberate and full of rectitude. These great pillars of righteousness, from Wilberforce to Martin Luther King, have followed, as it were, like solemn funeral mutes the long obsequies of western civilisation; as they fell by the way, others coming forward to take their places. Now the time has nearly come for the coffin to be actually interred. Then at last their occupation will be gone for ever.

Lady Courtney herself, though by this time quite old, had the black and white colouring of the Potters, with a noticeable moustache on her upper lip, which, clearly untended, was silky rather than bristly in an embrace. There was said to be a gipsy strain in the family; plausible enough in Lady Courtney, and in Mrs Dobbs quite noticeable, particularly in her last years. She had a great fancy for picking over things, and gathering faggots, especially on a beach; as well as for cooking over an open fire. When only an electric radiator was available, she would turn it over on its side and brew weird concoctions on it. People quite often took her for an old gipsy woman, and offered her charity, which she invariably accepted. A kind gentleman on a bus, she told me once, had given her a shilling to pay her fare, and told her to keep the change. Did you? I asked. Of course, she answered primly. Though Lady Courtney herself looked and lived like an upper-class lady, even in her one sensed a vagrant strain just under the surface. In all the Potter households I visited, this was particularly noticeable in connection with meals, which, however lavish and elegantly served, were always somehow fragmentary and furtive, as though wrapped in a newspaper and hastily gobbled. One was aware of one's hostess's eye on one as one sliced into the butter or poured out the cream. Similarly with money; Mrs Dobbs's cheques looked old and stained, as though taken out of some secret hoard under the floorboards.

In her widowhood, Lady Courtney continued to support all her husband's causes, especially peace. She was closely associated with organisations like the Women's International League for Peace and Freedom. Indeed, there was a lady from this organisation – a Miss Sheepshank – present at our luncheon. Lady Courtney had, she told us, just finished embroidering their peace banner, a white dove on a green background. After lunch, she proudly and reverently showed it to us. It was, she said, to be hung in the Chelsea Town Hall. Where is it now? I wonder. Carried into battle by Women's Lib battalions, maybe; or in some celestial museum laid beside the Stalingrad Sword. Her house was packed tight with furniture, pictures, objets d'art, ornaments, knickknacks. Until I got used to them, upper-class houses always seemed to me like antique shops by comparison with the ones I knew. So chock-ablock with things; many of them so fragile that one scarcely dared to move or stretch for fear of breaking something enormously valuable. As it happened, I witnessed the dismantling of Lady's Courtney's establishment. When she died, we were notified by Mrs Webb that she had expressed in her will a wish that every descendant of Richard Potter (she had no children of her own) should choose some memento of her from her effects. On a fixed day and time, we were all to come to Cheyne Walk and make our choice. Kitty and I went along. It was a remarkable scene. Mrs Webb watched, hawk-eyed, over the proceedings. When we arrived, there were some hundred and fifty Richard Potter descendants roaming about the house like stampeding cattle. The niceties of polite behaviour were all laid aside; people picked up chairs and tables and brought out magnifying glasses to fix their period, carried objets d'art to the window to examine them more closely, eagerly turned over the pages of books in search of rarities. By the book-shelves I heard someone exclaim bitterly: 'They've taken away the Shelley and the Brontë first editions!' Any efforts to circumvent the conditions and make off with more than one memento were spotted by Mrs Webb, who resolutely took counter-action. By the time they had finished, the place looked like some of the interiors I remember in the 1939–45 war after a looting session. Confronted by this scene of confusion, Kitty contented herself with picking up a jewel – a little starfish, set, as we fondly hoped, in diamonds – as being easily removable and disposable. When, in subsequent hard times, we tried to flog it, it turned out to be only paste, and worth no more than ten-and-six.

In the matter of meeting Kitty's distinguished relatives, for me the big occasion, of course, was going to spend a week-end with the Webbs. I had heard them spoken of in tones of reverence by my father and his friends from my earliest years. So I approached the house they lived in at Passfield Corner with a decided feeling of awe, riding in an ancient hired car which had met us at Liphook Station. The Webbs never had a motor-car of their own. A Scottish maid – one of a pair who served Mrs Webb for many years – let us in. They were women of the utmost discretion who remained completely unaffected and uncontaminated by the procession of cranks, crackpots and egomaniacs who flowed through the house; in some mysterious way, they kept to the very end their Scottish self-containment and impregnable complacency. One of them asked Kitty, after we had returned from the USSR, whether the Five-Year Plan answered. It was a question which indicated, I thought, a very creditable scepticism in spite of the concerted insistence of their employers and most of their guests that the success of every Soviet venture must be assured.

Mrs Webb was waiting for us in the sitting-room, standing, as she so often did, with her back to the fire, and swaying slightly to and fro. So completely different from her sister Kate; frail and white, almost ghostly, by comparison with the other's solidity. She rushed at Kitty in a way the Potter women had, hurling herself upon her with a kind of avidity, as though to assure herself that Kitty was indeed there in her bodily presence. Jewish women, I have noticed, do likewise with children; kneading their cheeks, feeling their arms and legs, fingering their ears and hair. I also was asked to implant a kiss upon Mrs Webb's cheek; an experience comparable, I imagine, with kissing the big toe of a marble saint. The thing that struck me about her at once was her beauty, so reminiscent of Kitty's. A beauty of bone rather than of flesh. She was also, as I sensed, tragic; not in any trivial way of deprivation – like losing the lover she fancied (though that had happened, as I learnt afterwards, in the person, ridiculously enough, of Joseph Chamberlain; a preposterous engraving of a man, with wooden features and a monocle, who habitually wore an orchid in his button-hole; a Birmingham industrialist and Radical turned Imperialist). Hers was some deeper tragedy, with which I felt instinctively in sympathy. To do with her restless walks along the Embankment; with her prayers, offered in a silent cavernous Westminster Abbey, but alas wrongly addressed – dead letters that were never delivered; with sleepless nights, and the longing so often expressed in her journal for the long, definitive sleep of death.

Webb came toddling in. He really was a ridiculous looking man, with tiny legs and feet, a protruding stomach, and a large head. A sort of pedestrian Toulouse-Lautrec. It was as though Mrs Webb, not being able to have her monocled giant, chose this dwarf in pince-nez instead. Such temperaments as hers always try to ridicule their own passions by making a moral tale of them; planting gargoyles where the steeple should have climbed into the sky. Webb was her gargoyle; the *reductio ad absurdum* of love and lovers; a Blue Book Abelard, or computer Casanova: Sancho Panza to their friend Shaw's Don Quixote. Maybe, I sometimes used to reflect, Shaw would have provided a compromise mate for her; something between the monocle and the pince-nez. She told me once that, the first time they were alone together, Shaw 'simply threw himself upon me'. It was something, she went on, lest I should suppose this experience had any significance in her eyes, or, for that matter in his, that he did to every woman, and she had so sternly rebuffed him that nothing of the kind ever happened again. If the thought had crossed her mind that the tall, red-bearded, pale-faced jester would have been a more diverting companion than the partner she chose, and *Plays Pleasant and Unpleasant* a more diverting *oeuvre* than the forbidding tomes the Webb partnership produced, about which she always spoke disparagingly, she took a characteristic and terrible revenge by ensuring that Shaw was married, not to one of the luscious actresses like Ellen Terry, or ad-

vanced ladies like Annie Besant that he occasionally fancied, and she so
disliked (she made the word 'advanced' somehow more detestable by
accentuating the second syllable and shortening the 'a'), but to Charlotte
Payne-Townshend, an Irish lady of great plainness and considerable
wealth. He met her at the Webbs' house; it was Mrs Webb who made
the match, and resolutely cut off his retreat when he tried to make a
getaway.

Mrs Webb's household rose early; before breakfast one would see her,
if the weather was fine, roaming about the garden; not with the eye or
step of a gardener, more in the style of a tigress pacing up and down its
cage. If she caught sight of one looking out, she would pause and begin
a conversation, liable to be even less discreet then than at the indoors
sessions. I remember on one such occasion leaning out of the window to
hear from her the most scabrous particulars of eminent Fabian Society
and Labour Party figures like MacDonald and Bertrand Russell and
Wells, most of whom she intensely disliked or despised. 'Poor little
Wells,' she always called him. This side of her nature – curious, gossipy,
scandalous – which gives piquancy to her enormous Journal, brought
out all the true vivacity and charm, the audacity and insolence, in her, so
muffled in the partnership with her dreary little consort and their joint
enterprises, in which, in my opinion, she had little real interest, and
played little real part. Certainly, her own writing, in the Journal and in
her autobiographical works, is quite different in style and mood from
their joint efforts.

After lunch Mrs Webb rested, and Sidney was instructed to take a
walk along with any male visitors who happened to be present; ladies
were expected to follow Mrs Webb's example and lie down – which did
not please Kitty. Exercise was considered to be good for Sidney; though
his diet was strictly controlled by Mrs Webb, and certain things like
bacon and egg which he particularly appreciated denied him, he still
was a hearty eater, and liable to put on weight. Once out of sight of the
house, his zest for walking markedly diminished, and he usually looked
round for some convenient haystack where he could take a nap. If it was
hot and there were flies about, he would knot his handkerchief and wear
it on his head. It was on one such occasion that he complained to me
that there were no novels of business life which he had been able to
discover, and asked whether I knew of any. I mentioned *Dombey and Son*
and Upton Sinclair's *The Jungle*, but the suggestion was not acceptable.
After a discreet interval, he would shake himself awake, get up and
return to the house, quickening his step so as to arrive in a convincing

condition of breathlessness and lather. His physique facilitated this mild deception, since he easily perspired. Mrs Webb was in the habit of, as it were, issuing brief bulletins about his bodily propensities – as, 'Sidney sweats!' or, explaining the impossibility of their sharing a bedroom, 'Sidney snores!' – which he seemed to find totally inoffensive; even, perhaps, endearing.

The evening was given over to talk, and in Mrs Webb's case, to an occasional herbal cigarette; in his, a cigar. If there were several guests, Mrs Webb would arrange them hierarchically. Thus her nephew Stafford Cripps would take precedence over Kitty and me, but we would be more considered than some mousy little secretary or archivist allowed to join the company. An earl, actually Bertrand Russell's brother, who who had recently come into the Labour Movement, got better treatment than a don like Harold Laski who had been in it for years. Only in Simla in the days of the British Raj did I come across such careful *placement*. Sometimes her hierarchical arrangements were enforced at the risk of being thought rude; as in the case of the Dean of Canterbury, Dr Hewlett Johnson, who turned up after a telephone call inviting himself had given Mrs Webb the impression that it was the Archbishop who proposed a visit. The Dean was amiably but firmly put in his place. All opinions and anecdotes from our hosts were joint ones, delivered with the editorial or royal 'We'. For instance, describing a visit to Trotsky, when he was in exile on the Turkish Island of Prinkipo, Mrs Webb recalled how the sometime Soviet Commissar for War had remarked that even in England a bloody revolution would be required. 'We told him *No!*' she triumphantly concluded. While Mrs Webb regaled us with anecdotes, Sidney sat stroking his beard, with a look of sly contentment on his face; as though just being a party to such glories was enough for him. His little legs seldom reached the ground, and I wondered how it would have been possible for Mrs Webb's long, lithe body to curl up on so tiny a lap; as she claimed happened when they broke off their labours for a little – her term – 'spooning'. It seemed an impracticable proposition to me; like the angels dancing on a needle-point which so troubled medieval schoolmen.

By the time the ancient vehicle arrived on Monday morning for the return journey, the Webbs were already at work. I once, greatly daring, peeped in at them. He was seated at a desk; as it might have been, back at the Colonial Office, where, before his marriage, he worked as a civil servant. A gnome-like amanuensis, pen strokes steady, stance assured. She was prowling about the room as, earlier, she had about the garden.

There they were, planning our future, and along lines that actually came to pass in a matter of a very few years. A weird enough pair to be so engaged, to be sure; Beauty and the Beast, twentieth-century style, I thought. Or, better, following Blake, he the mole watching the roots, she the eagle, watching the fruits; he burrowing about underground, she soaring into some wild sky of her own imagining. A two-man demolition squad, enormously effective, as it turned out; operating in their snug Hampshire home, with the two Scottish maids keeping everything ship-shape, preparing the special scones and shortcake Mrs Webb found so palatable, and everlastingly asking themselves what, if anything, answered. What the mole got out of it all was obvious; when, as Lord Passfield, he found himself sitting in the Secretary of State's chair in the Colonial Office he felt so contented that, for once, his mind lapsed into total quiescence. It was, after all, the same chair that Joseph Chamberlain had once occupied; and the mere being in it sufficed.

But what of the eagle? What did she hope to get out of it? This was a more complicated question. I got the clue, I think, the very last time I saw her, not so very long before she died. We had been quarrelling, more or less publicly, about the Soviet régime, which she had come to adulate, and I to detest, thus reversing our positions when we first met. At the same time, she continued to fascinate me, for her beauty, and for that tragic quality in her which she retained to the end; both characteristics which intensified with age. She, likewise, for some reason, went on wanting to see Kitty and me. So we still visited Passfield occasionally. On this last visit, just as we were leaving, she said she had something to show me. It turned out to be a portrait of Lenin, presented to her by the Soviet Government; as stylised and cheap, artistically speaking, as any print of a Saint of the Church or Blessed Martyr offered for sale in Lourdes. She had set the picture up as though it were a Velazquez, with special lighting coming up from below, and a fine vista for looking at it. It was vivid in its way, showing the tiny eyes, the Mongolian features, the resolute chin and cruel mouth of its subject. For her, I realised, the place was a shrine; she looked positively exalted there – uplifted, worshipful, in an almost frightening way, like someone possessed. A frail, aged bourgeois lady, wearing, as she usually did, a grey silk dress and pretty lace cap on her head, prostrating herself, metaphorically speaking, before the founding father of the twentieth-century totalitarian state, the arch-terrorist of our time! It was extraordinary and rather horrifying. Afterwards, I reflected that the two scenes I had witnessed – the Webbs at work, and Mrs Webb at prayer before her

Lenin picture – embodied the whole spirit of the age, showing her to be a true priestess and prophetess; pursuing truth through facts and arriving at fantasy, seeking deliverance through power and arriving at servitude.

I went on with my supply-teaching in Birmingham, looking forward more than ever to 'Now the day is over' on Friday afternoon, and the two days of freedom in Kitty's company that followed. In our new intimacy together, as I got to know her better, I found her companionship ever more delightful. This has continued to be so throughout our forty-odd years together; despite rows, separations, jealousies, infidelities, all the usual wear and tear of a marital relationship. Troubles which, at the time, were very agonising, sometimes desperately so, now, looked back on, seem rather trivial by comparison with the love between us that has steadily grown, like a tree, in the soil of our discontent, striking ever deeper roots, reaching ever higher into the sky.

From Mr Dobbs's point of view, with his old-fashioned Anglo-Irish views as to what constituted success in a career or socially, a son-in-law who was an elementary school supply teacher was not to be brooked. It was he, therefore, who drew my attention to an advertisement for teachers at government schools in Egypt. The salary was appreciably more than I was getting in Birmingham, the conditions of employment seemed satisfactory; what, above all, recommended the job to me was that it involved making off. One more fix with the going-away drug! I applied, and was accepted. There was not much competition, anyway; employment with the Egyptian P.I. (Public Instruction) offered no prospects in the way of advancement or pensions, and most of the applicants were very young, and from what are now called Red Brick universities, or middle-aged to elderly, with indeterminate qualifications and an air of having failed or run into trouble somewhere along the line, characters for Evelyn Waugh. Kitty and I packed up our effects, such as they were, and set off cheerfully for Minia in Upper Egypt, via Paris, Genoa, Alexandria and Cairo.

Life in Minia was rather reminiscent of India, except that the erosion of British power had proceeded farther. As the Empire ran down, the former beneficiaries – the putative colonial governors, district administrators, collectors and all the other recipients of the vast and varied patronage it offered to the middle and upper classes in its heyday – displayed a remarkable flair for knowing when to leave the sinking ship. It seems to be almost their sole surviving talent. There was a British Consul in Minia who was also district manager for a large British cotton firm. He maintained a position of sorts, had the Royal Arms over his door and gave parties; there was even a club where local English gathered, along with Egyptians of standing like landowners and important civil servants. The local Greeks were mostly excluded as being outside the pale; we in the P.I. were accepted, but only just, our academic qualifications compensating for our lowly position as teachers under an Egyptian headmaster. Our school work was mostly no more than elementary language teaching; even then, I am doubtful if the boys learnt much from me. I stood in front of the class just as I had in Alwaye and in Birmingham, a blackboard behind me and faces before me, only vaguely aware of what I was supposed to be doing, and listening for a bell to ring, bringing my release. Kitty and I spent most of our time in one another's company; we went for walks by the Nile, and in the evenings I sat at my typewriter, expecting her to listen appreciatively to the results of my labours and bolster up my so easily sagging spirits, which she valiantly did. Occasionally, we strolled into the centre of the town where there was a rickety hotel and a Greek grocer with extraordinary protuberances on his head. The only dissipation offered was to sit at a café table and drink a cup of sweet Turkish coffee. From the window of our flat we looked across the Nile, with the desert always in view; the river running like a silver vein through strips of brilliant green vegetation, and, parallel with it, a road, a railway, and a canal. Whenever I see an Egyptian head or stone figure, I think of these parallel lines and the built-in symmetry of so narrow a land. After two terms in Minia, I was summoned to Cairo to join the staff of the university there.

In Cairo we lived in a little house on the edge of the desert in Helmia Zeytoun. For my walks I strode over the desert, where the sand was hard; sometimes in the scorching sun, sometimes, when the *hamzin* wind was blowing, breathing in dust which gritted one's nose and throat; best of all, in the evening when the sun went down, leaving the empty sky bloodshot, and dripping lurid colours on to the yellow sand. Wherever I have been – in town or country, desert or jungle, in rain or snow or ice or tropical heat, up mountains or by the sea-shore or along urban streets – I have always walked; not caring particularly about the surroundings or the conditions, often scarcely noticing them, so that for all I knew I might be in Thornton Heath or the Himalayas or Park Avenue or the Alpes Maritimes. Just pounding along, from nowhere to nowhere; sometimes with thoughts likewise pounding through my mind, sometimes not. Sometimes just vacant; unthinking, unseeing, unfeeling. In motion merely.

The university at this time was in the Zaffaran Palace; a building formerly used by the Khedive for the accommodation of his harem. In the classrooms and along the corridors there were still odd traces of the previous usage. Little frivolous twists and turns in the masonry and woodwork, fragments of marble frescoes; up in the ceilings, coloured designs and figures, now faded, and in the neglected garden a rusty disused fountain in the middle of what had once been obviously an ornamental pool. It added an extra dimension of fantasy to our disquisitions on *Antony and Cleopatra*, chosen for its topicality. Later, the university moved to new premises in Giza. The students all wore tarbooshes and suits with narrow trousers bunched up round shoes with narrow pointed toes. They seemed to be faraway, lost in some distant dream of erotic bliss; a consequence, no doubt, in the case of many of them of their addiction to hashish, widespread among the *effendi* class, and prevalent among the *fellahin*, especially the ones who had moved into the towns. The deleterious effects of this addiction were, in those days, universally taken for granted; and the Egyptian authorities, following a plan of modernisation and national revival on the general lines of Kemal Ataturk's in Turkey, spent a lot of money and effort in an attempt to stamp it out. Russell Pasha, the head policeman and the last Englishman to hold the post, was particularly active in trying to prevent hashish getting into the country, and in reducing indulgence in it. At the League of Nations, too, the suppression of the traffic in hashish was one of the few things the member states unanimously agreed about. If anyone then had suggested that all this endeavour was misplaced because hashish did little harm, and was anyway non-addictive, the suggestion would have been received with incredulity and derision. To the best of my knowledge no one at all reputable, or for that matter disreputable, ever did make such a suggestion. I had to wait forty years to hear it made, and then not just by crackpots and wild libertarians; but by respected citizens, clergymen, purported scientific investigators, and other ostensibly informed and enlightened persons. When I hear or read their apologies for hashish, I recall the Zaffaran Palace and the stupefied faces and inert minds of so many of the students there; the dreadful instances of the destructive effects of this drug on bodies and minds which any resident in the Middle East was bound to encounter. I know of no better exemplification of the death wish at the heart of our way of life than this determination to bring about the legalisation of hashish so that it may ravage the West as it has the Middle and Far East.

As at Alwaye, my duties were not arduous; the students anyway were frequently on strike, and did not even, like the Indian students, take their examinations seriously, let alone their studies. They were expected to be able to follow lectures in French as well as English, and, of course, in Arabic. My impression is that, hashish apart, only very few of them had the faintest notion of what we lecturers were talking about. The head of our department, successor to Robert Graves, was Bonamy Dobrée, a fidgety, eager man with a beard (not then as popular as now among literati) who had been a regular army officer before he became an academic. Major professor or professor major. We became and remained friends, though there has always been a certain basic dissidence between us, due partly at any rate to his attitude to literature – Bloomsburyite, topped up with D. H. Lawrence, with just a dash of Marx and a good slice of Pound and Social Credit. He spoke always of T. S. Eliot as Tom, and E. M. Forster as Morgan, and on his passport described himself as 'man of letters'. He is another figure I have found myself unkindly introducing in fictional guise; in Dobrée's case, a high-pitched voice echoing along an empty street declaiming some lines from 'Lycidas', and then breaking off to proclaim his belief in life and in living.

It was from Dobrée that I first heard of 'The Waste Land', of which we were all going to hear and say a great deal more before we were finished. This was at a public lecture he gave; one of those occasions at which a few people manage to seem a lot, like a levee or reception on a small repertory stage or in a television play. Some elegant females, expensively dressed, of indeterminate age and race, called Levantine in those days; an Egyptian or two who had been to Oxford and looked it, wearing club ties, tarboosh-less; some indeterminate clergy, an Archdeacon of Port Said, a Canon of Wadi-Halfa; a bank manager, an officer from the garrison who read the *New Statesman*, an American missionary in alpaca, and a sulky-looking third secretary from the British High Commission, present under compulsion; a sprinkling of elderly, wispy ladies who might once have been governesses, or companions, liable to emerge mysteriously in Cairo, as in other out-of-the-way places, for anything free and respectable and English like a lecture.

Dobrée was introduced by a French colleague, head of the Arts Faculty, also bearded, though with a thick, black tangle contrasting with Dobrée's tapering ginger, which he undoubtedly considered to be Elizabethan in the style of Sir Philip Sidney or even Drake. The French, in making cultural propaganda, always take the ball into the other court, going on about *votre paysage ravissant, vos mosques si mémorables, vos contributions importantes aux lettres contemporaines. . .* We play it straight; in this case, a discourse on the Metaphysical Poets. It was in the course of delivering this discourse that Dobrée looked up, paused, and then said with great deliberation, if not defiance, that he would stake his literary reputation that the publication of Eliot's 'The Waste Land' would be considered as being on a par with that of the *Lyrical Ballads*. We, the audience, felt that some response was due, but we scarcely knew what. Should there be cheers and some cries of dissent? Should someone get up and stump out in disgust? Someone else, stand up on his chair and applaud? It seemed unkind, even philistine, to let so dramatic a challenge pass seemingly unnoticed. We shifted in our places; one or two of us half smiled, others vaguely frowned or shook their heads. Certainly Dobrée was in on a good investment, if only a short-term one. On a longer term, who can tell? In the thirties and the war years, I occasionally ran into Eliot at the Garrick Club; he was extremely amiable and polite, but, as it seemed to me, a man who was somehow blighted, dead, extinct. I wrote of him once that he was a death-rattle in the throat of a dying civilisation, for which a contributor to *The Times Literary Supplement* took me severely to task. Yet that was how I saw him – actually, several cadavers fitting into one another, like Russian dolls. A New England one, an Old England one, a Western Values one. And so on.

We often used to go swaying and clanking into Cairo from Heliopolis on the Belgian-constructed tramway which vaguely recalled Knocke, Heyst and Blankenburg. On days when riots threatened, there would be more hats than tarbooshes. Foreigners were known as *howagas*, or hat-wearers; and as they still had their own Mixed Courts, and were not subject to the Egyptian courts, it was dangerous to involve them in public disorder. Thus, a hat provided a certain immunity. Cairo gave an impression of being inflammatory. In the dry burning heat, after weeks and weeks without rain, one expected the place to catch fire; as, indeed, it did some years after I left, with most of the places I knew, like Shepheard's Hotel, burnt to the ground, though, alas, 'The Awakening of Egypt', a massive monument standing outside the railway station, remained intact. I expect it is indestructible. For the time being, however, British troops were still stationed in Cairo and Alexandria; King Fuad was on the throne, and Lord Lloyd, the High Commissioner, was the effective boss, and behaved as such. I saw him once or twice driving about in a large car flying a large Union Jack, with motor-cycle outriders; a short, pale, nervously energetic man whom I afterwards got to know, when he was head of the newly constituted British Council. He told me that in his High Commissioner days King Fuad used quite often, literally, to weep on his shoulder. It conjured up a remarkable scene; that great swollen royal visage, with its thick, upturned moustache drawn to a point like the Kaiser's, tearful, and drooping on to Lloyd's little imperial shoulder; great sobs breaking from him, as well as a curious barking noise due to a hole in his gullet resulting from a shot fired at him by a jealous uncle. I was familiar with this barking noise, having heard it at a reception at the Royal Palace to which all professors and lecturers at the university were invited. It was so weird that a court chamberlain warned us in advance not to be surprised or disturbed if the King seemed suddenly to start barking. Even so, it came as a shock. At such receptions the regulation attire was a frock coat and tarboosh; most of us had to be content with just the tarboosh, but Dobrée, characteristically, had provided himself with an authentic frock coat with silk facings, and, with his tarboosh rakishly a little awry, looked every inch a Bey, if not a Pasha.

A favourite haunt was Old Groppi, a garden café in a courtyard with trees growing in it, and tables set under their shade or under coloured umbrellas. There, all day long sat the Pashas and Beys and Effendis consuming their tiny cups of sweet Turkish coffee, and keeping the flies at bay with their whisks; occasionally rising to greet one another with many courteous bows and gestures, but mostly, like my students, seemingly sunk in a long brooding reverie. Such a variety of faces, from dark Nubian to pale Greek, with many curious blends; as, ginger hair crowning a Bedouin head, or Negroid features contained in a pink skin. One or two, in majestic immobility, sucking at a hubble-bubble pipe; others scanning newspapers – the *Bourse Egyptienne*, *Al Ahram*, the *Egyptian Gazette*; none, as far as could be seen, engaged in any business or occupation, with appointments to keep or duties requiring their attention. Their inertia gradually became infectious, and one would likewise sit on and on, as the sun moved across the courtyard, with only the snores of a sleeping Pasha, the rhythmic gurgle of a hubble-bubble, the incursion of a newsboy, to disturb the scene's somnolence.

Once or twice a week I visited the residence of a rich Egyptian to give him lessons in English. It was well paid work, bequeathed to me by a colleague when he left Cairo. My pupil was, I should say, in his forties; rather darker than average in complexion, and usually, when I arrived in the mid-afternoon, and he opened the door to me, unshaved and in his pyjamas, though nonetheless, wearing a tarboosh, which gave an extra touch of grotesqueness to his appearance. The house, a detached villa in its own grounds, had all its curtains drawn. Within, it was dark and rather stale smelling. There were no signs that I could discern of any other occupant, though occasionally I thought I heard footsteps, and when tea was served some hand must have prepared it and set it out on a tray, ready to be brought in. My pupil would lead me into the large sitting-room whose furniture, except for a sofa and two arm-chairs on which we sat, was permanently covered with dust-sheets. A large glass chandelier hung over us, and on the walls facing us were some hunting prints bought, I was proudly informed, at Sotheby's. I addressed my pupil in English, speaking very slowly and clearly – 'It is a warm day, but here in your house I feel delightfully cool' – but it was obvious that the poor fellow had been unable to follow. His dark liquid eyes were full of sorrow, his unshaved chin moved convulsively. Perhaps, I managed to get across to him, it might be better if we read together. He agreed, and went to fetch a book. I was full of curiosity about what it would prove to be; maybe the *Kama Sutra*, or *The Arabian Nights*. He came back with Lord Beaverbrook's *Success* in his hand, in one of those cheap editions newspapers used to give away to boost circulation. It was, I understood, a book he particularly appreciated and admired; he passed it to me reverently, as he might a rare masterpiece. So for the rest of my afternoon sessions we worked through this turgid volume, with which I became abysmally familiar. He paid me the fee for each lesson as I left, in cash, which I thankfully pocketed. Of all the numerous and varied ways I have earned money in the course of my life, this seems to me to have been about the most bizarre.

It was at this time that Kitty first became pregnant. I found the whole process utterly wonderful; her stomach gradually swelling up, and the thought that out of our fleshly gyrations, beautiful and hilarious and grotesque all in one, should come this ripening fruit, this new life partaking of us both, and breaking out of its cocoon – her womb – to exist separately in the world. I had seen death, now I was to see birth. A white stomach rounding out, and inside it something growing, moving, living. It gave a point to every touch and caress and heave and groan; like print in a foreign language, laboriously spelt over, until suddenly it says something, and one understands. How beautiful are the Magnificats, the songs of birth! How desolate and ultimately disastrous and destructive is the pursuit of Eros for its own sake! The sterile orgasm; the bow passed across the strings and no music coming, the paddle dipped in the water and no movement following.

We spent our summer holiday in Austria by the Danube, at a place called Melk. Kitty's pregnancy progressed, and I wrote a play, *Three Flats*. A lot of our time was passed in the grounds of a monastery where there were portraits of all the Austrian Emperors up to Franz Josef, whose divided beard was as familiar to me as the German Kaiser's upturned moustache. The river was full of bronzed Germans who went gliding by in their canoes, noisily singing, and somehow, despite their seeming joviality, menacing. Too well fed, too hale and hearty, too boisterous for comfort. Back in Cairo we waited for the birth, which at last showed signs of beginning. I took Kitty into a German Deaconess's Hospital, and left her there; more aware of her presence when I had left her than when we were still together. Seeing her face on the pillow; as it were, saying it over, as I might some lines of verse committed to memory. The next morning I went back to the hospital, driving myself there in an ancient Chevrolet we had acquired; seated high up, and looking out, terrified, at the swirling traffic. At the hospital, the matron told me in her broken English, grinning, almost leering, that the labour had begun. So I waited, counting the passing minutes, until a nurse came to take me to Kitty and my son, already, as I thought, wearing the expression of cool, ironic detachment combined with infinite sweetness, which characterises him to this day.

Shortly afterwards Mrs Dobbs arrived to visit us. I met her at Cairo station. The arrival of the boat train from Alexandria in those days was quite an event; uniformed men with the names of hotels on their hats – Shepheard's, Mena House, Semiramis – stood at the barrier to coax any clients they could into their buses. When Mrs Dobbs, dressed, as ever, in collar and tie, hat perched well forward on her head, long billowing skirt and boots, appeared at the barrier, not one of them made any move to procure her custom. Only an Egyptian in a dirty galabieh whispered in her ear: 'YWCA! YWCA!' She, in any case, was too earnestly in conversation with two other Egyptians she had got to know in her third-class carriage to pay any attention. 'Ah!' she said when she saw me, 'here I am!' and proceeded to introduce me to her two friends, to whom, I gathered, throughout the journey from Alexandria she had been giving particulars of her sisters Beatrice Webb and Lady Courtney. I took her bag – she never used a porter if it could possibly be avoided – and we climbed into the Chevrolet. Seated side by side on our two high perches, and picking our way through the tumultuous traffic, she at once plunged into a conversation about the pyramids, and whether it was possible, as her psychic sister Teresa (Stafford Cripps's mother) had believed, that they contained information about the Lost Tribes of Israel. It was with reluctance that, when she saw Kitty and our son (whom we called Leonard after Kitty's brother), she switched from this subject on to more immediate personal matters.

During the days she was with us, she went off each morning with her sketching things into the desert, and sketched away through the heat of the day, returning only after sunset. She took provisions, and the inevitable Thermos with her; occasionally, she told us, one or other of the Egyptians who gathered round to watch her would make an offer for the sketch she was working on – forty or fifty piasters, which she of course accepted. Once, when she was alone, some hooligans forced her to give them the two pounds she had in her purse. About this she complained to the police, making it clear, however, that though she was prepared to try to identify the youths in question, she would only do so if she were given an undertaking that as long as they returned her two pounds they would not be punished. A parade of local bad characters was in due course arranged, which I attended with her; as they filed past, she would murmur from time to time as one of the more villainous faces came into view: 'I think it's him, but I'm not going to say so.' The result was indecisive. When the time came for her to depart for Upper Egypt, I took her to the station, where she was seized with a sudden panic as to whether she had her purse, which she kept in a body-belt round her waist. Checking involved largely undressing, which created some interest among passers-by. All was fortunately well, and she calmed down. As her train steamed out, I waved good-bye, with a sense of great relief, and also with a pang of regret. One always so wanted her to go, and then, when she had actually gone, missed that vivid crazy presence, that corncraking voice, those random, inconsequential, maddening remarks of hers.

The men in suits and tarbooshes, the Pashas and Beys and Effendis, whether somnolent in the cafés or garrulous along the streets, fly-whisks in hand, swallowing their interminable tiny cups of coffee, having their shoes shined, or their hair cut, being shaved or manicured, consuming enormous meals which left their breath onion-laden; then, replete, sucking sugar-cane, sometimes, as I have seen them, after a feast swarming into a nearby field, like stampeding cattle, grabbing canes, and there and then sucking at them – these constituted the new effective ruling class, able to bring the fellahin into the polling-booths to vote for this or that Pasha on behalf of the Wafd, the organ of Egyptian nationalism as the Congress had been of Indian nationalism. My Alwaye sermon needed to be brushed up again; here was another people rightly struggling to be free; more work for a Byron, a Garibaldi of our time. Never in human history, it is safe to assert, have there been so many actual and potential liberators as in the last half century, and so little liberation; so many and so loud shouts for freedom, and so much enslavement.

I became absorbed in the Egyptian political scene. It would have been far more advantageous to study Arabic, or ancient monuments like the Ibn Tulun Mosque with which Cairo abounded, or the splendid Tutankamen remains in the Cairo Museum. Alas, I did none of this, but spent my time arguing about the Wafd and its then leader, Nahas Pasha, a curious, distracted, almost Ramsay MacDonald-like figure; successor to Zaglul, considered to be the founder of modern Egyptian nationalism. My indoctrination at the Saturday evening gatherings in South Croydon came into its own; I found I had a lamentable facility for translating a particular political situation into a morality play or western, with an appropriate dénouement in which the Good Guy – in the particular case in question, Nahas – triumphs, and the Bad Guy – obviously, Lord Lloyd and his Egyptian toadies, the lesser Pashas and Beys – is cast into outer darkness; with King Fuad as the saloon-keeper, who is not actually in the camp of the Bad Guy, but needs watching. Once this technique is mastered – and God knows, it's easy enough – it is possible to be a successful and instant commentator in any medium, written, spoken, visual, on any situation in any part of the world. The style – studiously reasonable, and working up to occasional outbursts of idealistic fervour and satirical spleen – comes almost of itself. Thus: 'A certain amount of street turbulence, in any case greatly exaggerated in some of the reports, should not blind us to the vitality and vision of Egyptian nationalism, or induce us to think yet again in terms of conqueror and conquered, with the inevitable consequence of struggling on for a few more years towards predictable disaster. The awakening of formerly subject peoples like the Egyptians is an essential fact of the twentieth century. . .' One could easily have produced a prototype for this kind of composition, leaving blank spaces for the name of the country, capital city and local personalities, useable at any time anywhere.

I sent off an offering in such a vein to the *Manchester Guardian*. It flew into the window of the Cross Street office like a homing pigeon, and duly appeared in the paper; attributed to 'A correspondent in Cairo', the lowliest of all appellations. I got a letter from the editor, which greatly delighted and excited me, asking for more material along the same lines.

This I gladly provided, and had the additional satisfaction of seeing myself quoted in the Cairo press. Then, to complete my happiness, I received an intimation that Arthur Ransome was coming to Cairo as *The Guardian*'s special correspondent, and would be coming to see me.

Ransome, when he turned up, proved to be an amiable and attractive man, with a luxuriant blond soup-strainer moustache, a rubicund complexion, a large mouth from which more often than not a pipe protruded, and a hearty disposition. He was carelessly dressed in unseasonable tweeds, and wore a large, loosely tied coloured tie of the kind favoured in those days by middle-brow aesthetes of the C. E. Montague-J. C. Squire variety. As I came to realise subsequently, he was in a sense the epitome of all *Manchester Guardian* writers; amateurish, literary, opinionated, conceited, eccentric; immediately recognisable in any gathering of journalists, however large, by virtue of a certain self-righteousness of expression and bearing; the firm mouth and chin saying that news is sacred, the bright left eye, that comment is free. His great glamour in my eyes was that he had witnessed the Russian Revolution, and known and talked with Lenin, Trotsky, and the other leaders in the flesh. It all made him, to me, more remarkable than if he had actually been present at the Crucifixion, or accompanied Moses when he received the Ten Commandments carved on stone at God's hands. When he told me that he had actually played chess with Lenin, who proved to be rather a poor player, and with Litvinov, a much better one, I inwardly genuflected. I questioned Ransome eagerly and endlessly about his time in Russia. He went there originally to collect fairy stories; and, as I had occasion to reflect later, in addition to the traditional ones, managed to collect some of quite outstanding impact about the Revolution itself, though, ironically enough, these, like John Reed's in *Ten Days that Shook the World*, were put on the Kremlin Index in due course because they failed to make adequate mention of Stalin.

With such enthralling conversational material available, it was a wrench to switch to the matter at issue – the Pashas and their prospects. Truth to tell, neither Ransome nor I took them too seriously; with all our progressive pretensions, we had a somewhat lordly attitude to Egyptian politics and politicians, dwelling rather on their comic opera aspects. There would always, we felt, be a Pasha to form yet another government. Ransome described to me his encounters with them at the Mahomet Ali Club, where they foregathered in the evening, as well as conversations he had with Egyptian and British officials. As he talked, I could see the script being shaped for yet another version of the great morality play, in which virtue would once more be vindicated in the overthrow of Imperialism; heroes and villains given their parts and speaking their lines. The obtuseness of British official attitudes, the brutality of British troops in action; the reasonableness of Egyptian demands, and the advantage the extremists would derive from a stubborn refusal to meet them – it all fitted into place like a Willow Pattern. The Master Myth of our time.

My aptitude in this field was so marked that Ransome recommended me to the *Guardian* as a promising recruit, and in due course I received a letter from E. T. Scott suggesting that I might like to join the editorial staff for a probationary period of three months. I believe I have never received a letter which gave me so much delight; waving it triumphantly in the air, I rushed to tell Kitty, and then to the post office to telegraph my acceptance of the offer. Whatever feelings I may have had subsequently about the high proportion of my time and energy given to journalism, I cannot claim that harsh necessity drove me into the trade. No one could have embarked upon it more hopefully or thankfully or joyously. Though, or perhaps because, I had never so much as seen a copy of *The Guardian*, I was confidently of the opinion that it was the most enlightened, disinterested and progressive newspaper in the world. To be offered a chance to join its staff and write in its columns, seemed to me the most marvellous thing that could possibly have happened.

I owed this great opportunity to Ransome, and was duly grateful. He, as it turned out, went on only one more journalistic assignment – to China. Then he retired to a house in the Lake District with his agreeable Russian wife, Jenia, said to have at one time been on Trotsky's staff. Kitty and I visited them there several times. We watched him make flies for his line, with his great solemn face bending earnestly over the coloured threads as he selected them and fastened them together; then, in his boat on Windermere, dropping the hook, dancing the fly, still with the same solemnity, and hushed silence – the beautiful solemnity of a child, though one with a large soup-strainer moustache sprouting out of a rubicund face. It was at this time that he wrote the first of his very successful children's books, *Swallows and Amazons*; a myth sans Commissars and sans Pashas; purer, sweeter, than the ones from Our Special Correspondent. Ransome never seemed to care much for children, which may well be a necessary qualification for writing successfully about and for them. Most adults like children because they are different from them; a child-like adult like Ransome dislikes them and is bored by them, precisely because he *is* like them. For that very reason, he can understand their games and attitudes as an adult cannot, and so his writings interest them. A. A. Milne, not at all a child-like man, was just the opposite; he really liked children (as Lewis Carroll did), and so wrote about them as it were from without, as an adult. The result was that his *Winnie the Pooh* books enchanted adults, as realising their picture of children, but rarely pleased children themselves, though sometimes they pretended otherwise to ingratiate themselves with adults. I had a curious encounter with Milne soon after I became editor of *Punch*. The poor fellow was in a nursing home in Tunbridge Wells, recovering from the after-effects of a cerebral haemorrhage, and understandably in a far from amiable state of mind; especially as he had hated *Punch* for many years. My visit was rather like Sir Hugh Greene going to see Lord Reith. Or John F. Kennedy dropping in on Harry S. Truman. Christopher Robin seemed very far away.

Kitty and our son went ahead, and I followed as soon as the term was over. It was the greatest possible relief to get away from Egypt. The place, to me, had an arid feel about it; I never put out any roots there, as I had in India, or made any close friends there, or had any sense of its past – of the great civilisations which had flourished in the Valley of the Nile. It was all just an excavation site as far as I was concerned; sand and shouts, and buildings that looked like one of those international exhibitions set up quickly to seem impressive for a little while, but soon growing shabby and derelict. Yellow sandstone turrets and domes and minarets standing amidst wide expanses of yellow sand. As for the so-called cosmopolitan society to which we always referred when we said how interesting living in Cairo or Alexandria was – I had never found them particularly alluring. The rich Syrians and Greeks and hybrid French who kissed hands and rolled their Rs as though they had never been off the Champs Elysées; the expatriate English public school homosexuals, aspiring T. E. Lawrences, burnous-wearing, with dusky Arab servants – Said, Hassan – who, bringing in the drinks or serving a meal, had a sly air of intimacy, even a touch of hauteur and insolence about them. Then the anglicised locals, the Maxes and Camilles and Georges, who had their suits made in Savile Row, and bought their cigarette cases and lighters at Aspreys; whose tarbooshes sat on their heads like red rimless bowlers, and whose slang came out of early Wodehouse; whose nearly Parisian ladies in nearly Parisian gowns, olive-skinned exotic beauties, had been reared on convent culture, and given a final polish in finishing schools in Gstaad or by the Lake of Lucerne, before being posted to Cairo, Beirut and Alexandria.

The only occasion that, for me, extricates itself from the general forgetfulness was giving a lecture on Swift in Alexandria, at Victoria College, alma mater of, among others, Rudolph Hess, and spending the evening afterwards with Kavafy, a local Greek poet about whom I had read in E. M. Forster's *Pharos and Pharillon*. He was a curious little grey fragile man, who, besides being a poet, worked in an orange exporting business; a passionate lover of the English language, which he spoke fluently, having learnt it almost entirely from reading works like Milton's *Areopagitica*, Johnson's *Rasselas* and Macaulay's Essays. The result was indescribably funny and touching; such splendidly rounded phrases and sonorous words coming from so seemingly alien and frail a figure, applied indiscriminately to any subject, weighty or frivolous, which might arise.

Revisiting Cairo from time to time in the years that followed, the process of decay was evident enough. The exotic beauties had all disappeared into the pages of Lawrence Durrell's novels; Max and Camille and Georges into the seamier haunts of Paris or London or Rome, whither their fat King Farouk, in due course, likewise decamped. Even 'The Awakening of Egypt' seemed sooty and slumbering; I had to hunt for Old Groppi, and when I found it wished I hadn't, so shabby and woebegone had it become, with the few ex-Pashas and Beys still seated there beneath the trees, shadows of their former selves, too listless even to whisk away the flies or eye over the *Bourse Egyptienne*. New Groppi, or Groppi Rotunda, in Soleiman Pasha, turned into a cafeteria, and even Lappas Frères, our majestic grocery, through whose spicy twilight one could see looming up every sort of rare delicacy, as well as local cheeses and fruits and yoghurt at their pristine best – even Lappas had grown seedy and shabby and stale. Was it like this, I wondered, in Hippo in St Augustine's time, when Rome was sacked, and the tide of civilisation which had washed through all the then known world, receded, leaving stagnation and decay behind?

I took a deck passage from Alexandria to Venice on an Italian boat, munching my own provisions, washed down with chianti, and sleeping by night where I sat by day, my little luggage beside me, the bright stars above me, and the moonlight streaming down, suffusing the sea and the ship; as it seemed, the whole universe made luminous. We sailed up to the Grand Canal and into the heart of Venice at dawn. I can remember now my exhilaration at the beauty of it; the delicacy of the Campanile in that glowing rose-grey first light, and all the hopes I had. Though far more alluring than Venice, in my thoughts, was Manchester, city of print rather than of churches, where all my future hopes were focused.

I arrived in Manchester on a Monday morning in August, 1932, and registered at the old Queen's Hotel, subsequently demolished. My instructions were to report to the *Guardian* office in Cross Street in the afternoon, so I spent the intervening time wandering about the streets of Manchester, several times passing the *Guardian* office, and staring in at a photograph in the window of the Lord Mayor of Manchester and the Lady Mayoress in their chains of office at some function or other. Also at one of some bathers on an Australian beach, the bill for the day being – all too characteristically, as I was to learn – SURF BATHING IN AUSTRALIA. The slight tang of smoke in the air was something that would always recall for me this first arrival – apart from my glamorised childhood visit to our Sheffield relatives – in the industrial North. Having read about the severe economic depression which had hit, particularly, Lancashire, I somehow expected to see queues and pinched faces and a general air of desperation. Actually, the city, matching my mood, seemed bustling and cheerful. Public reports are always misleading, and have been made more so by the camera's increasing part in them. Anyone who has had occasion, as I have, to participate in preparing compilation films about this period will know that the scanty available footage has to be arranged or doctored to produce the requisite effect. This will be easier for later periods; quasi-documentaries like *Cathy Come Home* realise the myth in terms of actuality, in the same way that, for instance, the assault on the Winter Palace in Petrograd, as presented in Eisenstein's film, has now been firmly incorporated in the documentation of the Revolution. When all the recording, compiling and documenting has been completed, it will be for ever impossible to know what happened about anyone or anything; history, in dramatising its records, abolishes itself.

Punctually at three o'clock, I presented myself at the *Guardian*'s Cross Street office, but was told that this was for receiving advertisements, not for journalists. It was, indeed, more suggestive of a travel-agency than a newspaper. The journalistic staff used a sort of stage-door at the side, much dingier than the other. Upstairs, on the editorial floor to which I was directed, things seemed pretty quiet. I was shown into the library and told to wait there. It was a long twilit room with solid-looking tomes lining the walls – mostly, as I observed, volumes of Hansard – and a bust of C. P. Scott by Epstein standing on the table.

Below me, I could feel, like a heart-beat, the steady throb of the presses turning out that day's *Manchester Evening News*; in the yard at the back of the building I had noticed the pony traps all waiting, tensed up, ready to rush away with the edition when it was ready. At once, I began to catch the fever of journalism, which even now I have not quite succeeded in shaking off; the working up each single day to a moment of climax, the frenzied effort to finish a story, sometimes actually running with copy to the stone and just getting it in; then relaxing; for good or ill, nothing more to be done about that particular edition. I suppose everyone recognises when he first finds his way to his own particular milieu or scene. The jockey-to-be first sniffing acrid stable air, his legs almost bending outwards as he sniffs; the priest-to-be catching a whiff of incense, the flash of a vestment, the throaty intonation of an exhortation or prayer – Dearly beloved brethren, I pray and beseech you . . . the palms of his hands drawing together of themselves, his eyes uplifting; the young wanton-to-be giving a lift to her gym-frock, a touch of accentuation to her budding breasts which she instinctively recognises as the tools of her trade. So, I recognised at once my native habitat in *The Guardian* office; in the tang of printer's ink, the yeasty aroma of newsprint; curious, aged figures carrying copy, or battered trays with dregs of strong tea and the debris of chops or fried fish; the clatter of teleprinters and typewriters, and the odd zones of silence somehow existing amidst the noise, like cloisters in a railway station. Paper everywhere, underfoot, clutched, pored over, discarded, even in the lavatories, agency copy available, brooded upon before using – from Georgia news of a man of a hundred and forty who remembered Napoleon; from Montreal, of a woman who had given birth to quintuplets; from Chicago, of an explosion which had flooded the neighbouring streets with illicit liquor. Pulp to pulp – this was my line.

Minutes dragged by slowly in the library. I fastened my gaze on Epstein's Scott, noting how the bronze head seemed to be about to jump off its pedestal at me. At last I was summoned by one of the aged messengers to the presence of Ted Scott, the E.T. who had written to me, and C.P.'s son; by this time nominally his father's successor as editor. He turned out to be a man in his forties with a large noble head, a grey complexion, soft dark eyes and a smile of great sweetness; the whole impression somehow vaguely sorrowful. I liked him at once. He was sitting in a small office, like an anteroom, and after we had chatted together for a while he asked me what subjects I was interested in.

Without thinking I said India, Egypt, the Labour Party – by this time my father was MP for Romford – and education. Then he got up to take me into the adjoining office where his father, the famous C. P. Scott, was sitting at his desk staring fixedly in front of him; his eyes bright blue, his flesh rosy, his beard white and truculent; a high-minded Sir John Falstaff, looking, as the old and famous often do, a little mad.

The memory of him sitting there, as I had first seen him, vividly recurred to me when in 1950 I spent some hours at Chartwell with Churchill; by this time well into his dotage, though with another government still to form. I happened to be briefly in the chair at the *Daily Telegraph*, then serialising his War Memoirs, and it was in connection with some dispute arising over his excessive proof corrections that he had required my presence. His physical condition was vastly inferior to Scott's; flabby and puffy, and, in some indefinable way, vaguely obscene. Like an inebriated old sea lion, barking and thrashing about in shallow water. He was wearing his famous siren suit, with a zip-fastener up the front; various of his collaborators were there, familiarly sycophantic, as is the way with such people, especially the service ones. At four o'clock, in lieu of tea, a tray of highballs was brought in, and as others followed my senses began to swim. I cannot recall that the subject of the proof corrections was ever broached, except perhaps very casually. At one point Churchill took me out into the garden and showed me his goldfish and water works, and some not very distinguished paintings connected with Marlborough, that his nephew John Churchill had done on the walls of a little pavilion. Inside the house, he drew my attention to a handbill offering a reward for his capture in the Boer War. All, as I realised, a standard routine and patter; a conducted tour often provided to all sorts and conditions of visitors – for instance, Molotov, who must surely have been taken over the course, and whose wooden attention I could easily imagine.

Seated again, I raised the question of Yalta; the only incident in the late war about which I had any particular curiosity or concern. It produced a great splutter of talk about how, if he were to say what he knew, it would 'bring the United States Government down'; at that time, President Truman's second administration. I particularly remember the phrase about bringing the United States Government down because of its absurdity. Then he went on to tell me about how he had been invited to speak at a great meeting in Cologne, when he would be bound to be given the greatest reception of his life. Striding up and

down and gesticulating, he proceeded to deliver the speech he proposed
to make; all about the valiant fighting qualities of the Germans, the
disastrous consequences of our two wars against them, and how our two
nations must henceforth walk together; their combined strength a great
stabilising factor in the world. I reflected afterwards how the only thing
our politicians learnt in the two world wars was to admire the Germans.
It was a really ludicrous and embarrassing performance on Churchill's
part, even as grasped through my highball stupor. He was at that time, I
suppose, the most famous and admired man in the world. Yet I had seen
him delivering himself of a rhetorical rodomontade such as one might
expect to hear from some retired colonel at an Old Comrades Association
dinner. Whether the proposed Cologne speech was ever actually delivered, I have no idea. I should suppose not.

Only later, going over in my mind this brief encounter with Churchill,
did the comparison with C. P. Scott suggest itself. It was intrinsically
implausible of course – the puffy, loose, self-indulgent, baby-smooth
face of the one, and the taut, well-groomed and brushed appearance of
the other. In Scott's case, the intent purposive look, the expensive tweed
suit, the large loose tie, not, as might be expected, with a ring over it;
the everlasting expectation that somehow Whitehall leads to Damascus.
In Churchill's, a certain slackness, not exactly easy-goingness, nor even
good-nature (in fact, as far as that's concerned, the reverse – something
malign and disagreeable, as it seemed to me, behind the image-mask of
high living, low thinking and general amiability). Ribaldry is perhaps the
word; a Lear who has changed places with his Fool, but kept his blank
verse. What, then, did they have in common that made my mind go back
to that other occasion, two decades before? I suppose, that they had the
same addiction to power which stamps itself unmistakably on all who
succumb, whether they get the stuff in courts, or parliaments, or board
rooms, or at mighty demos; whether in the Kremlin's obscure recesses,
or exposed to millions of eyes in a television studio, or at the high altar at
St Peter's. In the same sort of way promiscuity gives a greedy, hungry,
coarse look at the corners of the mouth, equally in a duchess and a
whore. They had different parts, of course; Churchill a poor man's
Chatham, Scott a rich man's Good Samaritan; the one decked out in
funny hats and uniforms, the other in sartorial righteousness; one hairless
and the other bearded, one ebullient and the other dry, one a man of
fraudulent rhetoric, the other of equally fraudulent principle. On
different paths, but going in the same direction and making for the same
destination.

Scott was very affable to me, and I tried to dazzle him with my knowledge of Indian and Egyptian politics and politicians, none of whom I
had even seen, let alone met. (When, subsequently, I did see and meet
them, I did not find that I gained much thereby in knowledge or in
wisdom compared with when I only pretended to have seen and met
them.) It was difficult to decide whether Scott was listening or not; he
had the faraway air of someone preoccupied with another scene and
other words than the ones being spoken. His memory by this time was
very sketchy, but it required exceptional courage to risk correcting it
when it seemed to have led him astray. I remember how, on one
occasion, he put in the paper the obituary of someone who was still
alive; only at the very last moment before the edition went to press did
anyone – actually, the news-editor – manage to summon up courage to
tell him. When Ted and I withdrew he was still seated at his empty desk
staring in front of him. Presumably, as the evening wore on, proofs were
brought in, there were telephone calls – though there was no telephone
on his desk – to take, before he finally made off, riding his bicycle
deliberately and sedately along the dark Manchester streets, out to
Fallowfield where he lived. A majestic figure in his way; worried, maybe,
about Bulgaria, whether the British Embassy should be transferred from
Peking to Nanking, Lloyd George's perfidy, Asquith's somnolence,
Ramsay MacDonald's confusion. So many worries, turning the pedals –
O! troubled world. Pedalling along Oxford Street, into Victoria Park,
then turning into his front garden; the dark silent house, a light in his
study, soon the first edition specially delivered. One more to eye over
anxiously. Whither Bulgaria? Nanking be of good cheer, their Excellencies are coming! Steady Lloyd George! Wake up, Asquith! Ramsay,
time is running out! And so to bed.

I was allotted the task of doing a short leader on corporal punishment.
Ted handed me the relevant copy with diffidence. Not much of a subject, he seemed to say, but nothing else available. Blotched teleprinted
words, from the Press Association, about a headmasters' conference at
which some worthy or other had pronounced himself against this
barbarous custom, damaging alike to chastiser and chastised, etc., etc. I
returned with the copy to the library, where, pending a perch of my
own becoming available, I was to work. Anxiously, I added up the
wordage of a short leader in that day's paper; it worked out at between
a hundred and a hundred and fifty words. I had three hours to produce
my piece. It seemed quite long, but how to begin? Were we for corporal
punishment or against it? I supposed the latter, but sought confirmation.

It would not do, I decided, to ask Ted, since this would suggest to him that I was someone without principles, and also ignorant of the, no doubt, firm line already taken by *The Guardian* on the subject. So I ventured out of the library and into the corridor outside, this being, as I afterwards discovered, the seat of the editorial department, each door in it opening into a small room where a leader-writer was sitting like a broiler bird ready to lay an egg. Opening one of the doors at random, I saw a figure bent over a typewriter who turned out to be Paddy Monkhouse; a youngish man with already greying hair and a large kindly mouth; the son of A. N. Monkhouse, the literary editor. I grew to love him dearly when I got to know him. After a brief and unsatisfactory foray into Fleet Street on the *Evening Standard* (I was also on it at the time), he returned to *The Guardian*, where, as it seemed to me, the life was slowly and systematically drained out of him. This Liberal Moloch ate its children.

With great diffidence I announced myself to Paddy as a newcomer, and asked him if he would kindly tell me what was the paper's line on corporal punishment, as I had to write a leader on the subject. Without looking up, or stopping his typing, he muttered: 'The same as capital, only more so.' This had to suffice by way of a directive. I returned to the library and began my labours. Did I write or type? I cannot now remember. I fancy I must have taken a typewriter along; my handwriting has always been hopelessly illegible, I think because I can never bring myself to finish words of more than one syllable – least of all my own inordinately long name. With a shorter name I might have written more legibly.

So I began, and the words seemed to come of themselves; like lying as a child, or as a faithless lover; words pouring out of one in a circumstantially false explanation of some suspicious circumstance. The more glib, the greater the guilt. First the originating observation – *As Mr so-and-so, headmaster of such-and-such a school, justly observed at the Headmaster's Conference meeting yesterday.* . . . Then the qualifying counter-observation – *Some of his colleagues took him to task* . . . ('Taking to task' is better editorialese than 'criticised' or 'attacked', as it is better to say that Mr So-and-so's withers remain unwrung than that he is unrepentant.) Followed by a touch of facetiousness; out with the *Oxford Dictionary of Quotations*! – *That eminent pedagogue, Mr Wackford Squeers of Dotheboys Hall, might not agree* . . . Preparing the way for the ascent to total seriousness – *It is surely high time that this reprehensible practice were discontinued* – and working up to the moral point on which every leader must hinge – *inflicting, as it does, quite apart from any purely physical pain or discomfiture, serious psychological damage on punisher and punished alike* . . . Finally, a note of hope, on which all good leaders must go out – *While not for one moment suggesting that punishment, as such, can be wholly dispensed with, it is greatly to be hoped that the use of the cane will be, if not abolished altogether, then reserved for only the most drastic occasions* . . . In editorialese time is always high and punishment as such.

It is painful to me now to reflect the ease with which I got into the way of using this non-language; these drooling non-sentences conveying non-thoughts, propounding non-fears and offering non-hopes. Words are as beautiful as love, and as easily betrayed. I am more penitent for my false words – for the most part, mercifully lost for ever in the Media's great slag-heaps – than for false deeds. Discussing once with Kingsmill this obliteration of language, we decided that there was no need for politicians to finish their sentences, the end being implicit in the beginning. Thus, taking the case of the then looming opening of the United Nations, the following all-purpose cues would serve for any orator:

On this historic occasion when . . .
There can be no one here present who . . .
We have just passed through an ordeal that . . .
No thinking man will underestimate the . . .
While there are many circumstances which . . .
There are solid grounds for hoping that . . .
It is surely incumbent upon all of us to . . .
While recognising the reality of . . .
No mere conflict of interest should . . .
The immeasurable strides that Science has . . .
Such is the choice that at present confronts . . .
It is idle to think that politicians can . . .
It rests with the common people to . . .
With head erect and clear purpose we . . .

For the time being, however, I was well satisfied with my first offering to *The Guardian* as I laid it on Ted Scott's desk, and returned to the library to await the outcome. Paddy Monkhouse looked in to see how I was getting on with corporal – or was it capital? – punishment. His own piece (on, if I remember correctly, footpaths in the Peak District which were threatened with closure) – being likewise finished, we repaired to the Stock Bar, a conveniently situated underground bar which the editorial staff frequented. Standing there already were A. P. Wadsworth, a quick, eager, squeaky little man, then industrial correspondent and afterwards editor, and Kingsley Martin, who had heard of me through the Webbs. I have always thought of Kingsley as the prototype of all Leftists; Mr Lefty of our time. At this, my first encounter with him, I formed an impression which was scarcely modified in the succeeding years. Even his appearance changed little – the tousled hair greying but never thinning, the great beak of a nose like a shadow over the face, the sallow complexion which Mrs Webb, wrongly, took to be a sign of grubbiness (the grubbiness, if it existed at all, was inward). He gave an impression, not exactly of being shifty; rather, of constant mental pullalation. Like a marsh, bubbling and oozing and glistening; his very speech somehow tortured, words breaking and bubbling out of his anguish. Bred in Nonconformity, his father being one of those ministers who, in the spirit of the age, moved on from Calvin to William Morris, and then to a sight of Keir Hardie, Kingsley continued the journey to Marx, with many a detour and backward leap; as he would hover round the stone in his *New Statesman* days to insert or delete a last-moment 'not'. Indecision the very heart and soul of him; 'Shall we? Shan't we?' A man for all causes. He still had his father's pulpit manner; unction of righteousness, and, in his political leaders, the flavour of extempore prayer – Lord, we *do* beg thee to raise the school age . . . I remembered an old song I had heard; 'I am myself my own fever and pain.' Kingsley was himself our own fever and pain; he was crucified nightly (later, weekly) as the paper went to bed, and rose again from the dead when it was delivered with the milk. Every age has its own man; Medieval Man, Renaissance Man, Industrial Man, etc., etc. Ours was Kingsley – Socialist Man. At once our battle and our battlefield, our message and our medium. At the Stock Bar he was holding forth about regulations he had been endorsing for humane killing – of animals, as it happened. It might perfectly well have been men; he had a way of airily abolishing huge concourses of people, as when he considered in a leader whether or not Mao Tse-tung had been justified in liquidating some million recalcitrant Chinese.

Back in the library, I found that the proof of my leader had been laid on the table. The first galley I had ever seen, with galleys to come that would make a paper-chase round the earth's circumference. This the very first one, still damp, so that, when I tried inking in corrections, the ink spread in little rivulets. Yet somehow my morsel of newsprint with its ridiculous sentences and rivulets of ink seemed unearthly in its wonder. My words, printed! I could scarcely contain myself; I felt up-lifted, and walking back to the Queen's Hotel through Manchester streets already emptying, I scarcely felt the pavement in the thought of all those *Guardian* readers, over the breakfast table, or swaying from side to side in crowded railway compartments, or dozing in their clubs, or strap-hanging in trams and buses, confronted with my broadside on corporal punishment. Stopped in their tracks, maybe; stunned, over-whelmed by the well-chosen, well-directed words, resolving that hence-forth the cane should be laid aside for ever. In the morning I lay in bed listening for the footsteps of the man taking round the papers; at last I heard him, rushed to the door, and there it was, the day's *Guardian*, fresh and fragrant as a newly picked rose. On the leader-page, sure enough my piece. I read it over and over – headed: 'Spare the Rod' – as though it had been some exquisite sonnet. It would be nice to feel now, and gratifying to say, that all the fatuous lucubrations of which this first one was the herald were so much waste product, preventing a more particular and lasting use of one's own verbosity. In truth, I feel about them as Falstaff did about the riff-raff he recruited to fight in the king's wars – mortal men! In my case, mortal words.

When Kitty and our son came, we moved into Kingsley's house in Didsbury while he was away. He had a special contract with the *Guardian*, much resented by Scott even though he made it, whereby he could be away from Manchester for three months in the year in order to refresh and re-fertilise his mind. Whether this purpose was in fact achieved, may be doubted; his mind always seemed to me like one of those small plots whole Indian families live off, which never lie fallow for a single instant – endlessly tramped over by buffaloes; ploughed and sown and harvested in endless succession. I stayed with him while awaiting Kitty's coming. His then wife, Olga, a spare lady with a fringe and a sharp chin who was reputedly engaged in writing fantasies, called him 'Kingly'. When we left for the office together, they would embrace warmly, she murmuring as she broke away: 'Nuffs, Kingly; nuffs!' Physically, she was fashioned very much in the style of Katherine Mansfield, a then popular model in such circles; and no doubt the fan-tasies – though I never saw one – were likewise in the Katherine Mans-field manner. (Come to that, Kingsley bore a decided resemblance to Middleton Murry, Katherine Mansfield's husband.) Warm sand trick-ling through bare cool toes; impulsive, elfin (that's the word), floor-squatting, head on one side – Do I love you? What's love? Voices crying in the wilderness to make straight the way for Virginia Woolf. To the

Lighthouse! Oh, to the Lighthouse! Long afterwards, abruptly, *à propos* of nothing, Kingsley told me how Olga came to die. They had been separated for many years; Olga drifted in and out of mental homes, weaving her fantasies therapeutically. Leaving one such mental home, carrying her suitcase, she incautiously crossed the road, and was knocked down and killed. The suitcase gave me a pang; contents scattered about the tarmac – bits of clothing, books, scribbled sheets of fantasy. To the Mortuary! Oh, to the Mortuary!

Driving from Didsbury to Cross Street with Kingsley was a hazardous business; in a car so ancient that it had no mechanical wind-screen wiper, requiring the driver when it was raining (which it usually was) to move the wiper to and fro by hand, which Kingsley did vigorously, the other hand on the steering-wheel, and, at the same time, discoursing fluently on the world situation. Poincaré, that implacable militarist, with the xenophobic French behind him, and only a few virtuous lone voices – Barbusse, Albert Thomas, Romain Rolland – protesting, the virtuous Germans, encircled by the Little Entente, malignantly kept on the edge of bankruptcy, wickedly and foolishly excluded from the comity (an editorial favourite) of nations. MacDonald's fine speeches at Geneva, but would they butter parsnips (another editorial favourite)? Kingsley had it all worked out. Later, he would have occasion to shatter this pattern of events in favour of another. The French promoted in virtue, the Germans drastically demoted, with other consequent adjustments of smaller fry like the Poles and the Czechs. It was wonderful how quickly and wholeheartedly such re-arrangments could be managed. Like a man racing after a bus, falling, picking himself up and dusting himself down, and then catching another going in the opposite direction. At the time of the Nazi-Soviet Pact, for instance, when other enlightened voices grew hoarse, were muffled and even silenced, Kingsley soon got a second wind and was off again. Similarly when Khruschev delivered his anti-Stalin broadside at the twentieth Party Congress. It was not that he was unprincipled; rather the converse. He had a super-abundance of principles; enough and to spare for all possible eventualities.

Though Kingsley was so completely tuned in to the spirit of *The Guardian*, more so than any of the rest of us, oddly enough he failed to please the Scotts, and was not a success on the paper. Quite soon after I joined, he left it to become editor of the *New Statesman*; a position in which he throve mightily. I inherited his room along the Corridor; a small cubicle with windows looking on to nothing, and a coal fire which I tended to over-stoke, generating a fug, soon laden with tobacco smoke.

Through this haze occasionally the figure of C.P. loomed up on one of his visitations. He appeared and disappeared unaccountably; the Corridor in any case was full of ghosts – for instance, a figure in a winged collar with a shining forehead, and occasionally glimpsed muttering, or passing silently by – and C.P. might well have been one of these. On one of his visitations he spoke to me about Kingsley, telling me how, almost from his very first appearance in Cross Street, he had found his physical presence distasteful; to the point that he could not bear any bodily contact with him, like shaking hands, or reading copy over his shoulder. Was this feeling, expressed so emphatically, perhaps a premonition of the moral squalor and confusion which the attitude of mind Kingsley so perfectly exemplified was bound to produce, and of which *The Guardian* would be a leading exponent, rather than a comment on his actual physical presence? Mrs Webb, in any case, reacted to him similarly, in her Journal; and so, as I had occasion to learn, did George Orwell. Once when I was lunching with him at a Greek restaurant in Percy Street he asked me to change places with him, which I cheerfully did. He explained that the reason for the change was that, from where he had been sitting, he looked straight at Kingsley lunching at an adjoining table; and the sight of so corrupt a face, he said, would spoil his luncheon. When I took his place I had to admit that I felt no particular distress at having Kingsley in vision. Was this because I was part of the same corruption? Or just that over the years the stench of it had so got into my nostrils that I didn't notice it any more.

The body comes into our moral struggles more than is commonly recognised. There is nothing out-of-the-way in Jacob's long wrestling match with his God, or in the bloody battle between Christian and Apollyon in *The Pilgrim's Progress*. Everyone with experience of mental derangement – and there are few to-day without it – will know that the sickness of the mind goes with a horrifying intensification of the body's animality; a wild animal staring out of the eyes, or dim windows of the soul, as Blake calls them. Dreadful grunts replacing human speech, froth at the corners of the mouth, and the flesh exuding smells and rankness. My own most vivid experience of the bodily implications of mental strife came in a radio session I once had with Bertrand Russell. I had spoken in praise of Christianity, and he rounded on me with unexpected ferocity, shrilly insisting that everything most cruel and destructive and wicked which had happened in the world since the end of the Roman Empire had been due to the Christian religion and its founder. I shouted back; it was an absurd and unedifying scene which nonetheless left me physically exhausted, as though I had been engaged in a physical wrestling match. I remember still with a lively sense of horror how, as Russell's rage mounted, a flush rose up his thin white stringy neck, like a climbing thermometer, to suffuse his simian features, making of the great philosopher a flushed ape.

C.P. himself, in any case, was physically very fastidious, well scrubbed and brushed and groomed. His thoughts and attitudes were similarly hygienic, though his ear was attuned to the first tiny rustlings of the permissive tornado to come, which was to sweep *The Guardian* so notably along with it. I wrote a long leader for him one hot summer's day when there seemed no other subject, on the cult of sun-bathing, in which I quoted a line from D. H. Lawrence about the genitals of space. This he passed, though a cloud hung over our relations in the succeeding few days which suggested he may have been criticised for so doing. On one of his ghostly visitations we got on to the subject of a remark of Goethe's to the effect that women wearing spectacles put a barrier between themselves and male approaches. Yes, he said, looking knowing, he had found it so. It reminded me of Dr Johnson saying that if ever he had a harem he would dress the ladies in linen rather than silk. On another occasion, in connection with some story about racial trouble in Cardiff, we discussed whether Africans were better equipped sexually than Europeans. He had heard they were, he said. Though he was completely devoid of humour in the ordinary sense, there was a strain of impishness in him which came out from time to time; even a touch of irony – as when he remarked that printing *The Guardian* in London would be disastrous because then people would *read* it instead of just praising it. I did not venture to point out – what was, indeed, the case – that as things were, this was, with the best will in the world, impossible, because of the many misprints in the London edition.

Sometimes C.P. bicycled out to Didsbury to have tea with Kitty and me in the flat we had moved into from Kingsley's house. He was so amiable and flatteringly appreciative of my work that I should in the ordinary way have responded by liking him. Actually, I never did; I sensed something false and phoney in him – or thought I did. This feeling was heightened by my great and growing fondness for Ted, who submitted to being bullied by his father with sullen acquiescence but much inward resentment. He told me once that he had never known C.P. do any truly disinterested act in the whole of his life; everything he said and did, however ostensibly high-minded, had an interested notive. Even his bowing out of the editorship in favour of Ted was more nominal than real; he continued in practice to hold all the strings in his hand. He represented, indeed, to a superlative degree, the great moral fallacy of our time – that collective virtue may be pursued without reference to personal behaviour. Thus he believed passionately in equality as long as he himself could enjoy the company of Oxford men who had read Greats; in security as long as he did not have to foot the bill for his own employees. His passion for freedom varied in direct ratio with the distance from Manchester of those demanding it, and he loved all mankind except those among his associates and underlings he considered to be socially or intellectually inferior. These were made all too well aware of his lofty disdain.

In our cubby holes along *The Guardian* corridor we expounded all the hopes and apprehensions this righteously exalted old man entertained for mankind. We, as it were, wrote him down nightly for the edification of his paper's readers, in words that, as we fondly believed, would reverberate round the world. Bringing cheer to Asian peasants as they followed their wooden ploughs, uplifting bearded Bedouins as they rode their camels along desert tracks; spreading enlightenment over palm and pine, over campus and conveyor-belt, wherever there were minds to think and hearts to feel. Tapping away at our typewriters on his behalf, we called upon moderate men of all shades of opinion to draw together to ensure that wiser counsels should prevail. Wars which threatened, all to be averted; wrongs which the downtrodden and oppressed suffered, all to be righted; conflicts all to be honourably resolved, and injustices all to be honourably corrected. The people of this country will never for a moment countenance, we sternly proclaimed; ourselves, the people of this country and C.P., momentarily identified; one in three and three in one, another Holy Trinity. They will recoil as one man, they will speak with one voice, they will scornfully repudiate; there was no end to the honourable capers the people of this country might be expected to cut – on our typewriter keyboards. We charted their best course, spelt out for them their finest destiny. If fingers faltered – because false sentences will never finish, sprouting clauses as profligately as gluttons stretch out their meals or spendthrifts accumulate debts – one had somehow to press on, resolutely raising the little hammers to pound out the requisite number of words. Lubricated with strong tea, fortified with buttered toast, stupefied with tobacco smoke; dog-eared press-cuttings once more turned over, past exhortations resuscitated and refurbished, shuffling along in other men's cast-off hopes, until the home-stretch

reached at last – In this day and age surely not beyond the wit of man . .
To be hoped . . . Greatly to be hoped . . . Devoutly to be hoped . .
What, I sometimes cried out in anguish – what, oh what is to be hoped

This is the dark night of the leader-writer, when there seems to b
no wit in men in this or any other day and age; no moderate men and n
shades of opinion to draw them together; nothing at all to be hoped. A
with that other dark night of the soul described by St John of the Cross
for those who endure to the end, it passes, giving place at last to fulfil
ment and peace. Easily, smoothly, the concluding words are ejected lik
brushless shaving cream from a full tube – Devoutly to be hoped tha
resort to brute force will be eschewed . . . Self-interest in the narrowe
sense put aside . . . Solution hammered out at the conference table . .
On the one hand safeguards . . . on the other provides for the possibility
of . . . thereby ensuring that . . . Hurrah! The job is done. Wise
counsels after all *have* prevailed, moderate men of all shades of opinior
have drawn together. Positively glowing with the nobility of the fina
sentiment, I put back the cuttings in their folder and hand in my copy
to be fed in due course to the rotary machines. Soon I hear them
chewing it over like giant molars.

Convivial in the Stock Bar; then in the Press Club, where, when
Parliament was not sitting, the solid, dignified figure of the Honourable
Member for Salford South was usually to be found. Back to the office
for a last look at the news, and to pick up the first edition – pale shadow
of the others to come, but still indubitably the next day's paper, whose
possession the night before bestows a certain distinction; like eating
strawberries out of season. Bearing it, I make my way homewards,
along Oxford Street (Manchester being, with all its ostensible local
glory, full of metropolitan echoes – Piccadilly, Leicester Square, etc.)
and on to Didsbury. In winter more often than not, houses shrouded in
mist, with only occasional dulled vagrant footsteps to be heard, and dim
shadowy passing figures to be seen; in summer, long evening shadows,
and occasionally, when a late story had to be waited for, the first intimations of dawn breaking across Victoria Park. At home, Kitty waiting;
not pleased. Already the strife of egotistic living, of spent appetites and
surreptitious actual or envisaged infidelities, charging the atmosphere
with currents of rage and mutual reproach and accusation. Old rows
that go on echoing in the limbo between deed and intent; lightning and
thunder in the dark jungle of our human will.

Ours was the standard interior of our kind; shabby divan, three book-
rows will I have there, and a flagon for the cheap chianti. A set for *Look*

Back in Anger and a hundred other like productions, assembled some two decades ahead of the Royal Court. The characters, too – we live out the plays long before their vogue upon the stage, which is why they have so often a stale *déjà vu* air about them; why, as the applause breaks, there are sour looks among those who waited for Godot years and years ago, played football on The Wasteland when its only begetter still wore a monocle and called himself Captain Eliot; who howled and howled when Ginsberg in tiny ringlets was lisping out the Torah under a Rabbi's spreading beard.

So, before going to bed, I sit surlily reading my first edition; mopping up the news like an avid eater cleaning up his plate with bread. The addiction had already gripped me. In the morning all the papers delivered, a daily pile of soggy newsprint on our doorstep; then the evenings, the Sundays, the weeklies, the monthlies. It was to be a life-long passion, only now, belatedly, beginning to wane; later, of course, to be augmented by listening and seeing. Impossible to calculate the vast expense of time and concentration on this evanescent pursuit; the equivalent, maybe, of painting twenty Sistine Chapels, or writing the Decline and Fall of several Empires. Words tapped out or scribbled or telephoned; then printed, rushed to delivery vans, trains and aeroplanes, put under door-knockers or laid beside bottles of milk, held up at break-fast tables, uncomfortably squinted at in buses and trains; by midday discarded, by tea time superseded, by evening relegated to lighting fires or wrapping fish. My own role a voyeur one; peering in through a keyhole or camera-shutter at the antics of those set in authority, and deriving therefrom some sort of perverse vicarious satisfaction, which, passed on, catered for a similar addiction in others. News an expression of the hypochondria of a sick society – like endlessly sucking at a thermometer, standing on the bathroom scales; for ever anxiously examining the tongue's colour, the breath's odour, the urine's consistency; pressing the gut for intimations of ulcer or cancer, dreading the appearance of a chancre, a gonorrhoeal emission. In a civilisation dropping to pieces, news takes some of the sting out of happenings. So, more and more of it; all day long, and often all night long, too. A sort of Newzak, corres-ponding to Muzak; instead of a melange of drooling tunes endlessly played, a melange of drooling news endlessly heard. As the motor-cars sweep along the broad highways, Newzak is absorbed; the face at the wheel, intent, almost religious and uplifted, detached from the whole mundane stationary world in this other ethereal world of perpetual motion from nowhere to nowhere, cigarette drooping, suit newly come from the cleaners swinging to and fro on its coat-hanger like a clock's pendulum. In distant Peking, in nearby Washington D.C., in London and Paris and Rome, and everywhere, happenings, coming into view like coloured balloons. An endless succession of balloons of all colours and sizes. News.

Such was now my trade; part of the process of translating life and its meaning and significance into pictures, thereby draining it of its blood and flesh, its livingness. Surely it was not by chance that the age's essential invention in communications has been the camera. We needed it, and so invented it. Needed it to provide us with these very pictures; first stills, then moving; first black-and-white, then in living colour; first silent, then speaking; one-dimensional, two-dimensional, stereoscopic. As for the script, where my business lay – it, too, had to be what was seen *with* the eye rather than *through* it. Actualities rather than imaginings. Literature would not do, art would not do, these being through-the-eye activities. (Having no role, they were, in fact, to expire.) All that remained was pictures; the cameraman's, or the commentator's. Ultimately, a combination of both, when the deception would be complete; between the Action! and the Cut!, between the first clapper-board and the last, only fantasy.

Over and above the cotton trade, the screeching trams, the massive blackened public buildings and statues of forgotten worthies – champions of free trade, abolishers of slavery, instituters of polytechnics and public libraries; beyond the slums and the shops, the warehouses beside the stagnant Ship Canal, the clatter of occasional surviving clogs, the Midland Hotel with its majestic palm court – over and above all of them, like seraphim and cherubim high up on a white cloud in one of those vast Renaissance paintings of Creation or Transfiguration, there perched a little cluster of the culturally elect. Professors and teachers from the university, among them the massive swollen figure of Namier and the more whimsical one of A. J. P. Taylor, then his acolyte. Enlightened manufacturers' ladies with piled up hair and embroidered bodices who provided buffet and claret cup, and the presence of some distinguished visiting flautist, or bearer of good tidings from the League of Nations; even, on occasion, an Ouspensky, or Theosophist from Adyar with words to say on transmigration. The Hallé Orchestra, the Rep (then performing in a cavernous converted tram depot), *The Guardian*, of course, all provided their quota, along with an occasional museum or art gallery curator, librarian, local scribe or lady novelist from the West Riding, Jewish or Armenian *aficionado* from Cheetham Hill (Harold Laski or Michael Arlen progenitors), rumbustious magnate with a taste for Trollope and a son at Bedales. The north country accents, muffled or defiant, seemed even then to contain a hint of migratory intentions southwards, with conquest in view; Arnold Bennett, J. B. Priestley, D. H. Lawrence beckoned, and many another cultural pilgrim would follow. Likely Lads in Eng. Lit., aspiring novelists-in-the-raw, rough but rewarding bedfellows for randy debs and girls with cultural aspirations from Girton and the Cheltenham Ladies' College, to be picked up at the Tate Gallery on a warm summer's afternoon. They, too, dramatis personae for a multitude of plays, novels, films and, above all, television documentaries yet unborn.

Kitty and I were no more than occasional frequenters of this society. For relaxation we used often to go into Derbyshire for long walks, battling our way across bleak moors and up windy hillsides, and often arguing or quarrelling as we went along; the wear and tear of two egos in two bodies laid side by side, each seeking fulfilment in the other's flesh under the watchful eye of the other's ego. It was tempting to look for answers to our dilemma, and, in exploring them, we joined in the great contemporary cacophony on the same theme. The marriage tie must not hamper or hinder us; marriage and the family were things of the past, as was jealousy, fidelity, parenthood. We abolished the lot, along with property, capitalism, money, and all other appurtenances of what we had already begun to call the Establishment, deriving the term from the Anglican Church as by law established. Having cleared away all this jungle, we should, we confidently believed, be free to live together of choice, not necessity. Finding satisfaction in one another's bodies without any sense of guilt or possessiveness; our appetites a great ecstasy rather than a great anguish, the Apostle Paul with his 'To be carnally minded is death' cast out in favour of the Apostle Lawrence with his 'To be carnally minded is life.' Phallic purification, as it were, cauterising and restoring our mind-infected flesh.

A more regular walk for me was what I called the Round; following the raised bank of a turgid stream that wound its way through a stretch of wasteland for some reason unbuilt on, just behind where we lived. It could scarcely be called country. Smoke and soot had settled upon it; the water of the stream seemed thick and lifeless, and though fishermen sometimes stood with their lines beside it, I never saw them pull any-thing out except old boots, and once a lady's hat. The very green of the trees and grass seemed faded and stale. In every direction, the skyline was houses or belching chimneys; there were some adjoining allotments, heroically cultivated, and a football ground of sorts where in the school holidays and on summer evenings urchins played. The memory of this place has stayed with me more tenaciously and vividly than the Derbyshire or Cheshire countryside, or even than the Yorkshire moors or Lake District of our more ambitious outings. I must have pounded through it in all sorts of weather and temperature, some hundreds, if not thousands, of times; sometimes, in moods of special restlessness, completing the Round, and then at once beginning on it again, to the surprise of anyone who had happened to notice me on my first circumlocution. Always conscious of being incarcerated, a prisoner, the Round so pleased me, perhaps, because it was like what I imagine prison exercise to be. Not to get anywhere; always, essentially, remaining in the same place, yet moving, footstep following footstep, arms swinging, sweat accumulating, and in the mind the everlasting questions that were never answered, the everlasting desires that were never satisfied, the everlasting longings that were never realised. Curiously enough, returning to Manchester after many years, and looking for familiar landmarks which I could not find, I came upon the Round exactly as it had been. It alone survives unchanged and intact; *The Guardian* office in Cross Street has disappeared.

I habituated myself to relating my life to news as farmers do to weather. This soon became second nature, and long after the necessity was passed the habit persisted; like the man in *Rasselas* who had convinced himself that without his exertions the sun would never rise or set. We leader-writers were expected to turn up at the office in the early afternoon; one mooned around, dropped into the sub's room to see what had come in, pored over the early editions of the evening papers. At some point or other one would usually be sent for by Ted or C.P.; if not, one felt anxious and unwanted. Then, the subject of that day's leader agreed on, one would settle down to it, cuttings spread out, *Encyclopaedia Britannica* or some other relevant book or work of reference consulted, maybe even a telephone call made; though the telephone had not by any means yet come into its own as the constant instrument of daily journalism, and, in any case, on our penurious paper, its use, except for local calls, was frowned upon as an extravagance. A piece of paper fixed in the typewriter, a heading underlined – as it might be, Trouble in Panama – and off we go: 'The overthrow of Sr Farrago's (one had to be careful about **Signor, Senor, Senhor; Sr** was safer) Government and replacement by a military junta (junta had a nasty sound, and could safely be applied to any régime displeasing to the *Guardian* which had an officer above the rank of major in it) under the leadership of the notorious General Fandango ('notorious' was safe enough for any Panamanian general) would seem to be a retrograde step . . . and so on, leading up to the anchor- or hinge-word 'Meanwhile'. After 'meanwhile', came, almost as a matter of course, 'it remains to be seen', the equivalent, in distant and doubtful situations, of 'it is to be hoped'. What precisely remained to be seen in Panama just then, now escapes me, but doubtless it was to do with whether the general's strong-arm men would be able to terrorise the peasants and factory workers into acquiescence, and tranquilise a population, divided between *Moderato* and *Exaltado* factions (two easily invented words betokening a deep knowledge of the subject), and notoriously subject to political instability.

Or one might have some other additional task like an editorial paragraph for the *Manchester Guardian Weekly*, remunerated at the rate of twelve-and-six a time. Or a back-page article to finish off, these being fictional pieces of about a thousand words for which one received four guineas; only three, however, if the background was derived from an expenses-paid *Guardian* assignment. Or a book review to do. I easily took to this work, which I have gone on doing more or less regularly ever since. My only steady occupation, and the only 'serious' reading that, with a very few exceptions, I have ever undertaken. I soon became versed in sampling a book here and there; like a wine-taster taking a mouthful, washing it several times round his mouth, and then spitting it out. Versed, too, in digesting a blurb (Miss So-and-so's vivid account of a relationship between a young aggressive village schoolmaster and a middle-aged recluse whose archaeologist husband thinks of nothing but his digs), in grubbing up a sentence here, a sentence there, to suggest familiarity with some unknown subject; in playing with phrases which find their way into publisher's advertisements: I could not lay it down . . . Essential reading for all students of contemporary affairs. . . . Unique contribution to . . . Alas, how easily the hack acquires his tools! In A. N. Monkhouse's absence on holiday, I even sat in as Literary Editor, and in that capacity included in the Book Page a review by myself of Mrs Catherine Carswell's book on D. H. Lawrence, *The Savage Pilgrimage*, the first of a long grisly line of female outpourings about him. In view of the fact that Mrs Carswell was a valued contributor to the *Guardian*, my closing peroration caused much indignation, within and outside the paper: 'How sick one gets of Don and John

Patrick (Mrs Carswell's husband and son)! How sick one gets of Lawrence himself! How sick, how unutterably sick, of Mrs Carswell!' On the whole I welcomed Monkhouses's return with relief.

I struggled on with my own writing, fitfully but ardently. To my great surprise and delight, it was finally arranged that my play *Three Flats* was to be produced by the Stage Society. The producer was Matthew Forsyth, and I note in the case several names that afterwards became well known – Barry K. Barnes, Dorice Fordred, Mary Hinton, Margaret Yarde; among the extras, Anthony Quayle. I went up to London for a dress rehearsal, and sat beside Forsyth, but was too overwhelmed to say anything much. The play did not seem to be by me; the set – a ground-floor flat and, above it, two adjoining first-floor ones – and the words as I heard them spoken, were quite unfamiliar. Nor have I now the courage to read them in the published version, of which I still possess a copy. I went with Kitty and my father and mother to the Sunday evening production at the Prince of Wales Theatre. It was an occasion of delirious happiness; there were shouts for the author, and I took a curtain with the cast. My father's pleasure was a great satisfaction to me, and I hope it offset some at least of his disappointments. His eyes were shining. I still had the feeling, though, that the play was by someone else; even when I read the notices, which were reasonably encouraging, especially *The Times*, whose dramatic critic wrote (I quote from a faded cutting pasted in a scrapbook): 'All is vain, all is scattered and seemingly unrelated, all is at once sad and absurd. What is the unifying cause and truth? The author asks his questions with skill and sympathy, pointing it with faultless observation, that he never permits to become shrill ... In brief, a play distinguished by the sureness of its detail and the economy of its writing.' I read those words over a good many times at breakfast on the Monday morning. Subsequently I learnt that the writer of the piece was Charles Morgan. There is always a catch in everything. Shaw was in the audience, but my attention was focused on the stage. He wrote a long letter to Mrs Webb about the play, which I only saw recently. Though quite appreciative, it showed a total unawareness of what I was getting at. This did not really surprise me, since I came to realise that Shaw got everything wrong – Shakespeare, Caesar, the Soviet Union, Mussolini, St Paul. He had a sparkling intelligence but a low understanding; this enabled him to be very funny, but whenever he was serious he was absurd. In any event, he was too encased in his own narcissism, too remote from real life ever to do more than grimace at it through a long-distance telescope. Once Lady Rhondda asked me to accompany her to lunch with him, but afterwards telephoned in some embarrassment to call the invitation off. When pressed, she told me that it was because I had referred to Shaw in something I had written as 'that absurd vain rich old man'. He particularly resented, she said, being called rich. It surprised me at the time that he should be so touchy; now I can see that it was understandable enough. He wanted to make a lot of money without being considered rich, as Casanova wanted to have women without being considered lecherous, or as Stalin wanted to operate a terror without being considered cruel. James Agate's notice was patronising but kindly, and advised me to change my name at once. Though Ransome had proffered similar advice, I resolutely declined to follow it.

When, a few days later, I heard from my agent, Walter Peacock, that Universal Pictures had bought an option on *Three Flats* for five hundred pounds, and that if and when they made a film based on it I should get some thousands of pounds (I can't remember how many, but it seemed a great many at the time), I thought my fortune was made. Of course they never did make a film, and though I wrote a number of other plays I never had another professionally produced. So it all came to nothing. At one point, Peacock arranged for me to meet Charles Laughton with a view to writing a play for him, and we lunched together in his hotel room in Manchester. I can't now remember what sort of play I suggested, but I know we only got to it in the last ten minutes of our luncheon. Before then, he had been telling me how, to get in the right state of mind when he was playing Al Capone in Edgar Wallace's play, *On the Spot*, he used to remember how as a schoolboy he had believed that his fingers were going to drop off as a result of masturbating. This was my only brief, and not very pleasing, encounter with the theatre and actors, though Peacock remained a friend to the end of his life. He was a curious melancholic figure, in a permanent state, as it seemed to me, of faint uncomplaining excitation by constant contact with pretty aspiring actresses anxious to please him. A sort of lovable green-room sage or oracle. He did not care much for my plays, though he did his best to get them put on. I expect he was right; my impression is that the themes were too abstract and symbolic, and the dialogue correspondingly stilted.

A mellifluous American named Constant Huntington, managing director of Putnam, the publisher of *Three Flats*, urged me to write a novel. It was my first acquaintance with the world of Henry James and the Europeanised New Englander, beautifully dressed, elaborately courteous, enormously *slow* – in Huntington's case, this slowness accentuated by his practice of carefully masticating his food a fixed number of times, which meant that, lunching with him, one was liable to find oneself well into the celery and cheese when he had barely finished his soup. I suppose T. S. Eliot represented the last fine flower on this particular plant, unless, indeed, you count Joe Alsop, which would be to reduce the whole thing to absurdity. On one occasion Huntington took me out to lunch with Lloyd Osbourne, Robert Louis Stevenson's step-son, with whom he collaborated in writing *The Wrong Box*. I was very excited about it, and planned to get Osbourne talking about life in Samoa with his mother and step-father; alas, as has so often happened to me, I talked myself, and he barely uttered. He seemed, in any case, a rather taciturn sort of person, with a round, dull face and a rumbling American accent. All the same, it was an opportunity missed; one of many such.

The novel I wrote at Huntington's behest was called *Autumnal Face*; about an ageing dispirited suburban lady, and her longings for a more exciting, full-blooded life, but patient acquiescence in her lot; based, of course, on my Croydon memories. I wrote it in the mornings in Didsbury, between Rounds, going over it with Kitty as I went along; as I have everything I have ever done. It is dedicated to her. In the same scrapbook as the notice of *Three Flats*, there are some reviews – 'Skill and insight . . . fascinating picture . . . first novel of a genuine artist . . .' I could go on culling such choice items from an otherwise moribund expanse of print. I note with a pang that one notice in the old *Sunday Referee* has a 16 pt headline: A YOUNG NOVELIST TO WATCH. Until I looked at these notices I had forgotten that, with prophetic insight, I gave the dreary suburban family I atomised the all too apt surname of Pill!

The reception of my play and first novel, I suppose, along with whatever kudos derived from a fairly brisk start on the *Guardian*, would have qualified me to set up there and then as a professional writer, without any necessity to be on the staff of a newspaper, and undertake the writing and other chores this entailed. I cannot recall that I even considered such a thing, or claim that I was held back from dedication to letters by financial or family considerations. Kitty would not have minded – she never has minded anything of that kind; we should have rubbed along perfectly well, as later on we did. The truth is that I have no fancy for a writer's life as such; some instinct told me that in contemporary circumstances it would prove sterile, and, ultimately, absurd. It would be Eng. Lit. and Little Dowden all over again. Living in some country retreat, by the Mediterranean if prosperous enough, or otherwise exotically situated. Coloured-shirted, sandalled, panama hatted for day-time wear, broad-brim for the evening, and maybe velvet jacketed. Puffing away at a pipe, dreaming of young girls, turning out a daily quota of words – 'Mrs Farquharson sat in the sun, a novel with uncut pages listlessly held, her neat, trim figure elegantly disposed in yellow – a colour that suited her still flaxen hair coiled round tiny, shapely ears. Would Henry speak at last when he came to dinner; just the two of them? About Angela, and all that had happened since that so strange en-counter . . . ?' Or some ferocious tirade in the Wyndham Lewis manner. Or Poundian? Or Joycean? Or, culled from Belloc, about the Faith, and Richard Coeur-de-Lion, and Thomas Aquinas? Or, perhaps worst of all, the Workers, and some champion of the down-trodden and op-pressed from Balliol, in baste shoes, who joined the hunger marchers, and reviewed the collected works of Lenin in the *Worker*, and supped at the 1917 Club with Ethel Mannin after Brecht. Or getting invited to Garsington, with a chance of catching a glimpse of Aldous Huxley, and hearing D. H. Lawrence shout across the dinner table at Bertrand Russell: 'You're all doomed!'

Kitty's and my feelings in this matter were no doubt coloured by our friendship with Gerald Bullett and his wife, whom we occasionally visited, and they us. Gerald was a fairly successful novelist, always at work on a book, with the next one already at the planning stage; this one maybe to include a touch of incest – and why not after Oedipus? A plump man with a round face, humorous eyes and sad jowls, he and his wife lived in the usual two cottages run into one, with a thatched roof – so difficult to get repaired nowadays because all the delightful village arts and crafts were dying out, but fortunately they had a man, a droll delightful old fellow who was prepared to take it on. Gerald's study was a large dark room with a lot of books lying about, mostly in their dust-jackets; he did a bit of reviewing for the T.L.S. and other literary publications, but not enough to get in the way of his creative work. His wife typed for him, very energetically; one could hear her in the morn-ings bashing away at her keyboard – like volleys of machine-gun fire. In the evenings, likewise energetically, she crocheted or knitted while the rest of us talked; only very occasionally joining in, her voice sharp and bright and cheerful. Theirs had been a runaway match; they were deeply attached to one another, kind and considerate by nature. Yet somehow there seemed to be something weighing them down; especially him. If they had some unexpected windfall, like unexpected translation rights for one of his novels, they would launch out on a trip to the Greek Islands, or even farther afield. Their only child was at an ultra-progressive school, and Gerald was a member of the Savile Club.

He and I often went for country walks together over the downs when we were staying with them; laughing a lot as we went along, and maintaining together the fantasy that we were aloof from the ordinary world where people cashed cheques and grabbed girls, as well as a little fame, when a chance offered. All that, we implied, was outside our ken. To sustain the fantasy, we would sow our conversation with qualifying phrases like 'what's called'. Thus, we would say, 'I take it, he was what's called "in love",' or: 'I believe that, actually, she's quite comfortably off, and moves in what's called "Society"'! As 1939 approached, Gerald tended to emerge from his terra-cotta tower and write furious letters to *The Times*, or, if not accepted there, to *Time and Tide*, denouncing Neville Chamberlain in unbridled terms, or advocating World Government based on the transferred vote as a solution to all our troubles. Sometimes, so intense was his rage, he compressed it all into a postcard, as a man might express all his pent-up fury in a single expletive In the war years, he worked in the BBC, beaming programmes on Milton or Wordsworth to the Nazi-occupied countries with a view to raising their morale. In a nearby studio Orwell was doing the same sort of thing to India. I think Gerald enjoyed this work, especially when the Blitz was on; in an underground studio in Oxford Street, holding forth on *Lycidas* or the *Ode on the Intimations of Immortality*, while the Luftwaffe roared overhead and the ground shook below him. The last glimpse I had of him was when he stood in the doorway of a flat Kitty and I had in Regent's Park, on his way to the Savile Club to dine with some choice spirits – Gilbert Harding, Gerald Barry, C. P. Snow; his large moon face crumpled and woebegone as he told me that he didn't want to write any more novels; hadn't anything more to say, his act being, as he put it, played out. Like an old recitative man with a funny bowler and a nose that lit up, wanting to get off the stage. Well, he did, as it happened, because shortly afterwards he died.

I had an instinctive aversion to this role of man-of-letters, as I had to being ordained. Both roles related to things I cared greatly about, but somehow, in the existing state of affairs, neither seemed appropriate. As I see it, in the twentieth century the genius of man has gone into science and the resultant technology, leaving the field of mysticism and imaginative art and literature almost entirely to charlatans and sick or obsessed minds. The result has been that, whereas in the last half century more progress has been made in the exploration of man's material circumstances, and in the application of the knowledge thereby gained, than in the whole of the rest of recorded time, the corresponding contribution to art and literature has been negligible and derisory. The circumstances of the age are just not conducive to such activities, and those who nonetheless pursue them tend to become unhinged or junkies or alcoholics, if not all three. This is particularly true of American practitioners; as Gore Vidal has pointed out, it is difficult to think of a single contemporary American writer of any note who is not either an alcoholic or on the way to becoming one.

In such circumstances, reporting and commenting upon contemporary happenings seemed preferable to dancing and grimacing on the grave of a dead culture. News was the raw material of this new trade, consisting of jerkily written messages torn off teleprinter machines, or long screeds, sometimes difficult to decipher, from Our Own or someone else's Correspondent. Sometimes the Correspondents themselves made an appearance; arriving, as it were, booted and spurred from distant places, and inclined to be somewhat contemptuous of editorial scribes toiling away at typewriters to produce sententious comment on the news they so heroically tore with rough strife through the iron gates of censorship and other natural and artificially imposed impediments. It was in the nature of things that they should appear to be in fancy dress; as Robert Dell from Paris, with his white gloves and cane and rakish felt hat and neat white moustache; like a seaside repertory Proust. At the Stock Bar we delighted in his tales of who was whose mistress in the Gauche Radicale, and listened attentively to how he outwitted the Quai d'Orsay, and what was said at his tête-à-têtes with Maxim Litvinov.

Then there was the Rev. C. F. Andrews, hot foot from Gandhi's ashram in Ahmedabad. Bearded, every inch a guru, with meek downcast eyes, he seemed to be saying that his heart sank when he reflected how, though well past thirty, he had still not been crucified. One could not but share his sorrow, more particularly as there now seemed little possibility of this unaccountable gap in his range of experience being rectified. He was also fond of comparing Gandhi's various appearances before the Indian courts with Christ's before Pilate. Scott leant a good deal on Andrews, whom he liked, in shaping *The Guardian*'s attitudes towards British policy in India, though curiously enough when he met

Gandhi himself, despite Andrew's mutual recommendations, he found the experience distasteful. I think perhaps they were too alike to get on well together; if Gandhi had been born of Unitarian parents in Lancashire he would almost certainly have become owner-editor of *The Guardian*, and likewise, if Scott had been born the son of a Kathiwar State Dewan, he could almost certainly have become a Mahatma. They met when Gandhi was over in London for the Indian Round Table Conference. C.P. had to fight his way to him through a posse of Quakers and even then found the Mahatma at his spinning-wheel and little inclined to talk, which was calculated to irritate him inordinately. Gandhi's meeting with Charlie Chaplin round about the same time was as successful as the one with Scott had been disastrous; the clown and the Mahatma were complementary images of the same thing, a gargoyle and a steeple in juxtaposition. I attended the official opening of the Round Table Conference by George V on behalf of *The Guardian*. It was a tremendous turn-out – Maharajahs and other Indian princes, the Aga Khan as huge as Chesterton, knights brown and white, turbans and shining pates, politicians, policemen, and even an odd member of the public vaguely curious to know what, if anything, was to happen to the brightest jewel in their sovereign's crown. Presiding was the then Prime Minister, Ramsay MacDonald, already well on the way to the condition of total incoherence and irresolution which marked the last stages of his political career. His opening address was vintage stuff, containing, as I recall, a remarkable appeal for 'the lion (I don't know which is the lion) to lie down with the lamb (I don't know which is the lamb).' It gave rise among those present to a sort of lions and lambs game, with everyone trying to decide to which category they belonged. Only King George V seemed quite certain; he, it was clear, considered himself as indubitably belonging to the lions. Despite the opening pomp and circumstances, the Conference soon got bogged down in a plethora of words, to which I contributed my quota in the shape of long messages to *The Guardian*. In making our getaway from India we laid down a vast preliminary smoke screen of words in the shelter of which we were able to make our dispositions for withdrawal.

To me, far the most interesting and impressive of the correspondents was F. A. Voigt from Germany. He did not need to dress up as a German; he was one (his family belonged to the sizeable German community in Manchester, and had a music shop there), with the raw features, desperately emphatic speech, powerful mind and ultimately tragic disposition of the race. If Dell was a pinchbeck Proust, he was a Nietzsche; a wild swordfish put to swim in *The Guardian* aquarium among the minnows and the goldfish and the Portuguese men-of-war. I admired enormously the furious indignation with which he described the growing threat of a Nazi takeover in Germany, of the mounting terror and violence that was building up there. Unlike other correspondents, he stressed all the time the moral consequences of what was happening; showing that it was not just war that threatened, but a moral catastrophe which could engulf whatever remained of western civilisation. Voigt's strong unequivocal attitude made him an alien element in *The Guardian*'s measured columns, especially after the outbreak of war in 1939. After he left the paper, he became editor of the *Nineteenth Century and After*, providing in it almost the only free comment and criticism of Allied policy – apart from *Tribune*, under Aneurin Bevan, with George Orwell as literary editor – which stands to-day as a shining exception to the prevailing servile acceptance of Churchill's leadership in all its aspects and with all its implications. When Voigt turned the furious indignation with which he had lambasted the Nazi terror on to Stalin's, his former liberal friends and associates discovered in him a Nazi sympathiser. Another liberal newspaper, the *News Chronicle*, ran an article about the *Nineteenth Century* headed, HITLER'S FAVOURITE READING, with pictures of the Führer and Voigt looking amicably across at one another. For this, the *News Chronicle* was sued, and I was proud to appear in court to testify to Voigt's record of integrity and distinguished journalism.

The case was heard during the Blitz, and every so often an alert sounded and the court was adjourned. It was an eerie experience, but somehow I felt that the proceedings were more relevant and important than the war itself. In a sense, they *were* the war – the true war. The judge – Scrutton – conducted the case with impeccable impartiality, and I was uplifted to think that, in a world gone mad, being torn apart and destroyed by rival fanaticisms and power-maniacs, it was still possible for a case involving these passions to be dispassionately heard and justly concluded. Voigt got damages and an apology from the *News Chronicle*, and I returned to my military duties, such as they were. After the war I saw Voigt occasionally; he fell on evil days, no one wanted his work, and he found a sanctuary on *Time and Tide*, that Salvation Army shelter provided by Lady Rhondda for destitute ideologues, where I, too, in my time, was glad to take an occasional cup of hot soup. He died largely forgotten and in poor circumstances despite a charming and devoted wife; his book *Unto Caesar*, in my opinion the most powerful and perceptive political work of our time, has long been, and to the best of my knowledge remains, out of print.

Whenever I was in London I used, of course, to look in at the House of Commons to see my father. I would wait for him in the public lobby; one of those points of intersection where rulers and ruled consort. Always crowded, with many anxious faces such as people wear before an examination; whenever they are confronted with some test of character or occasion for self-assertion. There were the usual cranks, bearded or strangely dressed, their pockets bulging with petitions, liable to mutter to themselves and make weird gestures; the women in long skirts and hats decorated with fruit and flowers, sometimes with veils – rather in the style of Mrs Dobbs. These were always interminably waiting, and one wondered if they really had any serious possibility of an appointment with an MP, or had just chosen to come there as a change from their usual haunts like the British Museum Reading Room and Hyde Park Corner and Lincoln's Inn Fields. From certain points of vantage one could see the MPs coming towards the lobby, and observe how, when they heard their names called by the policeman in attendance, they threw out their chests, and summoned up a smile, assuming a bland and jaunty air, like actors coming on the stage. So I would hear my father's name called, and it was exactly as though I were back at East Croydon Station, and had spotted him coming up the slope from the arrival platform; stepping out, ahead of the others.

We usually made for the terrace, to walk up and down there, or stare at the river; or, if the sun was shining, take tea together, and watch other MPs and their guests; just occasionally catching a glimpse of one of the great ones – a cabinet minister, a face familiar from photographs or cartoons, and now seen in the flesh; MacDonald himself, or Baldwin, or Lloyd George. Inside, whatever the season or the weather, the atmosphere always seemed dry and stale and sour. There are certain smells that remain with one – an elementary school cloakroom on a wet day; the combination of Gauloises cigarettes, urine and pungent scent which assails one's nostrils on arriving anywhere in France; a barrack-hut on waking, with one's thirteen fellow-inmates still asleep, and all the windows firmly closed. This House of Commons smell is one of them. I recall a rather similar smell in public transport vehicles in the USSR, especially on the underground. It is, I suppose, the smell of power, as in a brothel there is a smell of sex. My father liked introducing me to his fellow-members, most of whom seemed to have little to do, and spent their time sitting around in the bars and cafés interminably talking, and listening for the division bell, which spurred them into sudden, and often unthinking, action. They had, I thought, a flaccid air; like under-exercised animals in the zoo. Even my father, most energetic of men, seemed to have lost his momentum and settled into a kind of inertia, with a predisposition for doing nothing about anything. It was particu-larly noticeable in the trade union members, the only authentically proletarian ones. They were out of condition, sagging, running to fat; their faces creased and indolent, as though they were half-drunk; as, indeed, they sometimes were. The ostensible fanatics like Maxton gave an impression of character actors who had just come out of the make-up room; the lock of hair falling over the forehead, the wild eyes and accentuated eyebrows, the ardent words soulfully spoken. Likewise the Clydesiders, the sea-green incorruptibles. Years later, from the press gallery, I happened to see one of them – David Kirkwood – introduced into the House of Lords; in his robes and floppy hat, bowing religiously at the appropriate moments in the ceremony, a fellow-peer on each side of him, and Silver-Stick-in-Waiting presiding. It was a perfect exposi-tion of the humble and meek being exalted. From Saint-Simon one gathers that things were much the same at the court of Louis XIV, from Swift that they were not dissimilar at Queen Anne's, from Djilas that very similar arrangements prevailed in Stalin's; not to mention Nebuchadnezzar, Herod and the Emperor Nero.

Journalism is, I suppose, among other things, an exploration of varieties of political experience in all their wild diversity, as William James explored varieties of religious experience. Some colonel screws a monocle into his eye and takes over a government. Or a bearded arch-bishop with a ring to kiss manoeuvres himself on to a throne. Or a black corporal breaks ranks and becomes a president. Or an obscure figure playing interminable games of chess in Geneva cafés, boring everyone, quarrelling with everyone, is suddenly whisked off to rule over a fifth of the world. Or a convention demagogue shouting and sweating and fixing, at last arrives in Connecticut Avenue, to occupy the White House and imagine that it falls to him to decide there whether or not the world is to be blown to smithereens. At fantastic levels of seeming splendour – a Viceroy moving from his law chambers to sit on a silver throne and accept the homage of maharajahs with diamonds as big as ostrich eggs stuck in their turbans. Equally at levels of infinite obscurity, as I once saw two archdeacons in gaiters sitting meekly side by side on a bench outside the door of the patronage secretary's office at 10 Downing Street in Mr Attlee's day, waiting, presumably, to be summoned inside to hear about preferment possibilities. Helping a brigadier on with his coat, attentive in a board room; gallant to wigs and dentures elegantly mounted on scrawny flesh, as Drake and Leicester and the other Eliza-bethans were to the hideous old scarecrow they served – all manner of calculated obsequiousness directed to the same end. My collector's item is Brindisi after Mussolini's fall, at the Hotel Imperiale where Marshal Badoglio had formed a government under Allied auspices. What a turn-out that was! Teeming with Intelligence officers, Italian generals in enormously wide riding-breeches, hurriedly assembled diplomatic excellencies, journalists, exiled venerable anti-Fascist liberals trans-ported from their Kensington lodgings to accept portfolios in the Marshal's cabinet after many penurious years of patient endeavour in Bush House on behalf of the Overseas Service of the BBC. All manner of personnel pushing and shoving, in the dining-room and elsewhere, with a view to restoring the Four Freedoms and other democratic blessings to Italian soil; the only notable absentees being the beneficiaries of all this – the Italian people. Unless, indeed, the Imperiale staff could be considered such, as attentive to Marshal Badoglio and his entourage now, I noticed, as they had been in the days when he was the Duce's com-mander-in-chief.

My father's pleasure in being an MP and in spending his evenings at Westminster was scarcely marred by public anxieties. These, in a way, sharpened the pleasure by giving the whole experience a flavour of drama. He even appended his signature to a memorandum calling for drastic action on the Government's part, drawn up by Sir Oswald Mosley, then still a Labour MP and beloved of the Left-Wing. There were furious exchanges about ever rising unemployment and cuts in the social services; all-night sessions when Honourable Members emerged dishevelled and bleary eyed, with a sense of having been engaged in a ferocious bloody battle. But with whom? About what? No one really knew. The economic blizzard, as it was called, implying that no one could do anything about it except take shelter and hope for it to pass, blew as it listed, until there came a day when MacDonald went to the Palace and returned to announce that he had resigned as Labour Prime Minister and been entrusted with a mandate to form a National Govern-ment comprising both Tories and Liberals. No item of news has ever given me quite so overwhelming a feeling of outrage mixed with in-credulity as this one. All the pent up hatred of MacDonald and Snowden and J. H. Thomas, the three leading defectors, exploded. They had gone over to the enemy, betrayed the cause, shattered the work of years in a single act of treachery.

I remembered my father telling me the last time I saw him how the members of the Parliamentary Labour Party had assembled to hear MacDonald explain the Government's policy to them. He arrived late, in full evening dress and smoking a cigar; then, waving a condescending hand, had spoken a few meaningless words – my frrriends! . . . – and hurried off to a reception given by Lady Londonderry. Now he would be able to attend as many such functions as he liked ('Tonight every duchess in London will be wanting to kiss me,' Philip Snowden quoted him as saying) in whatever rig he liked. Grinding my teeth, I saw him as the typical figure in the Soviet satirical paper *Krokodil*'s cartoons; the flunkey in some ridiculous uniform bowing and scraping to bankers carrying money-bags and noblemen wearing coronets. For the moment he and his accomplices were riding high, but, some dreadful fate must surely await them. As, indeed, it did; MacDonald, broken in health was finally turned out of office by his Tory associates, and died at sea – he, the great pacifist, brought back on a battle cruiser in a coffin draped with a Union Jack. Thomas was convicted of using budget secrets for personal enrichment, and disappeared without trace; Snowden likewise withdrew from politics, continuing to mutter to the end of his days about Free Trade, the only article of faith left to him. It was an appropriate end to the three lost leaders, each of whom, in his own way, symbolised essential elements in the Labour Party. MacDonald, the romantic elevation of the down-trodden and oppressed to cultural and intellectual heights, Thomas the jovial proletarian at ease in his own breezy way with captains and kings alike, and Snowden the canny Yorkshireman, looking after our pennies so that the exchequer's pounds could look after themselves.

When afterwards I heard from Sidney Webb the full story of what happened, the drama seemed even more appropriate. In his soft, sibilant, toneless voice he described how he and the other cabinet ministers sat in the garden at 10 Downing Street on that warm August evening waiting for a telephone call from New York to tell them whether American banking houses were prepared to put up a loan sufficient to enable the Treasury to go on supporting the pound on the gold standard. When the answer came as no, there was nothing more they could do. They just shook their heads and departed, leaving MacDonald to go to the Palace and resign. Webb, now the first, and last, the one and only,

Baron Passfield, was the perfect narrator; seated in an arm-chair, his tiny legs not reaching the ground, his goatee beard wagging, his pince-nez with their black ribbon steady on his large nose, he showed no awareness that the occasion he described had any particular momentousness. To me it seemed – and, for that matter, still seems – to mark the end of any notion that the Labour Party, or any Social Democratic party similarly constituted, can be an effective instrument of fundamental social change. Whenever, subsequently, I read or heard prospectuses of the great things a Labour Government might be expected to achieve, I remembered that little cluster of respectable-looking men in the garden at 10 Downing Street, drawing at their pipes, occasionally getting up to stretch their legs, while they waited for Wall Street to decide their fate.

Now the rage and fury at what I considered a great betrayal has long ago passed. Even the three traitors seem more absurd than villainous. One sees MacDonald as a victim of history rather than a shaper of it; a Scottish loon who found himself on the captain's deck of a sinking ship, the less able to navigate it because he had got there by insisting that it was unseaworthy. He and the others might say with General Mihailovitch: 'There is a storm in the world, and a gale and a whirlwind have carried me and my work away.' So furious a storm, so wild a gale, so fierce a whirlwind, and such featherweight men and work.

When the news came of MacDonald's betrayal and formation of a National Government, Ted was away on holiday, and W. P. Crozier, the then news editor, was in charge of the paper. He was a rather unhappy, dyspeptic man with a bright red face and a buttoned up mouth, who hated the sight of me, and found my copy highly distasteful. In Ted's absence I made no effort to come to terms with him, but just coasted along doing little or nothing. I looked on him as someone infinitely boring; a Nonconformist who had lost his faith but retained its scaffolding of self-denial. It is one thing to resolve to give up self-indulgence like drinking and smoking in order to foster and sharpen spiritual awareness, but to give them up, as Crozier had, just for abstemiousness's own sake is itself a form of self-indulgence, and a rather particularly repellent one at that. If he altered anything I wrote, it was always, as I considered, to make it more banal and flat. That scarlet face looming across a laden desk at one, those fishy hostile eyes seeking an opportunity to cause unease and embarrassment, the dreadful silence that fell as I reached round in my mind for something, anything, to say – it all was so painful that, as far as possible, I avoided ever going in to see Crozier.

An extra touch of the macabre was added because the women's page editor was often with him for consultation, leaving behind a heavy cloud of pungent scent which hung over the office like sweet smog. In my youthful arrogance I failed to notice that, though Crozier happened to think little of me, he was an exceptionally able journalist, devoted to *The Guardian*, and even to the Scotts, though, I daresay, embittered by the way he had been passed over in preference for members of the family.

Crozier's immediate impulse was to support the National Government, which he did in a leader containing the unfortunate remark that J. H. Thomas was a dab hand at preventing 'that sinking feeling' (a reference to a then famous Bovril advertisement), and so a boon to any government. In the Stock Bar that evening we raged over this piece of bad taste facetiousness. Crozier was never popular, partly because he held aloof from convivial gatherings, and seldom unbent. Now he was more unpopular than ever. Like all the dyed-in-the-wool *Guardian* men, including even Paddy Monkhouse, he was somehow stricken. Some sort of liberal lightning came down from heaven, so that they actually looked as though they had suffered a paralytic stroke; slumping along the Corridor wrapped in their own internal gloom, sometimes, as I have heard them, actually muttering to themselves. What was it that afflicted them? I suppose just the anguish of pretending – always pretending that it was possible to make virtue out of benevolence, happiness out of well-being, peace out of accommodation and freedom out of emancipation. The wish wrestling with the reality produced strain, which in turn produced despair, at last transforming the wish itself into a kind of annihilation, or death-wish.

My dislike of Crozier took the form of totemising him, constructing my own hateful image of him; making his scarlet face even more scarlet, pursing up his lips even tighter, squeezing banalities out of him like pus. In the same sort of way, Africans seek, and sometimes manage, to injure their enemies via their likeness in some crude image or picture. We who pass for being more civilised can do the same thing in our imaginations. It is a form of diabolism to which I have been prone.

When Ted returned, we all worked on him, inducing him to reverse the paper's line and show up the fraudulence of MacDonald and his National Government. The turning point was at a luncheon in Ted's house when we all held forth eloquently; one could see him yielding – as, indeed, apart from our persuasion, all his personal feelings strongly induced him to do. It was very humiliating for Crozier. Thenceforth, we thoroughly enjoyed ourselves lampooning the Government, the re-

criminatory rows inside the Labour Opposition, and the three recusants
with equal zest. I have to admit that, for me, journalism is only exhilarating in opposition; I have never, happily, been in the position of having
to support a government. When Mr Attlee got his huge majority in 1945,
I got a job on the *Daily Telegraph*, and shortly after the Tories came
back into power in 1951, I niftily transferred to *Punch*.

C.P. had played little part in these events; at last his vitality was
ebbing, and in the early hours of New Year's Day, 1932, he died. One
final rapturous burst of adulation and he was soon largely forgotten; or
remembered only as a symbol of good, noble journalism as distinct from
the sensational kind instituted by Northcliffe. 'C.P. would never have
agreed to that,' people would say, shaking their heads, and recalling his
refusal to allow racing news, or liquor advertising, or the publicising of
the Irish Sweep in *The Guardian*. Why, in the early days, he even, it
seems, on one occasion turned down a full-page advertisement for
corsets, worth £260, because it showed a picture of a lady wearing the
advertised product. What was conveniently forgotten was that *The
Guardian* subsisted on the profits of its sister-paper, the *Manchester
Evening News* (does, indeed, to this day), in whose columns racing, the
Irish Sweep, liquor advertising and uncorseted bosoms got the fullest
play. Every now and again someone would write in to the effect that the
malicious rumour was circulating in Manchester that the great C. P.
Scott had some connection with that odious sheet the *Manchester
Evening News*, and might this lie please be nailed. Such letters were put
on C.P.'s desk, whence they disappeared without trace. Northcliffe is
alleged to have undertaken a special pilgrimage to Manchester to salute
Scott as the man who had uniquely shown that truth could be made to
pay. The encounter between them must have been interesting, revealing,
I should imagine, that they had more in common than might superficially be supposed. If Scott had made truth pay, a lot of his truth was
lies; whereas Northcliffe, in making his lies pay, sometimes told the
truth. So the contest in a way evened out.

When Ted finally took over, he could not bring himself to move into
his father's office and sit in his chair. I found this somehow a sombre
circumstance, as boding ill for his editorship. Actually, C.P.'s office
never was occupied by anyone else; when the Cross Street premises were
finally evacuated in August, 1970, having been sold for demolition, it
was still empty, and just as when he had last used it. Now it has finally
gone, along with the whole building, and the legend of C.P. with it. The
first months under Ted's editorship were among the pleasantest I have

ever spent on the staff of a newspaper. We got on very well together; he had one of those receptive minds, always ready to discuss anything and consider anything, which made working under him pleasurable. No doubt I liked it the better because he tended to lean more on me than anyone else. I even got an unsolicited pay rise; something very unusual, if not unique, on *The Guardian*. It came about because I happened to remark, unthinkingly, that with a wife and child I didn't pay any income tax. This led Ted – an expert on such matters – to look up what I was paid, and increase it quite substantially. He had to a high degree the virtue I most admire, perhaps because I so notably lack it, and, however hard I try, even now fail so miserably in my efforts to acquire it – a true humility. This was combined with a passionate honesty; a reaction, I daresay, to his father's self-centredness masquerading as disinterestedness. There are few pleasanter things in life than the companionship of a totally honest mind, which is what Ted had. This may have accounted for a certain fixed melancholy in his disposition; *The Guardian* was no place for mental honesty. An honest mind was as out of place there as a virgin in the pages of Casanova or a pregnancy in D. H. Lawrence's.

In April following his father's death Ted decided to go to the Lakes with his son Dick for some sailing. I drove up with them on the Friday evening. He had just bought a new Vauxhall car (I remember the grooves along the bonnet), and was in a particularly cheerful mood. I was to stay with some friends at Sawrey – the Spences – for the Friday and Saturday nights, returning to Manchester on Sunday because I was working that day. Ted dined with us on the Saturday evening; we all laughed a lot, and it was altogether a carefree, happy occasion. The next morning Mrs Spence drove me to Windermere, where I caught a train back to Manchester. Sunday afternoon on any newspaper is fairly drear, and *The Guardian* was no exception. News comes in laggardly, mostly from correspondents with hangovers; one turns over the Sunday papers listlessly, looking with jaundiced eyes at stories which already seem about a thousand years old. Even the arrangements for getting tea at one's desk usually don't function. I was toying with the notion of proposing yet another leader on a project for an All-India Self-Governing Federation then under consideration, when I was called to the telephone. It was Mrs Spence to tell me that Ted and Dick had been involved in a sailing accident on Lake Windermere, and that Dick had been rescued but Ted was drowned. I found some difficulty in registering what she had said; bad news transmitted on the telephone is particularly bleak and unconvincing. 'You mean it's all over; that Ted is . . .' 'Yes,' she said, in a flat definitive voice. The time was round about five o'clock, and I realised that this would mean a crisis in the office. The first thing to do was to tell Crozier. I went into his room, and he looked up expecting me to propose a subject; I felt that the very words were shaping themselves with which he'd manage, as was his way when he was in the chair, to deflate whatever I suggested, and make it seem dubious and not worth doing. Instead, I just blurted out: 'Ted's dead!' The effect on him was instantaneous and extraordinary; I saw, or thought I saw – the impression was very strong – some strips of bright yellow come into the scarlet of his face. When he had collected himself, he asked me if I was sure. I said I was, and gave him Mrs Spence's telephone number so that he could speak to her himself. Then I went back to my room, understanding that Crozier would have to get into touch with John Scott, Ted's brother, who was the paper's business manager, and so not in the office on a Sunday evening.

It was the first time I'd felt this particular sort of shock; a numbing sense of utter desolation and lostness. I telephoned to Kitty to tell her; whenever anything happens to me, good or bad, anywhere in the world, my first impulse is to find her and tell her. She has that wonderful capacity for being neither unduly alarmed nor unkindly calm; above all not *curious*; just calm and near, and conveying without saying anything her total readiness to take any shock and share any burden. A kind of fathomless, unquestioning sympathy and support. After speaking to Kitty I just sat doing nothing; it was impossible to even think of tackling the All-India Self-Governing Federation. Then Crozier came into my room and asked me to write Ted's obituary; it seemed that nothing whatever had been done about it, and there were no cuttings. I rather fatuously asked Crozier how long it should be. It was the kind of question he was easiest with, but in this particular case he just shrugged and left me to it. Time was pressing for the first edition, and I got to work, sending the copy into Crozier sheet by sheet as I did it. All I had to help me with facts and dates was Ted's *Who's Who* entry. Crozier passed it all without altering a word – the last time this was to happen to anything I wrote for *The Guardian* until quite recently, when I did a leader-page article at the request of the present editor, Alistair Hetherington. When I came to Ted's editorship, I described with unnecessary gloating how he had drastically and courageously reversed the position first taken by the paper about the formation of MacDonald's National Government. As I worked on, I was aware of Crozier standing in the doorway of my room holding that particular sheet in his hand. He was looking distressed, and said he thought I had over-stressed the change in the paper's attitude. Without stopping typing, I said I left it to him to make any changes he considered desirable. Actually, he didn't make any changes, and nor did I. The episode, which I consider to be very discreditable, if not contemptible, on my part, sealed the hostility between us.

Otherwise, the obituary came out quite well, and I received a congratulatory letter about it from J. L. Hammond, who wrote the official life of C.P. While writing it, and after, the thought had been in my mind that somehow Ted's death was connected with his father's. People die when the momentum of their lives is spent, and C.P. had, as it were, suffocated Ted; like an old tree keeping the sun, taking all the goodness of the soil, and thereby precluding an offshoot from growing and thriving. When at last the old tree died, the other withered from the unaccustomed light and sustenance instead of burgeoning. This explained, as I thought, Ted's reluctance to sit in his father's chair; he was not strong enough to be him, and the long years of subservience prevented him from being himself. By the time he took over, he had no self to be. I felt, too, that Ted was a victim of the paper itself, succumbing where others had been maimed and stunted; fed to the rotaries, like our leaders. I tried to work all this out in a novel called *Picture Palace* about a liberal newspaper in a North country town. When it had already been sent out for review, *The Guardian* got an injunction and threatened legal proceedings, in consequence of which it was withdrawn and suppressed. The particular passage to which exception was taken described the dependence of a newspaper as high-minded as *The Guardian* on a stable companion as low-minded as the *Manchester Evening News*; a relationship I compared to someone living off the immoral earnings of his daughter. Subsequent efforts to get the novel published came to nothing; *The Guardian*'s passionate advocacy of freedom of publication did not extend to books about itself.

In the weeks that followed Ted's death my position in the office was rather curious. Crozier continued to edit the paper, and was in due course confirmed as Ted's successor, but John Scott had told him that as far as possible he should continue to follow the guidelines laid down by Ted, and that I, having been closest to Ted, was the best person to advise him on this. So for a while I was a kind of assistant editor. Crozier would come awkwardly into my room – I never went into his if I could possibly avoid it – and go through the motions of discussing with me points of policy and the choice of leaders. I suppose if I had been ambitious in that sort of way, I could have pressed home my advantage and got into the line of succession on the paper. Actually, I had no interest in anything of the kind; the thought of working under or with Crozier was hateful to me, and anyway I was sick to death of liberalism; of drawing together with moderate men of all shades of opinion. All I wanted to do was to kick them in the teeth and be gone. This suited Crozier perfectly, and for my part, I have never found any difficulty in leaving a job, or in disengaging myself while nominally still in it.

To heighten my mood, there was the more or less total collapse of the Labour Party in the 1932 Doctor's Mandate election, which returned MacDonald and his Tory allies to power with an immense majority. My father, of course, lost his seat at Romford. I spent the last two days of the election campaign with him. It was obvious that the tide was flowing strongly against us, but he refused to succumb to low spirits, and kept up the fight to the very last moment. We went prowling the streets together trying to rally our supporters, until the polling booths closed. It was a hopeless task; hoarse-voiced, exhausted, my father still could not bring himself to pass a street corner without addressing a non-existent meeting: 'Ladies and Gentlemen . . .' Only a few ribald children gathered round him. It carried my mind back to those magical Surrey Street meetings, and the joke about the national debt which ought to be His Majesty's. Now, suddenly, he seemed very old and tired; no more that prophetic figure against the skyline, but shrivelled and bent. In his case, too, a storm in the world and a whirlwind had carried him and his work away. We desisted at last and repaired to a nearby committee room; the same empty shop, the same posters and slogans, the same elderly lady helpers with grey dishevelled hair and drooping cigarettes; the same cups of strong tea, the same smell of stationery, ink and gum. They affected still to be confident of victory, but we knew we had lost – as, indeed, we had, by a huge turnover of votes. It was my father's last election; the end of the road to that promised land I had so often rejoiced in on Saturday nights, securely tucked away in the tall red cosy corner in our South Croydon sitting-room.

I decided on an impulse to drive back straight away to Manchester; through the foggy night, everything muffled and misty, past the slag-heaps and the furnaces; leaving Birmingham behind me, then the Potteries, dimly glowing clusters of yellow lights that seemed to be floating on banks of cloud; across wild moorland, with no sign of a fellow-human or a human habitation. No stars, no anything; only the wind screeching and, maybe, an owl hooting, a voice wailing. Heartland of the industrial North, once pulsating with life and energy; the world's workshop and arsenal, now sleeping under its eiderdown of mist. Or dead? When the day came, the queues would form at the Labour Exchanges, the groups gather at street corners to while away an empty day; the old red-brick factories with a hint of the chapel in their structure, standing idle and empty, their obsolete machines rusting from disuse. By the time I got to Manchester dawn was just dimly breaking; in Cross Street nothing stirring, the last edition recording MacDonald's great triumph already on its way. Would it ever revive, this birthplace of twentieth-century prosperity, this cradle of the affluent society, this technological kindergarten where the first faltering steps to an everlastingly expanding Gross National Product were taken, this beginning of the rainbow at whose end lay buried the crock of gold, the green stick, holding the secret of perpetual happiness for everyone? I thought not; it was a falling citadel, at the mercy of any marauder; the piled up debris of a greedy past, inhabited by ghosts demanding rights that were already lost and their fair share of wealth already squandered. I had resolved to go to where I thought a new age was coming to pass; to Moscow and the future of mankind. Crozier was all too ready to expedite my going; *The Guardian*'s Moscow correspondent, William Henry Chamberlin, was going back to America for a lengthy stay, and I could take his place. So it was arranged.

Kitty had gone to stay with her parents in Vevey, in one of those hotels overlooking the Lake of Geneva from whose terrace Mrs Dobbs could continue to add to her collection of paintings of the Castle of Chillon. I joined her there for a short holiday before we left for Moscow. Our son was already placed at a school in Windermere where he was to stay until we were settled in Moscow and could fetch him over. It was an arrangement hateful at the time, and seems even more hateful in retrospect. On the Channel boat I ran into Arthur Henderson who had been MacDonald's Foreign Secretary. Refusing to follow him into the National Government, he had lost his seat in the recent General Election, and was now on his way to preside over the opening session of the Disarmament Conference in Geneva, having been elected President on Briand's recommendation before the electoral debacle. A former Liberal Party agent, a lay preacher, an eminently respectable figure wearing a bowler hat, a decent overcoat and suit, his face was full of woe and bewilderment. We walked up and down the deck together, and every now and again he paused, as though collecting his thoughts; took off his bowler and muttered more to himself than to me: 'The unemployed in Burnley voted against me!' It seemed like a perfect finale to all our revolutionary postures and hopes; our renderings of 'The Red Flag' and the 'Internationale', the canvassing, the addressing and the licking, the speaking and the cheering. All ending in one broken-hearted, bewildered little man taking off his bowler hat on a Channel steamer on his way to Geneva, as he remembered once again that the unemployed in Burnley had voted Tory.

5 *Who Whom?*

I no longer wished for a better world, because I was thinking of the whole of creation, and in the light of this clearer discernment I had come to see that, though the higher things are better than the lower, the sum of all creation is better than the higher things alone.

– St Augustine

KITTY AND I were confident that going to Russia would prove to be a definitive step, a final adventure. Our plan was, as soon as we were settled, to fetch our son over and live there for evermore. We wanted him, we told everyone with great emphasis, to grow up in a sane world with a future instead of in our crazy run-down one with only a past. What we were leaving behind, we felt, was derelict, moribund. A preposterous Ramsay MacDonald grimacing and posturing, contemptuously retained in office by his political adversaries for a little while longer so as to hold up to ridicule everything the political movement which made him Prime Minister in the first place, had ever stood for or aspired after. The depression hanging like a dark cloud over the industrial North, Lancashire especially; *The Guardian* under Crozier abysmally second-rate and flat; another war looming, which would surely come, and complete the moral and material destruction of the previous one. Where we were going, we assured ourselves and one another, there was hope and exhilaration. It was the wave of the future – a phrase even then current.

Feeling so, we sold off pretty well everything we had, making, as it were, a bonfire of all our bourgeois trappings; my dinner-jacket, for instance, and Kitty's only long dress, as well as some little trinkets and oddments, and most of our books, which we considered to be bourgeois literature of no relevance in a Workers' State. We even wound up our bank account, taking what money we had – some two hundred pounds, as I recall – in traveller's cheques. What possible use would a bank account be in a country where bankers, along with industrialists, landlords and priests, had all been eliminated? I took particular pleasure in jettisoning our marriage lines, and my ridiculous B.A. hood and certificate; these being also, in my eyes, badges of bourgeois servitude, now to be discarded for ever. We were fully prepared to exchange our British passports for Soviet ones; indeed, we were looking forward to making the exchange. Nor did I have any anxiety about going off *The Guardian*'s pay-roll and becoming dependent on freelance earnings; the arrangement Crozier had proposed. The connection with the paper would only be useful while I was fixing myself up with a job and somewhere to live in the USSR; then, I looked forward to forgetting *The Guardian*'s very existence. Finally, to my great delight, Kitty was pregnant again, so that our next child would be born a Soviet citizen. It all seemed wonderful.

One last thing remained to be done; before sailing for Leningrad, we felt we must pay a farewell visit to Passfield to receive the blessing of the venerable couple under whose sponsorship we were venturing into the New Civilisation they had proclaimed. For us, it was the laying on of hands. 'Sidney and I,' Mrs Webb had told me, 'have become ikons in the Soviet Union.' Kitty and I hoped to participate in this sanctity they had acquired by virtue of the fact that Lenin, while a political prisoner in Siberia, had translated their *The Theory and Practice of Trade Unionism* into Russian – an example of the quality of boredom being twice blessed.

Everything at Passfield was just the same. Webb, complacently stroking his goatee beard, explained how under capitalism there might be as many as thirty or more varieties of fountain pen, whereas in the USSR we should find but one. A much more satisfactory arrangement. As he made the point, his bulbous eyes positively glowed behind the pince-nez. She, fluttering her hands like a mesmerist to shut him up, spoke about Man as consumer and Man as producer, and how under Socialism ever the twain should meet. He was seemingly delighted by the notion of reducing a plethora of pens to a single one, but she, it seemed to me, had no real interest in consuming and producing Man, and only addressed herself to the theme with the distracted over-emphasis of a sceptical Monsignor dispensing the Blessed Sacraments.

The Soviet Ambassador, Sokolnikov, and his lady came to luncheon on the Saturday, arriving in a sleek black limousine driven by an Embassy chauffeur, he doubtless being, as I came to realise later, the GPU policeman in attendance. At the time, I just marvelled at how, as my mother would have put it, wonderfully superior he was, and wondered how he would make out with the two Scottish maids, accustomed, as they were, to capitalist subservience. Actually, I don't believe he addressed a single word to them, but just sat in the car, a still, ininscrutable figure, until the time came to depart.

Sokolnikov was a pasty-faced, uneasy looking man. At one point he had been concerned with stabilising the rouble, which greatly appealed to Webb, who tried, as far as I could judge without much success, to pump him on Soviet banking. He clearly hoped to hear that the same simplification prevailed in distributing cash in the USSR as in distributing fountain pens. An important factor in the admiration of the Webbs and Shaw for the Soviet régime was what they considered to be its financial soundness and rectitude. Shaw was always going on about its budgetary surpluses in a world of deficit accounting, and the Webbs actually held some Soviet Government stock on which, they would complacently observe, the ten per cent interest was punctually paid. How far this stock represented a negotiable asset when they died, only their heirs, the Passfield Trust, and the governors of the London School of Economics, know; but it is possible to guess.

Mme Sokolnikova was livelier altogether than her spouse; a large ebullient woman, dark and hairy, who, had she been English, might well have espoused the cause of family planning, and perhaps married a clergyman. If American, I see her more as a popular novelist in the style of Mrs Parkinson Keyes; or maybe an anthropologist exploring the sexual ways of Papuans in the manner of Margaret Mead. In the circumstances of our meeting, I found her rather attractive; there is, I fear, an incipient gigolo in my make-up, and I have been conscious occasionally of an unseemly taste for public ladies like millionairesses, and female racing-motorists, politicians, and champion show-jumpers. Amy Johnson's rusty voice took my fancy in her flying days, as did Eva Peron, but not, I am happy to say, La Passionaria or the Duchess of Windsor. Mme Sokolnikova had already had one of her books – a collection of profiles of revolutionary women, including Charlotte Corday – published in England, which, by a fortunate chance, I had read and reviewed in favourable terms in *The Guardian*. It was arranged that Kitty and I should call on the Sokolnikovs in Moscow, whither they were shortly returning, to be succeeded in London by Maisky, one of those indomitable survivors the Soviet régime throws up from time to time (Ilya Ehrenburg was another), who somehow managed to survive despite all the perils and dangers of life under Stalin. By writing occasional letters to *The Times* in support of the latest version of Party orthodoxy, Maisky even continues to have some sort of public existence, unlike more important figures like Molotov and Malenkov who, when they fall from power, get obliterated.

We did go and see the Sokolnikovs at their flat in Moscow. The Purges were looming, and there had been rumours of his arrest. The poor fellow looked very nervous and shifty, and there was a noticeable greenish tinge in his sallow face. He kept glancing anxiously over his shoulder as though at some invisible intruder. With one of the most mirthless smiles I have ever seen, he remarked over tea that, if the capitalist press was to be believed, he was languishing in Lubianka Prison. Did he look like it? he asked, getting his teeth into a chocolate eclair. Alas, he did, and I was not surprised to hear, in due course, that he had been liquidated, not even being considered important enough for rehabilitation when the climate of opinion changed under Khrushchev. She, too, disappeared for a twenty years' sentence, but to everyone's amazement reappeared, to resume her career as a woman-of-letters. Survival would seem to be the single enduring gift we humans possess, especially among the female of the species; providing the only sure foundation for Women's Lib.

After luncheon, we were joined in the course of the afternoon by Sir Stafford Cripps, another member of the Potter clan, accompanied by the chairman of his constituency (Bristol East) Labour Party, whose name Mrs Webb made little effort to discover. There was also present a grey-haired nondescript lady in sackcloth and gold chains from the Fabian Research Bureau. She must have had more audacity than her appearance suggested because she took one of Mrs Webb's herbal cigarettes and smoked it – something I had never before seen anyone do. As usual, Mrs Webb disposed us about the room like a cricket captain arranging his field, and then the conversation got under way. We began with participatory democracy, which, the Webbs insisted, was perfectly exemplified in the system of representation laid down in the Soviet Constitution. As they elaborated upon this theme, I could see that Sokolnikov was trying to say something; his lips were moving and his hands gripping the sides of his chair. By the time he managed to get the words out against the Webbs' duet – like a muted trombone and a particularly shrill flute – he was understood to say that his country made no bones about being a . . . Even then he could not bring himself to say it in English. So he tried it in French . . . a *dictature*. The word caused a stir even in French; Webb paused in mid-sentence, and then changed direction, going on to point out that, like the Roman Catholic Church, the Soviet system was hierarchical. This parallel with the Church, equating Commissars in the Politbureau with Cardinals in the Consistory, got over any awkwardness the Ambassador's hasty remark might have occasioned.

Cripps looked delighted; he stroked his jaw as counsel do when making an advantageous point in court. *Dictature* or dictatorship, it was all one to him. How is it, Dr Johnson asked, in *Taxation no Tyranny*, that we hear the loudest yelps for liberty coming from the drivers of slaves? How indeed? One might equally well ask how it is that those with the greatest aptitude for applauding the arbitrary exercise of power are most insistent in proclaiming the virtues of freedom. Cripps went on to explain that social democracy was now discredited, that what was needed was a revolutionary dictatorship enabling the workers to take over. Mrs Webb did not fancy being lectured by a nephew, especially in terms that, if only by implication, put her among the despised Social Democrats, rather than with the proletarian elect, and anyway suggested that her ideas were behind the times. Even so, Cripps was in the category of being 'a very clever young man', and earned enough at the bar to qualify for equal billing with her successful brothers-in-law. So she left him unrebuked, and there the matter rested. Sokolnikov, having made his point about the *Dictature*, relapsed into silence, and the Webbs turned their attention to Consumers' Co-operatives, which ensured, they intoned, that the interests of the consumer were adequately safeguarded as against those of the producer and the State. Cripps scarcely seemed to be listening; his thoughts were doubtless far away – on a barricade, Red Flag in hand, leading the oppressed to revolution and freedom. Stafford Egalité.

The Sokolnikovs left in the early evening; Cripps and his local party chairman shortly afterwards. Webb soon began to doze noisily in his chair, fulfilling Mrs Webb's favourite dictum about him: 'Sidney snores!' She sat warming her hands at the fire, holding them out as though warding someone or something off. 'It's true,' she said suddenly, *à propos* of nothing, 'that in the USSR people *disappear*.' She accentuated the word, showing her teeth as she did so. Clearly, she would have been well content to promote the disappearance of tiresome people in the asme expeditious way, with no questions asked. Some of the more difficult and obscurantist figures in local government, for instance. And among trade union leaders, no lack of candidates. Yes, people *disappeared*. She looked very unearthly just then, with her white hair and white face. Very unsubstantial. It was probably, I reflected, my positively last glimpse of her and of bourgeois life; and I wanted to fix the scene in my mind so that I should never forget it. Webb asleep in his arm-chair, grunting occasionally; the glowing fire, the sofa, the little tables and knick-knacks and photographs in silver frames. The warmth, the snugness; the wonderful insulation from what is harsh and bitter and inexorable. Those two Scottish maids sitting by *their* fire and in their own arm-chairs, but ready at any moment to spring into action, and make a hot drink or prepare a hot water-bottle. Mrs Webb hovering over it all, the genie escaped from the bottle; pronouncing a doom – that in the USSR people *disappeared*, as would we all, along with that room, that whole way of life. Set, scenery, actors and props, all due for disappearance.

On the Sunday morning the Webbs came to the front door to see us off. It was an unusual attention; except in the case of particularly important visitors, adieus took place in the sitting-room. This was a special occasion; we were going to the USSR where they were ikons. Standing side by side, she looked ridiculously tall and thin, and he squat, almost a dwarf. As the ancient limousine lurched forward to take us to the station, they waved in unison. Standing behind them, also discreetly waving, we could see the two Scottish maids. So, from this warm, snug bourgeois nest we took off on our migratory flight, saying to ourselves with the monkish author of *The Cloud of Unknowing*: 'Look now forwards, and let the backwards be.'

Sailing down the Thames again, this time with Kitty beside me, in the Soviet ship *Kooperatsia*, there was the same sweet music I remembered from when I set sail for India – a prow piercing the water; a ship's stealthily onward push as it followed its determined course. The sweet music of departure. This time I was on my way, not to tired imperial glory, but to the veritable future of mankind. Our ship's Red Flag flying proudly at the very heart of London; within sight of Westminster and Honourable Members on their terrace; within sound of their division bell and Big Ben; the Unholy City, gathered by the Thames, harbouring, without knowing it, this crimson portent of the wrath to come.

Kitty and I waited on deck as long as there was anything to see, and then explored the ship. Somehow, we expected it to be different from other ships, but apart from having a picture of Lenin and Stalin in the dining saloon where a P & O boat would have had one of King George V and Queen Mary, it seemed in no way peculiar. I even noticed that the ship's engines had been made in Glasgow. It was, in fact, a pre-Revolution ship that had been taken over by the Soviet authorities and renamed. Our cabin was deep in the bowels; we had booked in the cheapest category, for economy's sake, and also because it seemed appropriate. The more privileged passengers in the upper regions consisted mostly of a party of miscellaneous Leftist intellectuals, or, as they were later to be called, Fellow-Travellers, on their way to see for themselves what the world's first Workers' State was really like. They recalled lectures in Croydon with my father in the chair, and visits to our house afterwards. Several were already well on the way to becoming important personages; beneficiaries of the new enlightenment, honoured, comfortably off even; in due course, persistent pundits of the air. The *Kooperatsia* echoed with their resonant, donnish-demagogic voices; their tweedy suits and coloured ties were everywhere. They had the shambling gait, the roving eye, the air of being the elect or chosen ones, which I had come to associate with those who felt they knew the answers, and could steer us aright to peace, prosperity and the everlasting brotherhood of man.

On their way to the USSR they were in a festive mood; like a cup-tie party on their way to a match, equipped with rattles, coloured scarves and favours. Each of them harbouring in his mind some special hope; of meeting Stalin, or, alternatively, of falling in with a Komsomolka, sparkling eyed, red scarf and jet black hair, dancing the *carmagnole*; above all, with very enlightened views on sex, and free and easy ways. In any case, of equipping themselves with special, authoritative knowledge which would enable them to embellish their articles and lectures, and shut up hecklers with lordly data like: Dairy produce increased last year in the Ukraine by X per cent; slightly less in White Russia, but still well above the national average of Y per cent. Or: article PQR of the Criminal Code clearly states . . . Oh, to be in Russia, now that Stalin's there.

In their dealings with the crew and the stewards they were punctilious in cultivating an egalitarian attitude; the word 'comrade' was often on their lips. What a relief it was, they seemed to be saying, not to have to cope with obsequiousness and servility on the part of the lower orders! In this new society, as most of them would shortly be tapping out on their typewriters, 'there was an agreeable absence of cap-touching. One noticed a certain confident bearing among working men and women; a new social equality divorced from a worship and evaluation of success in money terms, and from deference to the man who has won a financial position above his fellows and shows it in his habits and dress and bearing . . .'

In order to fit in with this social climate it was obviously necessary to eschew tips, which anyway, we were given to understand, were considered gross and ill-mannered, and, especially to the younger Soviet citizens, nurtured in the régime, quite inadmissible, if not incomprehensible. To settle the matter a meeting of passengers was called, presided over by one of the intellectuals with a particularly booming voice, at which it was decided that the best procedure would be to make a collection for the crew and officers, and to spend it on books for the ship's library. This was explained to the chief steward, who, as it seemed to me, failed to kindle at the suggestion. Perhaps he dreaded, not without reason, that some at least of the books provided would be works by the present company. To clinch the matter, and to show our good will and high spirits, it was further decided to present a pageant or charade for the diversion of the crew. The subject chosen was the Genesis story of the creation, with the booming intellectual as God, and a Montessori teacher from Leeds as the serpent. Such a theme, it was calculated, would conform with the anti-religious sentiments of our audience, and show them that, however bourgeois we might seem outwardly, at heart we were as proletarian and anti-religious as they were.

When it came to the night, the performance seemed to please the players better than the audience, who for the most part sat woodenly in their seats, more bewildered than amused. God, it must be admitted, was somewhat elephantine in his antics; the serpent lacking in the deadly attractiveness which the Genesis original must be supposed to have possessed. It proved to be a *mea culpa* which quite failed to register with those for whose edification it had been intended; an unheeded act of abasement. The crew retaliated by offering a musical evening at which *Stenka Razin* and *Ochi Chornye* were sung; two songs that were to become all too familiar in the months ahead. One of the sorrows of life for a western journalist or diplomat in the USSR was the enormous repetitiveness of everything. Thus, there were veterans who had been forced to sit through *Swan Lake* on thirty or more ceremonial occasions. I myself sat through it five times; it seemed like fifty.

These fellow-passengers provided my first experience of the progressive elite from all over the world who attached themselves to the Soviet régime, resolved to believe anything they were told by its spokesmen. For the most part, they were academics and writers – the clerks of Julien Benda's *La Trahison des clercs*; all upholders of progressive causes and members of progressive organisations, constituting a sort of Brechtian ribald chorus in the drama of the twentieth century. Ready at any moment to rush on to the stage, cheering and gesticulating. The fall guys of history; a western version of the devotees of Krishna who throw themselves under the wheels of the great Juggernaut. I was to speculate endlessly about them, rail against their credulities and imbecilities, ridicule their absurdities and denounce their servility before the naked-ness of Soviet power. The more so because I knew inwardly that I was one of them; in my heart, too, the same death-wish.

It was perhaps because such thoughts had already begun to occur to me, or, more probably, because of a certain drabness in the ship itself and in the crew, an air of oppression which seemed to hang over it and them, that somehow or other I felt less confident than I had about the Soviet régime as an answer to my own and society's problems. As we approached Leningrad my excitement at the thought of actually landing, and putting to the test all my hopes, was tinged with apprehension. This was intensified by an incident while we were at Hamburg, where we put in for a day to take on some cargo. I was loafing about on deck as the time of departure drew near when I noticed three men, arm in arm, coming up the gangway. The middle one was the ship's doctor, whose face I knew, having observed it at times rather closely as being somehow like Chekhov's. With the same kind of sparse beard, and loose, whim-sical, weak mouth; even with the same kind of spectacles fastened on the end of his long nose, and thin cigar drooping from his lips, the ash powdering his beard. There was also the fact that he was different from the crew, who all had what I came to recognise as Soviet faces; as characteristic as the equivalent American ones – rather grey and im-mobile, like lumps of stone on which features had been drawn, rather than living flesh. The doctor's face was, on the other hand, mobile and European, and would have passed unnoticed in any café in Paris or Brussels or London.

On this occasion he was obviously hopelessly drunk; his head lolled, his eyes were dead, his legs scarcely touched the ground. It was clear that without the support of his two companions he would have fallen down. They held him firmly; not tenderly, or in a comradely way, more in the manner of policemen. I had noticed them about the ship, too, as seeming not to be ordinary seamen or officers; yet obviously exercising authority. Like the Sokolnikovs' chauffeur, they were doubtless GPU men, keeping an eye on everyone's orthodoxy and correct Soviet behaviour. It seemed to me that once they had got the doctor to his berth things might go ill with him. In any case, the incident depressed me out of all proportion to its ostensible importance. I priggishly felt that Soviet ships' doctors should not go ashore and get drunk like capitalist ones. Also, there was something Kafka-esque about the stance and relationship of the three of them which struck me as sinister; and as conflicting with the happier relationship between man and man over which we had so often cooed together at Passfield.

I had the feeling that landing at Leningrad should be different from landing anywhere else; more like the arrival of Bunyan's Pilgrim at the Heavenly City, with trumpets blowing, and shining ones waiting to welcome him. Actually, it was just like arriving anywhere; passports suspiciously examined, bags all opened and their contents gone over; then a final check to make sure that everything was in order. The custodians of entry and exit seem alike in every country and on every frontier. All the same, it was a wonderful feeling to be through the controls at last and at large in the USSR. Something I had dreamed about and longed for, and now at last it had come to pass.

Leningrad seemed a battered, shabby place, with crumbling stucco, chipped pillars, cracked masonry, paintwork in sore need of renovation; yet nonetheless somehow beautiful in the sparkling sunshine. In the streets few vehicles, on the pavement grey anonymous crowds padding endlessly along; the one constant factor throughout the USSR. I had a feeling that the place must have been lately bombarded, with only a bright shell remaining; which doubtless explains why the memory of my first glimpse of Leningrad came so vividly into my mind during the Blitz in London. Likewise, going into New York on just such a glittering day, and getting my first glimpse of the city across the Triboro Bridge, its skyscrapers, too, looked like the bombed out remains of once stately buildings arbitrarily arranged to be some weird, monstrous, luminous Stonehenge. It recalled what Brecht wrote: 'Long before the bombers appeared our cities were already uninhabitable . . . While we were still walking in our still upright cities our women were widows and our children orphans.'

In Moscow we took up our quarters in the Nova Moskovkaya Hotel, newly built for Intourists who came and went all the time. Quite often hanging about the lobby was a man named Wicksteed, vaguely known to Kitty from her Bedales schooldays. He was a Walt Whitmanesque figure, in a corduroy suit, with a high colour, an untidy beard, watery eyes, and wearing sandals, who had, it seemed, steered a course from Blake's Prophetic Books to Edward Carpenter's *Towards Democracy*, taking in Havelock Ellis and Housman (Laurence rather than A.E.) on the way, and casting many a sympathetic backwards glance in the direction of William Morris and even Ruskin. *Towards Democracy* turned out to be, as far as he was concerned, *Towards Moscow*, and there he stayed, sometimes with a burly Red Army soldier in tow; acting as a sort of unofficial tourist guide, glad to get a meal in the hotel restaurant and a drink or two in the hotel bar by way of remuneration. A bourgeois bum in Proletaria – spare a kopek, comrade! Broken down and pathetic, vodka-smelling, far from his native habitat of PEN Club meetings within sound of Sloane Square, and there's wind on the Hampstead Heath, brother; but still more sympathetic to me than the booming intellectual playing God and the Montessori serpent.

In order to start working as *Guardian* correspondent it was necessary to establish contact with the Press Department of the Soviet Foreign Office, housed, it turned out, in ornate gilt and red plush quarters unchanged from pre-Revolution days; more reminiscent in décor of the Egyptian University, or even the Vatican, than of a Workers' State as I had envisaged it. After a wait, I was shown into the office of the head of the Department, a youngish-looking man named Oumansky with crinkly hair and a lot of gold teeth. He later became Soviet Ambassador in Washington, and was killed in an air crash on his way to Mexico, to the undisguised joy of pretty well everyone who had worked as a newspaper correspondent in Moscow. He greeted me affably, complimented me on my connection with the Webbs who, he said, were held in great honour in the USSR, and spoke of *The Guardian* in the highest terms as being the newspaper above all others in the capitalist world which gave a true and fair picture of Soviet conditions and achievements. He felt sure I would maintain and enhance this reputation, and looked forward to our continuing collaboration. The gold teeth gleamed as he summoned up a toothy smile.

Being a newspaper correspondent in Moscow, I found, was, in itself, easy enough. The Soviet press was the only source of news; nothing happened or was said until it was reported in the newspapers. So, all I had to do was to go through the papers, pick out any item that might be interesting to readers of the *Guardian*, dish it up in a suitable form, get it passed by the censor at the Press Department, and hand it in at the telegraph office for dispatch. One might, if in a conscientious mood, embellish the item a little with back references or some extra statistics, easily procured from the Commercial Attaché at the British Embassy, where also the Press was meticulously gone through and analysed. Or perhaps, fancifully, sow in a little local colour, usually unobjectionable to the censor. Blow it up a little, or render it down a little according to the exigencies of the new situation. The original item itself was almost certainly untrue or grotesquely distorted. One's own deviations, therefore, seemed to matter little; only amounting to further falsifying what was already false.

This bizarre fantasy was very costly and elaborate and earnestly promoted. Something gets published in *Pravda* (meaning Truth); say, that the Soviet Union has had a bumper wheat harvest – so many poods per hectare. (It is always preferable to use foreign measures where possible.) There is no means of checking; the Press Department men don't know, and anyone who does is far, far removed from the attentions of foreign journalists. Soviet statistics have always been almost entirely fanciful, though not the less seriously regarded for that. When the Germans occupied Kiev in the 1939–45 war they got hold of a master Five-Year Plan, showing what had really been produced and where. Needless to say, it was quite different from the published figures. This in no way affected credulity about such figures subsequently, as put out in Russia, or even in China; any more than the repeated errors of public opinion polls affect the seriousness with which they are received. Truly, those who take to statistics will perish by statistics.

So we take the bumper harvest as having happened. The more ebullient drum it up a little – 'Down in the Ukraine husky girls and women hoisting wheat . . . Village markets flowing with eggs, fruit, poultry, vegetables, milk and butter at prices far lower than in Moscow . . .' The more sedate tone it down a little – 'The figure should be received with some caution in the light of present Soviet imports of grain, but without any doubt the collectivisation policy is beginning to pay off . . .' In any case, a statistic has been planted, and makes its appearance in tables, graphs, learned discourses, becoming part of the world's wisdom. In the beginning was the Lie, and the Lie was made news and dwelt among us, graceless and false.

I have a pile of the blacks of some of the messages I sent to *The Guardian* from Moscow:

DISCOVERY ANNOUNCED BY OGPU OF COUNTER REVOLUTIONARY ORGANISATION IN AGRICULTURE AND STATE FARM COMMISSARIATS PARTICULARLY IN UKRAINE NORTH CAUCASUS AND WHITE RUSSIA STOP NEWSPAPER REPORT SAYS ORGANISATION CONSISTED MOSTLY EXBOURGEOIS STATE OFFICIALS COLON MAJORITY CONFESSED GUILTY SABOTAGE WITH VIEW UNDERMINING SOVIET AGRICULTURAL ECONOMY AND SPREADING FAMINE . . .

FULL DETAILS 1933 ECONOMIC PROGRAMME AND BUDGET

PUBLISHED TO-DAY AS APPROVED CENTRAL EXECUTIVE COM-
MITTEE STOP IN INDUSTRY GENERALLY GROSS INCREASE ON
LAST YEAR PRODUCTION SIXTEEN POINT FIVE PER CENT
COLON ALLOCATION THREE MILLIARD ROUBLES TRANSPORT
DEVELOPMENT AND TWO MILLIARDS AND HALF SOCIAL SER-
VICES AND HOUSING COLON STATE FARM OUTPUT PRECISELY
ESTIMATED DASH FOR INSTANCE MILLION HUNDRED AND
FIFTY THOUSAND PIGS THIS YEAR STOP ESTIMATED
REVENUE THIRTY FIVE MILLIARDS AND EXPENDITURE THIRTY
THREE MILLIARDS OF WHICH TWO AND QUARTER MILLIARDS
ON FIGHTING SERVICES . . .

To the last figure for military expenditure I added in brackets
SUGGEST TELLING THIS MARINES. The significance of the addition
escaped the censor's eye; whether it caught that of *The Guardian* chief
sub I never heard.

I was still thinking of such work as merely provisional, and it had
been on the tip of my tongue to tell Oumansky that I was not really a
foreign correspondent but a comrade who had come to the USSR to
help build Socialism. Somehow, he did not seem to be the man, nor was
the occasion apposite; he looked so like a bank manager that he put me
more in a mood to ask for an overdraft than for citizenship in the
Kingdom of Heaven on Earth. Subsequently, I could feel my resolution
ebbing away, and basic questions about the whole validity of the Soviet
régime began to arise insistently in my mind. These doubts I wrestled
with while walking round the Red Square or passing through Lenin's
tomb; a spectacle of which I never tired. The little man in his glass case,
pink head resting on a red cushion, beard carefully trimmed, small hands
clenched, finger-nails daintily manicured; the khaki tunic with its single
decoration seeming to have nothing inside it – no body; just a head, and
that empty, the brain having been removed for separate examination
and preservation. Was he not the very materialist conception of history
in person? An empty skull embalmed in a vacuum to last for ever. Made
immortal. All day long there were people filing past, mostly peasants;
they just stared at him without showing any signs of emotion, though
once I saw an old peasant woman cross herself. Heaven knows what that
signified, if anything. For a short while he shared the tomb with Stalin,
his successor. I saw Stalin there, as it happened, during his short co-
occupancy. With his thick black moustache he looked almost jovial by
comparison with Lenin. Then he was turned out, and Lenin again left
in his solitary glory.

I never missed a chance of walking round the Red Square; fascinated by the massive Kremlin buildings, so extravagant a fortress, now housing, not an anointed king or emperor, not, like the White House, an elected President, nor, like the Vatican, a Pope chosen from among a College of Cardinals, but the Dictatorship of the Proletariat. This was authority in terms of a quite new abstraction, embodying a claim far transcending Louis XIV's *L'Etat, c'est moi*. *Le peuple, c'est moi*; that's what the ruler in the Kremlin claimed for himself. All the toiling masses everywhere, their will, their purpose, their very being, embodied in this one man, who spoke and acted, and even lived, on their behalf. And everyone else – kulaks, White Guards, Black Hundreds, down to Mr Pooters of the *Diary of a Nobody*, adding up their figures, puffing at their pipes, and maybe dropping a fishing line into the water on a Sunday afternoon – must be abolished. Then, at last, when this was accomplished, history would be over, and paradise have come to earth, and the Dictatorship of the Proletariat, in the person of the man in the Kremlin, reign for evermore.

The Red Flag flying above the Kremlin was illuminated at night; a little pool of blood suspended in the darkness. This was the true image of the Revolution; the mysticism of power, equivalent of the mysticism of sex in the other part of the world. Power versus sex. What I was looking for in the USSR – liberty, equality, fraternity – was irrelevant; just as the happiness Americans were under a statutory obligation to pursue, was irrelevant. The Knout or the Phallus – in any such contest, surely the knout must win. Opposite the Kremlin the onion domes of a sometime cathedral formed weird swollen shadows against the sky. Now it had become an anti-God Museum, with a great pendulum swinging to and fro to demonstrate the force of gravity in refutation of claims made on behalf of any divinity purporting to shape our ends. There were also fossilised saints on display, once fraudulently claimed to have been miraculously preserved against the ravages of time. Was the swinging pendulum, I asked myself, more god-like than the God it confuted? And that other contemporary saint across the way, preserved in his glass case – was he less fraudulent than the fossilised saints? The whole scene seemed abstract; like one of those models set up on army intelligence courses to demonstrate how a battle should be fought. But a battle between whom? About what?

For comfort I turned, as usual, to the streets, where the endless stream of anonymous people were somehow companionable, as the pendulum god and the refrigerated saint were not. Grey-faced; as winter came on, in padded coats and felt boots, their footfall mysteriously silent in the snow – they, too, seemed to be coming from nowhere and making for nowhere. Just drifting inscrutably along. There was little to look at in the shops except wooden cheeses and cardboard intimations of plenty to come. No neon lights, no spelt out pleasures; no whiff of flesh or snatch of music as a swing-door opened and shut. All drab and grey and restrained. And yet I had a feeling, stronger than I can possibly convey, that what was happening in Moscow must happen everywhere. That it was the focal point or pivot of the drama of our times, whose essential pattern was being shaped there. That these blank faces processing noiselessly through Moscow's blank streets were mankind processing through the twentieth century.

So it has proved to be. The Revolution has triumphed in an unexpected way, its ferment working rather through history than through the minds and hearts of men; its enemies' citadel surrendering, and the garrison opening the gates and putting out white flags, without any need for a siege or an assault. Jericho's walls tumbling down of their own decay before any trumpet sounded. So, the priests have chosen themselves to turn their churches into anti-God museums; and the image of our well-being and our plenty is shown in living colour on the television screen, like the wooden cheeses and the cardboard plenty in the Moscow shops. Above all, there were the *besprizorne*; the uncared for, or wild ones. These were children who had survived on their own, without parents or anyone else to look after them, from the famine and civil war of the twenties. Going about in packs, barely articulate or recognisably human, with pinched animal faces, tangled hair and empty eyes. I saw them in Moscow and Leningrad, clustered under bridges, lurking in railway stations, suddenly emerging like a pack of wild monkeys; then scattering and disappearing. I was to see them again in years to come on campuses anywhere between the Berlin Wall and the Pacific coast of America; waifs of plenty, spoilt children of affluence, graduate Calibans, with the same tangled hair and animal faces; likewise barely articulate, barely human.

Kitty and I continued to live in the Nova Moskovkaya, while making desultory efforts to find other accommodation. This involved visiting numerous apartment blocks where rentable rooms were allegedly available. They invariably turned out to be part of a room, with, at best, the possibility of hanging a blanket to curtain off the portion offered us, and the use of corporate cooking and washing facilities. I have often regretted that we did not have a go at living in this way, which was how the great majority of Soviet citizens lived. With Kitty increasingly pregnant, however, and the necessity I was under to do a lot of typing, it seemed as though it would have been an impossible arrangement. Our quest did at any rate give us a notion of what housing conditions were really like in Moscow. Only important officials like the Sokolnikovs and rich writers like Ehrenburg, enjoyed the luxury of apartments to themselves. Ehrenburg's flat actually had some Impressionist paintings – otherwise banned in the USSR – hanging in it. He also had a country residence near Moscow where, when I once visited him, he showed me with great pride a plant in his greenhouse that had been presented to him by the Queen Mother of Belgium. Later, we went for a stroll, and he pointed out to me nostalgically the house in which a rich merchant named Morosov had lived, entertaining the revolutionary intelligentsia like himself there at elegant evening soirées, and arranging amateur presentations of Chekov's plays; subsequently committing suicide.

Each morning a Russian woman named Klavdia Lvovna came to give Kitty and me a Russian lesson, and to read over the newspapers with me. She was a person of indeterminate age; she might have been forty or twenty, there was no telling. In ordinary circumstances one might have taken her for a governess or lady's companion. She had a high, piping voice and the nebulous colouring and dry texture of someone who has faded without ripening. There was something very ludicrous, and even at times vaguely tragic, in her high piping voice reading over to me in halting English the turgid, portentous, and often inflammatory sentences of some *Pravda* or *Iszvestia* article. Like playing 'Land of Hope and Glory' on a piccolo. Thus, she would begin: 'Comrade Stalin, addressing the Central Committee yesterday, declared that the world had never before seen so powerful and authoritarian a régime as the Soviet régime, or so powerful and authoritarian a party as our Bolshevik Party . . .' As she read one, she often faltered, appalled, and perhaps also frightened, at so unimportant and timid a person as herself getting involved in these weighty, explosive matters; then would summon up her courage and resolution to continue: 'Communists go on hunting for kulaks with beastly faces, red necks, harsh voices and guns like those on our posters; but present-day kulaks are quiet, sweet, almost holy men sitting inside collective farms as managers, secretaries, etc., leading village communists by the nose . . .'

She had to read it over again slowly while I tapped it out on my typewriter for the delectation of *Guardian* readers. Poor Klavdia Lvovna had no concern with kulaks, whether red-necked or quiet and sweet; it was all beyond her. Her interest lay in a few old dog-eared Russian classics she had managed to keep – Gogol, Goncharov, Lermontov – and the clandestine practice of Russian Orthodox Christianity. She would not accept any money for her services, but took payment in food, which I was able to get from a special shop for diplomats and journalists where one could buy for roubles more or less anything one wanted. Later, it was abolished in favour of Torgsin shops which only accepted foreign currency or the equivalent in jewels or precious metals. Their windows were full of otherwise unobtainable foods – hams and cheeses and butter – to induce Soviet citizens to bring out their secret hoards, or solicit money from their relatives and friends abroad. When they succumbed, it quite often happened that they were arrested for hoarding or having contacts with foreigners.

When Klavdia Lvovna got to know me better she told me that the food I gave her was passed on to a nun who, though her order had long ago been dissolved, still continued to observe her vows and engage in works of charity. Somehow this nun managed to send on the food she got from Klavdia Lvovna to fellow-nuns and other religious serving sentences in labour camps. Now I feel remorse that I did not help Klavdia Lvovna more; I may even have got her into trouble by the things I wrote after I left the USSR. Unfortunately, I never liked her; there was something mousy and prim and – absurdly enough in that particular setting – even snobbish about her which irritated me. Most of the translators and secretaries of the other foreign journalists in Moscow, I may add, were cast in a very different stamp. Blousy, brassy Red geisha girls; wearing unproletarian silk stockings, bras and underwear specially imported for them by their bosses, sometimes in diplomatic bags. Reputedly easy bedfellows who compensated for their deviant capitalistic ways by reporting regularly what they saw and heard to the GPU.

The housing situation was just becoming critical for Kitty and me – we were under notice to leave the Nova Moskovkaya – when we had the good fortune to make the acquaintance of Herr Schmidt, a German business man, at a party at the French Embassy. Such parties took place at one embassy or another almost every evening, and reminded me very much of the British Raj; more or less the same guests turned up at all of them – and one had the same feeling, as in India, of being a little privileged isolated community having practically no contact with the surrounding country and its people. Ideological sahibs. Herr Schmidt was very well turned out, gold wrist-watch on hairy wrist, sharp close-set eyes and a rather forlorn mouth lurking in the shadow of a large nose. When we told him of our difficulty in finding anywhere to live, he said that he had a dacha not far from Moscow which he only used at week-ends, and that we were welcome to stay there if we wished to while we were looking for suitable accommodation in Moscow. It seemed like a wonderful offer, and we accepted at once. Herr Schmidt kindly said that he would drive us down the next day, which he duly did, arriving at our hotel to pick us up in a smart convertible with a female beside him whom he presented as 'Die Kleine'. We never knew her by any other name; she had bleached hair, long coloured finger-nails, and a body so slender that it seemed surprising that she could, when absolutely necessary, hold herself erect. At the dacha she spent most of the time playing jazz records imported from Germany, and smoking cigarettes in a long holder. Herr Schmidt said that his wife lived in Vienna, and did not find the Russian climate suited to her. It was a set-up which would have been perfectly appropriate anywhere in the world, and Kitty and I endlessly speculated as to what business could put Herr Schmidt in so advantageous a situation. 'Chemicals,' I said, having vaguely gathered something of the sort from Herr Schmidt himself, but Kitty insisted it was just money. It was indeed the case, at that time, that foreign currency was sought after in Moscow with particular assiduity. We had not, after all, escaped from the kingdom of money. There are, I have discovered, certain constants in life which recur in all circumstances, Herr Schmidt and Die Kleine being one of them.

Herr Schmidt's dacha, which now became our home, was at Kliasma. It was a wooden house, rather like a Swiss chalet. There were other similar dachas nearby, but mostly already shut up for the winter. The pine woods round about had many long straight paths through them which I knew, as soon as I saw them, would be my walks. In among the pine trees, too, there was a large clearing obviously intended for recreational purposes, littered with cardboard slogans about building socialism. These had already begun to look rather disconsolate in the cold wind, with dead leaves swirling round them. It was a local version of the parks of culture and rest of which such a feature was made in taking tourists round Moscow, and where, despite the priggish name, on warm evenings lovers found a sanctuary though whether this usage came into the category of culture or of rest I never determined. On some days

Klavdia Lvovna came out to Kliasma, or I would go into Moscow on the electric train; preposterously crowded as all public transport was in the USSR. One just clung on where one could. I was wryly amused to find a picture of this train in a publication called *The USSR in Construction*, captioned: 'Eager Soviet Workers on their Way to the Capital'.

One way and another I managed to send off some articles and messages. The messages, of course, had to be stamped in the Press Department before the telegraph office would accept them. One took them in to be censored, like taking an essay to one's tutor at Cambridge; watching anxiously as they were read over for any frowns or hesitations, dreading to see a pencil picked up to slash something out. Later, the arrangement was changed, so that the journalists just turned in their messages, which were then processed in the Press Department and sent off without any further reference to them. It amounted to a sort of computerisation, in keeping with the exigencies of a technological society.

In my time, there were three censors, all Jews – Podolski, the most intelligent, with sad eyes and a thin pointed beard; Nehman, looking like a Rabbi, with a fringe of beard all round his face, and Ehrens, a ludicrous figure who had been in Magnetogorsk in some capacity or other, as a result of which he affected top boots and a rough pioneering manner which ill became his plump soft person. They all three disappeared into the labour camps in due course, never to be seen again. I was sorry about Podolski, who was really a very nice, intelligent, amusing man. Before the Revolution he had lived abroad, and one could even argue with him when he proposed censoring something. I remember on one occasion his shaking his head and saying to me: 'You can't say that because it's true.' It seemed like a basic twentieth-century text. I always liked to get him for my censor whenever I could; Nehman (described by Mrs Webb as 'that very clever young man') patiently and meticulously trod the Party Line. Ehrens was an oaf. The fact that they were all Jews had no particular significance. With the liquidation of the Russian bourgeoisie, Jews who had good revolutionary credentials, from Litvinov downwards, provided almost the only available personnel for Foreign Office jobs. The only non-Jew I can recall off-hand among Foreign Office personnel was a certain Fleurinski, the Chef-de-Protocol; a caricature of a pre-Revolutionary aristocrat, straight out of *Dead Souls*. He, too, was liquidated; not for being a class enemy, or a capitalist-imperialist running dog, but for pederasty when – to the great distress of, among others, André Gide – the earlier permissive attitude was reversed, and harsh penalties re-imposed against the practice.

Articles one could sometimes send by a diplomatic bag, which, of course, eliminated all censorship. The British were not particularly helpful in this respect, but other embassies were more accommodating. It was an article sent by this means – actually about the Soviet mania for discovering sabotage and treachery on every hand – that led to my first rebuke from Oumansky. He called me to his office, and there he sat looking very grave with the offending article on his desk in front of him. This will never do, he seemed to be saying, shaking his head and showing his gold teeth; and from you of all people! Writing in the sacred columns of the *Manchester Guardian*! With the Webbs' aureole shining about your head! He found particularly offensive my remark that one could say of sabotage in the USSR what Voltaire said of God – that if it did not exist it would be necessary to invent it. Somehow bringing Voltaire, a revolutionary hero, into my squalid argument made the offence worse in his eyes. This time, he indicated, a rebuke would suffice, but if anything of the kind occurred again, more serious consequences would follow.

I swallowed the admonition as best I might. The Soviet authorities were able to control foreign newsmen almost as rigorously as they did their own. They had perforce to live and work in the USSR under the constant threat of losing their visas. If this happened, their jobs automatically came to an end, which in most cases was something they wished to avoid. Also, any foreigner resident in the USSR was vulnerable, in the sense that just going about and displaying ordinary curiosity, in Soviet terms laid one open to a plausible charge of espionage. Then again, we all changed money on the black market, likewise an offence under Soviet law. The official rate of exchange was so unrealistic that it made living costs utterly exorbitant, whereas the black market rate – in my time something like two hundred roubles to the pound – was decidedly advantageous, and easily obtainable at some of the smaller Consulates. One would come away with great wedges of notes loosely wrapped in newspaper like fried fish. Add to this that most foreign correspondents, separated from their wives, acquired a Russian mistress of one sort or another who, if not planted on them by the GPU, was bound to report their doings and transactions. This provided a ready means of exerting pressure on them. Thus, one way and another, they were not free agents, and the messages they sent had to be slanted accordingly.

Newspaper managements and broadcasting agencies have nonetheless been ready to pay out large sums of money to procure this tainted news just in order to be able to say it came from Our Own Correspondent in Moscow. The image is, as always, preferred to the reality. Looking back, I can recall only one sentence I telegraphed from Moscow which was wholly true. It may even be the only wholly true sentence ever to be telegraphed from Moscow. This was when I was temporarily standing in for the correspondent of an American news agency, and received a cable asking for the Soviet man-in-the-street's reactions to the lavish scale of entertaining in Soviet embassies abroad. Without thinking I replied: MAN-IN-STREET'S REACTION STRONG DESIRE GET NEAREST BUFFET. Podolski passed the message with a twinkle in his eye. Such twinkles, I fear, were what cost him his life.

Our life at Kliasma was very happy. Moscow and the Dictatorship of the Proletariat seemed far away; as did the little bearded latter-day saint in his glass case. The great pendulum demonstrating the force of gravity and confuting the existence of God, continued to swing monotonously, but not for us. I had started work on a novel about a liberal newspaper in the north of England (*Picture Palace*), and managed to turn out enough casual material about the USSR to feel that I was earning our keep. A very nice Volga-German woman, Lena, looked after the dacha; Herr Schmidt and Die Kleine came at week-ends, when the gramophone played, reminding us of that other cinematic world we had left behind us, which seemed even farther away than the Kremlin. We took walks in the woods, and smiled at children playing, and felt, as we hadn't in Moscow, that we were living in a country rather than a régime. Then, suddenly, Kitty got ill, developing a very high temperature.

Herr Schmidt very kindly brought a German doctor, Dr Taubkin, to see her; a little gnome-like man who looked vaguely deformed – a near hunchback, with bright eyes and a soft, purring voice. He pulled a long face over Kitty's temperature, and after his examination – very delicately done; taking a white cloth out of his bag to put over her chest while he sounded her – he said she had typhus or paratyphus, the latter being a milder, but still dangerous, form of the same virus. When he told Kitty what was the matter with her, all she wanted to know was whether the child in her womb would be harmed. Reassured on this point, she closed her eyes again. There was nothing to be done except keep her in bed, and give her lots of water to drink and occasional enemas. In any case, medicaments were rare and difficult to come by. I asked Dr Taubkin anxiously whether she should go to hospital. A look of unspeakable horror spread over his gnomish face, and he crossed himself; otherwise making no reply. I used to recall his response to my question when I read articles by eminent doctors expatiating upon the excellence of the hospitals and public health service in the USSR.

For the next days I forgot everything except looking after Kitty. The thought that she might die filled me with desolation. All our quarrels and jealousies and harsh sayings and infidelities dissolved away; and all I saw in the universe was her flushed face, very youthful looking in its sickness, very alert and resolute, picked out as though spot-lit in the midst of an immense darkness. If she should die! A secondary terror was that I might catch the illness, and so be unable to look after her. What would happen then? Inevitably, I thought the symptoms were unmistakably developing, and secretly took my own temperature; positively dismayed, absurdly enough, to find that it was normal. Kitty's mattress was intolerably uncomfortable, so I gathered others in the dacha and piled them on it. Die Kleine, when she came at the weekend, very sweetly made no complaint about losing hers.

I slept on the floor beside Kitty's bed, waking up from time to time to look at her, taking her temperature far more often than was necessary; childishly enraged when it remained high, and equally childishly uplifted when it dipped down. In the morning I washed her as well as I could, very gently when I came to the swollen belly, and combed her hair. For an enema we had only rather crude sunflower oil, but I managed with this, experiencing a kind of blissfulness in the process. We had with us the Everyman edition of *Shakespeare's Tragedies* (I must, in jettisoning books before we left Manchester, have given this volume a non-bourgeois imprimatur), and I read aloud to her *Hamlet* and *Cymbeline*. In the evening, when Lena was in the dacha, I took a walk in the pine woods, up and down the straight paths. For the time being all my professional journalistic interest in the régime had evaporated; how many hours people worked, their real wages, rent, rations, whether the Consumers' Co-operatives, so dear to Mrs Webb, functioned successfully or not. My mind had momentarily stopped working in that sort of way. It just suddenly seemed to me that Russia was a beautiful place – these pine trees, dark against the snow which had now begun to fall, the sparkling stars so far, far away, the faces of the Russians I met and greeted, these also so beautiful, so clumsy and so kind. *Tovarich!* – it meant something, after all. Brother!

In the woods there was a little church, of course disused now. The fronts of such churches, like the Greek ones, are painted with bright colours; blues bluer than the bluest sky, whites whiter than the whitest snow. Someone – heaven knows who – had painted up the one in the Kliasma woods. Standing in front of this unknown painter's handiwork, I blessed his name, feeling that I belonged to the little disused church he had embellished, and that the Kremlin with its scarlet flag and dark towers and golden spires was an alien kingdom. A kingdom of power such as the Devil had in his gift, and offered to Christ, to be declined by him in favour of the kingdom of love. I, too, must decline it, and live in the kingdom of love. This was another moment of perfect clarification, when everything fitted together in sublime symmetry; when I saw clearly the light and the darkness, freedom and servitude, the bright vistas of eternity and the prison bars of time. I went racing back over the snow to K, breathing in the dry icy air in great gulps of thankfulness.

The next day I went into Moscow in quest of a bedpan. It happened also to be the anniversary of the October Revolution, and I had a press pass for the parade in the Red Square. The only possible place where I might find a bedpan, Herr Schmidt had told me, was in the commission shops; a sort of Soviet version of pawn shops, where the relics of the old Russian bourgeoisie brought their family treasures – ikons, pieces of furniture, books, stamp collections, Czarist medals even, anything that could possibly have a value – to exchange them for money to pay taxes and procure necessities. They were a great haunt of visiting Intourists, especially Americans, who eagerly poked about, looking for a bargain – Rasputin's breviary, a sometime duchess's fan, an ikon from some ancient monastery in remote Turkistan, to be carried away across the Atlantic and proudly displayed alongside wedding groups and college graduation trophies. The commission shops were recognised as capitalistic enclaves, their interiors dusty and shadowy as befitted such alien establishments in a Workers' State. They were tolerated as a means of relieving In-tourists of their Valuta – that magical incantation for foreign currency, breathed in one's ear at restaurants or when making a theatre booking, like an Ave Maria, to find out whether one proposed to pay in real or ersatz money.

When my turn came to be attended to, it was obvious that the shop-man assumed I was a seller rather than a buyer. He asked me arrogantly what I wanted, clearly anxious to hurry on to the more agreeable and rewarding business of Valuta transactions. The mistake doubtless arose as a result of my appearance, which did not at all suggest an affluent foreigner. I was wearing a short black leather jacket with a fur collar bought in an army surplus store in Manchester, dating back, as I was told, to General Ironside's force at Archangel at the time of the Allied Intervention in 1918. It was not a stylish or elegant garment. When I explained in my halting Russian that I wanted a bedpan for a sick wife, and that I would pay sterling, his interest kindled a little, and he produced a porcelain object which, if not exactly a bedpan, could be made to serve the same purpose. It was wrapped up for me in an old issue of *Pravda*; I paid in Valuta, and we parted amicably.

I went on to visit Cholerton, who at that time was still *News Chronicle* correspondent, before he joined the *Daily Telegraph*. He was far and away the nicest and most intelligent of the foreign journalists in Moscow, habitually stretched out on a couch, having a lung infection which made him subject to sudden temperatures; often with a bottle of red Caucasian wine beside him. He had a way of lining up bottles in the morning for the day's consumption. With his untidy beard, incessant conversation, wide-ranging, inconstant but scintillating mind, he was the very image of the Russian intellectual as portrayed by Dostoevsky. I once asked Podolski why, in view of the fact that Cholerton never bothered to hide his loathing and contempt for the Soviet régime, he was on the whole so tolerantly regarded, and always given his re-entry visa, when other ostensibly far more sympathetic reporters were persecuted and expelled. They were indulgent towards him, Podolski explained, because they liked him. He reminded them irresistibly of the good old days of their exile, when they lived penuriously in Geneva or London, arguing and quarrelling together, in and out of the British Museum Library, playing chess in cafés, bringing out obscure revolutionary sheets, splitting and re-splitting into ever smaller factions over minute doctrinal differences. Ah, too happy, happy times! Podolski seemed to be saying. I could see that Cholerton fitted perfectly into the scene, and that his detestation of of the régime somehow expressed theirs. He, as it were, hated it on their behalf, and so his presence was comforting. When they had all been shot by Stalin, this consideration no longer applied, and Cholerton's visa was at last withdrawn. He finally decamped to the Riviera, that last refuge of rebellious hearts, where I have continued to visit him from time to time, always with delight.

His household in Moscow consisted of a very sweet Russian wife, Katerina Georgevna, and their little daughter Katya, a sharp-tongued, aggressive secretary, Natalia Dmitrievna, who looked after his affairs, and numerous domestics and hangers-on. I felt happier there than anywhere else. He lived in an ordinary ramshackle Soviet apartment house, but his free-ranging intelligence, unpackaged in the ideologies of the age, irradiated the shabby room; as did a set of Stations of the Cross by some Ukrainian peasant artist he had somehow acquired. I remember them as being very beautiful in their strength and simplicity. He had neither the temperament nor the inclination to be a journalist; least of all for the *News Chronicle*, a sort of poor man's *Guardian*, which he abominated. If anything, he was a don (actually, a sometime fellow of King's College, Cambridge), with all the special donnish qualities of indolence and intellectual arrogance. His flat was littered with books; mostly paper-covered French editions in which he would forage from time to time, picking one up and opening it to read a few pages. Through him I first became acquainted with Taine's *Origines de la France Contemporaine*, from which I derived great enjoyment and enlightenment. How, in any case, could he be expected to provide nourishment for *News Chronicle* readers? With my experience of *The Guardian*, I, alas, knew the form all too exactly, and was happy to oblige occasionally on his behalf. His true spiritual home was Paris in the early twenties; he had flown to the USSR on the wings of the Gauche Radicale, not the Fabians, with Léon Blum and Marc Chagall for his ikon rather than Sidney and Beatrice Webb. It was the sheer philistinism of the régime that appalled him; its total humourlessness, its abysmal taste, its dreadful buildings, its flat, heavy representational paintings of Lenin and Stalin, like portraits of Lord Mayors in Manchester Town Hall; the long-winded cant and dull hatred which hung like an oppressive cloud over it. Reacting against this philistinism, by a quirk of history, he who had walked about Montmartre in a wide black hat, and looked on Hemingway and Joyce and the Shakespeare Bookshop, became almost the last voice to be heard in Moscow, if not in the world, expounding bourgeois virtues. The ultimate champions of a civilisation in dissolution, the Casabiancas who stand on its burning deck when all but they have fled, are, by the nature of the case, a weird lot, and Cholerton among the weirdest.

We went together to the Red Square for the parade, rather tipsy, and I still resolutely clasping my bedpan wrapped in an old edition of *Pravda*. As we approached the press stand, holding out our passes, one of the many security guards insisted on examining my parcel, no doubt supposing it to be a bomb. He was quite astonished when he saw what it was, and handed it back to me with a polite bow. From the press stand one looked straight across at the top of Lenin's Mausoleum where the Dictatorship of the Proletariat were standing; Stalin in the middle, with Kalinin on one side of him and Voroshilov on the other, and the rest carefully graded. They looked like a row of pygmies perched up there;

little clockwork manikins who might at any moment disport themselves when their mechanism was released, jerkily raising their hats and kicking their legs in unison, but for the moment completely still. The Red Square was densely packed; there, the Proletariat, and up on the Mausoleum, the Dictatorship. How were the two connected? As Lenin so succinctly posed the question: Who whom? The scene seemed pure fantasy; I couldn't believe in it. Not even as the mighty procession rolled past; the gymnasts, the troops, the bands, the armoured vehicles, the dashing cavalry. I wanted to raise my bedpan in the air in a special salute of my own; particularly when I noticed a little group of vaguely familiar faces behind a banner emblazoned CPGB; they, too, paying their tribute to the great Dictatorship of the Proletariat. We who are nothing shall be all; he hath put down the mighty from their seats, and hath exalted the humble and meek – it was the everlasting theme of revolution, here exemplified in all its majesty and fatuity.

I was so taken with the point that I turned to Cholerton to make it, but by mistake addressed a little red-faced buttoned-up Frenchman who turned out to be the correspondent of *Le Temps* – a Corsican named Luciani. He shrugged and agreed. On the stand next to ours were the diplomatic corps; the ambassadors all arrayed in astrakhan collars and fur hats, of varying size and splendour; the service attachés in their uniforms, which, in that setting, had a decidedly comic opera air about them, as though they had lately been fetched out of the property box and dusted down for the occasion. Altogether, they looked a nondescript, and even rather sinister lot assembled there, and so completely separate that they might have been seated together in a commodious tumbril which at any moment would begin to roll.

In the cold air, the Caucasian wine I had consumed with Cholerton began to wear off; he, too, looked somewhat pinched and abstracted, wondering, I daresay, what, if anything, could be gleaned for the *News Chronicle* from the turn-out:

TO-DAY FIFTEENTH ANNIVERSARY BOLSHEVIK OCTOBER RE-
VOLUTION MARSHAL VOROSHILOV STANDING NEXT STALIN
WITH REST POLITBUREAU TOOK SALUTE MASSIVE MILITARY
TURNOUT AMID SCENES GREAT ENTHUSIASM . . .

'An unforgettable experience,' I heard a voice say. It was Lord Marley, a recently created Labour peer who had come over with us on the *Kooperatsia*, his face full of rapture. The Montessori teacher said she wished the accent had been somewhat less military, but the enthusiasm of the people was infectious. If only we had something like that at home!

A nearby American warmly agreed. He was wearing a button which bore the legend '3%'. The notion, he explained, came from Professor Einstein, who had said that if three per cent of mankind were against war there never could again be one. He hoped in Moscow to recruit Stalin into the programme, which would mean, he figured, the involvement of the whole Soviet population.

I arrived back in Kliasma triumphantly bearing my bedpan, to find Kitty much better and sitting up and ready to laugh over my adventures. The sense of relief drove away all the fears that had been haunting me – only £90 left of our travellers' cheques, and very little money coming in; the impossibility of settling in the USSR as we had planned, or of going on being a foreign correspondent in Moscow, indeed, of working for *The Guardian* at all; the need to find somewhere for Kitty to have her baby, as well as a job for me. All these dilemmas seemed of no account in the light of her returned health and smile. A local woman doctor who visited her from time to time came in that evening, found that her temperature was normal for the first time since her illness began, and shared in our rejoicing. She was a cheerful amiable soul, the best type of Soviet product; simple, capable and pleasant looking, with a warm bright face. We managed to converse in a mixture of Russian and German. Her equipment struck me as primitive. For instance, her stethoscope was like a little wooden trumpet, and she had no drugs of any kind, not even aspirins. One of her favourite treatments, called *banki*, which she insisted on administering on this last visit, consisted of warming up a lot of little glass pots and then affixing them to Kitty's back. As they cooled, they sucked up the flesh, giving excruciating pain, and, allegedly, easing the bronchial tubes. The whole process was so bizarre that we couldn't help laughing, which, of course, made the pain all the greater.

This so painful laughter was the sign for me that Kitty was now alive. What an ecstatic experience to see someone greatly loved who has been languishing and dying thus come to life again! Blood moving through the veins and arteries, like traffic after a stoppage; nourishment again taken, gulped down greedily, each mouthful desperately needed, and preparing the way for the next, no less desperately needed. Likewise, air greedily breathed in. Talk returning, and laughter; even irritability – all manifestations of life. Like Lazarus raised from the dead. Even in plants this is wonderful; watering and easing the earth to coax some drooping, famished plant to lift its head and stand upright. Each morning's awakening similarly a miracle; beautiful to observe, especially in a child. Eyes slowly opening; consciousness coming back into them, chasing away the dreams, and focusing on the new day beginning; stretching, coughing, scratching, making ready. So, this preposterous laughter of ours, making the little *banki* jars quiver and shake, to poor Kitty's greater anguish, was particularly joyous as an outward and visible manifestation of her recovery. She was, after all, alive; the graph was upwards, not downwards; our journey was not over, the road stretched onwards.

Along the straight paths through the pine trees I tried afterwards to sort it out in my mind. How suffering, rather than pleasure, should be the sacrament of love. The imperfection of the flesh so much more crucial than its imagined perfection; the transports of tending it in sickness far transcending those of coupling with it in health. A contradiction, a mystery. Peeping in through a broken window of the little church with the newly painted front, I saw that it was used now for storing tools, as well as some of the fallen slogans from the nearby clearing, neatly piled for use the following summer. Yet at the back where the altar had been there was still the faint outline of a cross to be seen. Another statement of the same proposition. In its survival I read the promise that somehow this image of enlightenment through suffering, this assertion of the everlasting supremacy of the gospel of love over the gospel of power, would never be obliterated, however dimly and obscurely traced now, and however seemingly triumphant the forces opposed to it might seem to be.

By the time Kitty was really better we were able to move back to Moscow, where we occupied the flat of William Henry Chamberlin and his wife Sonia in the Borisoglebski Pereulok during their absence on leave. Chamberlin was the staff correspondent of the *Christian Science Monitor* and also worked as a stringer for *The Guardian*. He was a short, podgy, highly intelligent, droll man who neither drank nor smoked, his only form of self-indulgence being eating chocolate. As he read or ruminated, he chewed steadily, reckoning to consume his own weight annually. Perhaps because of this, he came increasingly to resemble a figure of the Buddha. Originally, he came to the USSR on a wave of pacifist-progressive sentiment, but soon soured on the régime, working off his resentment in little odd digs and innuendoes delivered on a wide front. Each week, for instance, he cut out of the *Manchester Guardian Weekly* an advertisement for a private mental home, posting it off to the public figure he considered most in need of it. One week he would send it to Mrs Eleanor Roosevelt, another to Rabindranath Tagore, always choosing the recipient with the utmost care in the light of his or her current attitudes and pronouncements. I was glad to know that one had been dispatched to the up-and-coming Anthony Eden, and another to Bertrand Russell.

Chamberlin, and more particularly Sonia – a Russian Jewess by origin – had every intention of staying in the USSR for some time to come, and very cleverly used his complaisant coverage in *The Guardian* to offset any sharp criticism of the régime he might essay in the *Monitor*. By playing off one against the other he managed to achieve the delicate balancing act of keeping on his feet in the USSR without becoming its committed stooge. Thus, when readers of the *Monitor* learnt from him that agricultural production was sagging alarmingly, the hearts of readers of *The Guardian* were uplifted by the news that the policy of collectivisation was producing undoubted results in the Siberian heartlands. This kept Oumansky happy, since he believed – no doubt correctly – that the USSR got the better of the bargain, *The Guardian* being a far more influential organ than the *Monitor*. After my floundering efforts in Chamberlin's absence to provide a less inhibited service from Moscow, Crozier was delighted to have Chamberlin back and resume the old arrangement. Substituting for Chamberlin on the *Monitor* presented its own special difficulties. For instance, I was given to understand that the subject of death was considered to be unsuitable in its columns. Unhappily, at the time, nearly all the stories out of Moscow were about humans and animals dying, and the various possible synonyms – like 'fell' – scarcely seemed appropriate. I did not fancy cabling Boston to the effect that x thousand kulaks had fallen as a result of the party instruction to liquidate them. Or that y thousand livestock had fallen, having been eaten by famished moujiks in the famine conditions induced by collectivisation.

The house in Borisoglebsky where we took up our quarters was an old-fashioned pre-Revolution one, and the Chamberlins' flat had a large tiled stove in it of the kind that occurs in so many of Tolstoy's and other Russian stories. I used to imagine Oblomov's servant Zachar curled up on top of it. We very soon got used to living there, so that we might have been back in Didsbury. Revolutions, like wars, upset things far less than might be superficially supposed. As the very word 'revolution' implies, they have a way of ending up where they began. Most days I would go to the Press Department, just as I had to the Cross Street *Guardian* office. There one met one's colleagues, also waiting for the attentions of Podolski or Nehman or Ehrens. The older hands knew the form perfectly, and brought in copy that passed easily through the censor's scrutiny. Newcomers might sometimes argue against the exigencies of censorship, and even shout and bang the table, indignant over excisions in what they supposed to be straight reporting. They had to learn that in the Soviet Union – as, later, everywhere – happenings occur exclusively on communication media, never in life. It is put out by *Tass*, therefore it is. Or, it has been shown on television, therefore it is. It amounts to the same thing.

The most notable activist among the press corps was Ralph Barnes, an earnest eager American reporter who kept us all on our toes. He used to pad about the streets of Moscow in rubber shoes hoping to come upon some newsworthy person or event, and endlessly apply for interviews with Stalin, which were rarely accorded, mostly to eminent visitors like H. G. Wells, and even then settled, if not drafted, in advance. When, as happened from time to time, Barnes disappeared from Moscow, there was great apprehension among the other correspondents. Where had he gone? What was he up to? On one such occasion he pulled off a coup of stupendous proportions, which made him the envy of all his colleagues. He went down to Georgia and managed to interview Stalin's mother, actually getting a photograph of her wearing an old-fashioned peasant dress, seated in the porch of her modest, but spotlessly clean cottage; like any American mum in Michigan or Minnesota. She was, as he put it, a little old lady in black, inordinately proud of her famous son in the Kremlin, her Soso. The story had a sensational success, and was widely reproduced. Later, doubts were cast on whether the lady in question really was Stalin's mother, or someone dressed up for the part. By that time, anyway, who cared? Her appearance in Barnes's story coincided, certainly, with a campaign mounted in the Soviet Press to show that Stalin was human – on any showing quite a sizeable undertaking. Nothing, however, could detract from the splendour of the scoop, which continued to have a special place in Moscow newspaper mythology.

Another coup Barnes pulled off, less noticed at the time but intrinsically more remarkable, was to procure an interview with someone who purported to be fairly high up in the GPU. In the course of their conversation, Barnes put to him the naïve but fundamental question: Why is it that in the USSR innocent people get arrested? The GPU man, it seems, fairly shook with laughter at this, to the point that it was quite a while before he could get his answer out. Of course we arrest innocent people, he said at last in effect; otherwise, no one would be frightened. If people are only arrested for specific misdemeanours, all the others feel safe, and so are ripe for treason. Probably without meaning to, he expounded the central doctrine of every terror, as well as of all dictatorial government, so brilliantly exemplified by Orwell in *Nineteen Eighty-Four*, and, more imaginatively, in Kafka's *The Trial*. By making justice subjective and arbitrary, every citizen can be plausibly arrested and charged at any time, with the result that they live in a permanent state of incipient guilt and fear; really feeling themselves to be miserable offenders, not just in the eyes of God, but of their earthly rulers as well. Hence the so easily procured confessions, which do not need to be invented or extorted, but truly come from the heart.

In those days foreign journalists were vouchsafed some contact with lower echelon Soviet bosses, besides an occasional sight of the top ones; even of the boss of the bosses, Stalin himself. He would walk into view on a platform, or appear in a box at the Opera House, or at the topmost end of a reception, always to the accompaniment of protracted cheers that were precisely timed by the GPU men in attendance. Their duration steadily increased, and at the time of Stalin's death had reached a minimum of seven and a half minutes. It was a preview of the studio audience. Sometimes, again, one would catch a glimpse of the back of his head, with its thick neck, as his heavily escorted car shot past, going to or from the Kremlin.

The receptions, whatever their occasion, were invariable. There would be a long table loaded with food and drink beside which officials would cluster like foraging bees, eating as hard as they could, and sometimes, when no one was looking, surreptitiously pocketing something portable to take home for their dear ones. A regular attender at these functions was Borodin, who at one time had played an important role in the execution of Soviet policy in China. Now, in semi-disgrace, he had been made, of all things, editor of the *Moscow Daily News*, an English language propaganda sheet published in Moscow. The unfortunate man had on his staff some ebullient English and American Communist and Communist-leaning girls of quite exceptional horror. When I read of his inevitable eventual arrest and disappearance, I thought that perhaps there might have been a tiny element of relief as he was taken off to Lubianka in the thought that he would no longer have to cope with these unspeakable harridans. At the reception he would sit alone, quietly drinking champagne and chain smoking, wearing an expression of oriental vacancy.

Another fairly frequent attender was Radek, a vivacious quick-speaking man with a beard like Nehman's, who might easily in other circumstances have been taken for a Rabbi. The first time I saw him he was the centre of an attentive group of sycophantic listeners, to whom, puffing away at his curved Meerschaum pipe, he held forth eloquently. At his subsequent appearances they dwindled, until he, like Borodin, sat alone. Then he, too, disappeared, to reappear in court to explain how, during his days as an active revolutionary in Germany, he was recruited into the British Intelligence Service, which he thenceforth faithfully served. The last article of his that Klavdia Lvovna translated for me was in the vein of the new spirit of nationalism ordained by Stalin, and described how, when he was in the arms of his mistress, he found himself speaking in his native patois, rather than in the Russian or German he used in his writings and public addresses.

Sometimes, too, Gorki was wheeled in, if he happened to be in Moscow rather than in the Italian villa the Soviet Government allowed him to keep. He looked like some extraordinary old performing seal, scarcely aware of what was going on around him, or of who anyone was. To me, he was an awesome figure because he had known Tolstoy and written so beautifully about him. I even made an effort on one occasion to get into conversation with him, but it was fruitless. The eyes were asleep; he was dozing behind his walrus moustache. In the end I usually gravitated to the side of D. N. Mirsky, a former prince in Czarist days, with whom I had a vague acquaintance in England. He was always invited to Moscow receptions to show any foreigners present that a prince could survive unhurt under a dictatorship of the proletariat. 'Look at him!' Oumansky would say, flashing his gold teeth. 'A prince! Just imagine!' Mirsky always turned up, I think largely for the free champagne. He was a great drinker, and not too well provided with money. In any case he only earned roubles – by writing articles in the *Literaturnaya Gazeta* tearing to pieces contemporary English writers like D. H. Lawrence, T. S. Eliot and Aldous Huxley, to whom, in conversation, he would always refer as 'Poor Lawrence!' 'Poor Tom!' 'Poor Aldous!' I found this sympathetic. In the civil war he had fought with the Whites, afterwards living as an exile in Paris, and associating himself there with the most extreme reactionary views. Then, he came to London, where, inevitably, he became a professor, and was commissioned to produce a book on Lenin. In the course of working on it, he came to see his subject as an enlightened saviour rather than, as heretofore, a degraded villain. So he changed from being a prince to being a comrade: a transformation which was celebrated on the dust-jacket of one of those yellow-covered, left-wing books of the period by showing his title struck through with a red line. When I outlined his career to Luciani, the *Temps* correspondent, he observed sourly that Mirsky had pulled off the unusual feat of managing to be a parasite under three régimes – as a prince under Czarism, as a professor under Capitalism, and as an *homme-de-lettres* under Communism. It was a just saying, but all the same I liked Mirsky.

He sometimes visited Kitty and me in our Borisoglebsky flat to take a bath; an amenity not available where he lived. I used to chat with him while he dried himself; his body white and tender like a boy's, and the old battered, bearded head, so ravaged and decayed, with its rotting teeth, seeming not to belong to it; like an old worn hood on a new motor-car. All the wear and tear of living seemed to have gone into the head, leaving the rest of his body fresh and new. Once, chatting in this way, and feeling totally isolated and secure – the bathroom having no windows, and being filled with steam, so that we might have been in some remote cave, or just floating about in space – I ventured, on an impulse, to ask him if he really believed the awful plays shown in Moscow theatres (apart from the Stanislavsky productions, which, after all, belonged essentially to the pre-Revolution period) were any good; Stalin and his unsightly gang, great leaders and seers; the unspeakable buildings, fine architecture; the new Socialist cities, other than instant slums, the empty slogans mechanically bawled, the dogma of a new religion; the stale Marxist notions, superficial in themselves, and even then misunderstood or deliberately distorted, the messages of the future.

Mirsky went on drying himself slowly and deliberately, as though anxious to delay as long as possible covering up his body and leaving only his stained head exposed. Then he turned on me in one of his sudden furies, telling me that I was a fool who understood nothing. Plays and people and buildings and slogans and ideas, he said, didn't matter in the least.

What did matter, then? I asked him. Now he stopped drying altogether, and just looked scornfully at me. What mattered was that what was happening in the USSR *had* to happen. That forces, interacting, produced a resultant force, which was irresistible. He might have been a Hebrew prophet, Jeremiah or Isaiah, proclaiming: Thus saith the Lord! Or Calvin preaching to the predestined the inevitability of their predestined salvation or damnation. Or Beethoven with his *Es Muss Sein*. When all the cant was put aside, I reflected, this was why all those ribald nondescript intellectuals so assiduously and cravenly followed their sour, Georgian Pied Piper – because in his wake they were among the Elect, and could count on salvation. They were ahead of history; propagandists for a victory which had yet to be won. Who Whom? – yes; but for ever Who!

One evening Mirsky took me along to a party at a sort of hostel where foreign writers were lodged. It was in honour of a Soviet writer whose play – *Cement* – had just been produced with great critical acclaim but little convincing audience enthusiasm. The guest of honour was a little man in top boots with a youthful lined face, like a jockey's. Whenever anyone spoke to him, he bowed, but said nothing. A group of Soviet poets in embroidered shirts stood round him like a bodyguard, who also bowed in unison when anyone greeted him, and, if he ventured a remark on his own account, gave it their respectful attention, or, if it was meant to be funny, fell into paroxysms of laughter; picked up by other guests, so that it echoed and re-echoed through the room. Again, there was a long table loaded with food and plentiful supplies of gaseous Soviet champagne, of which Mirsky partook lavishly. Drink made him more sombre and silent than usual; he sat looking balefully across at Elsa, the companion of the French poet Louis Aragon, for whom he had conceived a strong passion. She was, indeed, very beautiful.

At a certain point in the proceedings Aragon stood up and announced that he had just received a message from Paris that the members of the French Surrealist Movement had joined the Communist Party *en bloc*. At the news of this addition to the ranks of the World Proletariat there was a burst of cheering, in which, I noticed, Mirsky did not participate. This was doubtless due more to resentment over Aragon's favoured position *vis-à-vis* Elsa than to any scepticism about the importance of his announcement. Aragon read aloud an adulatory poem in *vers libres* that he had lately written about the French Communist Party, rolling out the words with immense gusto, his arms outstretched against the wall as though he was being crucified.

Leaving Mirsky's side, I wandered about the party rather disconsolately, trying to find someone to talk to. There were one or two American writers present of whose works, although apparently they sold in millions in the USSR, I had never heard, and quite a few Poles and East Europeans, some of them wearing decorated skull-caps. The only fellow-Englishman I came across was a man in top boots and a belted shirt who had, he told me, just come back from Baku, where he had been helping with the direction of a film reconstructing an incident at the end of the 1914–18 war when British forces executed a number of Soviet Commissars who had fallen into their hands. One of his tasks had been to teach the extras playing the part of the British troops to sing 'Tipperary', which had really been quite difficult; they had to learn the words phonetically, and he himself had been pretty shaky on the tune. He was deadly serious about his curious assignment.

Soon after this encounter I slipped away; there seemed no point in trying to stir up Mirsky, whose eyes by this time were quite glassy, and who had fallen into a deep trance. I walked briskly home, through the now almost deserted streets, near the Pushkin Memorial passing a bearded man in a sheepskin coat who was stretched out asleep or dead in the snow. Footsteps had made a detour round him; I followed them.

Mirsky never discussed with me how he felt about having returned to the USSR as a Soviet citizen. It was obviously an act of great imprudence, and it was clear that he disliked living in Moscow, and having to associate with other Soviet penmen. In London his position had been quite comfortable; as a crossed-out prince he had an assured social position both in upper-class and intelligentsia circles, besides being welcome at working-class gatherings. Even – perhaps particularly – the Communists were glad to have a prince with them on the plinth in Trafalgar Square when they assembled there. In Moscow he was completely at the mercy of the authorities. I don't, of course, know whether he ever meditated trying to escape, but once, when we happened to be looking at a map together, his finger moved to Batum, on the Turkish frontier, and stayed there. I never heard for certain what happened to him, but know that he was arrested and taken off, either to be executed or to die in a labour camp. The ostensible cause of his fall from favour was, it seems, an article he had written on the occasion of the centenary of Pushkin's death in 1937. Following what he supposed to be the Party Line, he wrote of Pushkin as a court lackey and toady. Alas for him, the Line had changed, and Pushkin had been reinstated as a national hero. So, as it turned out, Mirsky was liquidated for denigrating Pushkin – a delectable example of Fearful Symmetry, whose cruel whimsicality may well have appealed to his own savage temperament. When I heard how his fall had come about, I recalled Luciani's remark about him; of his three essays in parasitism, it was the last that had proved the most hazardous and exacting.

I saw Kitty off at Moscow station to go back to England to have our baby by herself. It was one of many partings which all seem hateful to me now; at the time my feelings were more mixed. I remember very vividly her face at the window as the train steamed away. Smiling and serene, as though she would be back in the evening. Actually, she was leaving with practically no money, and no certainty as to when, how, or even if, we should all be together again; with a baby due in two to three months, and only a dubious prospect of staying with my mother. Again and again I have been made aware of this rare quality of courage in her, taking refuge myself, with my easily failing heart, within the sanctuary it offers. I expect I should have gone with her; she never once asked me to, and I never thought of going. My callousness in such situations – a callousness the more abhorrent for being often quite unconscious – is something I look back on with particular disgust.

When the rear-lamp of the train had finally disappeared, I turned and walked away with Strang, of the British Embassy, whose wife had left for London on the same train. He was a diligent and kindly *fonctionnaire*, who later became head of the Foreign Office, serving sedately through the troubled appeasement years. Neville Chamberlain put him in the ignominious position of having to go through the motions of negotiating an Anglo-Soviet Treaty while Stalin was busily extorting the maximum loot from lining up with Hitler. He gave me a lift in his embassy car, and I tried to improve the occasion by questioning him about British policy towards the USSR. Without seeming to do so, he managed to evade my questions; like an experienced waiter managing not to catch the eye of a customer clamouring for attention. How fascinating they are; these gentle, diligent, honest souls, carefully buttoned and tailored, who somehow follow the twentieth century's Gadarene way without ever losing their breath or becoming dishevelled! For ever Jeeves, to an increasingly demented Bertie Wooster.

Shortly after Kitty's departure Sonia Chamberlin returned to Moscow without William Henry, and for some weeks we took our meals together in the Borisoglebsky apartment. Apart from this, I saw little of her, usually withdrawing to my own room as soon as I decently could to get on with my novel, or write articles and news stories for *The Guardian*. I also spent a lot of time with Cholerton, and roaming the streets. It is the kind of existence I have always fallen into very easily when relieved of the necessity to be in such a place, and to do thus and thus at such a time. Sonia was a low-built solid little woman with clumsy features and the shades of the ghetto still about her. There was also a strong flavour of Brooklyn, topped up with cultural and social aspirations, which took the form of wanting to have a salon frequented by professors and writers and musicians; people she regarded as having intellectual or artistic distinction.

In Moscow she was well placed to assemble a creditable salon; though no Madame du Deffand, a warmed house and modest refreshments were a big draw, and she had no difficulty in attracting to her evening parties quite an impressive collection of the more old-fashioned sort of Russian intelligentsia who had somehow managed to survive into the Stalin era, along with an occasional first or second secretary from one of the embassies, and itinerant European or American writers who happened to be in town. Rather like Cholerton (who perhaps for that reason did not find her sympathetic), she was another unexpected Casabianca, standing on the burning deck of the good ship *Bourgeoisie*. I caught a last glimpse of her in 1969, when she came to see us with William Henry, wearing, I noticed, white laced-up kid boots of the kind to be seen in old pictures of Baden Baden at the turn of the century. This was her period, and not even the Russian Revolution could deflect her from living in it. Soon after her visit to us I heard that she had died. William Henry did not wait long to follow. Theirs had been a very close partnership; I remember how, when the *Christian Science Monitor* arrived in his absence, she would point to some headline above his by-line likely to please Oumansky, and say, glowing with warm tenderness: 'He's thinking of me.' When he finally left the USSR, William Henry compensated for such indulgent marital signals by becoming an ardent supporter of Senator McCarthy and a regular contributor to the *Wall Street Journal*.

The battered, broken fragments of pre-Revolution Moscow intelligentsia who gathered at Sonia's salon had an apologetic air about them, as though saying: We quite recognise that in a manner of speaking we have a measure of responsibility for what has happened. But is it, when you come to think about it, such a calamity as might at first sight appear? After all, it *has* meant free universal education, and the emancipation of women, and birth control, hasn't it? Perhaps after a bit, when things have got into their stride, some of the harsher aspects will be softened, and we'll have proportional representation with the transferred vote, and a branch of the PEN Club here in Moscow, and available copies of the *Times Literary Supplement*, the *New Statesman* and *The New Republic*. My old *Guardian* editorials came wanly alive in them. They went on hoping, greatly hoping; the very last moderate men of all shades of opinion to draw together in the USSR. Eating tiny sweet cakes and sipping coffee in little cups at Sonia's salon, they were back twenty years before, when they talked about workers' control, and nationalising the land, and female suffrage; about making the past a *tabula rasa*, with no property, no family, and then the State would wither away, leaving labour to organise itself. They heard themselves proclaiming it all, in voices younger and more confident than their present apologetic whispers. *Tabula rasa* indeed; so it had come to pass. A clean slate, and they the first to be wiped off it. A lady with a raw face and little tufts of stiff black hair growing out of it began to talk about Chekhov. 'She knew him,' the other murmured. 'She's going to talk about Chekhov. It'll be such an interesting evening.'

Alexander Woolcott, a *New Yorker* mandarin who had looked in, suddenly gave his attention to what was being said. He saw a splendid piece in this, whimsically reporting how, at such a dingy, unappetising gathering in Moscow, new vivid reminiscence of the famous Russian playwright had been recounted. Mentally, he began to make notes of the scene; the old house, in what had doubtless once been a superior residential suburb; dark, musty passages, pieces of carpet and cloth draped over the walls, chairs and tables all likewise covered. A dusty, muffled, stale old house, and these people part of the dust and the staleness themselves. Ideological waifs and strays – he liked that phrase. He was a well-covered man himself, with a wide expanse of face, gleaming spectacles, and a camel-hair coat and fur hat hanging in the hall ready for when he went out. Clearing his throat noisily to attract full attention, he enjoyed telling them how that morning, when he stood on the steps of the Metropole Hotel where he was staying, a passer-by had come up to him and just gently passed his hand over his camel-hair coat, following the curve of his ample stomach, by way of a salute to his *en-bon-point*, his well-being, his affluence. The others laughed, but uneasily; they felt they were themselves rather in the position of the passer-by. They, too, metaphorically speaking, had been stroking Woolcott's stomach, so beautifully moulded, mounted and arrayed. The warmth of the flat, the talk, the refreshments, all brought them momentarily to life; like hibernating flies in sudden heat. When they put on their outdoor clothes, their shabby old coats and galoshes and nondescript knitted balaclavas, and went out into the street, they died again, creeping away to their holes.

For these residual ageing progressives who had not even been considered worth liquidating, the visits to Moscow of famous foreign intellectuals were gala occasions. Long-standing household gods come among them, whom they might even have known personally in the past; fraternal delegates at some conference or convention at which a Harold Laski or a Bernard Shaw or an Albert Thomas had been among the speakers. The fact that this link existed nourished the hope that it might somehow be possible actually to exchange a word with one or other of them, recalling past acquaintanceship. In practice, of course, it never happened. How could the distinguished visitors be expected to remember the last time they had seen these dismal relics of the past, when they, too, wore carelessly elegant suits, and had their hair in fine disarray; maybe with pince-nez like Webb's on a black ribbon; or even a monocle, like his fellow-Fabian, Hubert Bland? When, instead of creeping about apologetically in old balaclavas, they likewise stood on a platform, waving their hands in the air and proclaiming the coming of the great day when the workers would seize power, and mankind live happily ever after? Nor were to-day's distinguished visitors likely to reflect that, come another revolution or two, they might find themselves in their turn seedy citizens of a workers' paradise, with no return first-class ticket in their pockets to take them back to capitalist exploitation in London or Paris or New York whenever they had a mind.

For resident foreign journalists in Moscow the arrival of the distinguished visitors was also a gala occasion, for a different reason. They provided us with our best – almost our only – comic relief. For instance, when we heard Shaw, accompanied by Lady Astor (who was photographed cutting his hair), declare that he was delighted to find there was no food shortage in the USSR. Or Laski singing the praises of Stalin's new Soviet constitution. Or Julian Huxley describing how a 'German town-planning expert was travelling over the huge Siberian spaces in a special train with a staff of assistants, stopping every now and again to lay down the broad outlines of a future city, and then pushing on, leaving the details to be filled in by architects and engineers who remained behind.' Or – a collector's item – Maurice Hindus describing a young man at the reception desk of a Soviet home for reformed prostitutes who 'wears a modern suit of clothes, complete with collar and tie, and, what is more astonishing, spats.' 'Communist though he is,' he adds of this worthy, 'he deems it essential to keep up as presentable an appearance as the scanty supplies in the Moscow haberdashery shops permit.' Hindus, an American of Russian-Jewish extraction with black curly hair and a winning smile, wrote best-selling books in such a vein (*Red Bread, Humanity Uprooted*) about the Soviet régime. Future historians may well comment that the road to world revolution is paved with best-sellers.

We used to run a little contest among ourselves to see who could produce the most striking example of credulity among this fine flower of our western intelligentsia. Persuading church dignitaries to feel at home in an anti-God museum was too easy to count. So was taking lawyers into the People's Courts. The Webbs, too, were for beginners only. I got an honourable mention by persuading Lord Marley that the queueing at food shops was permitted by the authorities because it provided a means of inducing the workers to take a rest when otherwise their zeal for completing the Five-Year Plan in record time was such that they would keep at it all the time, but no marks for floating a story that Soviet citizens were being asked to send in human hair – any sort – for making of felt boots. It seemed that this had actually happened. A correspondent the *Neue Freie Presse* was commended for inducing the French Premier, Herriot, to believe, when he visited the USSR, that the milk shortage there was due to the large amounts allocated to nursing mothers. Cholerton, rightly, received the *Grand Prix* when, overhearing an eminent British jurist ask Oumansky whether Habeas Corpus operated in the USSR, he broke in to tell him, to his complete satisfaction, that, whatever might be the case with Habeas Corpus, the authorities strictly adhered to Habeas Cadaver.

I have never forgotten these visitors, or ceased to marvel at them, at how they have gone on from strength to strength, continuing to lighten our darkness, and to guide, counsel and instruct us; on occasion, momentarily abashed, but always ready to pick themselves up, put on their cardboard helmets, mount Rosinante, and go galloping off on yet another foray on behalf of the down-trodden and oppressed. They are unquestionably one of the wonders of the age, and I shall treasure till I die as a blessed memory the spectacle of them travelling with radiant optimism through a famished countryside, wandering in happy bands about squalid, over-crowded towns, listening with unshakeable faith to the fatuous patter of carefully trained and indoctrinated guides, repeating like schoolchildren a multiplication table, the bogus statistics and mindless slogans endlessly intoned to them. There, I would think, an earnest office-holder in some local branch of the League of Nations Union, there a godly Quaker who once had tea with Gandhi, there an inveigher against the Means Test and the Blasphemy Laws, there a staunch upholder of free speech and human rights, there an indomitable preventer of cruelty to animals; there scarred and worthy veterans of a

hundred battles for truth, freedom and justice – all, all chanting
the praises of Stalin and his Dictatorship of the Proletariat. It was as
though a vegetarian society had come out with a passionate plea for can-
nibalism, or Hitler had been nominated posthumously for the Nobel
Peace Prize.

When William Henry returned, I moved out of his Borisoglebsky
apartment and took up residence in the National Hotel. The decor was
in heavy marble and gilt, rather like the stations in the Moscow underground, then under construction, and to become a tourist show-place.
Once, sitting with Mirsky in the hotel lounge, I remarked upon its
excruciating taste. Yes, he agreed, it was pretty ghastly, but it expressed
the sense of what a luxury hotel should be like in the mind of someone
who had only stared in at one through plate-glass windows from the
cold, inhospitable street outside. This, he said, was the key to all the
régime's artistic products – the long turgid novels, the lifeless portraits
and landscapes in oils, the gruesome People's neo-Gothic architecture,
the leaden conservatory concerts and creaking ballet. Culturally, it was
all of a piece. There is no surer way of preserving the worst aspects of
bourgeois style than liquidating the bourgeoisie; whatever else Stalin
may, or may not, have done, he assuredly made Russia safe for the
Forsyte Saga.

The ceremonial opening of the Dneprostroi Dam, to which all foreign
journalists were invited, provided a welcome opportunity to get away
from Moscow. A special train was laid on for us, consisting entirely of
ancient international wagons-lits, in which we were allotted berths.
There was also, of course, a restaurant car. In over-heated carriages,
with vodka flowing freely, gossiping and laughing, we rolled southwards, looking vaguely out of the windows at the passing countryside,
which gradually, as we progressed, grew less wintry, more sunny and
salubrious. For the most part the small stations we rattled through
were cleared of people, but sometimes there were some bedraggled
looking peasants clustered together on the platform. Noticing one such
cluster, a large German correspondent carelessly threw out of the window a leg of chicken he had been gnawing at. There was a concerted
move to pick it up. The gesture and the response have stayed with me
through the intervening years like stigmata.

It seemed somehow symbolic of our whole situation that we, the reporters, should thus be coursing so cosily through this vast country that
was our territory. Seeing, and yet not seeing. In it, and yet inexorably
isolated and insulated; as it might be in a television control-room, and

looking down at a distant studio; faces, gestures and words there transmitted to us in recorded sounds and pictures. In the restaurant car a game of poker was in progress, round which a little group of spectators had gathered, including Ehrens, a keen player himself. With no deadlines to meet, no possibility of cabling, we could take it easy. Whatever happened would be a non-happening because unrecorded by us. I looked out of the window as night fell; such a beautiful countryside, luminous in the winter sunshine. The countryside of *War and Peace*, of *Oblomov*, of *Dead Souls*. I knew it as though I had lived in it all my life. What, after all, could Stalin and his henchmen do to it? It would surely outlast and outshine them. I had a notion even that I might live to go about in it cheerfully and freely, as in Sussex or Provence. Forty years later, this has not yet come to pass. Still, I do not despair, though there are now not many more years to go.

I was joined by an Englishman in shorts who carried his luggage in a rucksack, and was preparing material for a series of articles in the *New Leader*, then the organ of the Independent Labour Party. He was a nondescript sort of person, with a small black moustache, not as young as he looked or as old as he felt, who had been to prison as a conscientious objector in the war. It was easy to imagine him, at some ILP summer school, holding forth in his gritty, insistent voice about how, in the USSR, there were other motives than greed as the mainspring of action, nobler ideals to fight for than country or empire (not that he advocated violence in any circumstances; he meant mental fight, in the sense of striving after, seeking earnestly to attain); new standards of value, a new relationship between man and man. Now he had begun to wonder. There seemed to be a lot of violence about. Was all the talk about the Three Letters (a pseudonym used in conversation to avoid mentioning the dreaded GPU) justified and true? He was, I could see, troubled in spirit; like an evangelical clergyman who has suddenly been smitten with doubts about the Thirty-Nine Articles; with the same look of mute suffering in his eyes.

'Being actually in the USSR,' he said, 'drives one back to first principles, doesn't it?' Cholerton, who was standing nearby, said he thought it drove one back rather to last principles. Louis Fischer, correspondent of the American *Nation*, then chipped in to say that one mustn't expect too much; after all, the great experiment had only been going for fifteen years. We must give them time. Fischer was a sallow, ponderous, inordinately earnest man, dear to Oumansky as one who had never once through the years veered from virtuously following the Party Line.

Later, at the time of the Nazi-Soviet Pact, he did veer, quite drastically, afterwards turning for solace to Gandhi; a port in a storm for many an ideological wanderer. If the Mahatma had been present, I should have referred the troubled Englishman to him; as he wasn't, I told him to try Wicksteed who was, as being the next best thing. Wicksteed generally managed to attach himself to jaunts like the Dneprostroi one, if only to partake of the plentiful hospitality. I saw the two of them later in earnest conversation. I doubt if Fischer's defection, when at last it came, much troubled the Soviet authorities. His usefulness by that time was largely exhausted, and they might have reflected with Dryden that they had lost a villain, and his new patrons gained a fool.

I shared my compartment with a charming Bulgarian named Andreychin whom I had met at one of Sonia's salons. As we lay in our berths we talked together through much of the night. With the blinds up, we could look out of the window at a countryside now bathed in moonlight, most wonderfully still and serene, with just an occasional little cluster of lights coming into view and then disappearing. Andreychin had lived in America, where he had been a member of the International Workers of the World (the Wobblies). Describing to me with great zest and delight the antics they got up to with a view to undermining the economy of the State, he spoke of it all as though it had been an undergraduate frolic in his golden youth; something so delightful and gay and blameless that he could not hope ever again to recapture its spirit. Occasionally he broke out into one of their Wobblie songs, as it might have been a boating or a drinking song at some festive campus fraternity gathering, rather than a call to workers to rise up in their might and fury, and death to all bosses. He had been deported at the time of the Sacco-Vanizetti affair, making for the USSR, and remaining there ever since. Already he had done one stint in a labour camp.

But surely, I said, what you were striving after in America you've got here. Yes, he replied, doubtfully; it must be so. All the same, what would he not give to be back with the Wobblies in Detroit, engaged in bringing about the dissolution of the capitalist system! In the great purges of the middle thirties I heard that he had been given a further ten years' sentence. Then, to everyone's amazement, he turned up in Paris in 1946 as an interpreter with the Bulgarian delegation at the peace negotiations. He had lost most of his hair and all his teeth at the labour camp – tougher this time, he said, than at his first stretch – but was still liable to break into his Wobblie songs over a bottle in the evening. His western friends would have been glad to persuade him to stay in Paris, but he insisted on returning to Sofia, where in due course he was disposed of, like all the others, with a bullet in the back of his head. Did he give one more rendering of his Wobblie songs as they took him off? It would be nice to think so.

The next morning we arrived at Kharkov, now, instead of Kiev, the capital of the Ukraine. We were played into the station by a band; as it struck up the 'Internationale' in honour of Kalinin, nominally the head of State, who was travelling with us, everyone stood to attention, though in our Press carriages, where there was a general atmosphere of hangover, somewhat laxly. Kalinin was a small thin man with a wispy beard; so innocuous that, almost alone of Stalin's closer colleagues, he died unpurged. In the legend he was said to be a peasant, but I thought he had a decided resemblance to Sidney Webb – not by any means the same thing. Oumansky was waiting for us to take us to breakfast, wearing a cloth cap, breeches and top boots, which made him look woebegone; like a child at a Christmas party who has put on a cowboy outfit, and feels uneasily half aware that it isn't quite making the hoped for impression.

I was confronted with a similar sartorial surprise in the Ukraine when I accompanied Harold Macmillan there in 1959. In view of the fact that a visit to a collective farm was included in his itinerary, he arrayed himself for his arrival at Kiev in a plus-fours ensemble of the kind still considered appropriate for opening Conservative garden fêtes in the Home Counties. At the station he was met by local dignitaries, and delivered a speech which one of his staff had prepared about how in the twelfth century an English monarch had espoused a Ukrainian princess, and how ever since relations between the two countries had been particularly warm and cordial. On such occasions the ostensible Soviet public in attendance have in front of them a solid phalanx of policemen in issue civilian suits, with wide trousers, and plenty of room under the armpits for whatever they might wish to lodge there. I scrutinised the granite faces of some of these worthies to see whether there was any reaction to the British Prime Minister's remarks, and in one or two I thought I detected a faint flickering of the eyelids expressive of surprise, wonder, and maybe an impulse to laugh. That Christmas, greatly to my surprise, I got a telegram from the Soviet satirical magazine, *Krokodil*, asking me to let them have an account of the funniest thing that in my estimation had happened during the current year. In reply, I sent off a description of Macmillan in Kiev, but the editor wrote back very

politely to the effect that, though he personally thought my piece
decidedly funny, his magazine circulated among the broad masses, who
held Macmillan in the highest esteem and therefore would not be
amused. It might have been Crozier.

After breakfast Oumansky took us to see some newly constructed
factories. We traipsed rather disconsolately through them after him, to
a barrage of incomprehensible and unbelievable statistics. If any of us
allowed our attention to wander or lingered behind, Louis Fischer took
it upon himself to round us up. 'Come on! It creates such a bad impression if we don't seem interested.' A man from the *Chicago Daily News*
muttered under his breath that he *wasn't* interested anyway. Where's the
colour? Where's the human interest? he groaned. Visiting factories and
listening to statistics – unless of course, one happens to be a specialist,
and even then, readers aren't – is one of the major miseries of reporting
in Communist counties. There is no getting out of it; unavailing to
say, as I did when I was in China, that I was uninterested in heavy, or
for that matter light, industry, that I was perfectly ready to take on trust
the giant strides made in the way of industrial development, and only
interested in things like clergymen and co-education. It made no
difference; the dreadful ritual was inescapable. I imagine that pilgrims in
the Middle Ages were likewise required to go on all fours through the
Catacombs, and make their reverent but uncomfortable way to remote
desert shrines.

Our special train arrived at Dneprostroi late at night, and Oumansky
suggested that we should go at once and look at the dam and the hydro-
electric station. He was, one could see, already excited himself. So, we
piled into motor cars (in those days all the official Soviet cars were
Ford Lincolns), and there it was; looking like a huge theatrical set, with
searchlights flashing, sirens sounding, and written across the sky in
letters of fire: ELECTRICITY PLUS SOVIET POWER EQUALS COM-
MUNISM. A sort of Red Broadway. In the river below a great swirl and
rush of water; at the dam, soldiers on sentry-go, their bayonets gleaming
as they marched to and fro. Accompanying us there was a retired American colonel with several tremulous chins and a southern accent, who had
directed some of the construction. He, too, was uplifted. 'It looks great,'
he murmured. 'Great!' Louis Fischer warmly agreed, going on to ask:
'How have you found working here, Colonel?' 'That's been great, too,'
the other answered, adding, half to himself: 'No labour trouble!' Everyone knew what he meant; prisoners on forced labour had been available

as and when required. Fischer hurriedly changed the subject, moving on to the safer territory of how many kilowatts were being generated, and what volume of water the dam contained.

Oumansky climbed on to a little knoll and took off his cloth cap; he looked very Napoleonic standing there, and I almost expected him to tuck his hand into his overcoat in Napoleon's favourite gesture. The noise, the flashing lights, the movement; the sense of something immense that was reined in, controlled; power concentrated into a switch that anyone's fingers – his – could turn on and off; enormous wheels and turbines turning; silently, precisely revolving – all this went to his head. 'You see, gentlemen, what we have done,' he shouted at us, and went on to recite to us the tale of achievement – the largest hydro-electric station in the world; the world's record for cement-pouring, more electricity being generated than ever before in one single place; the whole thing finished in under four years, and now fully operative. 'Who,' he concluded, 'dare talk now of an interesting experiment?' Louis Fischer also took off his hat; it seemed the right thing to do, and he hoped the rest of us would follow his example. Actually none of us did. The ILP man certainly would have followed suit, except that, despite the freezing cold, he had no hat, though for some reason he had put on his rucksack to come to the dam. Fischer made up for our lack of response by a short formal speech: 'Mr Oumansky, we, representatives of many nations and many newspapers, would like you to know . . .'

The next morning Kalinin stood with the other notables on a raised platform and addressed a large audience assembled in an amphitheatre consisting mostly of delegations with banners and bands. Every so often one or other of these bands would play the 'Internationale', whereupon everyone would rise to their feet. Kalinin, with photographers hovering round him like insects with protruding eyes, delivered a speech which droned on and on, echoed and re-echoed by a series of loud-speakers, so that his words seemed to be chasing after each other across the amphitheatre. There was no response to them anyway; only an occasional rumble of drilled applause, and an occasional outburst of the 'Internationale'. He was followed by Henri Barbusse, author of *Le Feu*, a cadaverous looking Frenchman who spluttered over his words and waved his arms helplessly in the air as he spoke. It was impossible to hear what he said, but certain words and phrases came sizzling out of him; like *la Paix, la France, une journée inoubliable pour la classe ouvrière*. 'I see a vision,' he shrieked in his vibrant French, moisture glistening like dew on his moustache, 'of the toiling masses everywhere looking up from their misery and degradation, with hope in their eyes because of what you have achieved in your great workers' republic under the mighty leadership of Comrade Stalin.' Luciani aptly described him as *un homme décomposé*, and, indeed, his decomposition was such that one almost expected him to fall to pieces with the very vehemence of his oratory in so frail a body.

Compared with the night before, all the fire and mysticism of the occasion seemed absent; it needed the search-lights piercing the darkness, the letters of fire, the sentries and the sound of the swirling water, to provide a proper setting. Even Oumansky seemed subdued and dejected; the interminable speeches had a debilitating effect which not even the Commissar for Heavy Industry (Cholerton called him the Commissar for Heavy Income), an enormous Georgian named Ordshonikidze, was able to overcome. Cold and dispirited, we returned to our train, glad when it started on the return journey to Moscow.

Back in Moscow I felt at a loose end. My enthusiasm for dredging up items from the Soviet press with Klavdia Lvovna's help, had greatly abated. I spent more and more time tramping about the streets, or talking with Cholerton. My novel about *The Guardian* which I had sent off with Kitty was not, I now heard, acceptable to the publisher, who wrote complimentary things about it, but said the risk of legal action was too great to take. So I did not even get the £50 advance on which I had been counting. In the evenings I made a round of the theatres, often accompanied by Katerina Georgevna, whom I liked more and more. Her great simplicity of character and goodness shone in her face, making her beautiful. I have always loved such qualities and those who have them, and, contrariwise, been attracted sensually by those who lack them – who are egotistic and greedy and faithless. This is why happiness through the senses, even when I have sought it, has always seemed to me a vain pursuit, and also why, I suppose, I am often called a Manichee. No statement could possibly be, to me, more self-evidently true than St Paul's when he says that to be carnally minded is death, and to be spiritually minded life and peace. Unfortunately, I have wasted too much of my life in the death-camp of carnality.

Katerina Georgevna, in any case, was a delightful companion. She loved Russian drama and gave me the feel of it as no professional critic could. It was part of her life, something she treasured to keep alive a past that had been historically abolished. Thus, for instance, at a marvellous production of *Dead Souls* at the Moscow Art Theatre, then still being directed by Stanislavsky, she, as it were, introduced me to each of the characters, so that I knew them and can remember them perfectly to this day, even though I could not follow the dialogue. Afterwards, she gave me a set of postcard representations of them which I have kept carefully to this day and I have gone on reading Gogol's masterpiece from time to time; along with Don Quixote, Gulliver, Rabelais, Candide and Falstaff. In the interval we followed the pleasant Russian custom of joining the procession winding round and round the foyer, watching the others as they were watching us, and talking about the play.

One comment of Katerina Georgevna's that sticks in my mind was made about *The Cherry Orchard*. After agreeing with me about the excellence of the production, she added: 'But all the same, I couldn't see what they were bothering about. They had plenty to eat.' As a child she had been through the famine and the Civil War, and the memory was so searing that the sorrows and deprivations of Chekhov's characters failed to register. It was indeed a superb production, I think the best I have ever seen, and the first to be put on in Moscow since the Revolution. Up to then, Chekhov's plays had been banned as ideologically unsound and decadent. So, for the Art Theatre, and for Stanislavsky personally, it was a great occasion; the theatre's reputation had been built on Chekhov, and there was still a sea-gull on its curtain. Chekhov's widow, Knipper, played the lead, and the whole cast, down to the smallest part, perfectly recreated a society so rootless and without values that a revolution seemed scarcely necessary to bring about its destruction. The end was almost insupportable – the steel teeth of a saw biting into a tree-trunk; the downfall of a way of life, if not of a civilisation. Chekhov only foresaw the downfall, but this audience had lived through it. Many of them were in floods of tears, all were deeply moved; as was Katerina Georgevna despite her comment about the cast having plenty to eat; as, indeed, was I, despite my valuta origins and prospects.

We occasionally visited the other Moscow theatres – the Tairov, the Mayerhold, the Vakhtangov – but without caring much for them. After the Art Theatre, they all seemed rather spurious though, as can now be seen, making straight the way for Peter Brook, Peter Hall and other illuminati of the Arts Council. Their directors all in due course came to grief at Stalin's hands, as did Eisenstein, whose films, like *Mother* and *The Battleship Potemkin*, were part of the holy writ of all good Leftists. In the end, it was Stanislavsky alone who was given the Order of the

Red Banner and allowed to die in his bed. He, bourgeois of the bourgeois, flaunting to the end his soft black hat set rakishly on white locks, his astrakhan collar and flowing tie, as though he had just stepped out of the Hotel de Paris in Monte Carlo. The only production other than a Stanislavsky one which sticks in my mind is *Die Dreigroschenoper*, put on by the Moscow Judische Art Theatre, long since liquidated. It was my first acquaintance with Brecht.

Our stories from Moscow were increasingly concerned with the agricultural situation, which even the Soviet newspapers were featuring in, for them, a big way. In the circumstances, I decided that the best thing to do would be to have a go at visiting the agricultural areas in the Ukraine and the Caucasus by myself. Nowadays this would be quite impossible, since foreign journalists, like diplomats, have to get special authorisation to travel. Then, one could still, in theory at any rate, buy a railway ticket like anyone else. The odds were, of course, that one would be picked up at some point, but before this happened there was a chance of arriving unheralded somewhere, and talking to people other than under the shadow of the GPU. Actually, in my experience the Soviet security arrangements, once you get, as it were, off the moving stairway, are by no means as ruthlessly efficient as is commonly supposed. At a time when I had been persistently refused a visa to go to the USSR I happened to find myself in Peking, and on an impulse went into the Soviet Embassy there, and asked for a transit visa to stop off in Moscow on my way back to London. My passport was politely stamped, and handed back to me then and there; I stopped off in Moscow for ten days or so, without, as far as I could judge, my presence attracting any interest or attention.

Even so, I doubt if I should have had the perseverance or courage to join the immensely long queues always waiting in front of the ticket office at Moscow Station. Happily for me, Natalia Dmitrievna took me under her wing, and by dint of pushing, shouting and seeming to be important, made her way to the top of the queue, and procured the requisite return ticket to Rostov, with the possibility of getting off the train anywhere along the way.

The evening before I left there was a party at the British Embassy to which I went. Owing to the debourgeoisation of my wardrobe before leaving for the USSR, I had no appropriate clothes for such an occasion, and felt very self-conscious in a light grey suit, decidedly shabby, the only one I had. The ambassador was a man named Sir Esmond Ovey, a suave figure with brushed back grey hair and a small trimmed moustache. When I told him how my sartorial inadequacy had come about, he thought it very funny, and went on through the evening telling everyone he spoke to why I was so inappropriately dressed. I expect I deserved this. The only thing I can remember about Ovey is that he had a plan for solving the unemployment problem which on various occasions he tried to explain to me, no doubt calculating that *The Guardian* would be the ideal medium for launching such a proposal. Unfortunately, I never got the hang of it, maybe through my own inattention, or because he never managed to finish his exposition. So the plan must, I fear, have died with him. After Moscow, he was posted to Brussels.

On this occasion I managed to escape from his clutches quite quickly, and withdrew to a sofa where I found myself sitting between Anna Louise Strong and Walter Duranty, the *New York Times* correspondent. Miss Strong was an enormous woman with a very red face, a lot of white hair, and an expression of stupidity so overwhelming that it amounted to a kind of strange beauty. When in years to come I embarked on that Via Dolorosa, the American lecture circuit, I was constantly reminded of her; looking down on my audience from the podium, I saw row upon row of Anna Louises, as eagerly waiting for some crumbs of enlightenment from me as she did from Oumansky, or Borodin (under whom she worked on the *Moscow Daily News*), or the great Stalin himself. She had been around in Moscow from shortly after the Revolution, and allegedly, finding herself once in a car with Trotsky, the great man put his hand on her knee in what might have been taken as an amorous gesture. Whether because of this past anti-Stalinist deviation, or for some other reason, in the stormy days of the cold war even she got arrested; an item of news which, I regret to say, like Oumansky's fatal accident, gave great satisfaction among former newspaper correspondents in Moscow. Some of them even sent congratulatory telegrams signalising the glad tidings. Her incarceration proved to be brief – I imagine that even in Lubianka, her presence was burdensome – and she ended her days in Peking, where she was accorded a State funeral. A triumph of sheer staying power.

Duranty, a little sharp-witted energetic man, was a much more controversial person; I should say there was more talk about him in Moscow than anyone else, certainly among foreigners. By origin he was an Englishman from Liverpool, which probably means he was Irish; a conclusion supported by his proneness to hint at aristocratic connections and classical learning, of which, I must say, he produced little evidence. One of his legs had been amputated after a train accident, but he was very agile at getting about with an artificial one. His household, where I visited him once or twice, included a Russian woman named Katya, by whom I believe he had a son. I always enjoyed his company; there was something vigorous, vivacious, preposterous, about his unscrupulousness which made his persistent lying somehow absorbing. I suppose no one – not even Louis Fischer – followed the Party Line, every shift and change, as assiduously as he did. In Oumansky's eyes he was perfect, and was constantly held up to the rest of us as an example of what we should be.

It, of course, suited his material interests thus to write everything the Soviet authorities wanted him to – that collectivisation of agriculture was working well, with no famine conditions anywhere; that the purges were justified, the confessions genuine, and the judicial procedure impeccable. Because of these acquiescent attitudes – so ludicrously false that they were a subject of derision among the other correspondents, and even Podolski had been known to make jokes about them – Duranty never had any trouble getting a visa, or a house, or interviews with whomever he wanted. His subservience to the Party Line was so complete that it was even rumoured that he was being blackmailed by the Soviet authorities. Yet I do not myself think he was just a simple crook; in some strange way, his upholding of the Soviet régime was, besides being materially advantageous, a response to some need of his nature. Not, I hasten to add, because he believed in the Revolution, or in its beneficial consequences to Russia or to mankind – anything like that. Quite the contrary; I think he despised all that sort of apologetics, indulged in by Fischer and still more by Anna Louise Strong, more than anyone.

No, he admired Stalin and the régime precisely because they were so strong and ruthless. 'I put my money on Stalin,' was one of his favourite sayings. It was the sheer power generated that appealed to him; he was always remarking on how big Russia was, how numerous Russians were. Thus, for instance, in this last conversation I was ever to have with him, we got on to the subject of the agricultural situation and the famine. He admitted there was an appalling food shortage, if not a famine (something, incidentally, no one could have deduced from his messages to the *New York Times*, which were in an exactly contrary sense), but, he said, banging the sides of the sofa, remember that you can't make omelettes without cracking eggs – another favourite saying. They'll win, he went on; they're bound to win. If necessary, they'll harness the peasants to the ploughs, but I tell you they'll get the harvest in and feed the people that matter. The people that mattered were the men in the Kremlin and all their underlings; the men in the factories and the armed forces; us, too, the elite. The others were just serfs; reserves of the proletariat, as Stalin called them. Some would die, surely, perhaps even quite a lot; but there were enough and to spare in all conscience. It might have been a Burra Sahib talking about the natives.

I had the feeling, listening to this outburst, that in thus justifying Soviet brutality and ruthlessness, Duranty was in some way getting his own back for being small, and losing a leg, and not having the aristocratic lineage and classical education he claimed to have. This is probably, in the end, the only real basis of the appeal of such régimes as Stalin's, and later Hitler's; they compensate for weakness and inadequacy. It is also why their particular ideologies – *Mein Kampf, Das Kapital, The Thoughts of Chairman Mao* – are, in themselves, of no significance. Duranty was a little browbeaten boy looking up admiringly at a big bully. By the same token, if the *New York Times* went on all those years giving great prominence to Duranty's messages, building him and them up when they were so evidently nonsensically untrue, to the point that he came to be accepted as the great Russian expert in America, and played a major part in shaping President Roosevelt's policies *vis-à-vis* the USSR – this was not, we may be sure, because the *Times* was deceived. Rather, because it wanted to be so deceived, and Duranty provided the requisite deception material. Since his time, there have been a whole succession of others fulfilling the same role – in Cuba, in Vietnam, in Latin America. It is an addiction, and in such cases there is never any lack of hands to push in the needle and give the fix. Just as the intelligentsia have been foremost in the struggle to abolish intelligence, so the great organs of capitalism like the *New York Times* have spared no expense or effort to ensure that capitalism will not survive.

My journey to Rostov remains in my mind as a nightmare memory. The worn railway compartment, with glasses of tea endlessly served; other passengers coming and going, mostly party officials (who else could afford to travel first-class?), very companionable and amiable and ready to listen to my rudimentary Russian, but shutting up at once if I brought up the subject of what was going on outside. Then, their faces stony and expressionless again. Men in leather coats with briefcases, sucking at cigarettes, clearly used to giving orders and to being treated with deference in the Forestry Department, or the Audit Department, or I daresay in the GPU Department, but that also were unmentionable. The restaurant car, likewise cosy, with meals pleasantly served and plenty of vodka. There, too, the outside pleasantly remote, except for one intrusion; a bearded moujik in a padded coat, very drunk and wild looking, suddenly appeared, shouting out something – some sort of protest, I suppose, but I couldn't understand what. He was quickly disposed of; frog-marched out, still protesting.

It was tempting not to get down at any stations along the way as I had planned, but just to continue in the train. By comparison with its warmth and snugness, the stations looked very uninviting. I had no contacts, no transport, nowhere to go; the moment one arranged these amenities, one was back in Oumansky's charge. However, I did break my journey several times, and can never forget what I saw. It was not just a famine. No one, alas, news-gathering about the world in our time can fail to have seen quite a lot of famine. In India, in Berlin, in Africa – people picking over garbage, scrabbling about in rubble, maybe in their desperation cannibalising one another; swollen or skeletal, with huge stomachs suspended between bony arms and ribs, and heads that, while still alive, are already skulls. This particular famine was planned and deliberate; not due to any natural catastrophe like failure of rain, or cyclone, or flooding. An administrative famine brought about by the forced collectivisation of agriculture; an assault on the countryside by party *apparatchiks* – the very men I'd been chatting so amiably with in the train – supported by strong-arm squads from the military and the police.

As I wrote in *The Guardian*, in the course of three articles of mine that appeared on 25, 27 and 28 March, 1933: 'To say that there is famine in some of the most fertile parts of Russia is to say much less than the truth; there is not only famine, but a state of war, a military occupation.' The articles were held up to follow a series by Voigt on the Terror in the Polish Ukraine, and were run side by side with another series by him on the Nazi Terror, by way, I imagine, of neutralising some of their effect. In them I tried to describe it all – the abandoned villages, the absence of livestock, neglected fields; everywhere famished, frightened people and intimations of coercion, soldiers about the place, and hard-faced men in long overcoats. One particularly remarkable scene I stumbled on by chance at a railway station in the grey early morning; peasants with their hands tied behind them being loaded into cattle trucks at gun-point (this, incidentally, was the nearest I came to being in trouble myself; I was angrily told to make off, which I hurriedly did, fortunately without having to disclose myself as a foreign journalist); all so

C.W.T.—R

silent and mysterious and horrible in the half-light, like some macabre ballet.

Reading the articles over again, they seem very inadequate in conveying the horror of it all, which far surpassed just the human misery. *Rien de plus dangereux*, Taine writes, *qu'une idée générale dans des cerveaux étroits et vides*. Stalin's collectivisation of agriculture was just such a general idea in a narrow empty mind, pursued to the uttermost limit, without reference to any other consideration, whether of individual or collective humanity. To be oppressed by an individual tyrant is terrible enough; by an enraged deity, as the Old Testament tells us, even more terrible; but Taine is right when he contends that the worst of all fates is to be oppressed by a general idea. This was the fate of the Russian peasants, as it is, increasingly, the fate of us all in the twentieth century.

As it happened, no other foreign journalist had been into the famine areas in the USSR except under official auspices and supervision, so my account was by way of being exclusive. This brought me no kudos, and many accusations of being a liar, in *The Guardian* correspondence columns and elsewhere. I had to wait for Khruschev – who surely knew the truth if anyone did, having been himself one of the chief terrorists in the Ukraine – for official confirmation. Indeed, according to him, my account was considerably under-stated. If the matter is a subject of controversy hereafter, a powerful voice on the other side will be Duranty's, highlighted in the *New York Times*, insisting on those granaries overflowing with grain, those apple-cheeked dairymaids and plump contented cows, not to mention Shaw and all the other distinguished visitors who testified that there was not, and could not be, a food shortage in the USSR. I doubt if even Khruschev's testimony, let alone mine, will weigh against such honourable and distinguished witnesses.

In Kiev, where I found myself on a Sunday morning, on an impulse I turned into a church where a service was in progress. It was packed tight, but I managed to squeeze myself against a pillar whence I could survey the congregation and look up at the altar. Young and old, peasants and townsmen, parents and children, even a few in uniform – it was a variegated assembly. The bearded priests, swinging their incense, intoning their prayers, seemed very remote and far away. Never before or since have I participated in such worship; the sense conveyed of turning to God in great affliction was overpowering. Though I could not, of course, follow the service, I knew from Klavdia Lvovna little bits of it; for instance, where the congregation say there is no help for them save from God. What intense feeling they put into these words! In their minds, I knew, as in mine, was a picture of those desolate abandoned villages, of the hunger and the hopelessness, of the cattle trucks being loaded with humans in the dawn light. Where were they to turn for help? Not to the Kremlin, and the Dictatorship of the Proletariat, certainly; nor to the forces of progress and democracy and enlightenment in the West. Honourable and Right Honourable Members had nothing to offer; *Gauche Radicale* unforthcoming, free press Duranty's pulpit. Every possible human agency found wanting. So, only God remained, and to God they turned with a passion, a dedication, a humility, impossible to convey. They took me with them; I felt closer to God then than I ever had before, or am likely to again.

From Rostov I went to visit a German agricultural concession in the Kuban district of the North Caucasus, which had rather surprisingly survived from the early post-war years. It was like going abroad. Everything was completely different; the fields, the cowsheds, the piggeries, all in perfect order. I found it difficult to believe I was still in the USSR. A Bavarian in a green knickerbocker suit with a feather in his hat showed me round. Sensing, perhaps, that my attention was flagging, he asked me whether I was really interested in *Landwirtschaft*. I replied that I had to admit to being no specialist, but that I could not fail to notice how conditions in the concession contrasted with those outside. He agreed, and said that in consequence of the famine conditions all round them, they had been faced with a constant stream of famished peasants looking for work and food. In the evening I sat with him and a number of other Germans, all of them healthy and jovial and friendly and hospitable. While we were talking, one of them brought out a map, showing me just where the concession was situated, and going on to point out, *à propos* of nothing, how large the USSR was, and how rich agriculturally and in minerals. There was something vaguely ominous and menacing as his strong, short forefinger went moving about the map. Then someone turned on the radio, managing to get a German transmission. The news was that Hitler had become Chancellor. I had not been following the papers for some time, so it took me by surprise. 'How terrible!' I said, or something like that, expecting them to agree. They were, after all, professional people, agricultural experts, technicians; the sort of Germans, one assumed, who would find Hitler and his Nazis ridiculous and abhorrent. On the contrary, I could see that they were delighted. It was a good thing, they said; no doubt they and their class would once again lose everything they had, as had happened before; but this time Germany would recover her strength and resume her history. I had little inclination to argue, and, pleading tiredness, retired to bed. After I had gone they would, I felt sure, let their exaltation have free play; shaking hands, slapping one another on the back, drinking toasts. Late at night, I heard them, shouting and singing uproariously. Thenceforth, I never doubted that another war was inescapable.

When I got back to Moscow I found a telegram from Kitty telling me that we had another son. I managed to telephone to her, and we agreed that they should not come to Moscow. She told me that a chalet in Switzerland was available to us if we would run it as a guest-house for the Workers' Travel Association, a Labour Party tourist-agency with which my father was associated. It seemed a perfect solution, and we arranged delightedly all four of us now, to meet in Montreux. There seemed nothing left for me to do except write my articles about my visit to the Ukraine and the Caucasus, which I proceeded to do, getting them off by diplomatic bag unseen by Oumansky. When they were published, I should, I knew, have my visa withdrawn.

As it turned out, there was one last story to cover. The news got around in Moscow that some British engineers working on construction projects for the Metropolitan-Vickers Electrical Company in the USSR had been arrested, and were to be charged with sabotage and espionage, the chief of them being Allan Monkhouse, Paddy's cousin. I made use of this relationship in telephoning cryptic messages to *The Guardian* in the hope of thereby evading the censorship. Our first efforts to get news out by the usual channels met with a blank refusal. At the Press Department they said no arrests had taken place, and denied all knowledge of police raids on Metro-Vickers premises. In our fury and disgust at thus being deprived of our legitimate sustenance, we did something unprecedented, and late at night invaded the home of the censor on duty – who happened to be Ehrens. It was a cosy enough little apartment, with a wedding group in a silver frame, and crimson plush curtains, and a sofa with two round salmon-pink cushions on it, and a souvenir from Berne in the shape of a Swiss peasant doll. Ehrens appeared, to let us in, wearing pyjamas and a short embroidered coat with frogs, rather like a bandsman's tunic. We crowded in angrily, as though we were an insurrection; banging the table, shouting. The collectivisation famine, the Terror and the Purge, the Torgsin shops and the long queues outside the food shops

– all this, with some effort, we could take in our stride. But to be denied a story bound to get front-page treatment everywhere! That was too much. Poor Ehrens, too, was really troubled. What would the neighbours think? A GPU visitation? He pleaded with us to withdraw while he telephoned, which we did, standing in the passage outside until he had finished. Then he called us back to say that the bare facts of the arrests having been made could be telegraphed, and nothing more. We grudgingly and grumblingly accepted this meagre concession. I felt rather a Judas myself in the knowledge that, as I thought, my cryptic telephone call to Paddy Monkhouse some hours before would have given *The Guardian* an exclusive story. I need not have worried; only a drastically cut and sub-edited version of my coverage of the Metro-Vickers story appeared in the paper.

Later, Allan Monkhouse was released on bail, and we were called to the British Embassy to meet him. He turned out to be a quiet, solid sort of man who patiently answered questions of the kind that journalists, especially Americans, ask – How old was he? Married? Any children? How long in Russia? – to gain time before putting the serious ones they know won't be answered anyway. Like a juggler desultorily bouncing his little balls preparatory to getting them all into the air at the same time. It was a gentle enough curtain-raiser to what followed – the great Purge of the thirties mounted by Stalin; one of the most gruesome and macabre happenings even of our time, involving, according to Robert Conquest's careful estimate in his book *The Great Terror*, some twenty million souls.

In itself, the Metro-Vickers affair was rather a minor episode in this protracted *grand-guignol*, but it attracted a great deal of attention outside the USSR because of the appearance of foreign nationals among the accused. The brightly-lit court, the mechanically repeated confessions, the spectators baying in unison for the death penalty, the ravings and howlings of the Public Prosecutor, formerly Krylenko, and now Andrey Vyshinsky, subsequently eloquent Soviet spokesman at the UN – it was all to become part of twentieth-century folk-lore. Spreading in different versions throughout the world; to Leipzig for the Reichstag Fire Trial, to Nüremberg and Tokyo for the War Crimes Tribunals, to Washington for the Un-American Activities Committee, etc., etc., until it seemed that history itself had become a trial, at which, in Cholerton's words, everything was true except the facts. All the world's a trial, and all the men and women in the dock; Who whom? boiling down to Who's trying Whom?

Even now it is difficult to grasp the magnitude of what happened; a stupendous horror film conceived in the narrow, suspicious mind of Stalin, and produced and directed by him, in which every single Soviet citizen, from the Baltic to Vladivostok, willy-nilly participated, whether as extras, or with speaking parts. In Moscow one sensed the omnipresent fear in frightened, furtive eyes; sniffed the sour body-smell it gave out, which still, after all these years, remains with me. The endless interrogations; interrogators themselves in time interrogated, until no one knew who was confessing what to whom, who were the judges and who the accused. A fearsome morality play in which it had to be interminably demonstrated that, the system being perfect, as were all who had been submitted to the great baptism of the Revolution, any imperfection, whether in the system, or in individual beneficiaries of it, could only be due to malign stratagems, saboteurs, wreckers; to plots and subornings and conspiracies engineered by the powers of darkness – capitalists, imperialists, colonialists and their running dogs.

And how could the denizens of this dark, sub-human underworld find the strength to impede and frustrate the working out of Lenin-Stalin's revolutionary purpose? Only, obviously, when their efforts were reinforced by the very Revolution-makers themselves; all the Old Bolsheviks, who, one after the other, were required to make their public acts of penitence, beating their breasts, confessing their sins and misdemeanours, and receiving at the hands of a firing squad their just quittance. So the Revolution consumed its own children, reaching even outside its boundaries, and striking down a Trotsky in far-off Mexico. Power has its own mysticism of violence, symbolised in the USSR by what Stalin called the 'Flaming Sword of the Proletariat'; wielded on his behalf by the secret police, ever changing the initials of their name (Cheka, GPU, NKVD, KGB), one boss succeeding another (Dzerzhinsky, Jagoda, Yezhov, Beria; dreaded names until, in their turn, the purgers were purged), yet always remaining the same. As God's Flaming Sword was set at the entrance to the Garden of Eden to keep out the fallen children of men, so Stalin's barred the fallen children of the Revolution from his paradise. There was no need to set up a counter-revolution in the USSR; Stalin was his own counter-revolution.

As my increasingly hostile attitude to the régime became more apparent, my reception in the Press Department was correspondingly cold and hostile. Lost for ever now was my position of favourite son, as a protégé of the Blessed Webbs, and contributor to the beneficent columns of the

Manchester Guardian. I was the more surprised, therefore, to receive an invitation to dine with Oumansky, which, of course, I readily accepted. The occasion was set for the evening before my departure from Moscow, and the place the Spirodonovka, a former rich merchant's house which had been requisitioned intact, to be used for government hospitality, with all the furniture, décor, and other fittings kept just as they were. Such invitations were very rarely accorded to foreign journalists; not even to the tamest (in Soviet Double-Speak, most objective), like Louis Fischer or Duranty; least of all, one would have thought, to someone like myself who had proved, in the régime's terms, unreliable and unhelpful. Those that are not against us are for us, Podolski once remarked, smirking over some statement by an Anglican dignitary to the effect that if Christ were alive to-day he would probably be a communist. Even on that basis, I was an enemy now. Why, then, the invitation to dinner? Was it that Oumansky had some notion of plucking a brand from the burning? Or, at any rate, of moderating excesses of hostility I might indulge in on leaving the USSR? Or was it just that he saw a chance of having a good dinner for once? If so, a very human calculation. Or – an outside possibility – that he genuinely wanted to make a gesture of friendship before we parted, probably not to see one another ever again? An unspoken recognition on his part that my changed attitude represented a genuinely reached conclusion, not an interested calculation? Some support was given to this possibility by a remark he made to me; he had, he said, formed the impression when I first came to the USSR that I believed in nothing, whereas I went away believing in something. Yes, but in what? He didn't say, and I didn't know – then. Poor Oumansky, he was a sort of Soviet version of Maupassant's hero, Bel-Ami. It would be nice to think that the invitation was some sort of friendly gesture.

Oumansky was waiting for me at Spirodonovka when I arrived. He showed me over the house, which, he explained, had been built by a rich merchant; in very bad taste, of course, he added, but still use could be made of it. I followed him from room to room; tall, dimly lighted rooms, heavy with coloured marble; a décor of gold fleurs-de-lys on a blue background, with frail gilt candelabra hung from the ceiling. Oumansky, I could see, loved the house, and took great delight in showing it off – more so, perhaps, than in showing off the Dneprostroi Dam. The only other guest was Nehman, who had brought his photograph album to show me. We sat looking at it side by side on one of the delicate gold and blue sofas; so delicate that I half expected it to break under our weight and movements. There were a lot of snapshots of Nehman, his wife, and their little son wearing a sailor suit, on a Black Sea beach. I duly admired them. Then the three of us went into dinner.

The table was set for us in the centre of a black and white Japanese room, with many mirrors reflecting an endless series of Oumansky, Nehman and me. We sat underneath a massive candelabrum whose light shone down on us; again, a preview of television locations-to-be. The light, as it seemed, brought the confused pattern on the walls to life, so that it looked as though it was in perpetual motion; rippling and pulsating like a surface of dark water in a wind. Passfield had been, as I supposed, my last glimpse of snug bourgeois life; this was to be my last glimpse of proletarian life, and I wanted similarly to imprint the scene on my mind. As course followed course, and drink followed drink, my senses began to dissolve. I felt myself becoming absorbed into the Japanese room; the rippling, pulsating walls were closing in on me, as in an Edgar Allan Poe story; the mirrors revealed a long, long corridor along which I trudged, with no end in sight. The figure of Oumansky loomed up across the table, misty and remote. There was a question that I desperately wanted to put to him, but every time I got it into suitable shape, somehow or other he was off on another tack.

My question was, of course: Who whom? The only question to put concerning matters of power; all the other related ones, like justice, equality, freedom, representation, and so on, being diversionary. 'Yes, but look here, Oumansky, Who whom?' Did I actually say it, or only mutter it into my glass? Or just envisage saying it? I can't be sure – I was rather drunk by this time – but I do remember Oumansky going on about how, when the Provisional Government of Kerensky fell, the power passed to the broad masses, whence, via the first Congress of Soviets it found its way to the Dictatorship of the Proletariat, and, under the inspired leadership of Comrade Stalin and the Communist Party . . .

Did I then rudely interrupt with: 'No, but seriously, Oumansky, Who whom?' I doubt it, but something must have happened, for I swear that Oumansky's dissertation, as it were, changed gear. He dropped his voice to take on a more confidential note, explaining how the broad masses are like children; they need a father, a dictatorship of themselves; a force that is them, but that, working apart from them, makes it possible for everything to be subordinated to their interests. Any other force must, by its very nature, deceive and enslave them. It alone . . .

Perhaps he did say something of this sort, but it can't surely be true that, as I seemed to remember in my fuddled mind the following day, I once more interrupted, this time to say, pleadingly: 'Please, Oumansky; Who whom?', to which he replied, whispering softly, so that not even Nehman sitting with us could hear, but I just could: 'I they!'

It was time, anyway, for me to go. Oumansky and Nehman came to the door to see me off, as the Webbs and the two Scottish maids had at Passfield. As I walked unsteadily away, I could hear Oumansky say: 'Good-bye and *bonne chance!*' He liked speaking French; it befitted a diplomat, as it did his pre-Revolution prototype. '*Bonne chance* to you!' I shouted back over my shoulder. Before returning to my hotel I took a few turns round the Red Square. The place was deserted except for the soldiers with fixed bayonets on duty outside Lenin's tomb. I walked briskly; breathing in the icy air cleared my head. Suddenly, I thought I noticed a change in the wind that was blowing against my face. It seemed to be touched with warmth and fragrance, as though spring was already beginning. An extraordinary feeling of happiness welled up in me. Soon the river would thaw, the earth be green again. Thus it had happened a million times before, thus it would happen a million times again. Nothing could prevent it – the sudden, unexpected coming of spring. I filled my lungs ravenously.

I left the USSR via Riga, then the capital of an independent Latvia, breaking my journey at Leningrad, where, on an impulse, having some hours to spare, I decided to go and look for Dostoevsky's grave. It was by no means an easy quest. I found the cemetery where he was buried easily enough, but when I asked where his grave was, no one seemed prepared to give me any information other than pointing vaguely. At last, after much laborious spelling out of the names on tombstones, I did manage to locate it. The grave and the monument had a neglected, untended appearance, which was not really surprising since, following Lenin's view, the Party Line had pronounced anathema upon Dostoevsky as a reactionary who had rejected and ridiculed the very notion of progress and of Socialism. I wondered if anyone else had come there of late to do him reverence. Anyway, I was glad to take off my hat and stand for a while in silence, honouring his memory in the strange circumstances which had befallen his country – circumstances he had so uncannily prophesied in *The Possessed*, the book that of all others had been most in my mind during my time in the USSR.

What a scene it must have been, I reflected, at that very place when he died some half century before! What a turn-out of the great and the celebrated! He who, in his famous Pushkin Memorial speech, had proclaimed the great destiny of the Slav peoples to overthrow the corrupt, decadent civilisation of the West, and bring to pass a new, glorious era of Christendom reborn! Who had so brilliantly and devastatingly exposed the vain hopes and destructive purposes of the liberal mind, and, in the character of Raskolnikov, created its very prototype. Who, when he spoke of how now Russians must look to their roads southwards, had every general jumping in the air until his medals shook; every archbishop dancing about, his tall black hat askew. I could see it all, the carriages waiting, the exquisite ladies in veils, the splendid vestments of the officiating priests. And now just me!

But wait a minute. Go forward another forty years, to 1971, the 150th anniversary of Dostoevsky's birth, and lo! it turns out that Lenin put Dostoevsky only second to Tolstoy in a list he prepared of the greatest Russian writers, and that the judgement that 'Dostoevsky could not be in accord with our epoch was one of the errors of our young society, those errors which, in their own time, had their own truth and logic.' (Let other Mirskys, scavenging with their pens, watch out!) With the Great Soviet Encyclopaedia also suitably adjusted, there could well be another turn-out no less brilliant. As for the grave I found so neglected – it would surprise me if by this time it had not been refurbished.

Among several pieces I wrote about the USSR which never got published was one entitled 'Red Imperialism', in which I argued that the cause of liberating the toiling masses could lend itself just as well to Dostoevsky's brand of Slav imperialism as the notion of liberating Christians from the Ottoman yoke. In those days, with the worthy Litvinov advocating total disarmament whenever he had a chance, and every pacifist and internationalist cause sure of a warm endorsement in Moscow, my suggestion seemed too absurd. To-day, no one would print the piece because it would seem too banal. When I read in the documents from the archives of the German Foreign Office published in 1948 of the conversations between Hitler and Molotov relating to the Nazi-Soviet Pact, I realised that Dostoevsky would have found in Stalin's emissary an exponent of his views far more resolute and unscrupulous than any Czar; and one no less concerned than he was about roads going southwards.

Walking away, I noticed another funeral in progress; the coffin lifted off a red hearse, and the little group of mourners raising their hats while it was lowered into the grave. Some were in tears, and there was the same embarrassed expression on the faces of the less involved that one sees at all funerals. One of their number delivered a short exhortation, to which the others listened impassively. Dust to dust; or, in this case, a comrade who had faithfully followed Lenin's way, now departing. It was soon over, and the mourners dispersed, leaving the grave-diggers to fill in the grave.

There were not many passengers on the train to Riga. As we approached the Latvian-Soviet frontier, all of us with one accord went into the corridor to stare at the soldiers in their long grey great-coats, red stars on their caps, guarding it. Then, when we were safely in Latvian territory, we all began spontaneously to laugh and shout and shake our fists at the sentries. We were out, we were free. It was one of the strangest demonstrations of the kind I have ever been involved in. Subsequently, I have seen many Soviet frontiers, with barbed-wire, and land-mines, and dogs; with armed sentries in watch-towers ready to shoot on sight, like prison guards. All designed, not so much to bar people from coming in, as to prevent those inside from getting out. How strange, I have often reflected, that a régime which needs thus to pen up its citizens should nonetheless be able to make itself seem desirable to admirers outside. As though the purpose in taking the Bastille should have been to gain admission there and do a stretch.

The buffet at Riga Station seemed momentarily like paradise; the crisp rolls and butter, the piles of fruit, the luscious cheeses and succulent ham – who could ever believe in such plenty? My euphoria soon passed. Man cannot live by buffets alone, and the angels in this paradise were puffy, pasty men carrying briefcases instead of harps, with their beatitudes securely tucked away in wallets in their hip-pockets. On my way to Berlin, where I proposed stopping off for two days, my spirits steadily fell. I was, I felt, returning on my tracks; going deeper and deeper back into the bourgeois world I thought I had discarded for ever. Its very affluence made it the more abhorrent; I was a prodigal son puking over his fatted calf.

In Berlin the Nazi storm-troopers were out in the streets marking Jewish shops, and beating up their owners and anyone else who displeased them. Mostly not quite young; burly in their brown shirts, with incipient paunches filling out their breeches. The females likewise in brown, with blond plaits and pink cheeks, but also inclined to be outsize; more like women policemen than Rhine maidens. The city was hushed; like a theatre when the lights have been lowered preparatory to the curtain going up. Its glossy porn was still on display, and the transvestite shows still running; but the steam had gone out of it all.

To paraphrase Grey's alleged famous observation, they were shutting down the sex-supermarkets all over Germany, but we should, alas, see them opened again in our time. As for the then hippy model, the *Wandervögel*, in decorated braces, twanging their *Lauten*, and going ever *weiter im Blau*, further into the Blue – they had all become Hitlerjugend, and were marching and saluting and shouting in unison.

Always gloomy, Berlin seemed now under a permanent thunder cloud, a place of doom. I was not to see it again until 1945, when it was just an expanse of rubble, with occasional jagged fragments of buildings rising stark against the sky. If one looked carefully one could see that people were actually living in the rubble, having carved out for themselves little caves and cubby holes for dwellings, where they carried on commerce of a kind, with, for currency, cigarettes and spam, as well as their own bodies, if negotiable. I was reminded of the scene in the first pictures from the moon. Then, ten years later, back again, and this time I was amazed to find that a magical city of glass and lights, a Disney Deutschland, was rapidly rising; cafés crowded with solid citizens smoking cigars, sipping cognac; glossy porn back in the kiosks, *Schlag* back in the coffee, transvestites back in business. A city reborn. Or was it all done with mirrors? I am not certain even now.

I wrote to Crozier: 'From the way you've cut my messages about the Metro-Vickers affair, I realise that you don't want to know what's going on in Russia, or to let your readers know. If it had been an oppressed minority, or subject people valiantly struggling to be free, that would have been another matter. Then any amount of outspokenness, any amount of honesty.' I went on to describe the scene in Berlin, and the Nazis beating up Jewish shops, and everyone with his story of murder and folly, and concluded: 'It's silly to say the Brown Terror is worse than the Red Terror. They're both horrible. They're both Terrors. I watched the Nazis march along *Unter den Linden* and realised – of course, they're Komsomols, the same people, the same faces. It's the same show.' David Ayerst quotes this correspondence in his book on *The Guardian*, and says it read 'like a letter to end all communication'. So it did; I was finished with moderate men of all shades of opinion for evermore.

Montreux Station in the very early morning waiting for Kitty seemed about as far away from the USSR and Oumansky, from Berlin and the storm-troopers out in the streets, as it was possible to be. The coffee so hot and fragrant, the rolls so crisp, the butter so creamy; the waiter so obliging, his hair so sleek and black, his face so sallow, his coat so fresh and spotlessly white. Everything and everyone so solid and so durable. Even Kitty's train, roaring in exactly on time, was part of the omnipresent orderliness. There is always a dread on such occasions that somehow the rendezvous will not be kept; that arrangements which seemed so precise will somehow have gone awry. So one studies the gathering faces with mounting anxiety; every sort of face showing up except the particular one in question, until, at last, there it is; unmistakable, unique, infinitely dear. Waving to Kitty in the distance when I see her, holding one son's hand and another son in her arms, a Shakespearean tag comes into my mind: 'Hang there like fruit, dear heart, till the tree rot.' What is love but a face, instantly recognisable in a sea of faces? A spotlight rather than a panning shot? This in contradistinction to power, which is a matter of numbers, of crowd scenes. I heard of an inscription on a stone set up in North Africa which reads: 'I, the captain of a Legion of Rome, have learnt and pondered this truth, that there are in life but two things, love and power, and no man can have both.' Some twenty centuries later, I append my own amen.

We extravagantly hired a car to take us to Rossinière, where our chalet was, climbing up the still snow-covered valley under a blue sky and in bright sunshine. I took stock of our new son, very robust and hearty, and renewed my acquaintance with the older one, who even then had the air of slight aloofness and detachment, of being vaguely surprised at finding himself in so strange a place as this world, and in the strange company it offers, which characterises those who from the beginning walk with God. There we were, reunited, in the seemingly secure peace and security of the Canton de Vaud, with the rumblings of the wrath to come that I had unmistakably heard, well out of earshot. It was a moment of great happiness; as though, having found each other, we should never again be separated. As though, having found a blue sky, there would be no more grey ones; breathing in this fresh, clear mountain air, no more smog.

Such moments of happiness, looked back on, shine like beacons, lighting up past time, and making it glow with a great glory. Recollecting them, I want to jump up and shout aloud in gratitude at having been allowed to live in this world, sharing with all its creatures the blessed gift of life. Alienation is to be isolated and imprisoned in the tiny dark dungeon of the ego; happiness to find the world a home and mankind a family, to see our earth as a nest snugly perched in the universe, and all its creatures as fellow-participants in the warmth and security it offers. Its very components, the very twigs and mud of which it is made, likewise participating. Then, indeed, all the world in a grain of sand, eternity in an hour, infinity grasped in one's hand. So, such moments of happiness comprehend a larger ecstasy, and our human loves reach out into the furthermost limits of time and space, and beyond, expressing the lovingness that is at the heart of all creation. Curiously enough, of all people, it was of Karl Marx I thought as we rode joyously up to Rossinière; recalling how in one of his letters he describes to his wife the longing he has to return to Paris, where the family were then living, after one of his interminable quarrelsome conferences, and how the only lasting and satisfying joy he knows is to be with them and see around him their dear familiar faces. The memory of this letter stayed with me, I suppose, because of the contrast it offers with the efforts made in his name to promote the happiness of all mankind; in the result, so desolating, so bloody and so futile. Poor old Jewish enragé, whose furious indignation was to rumble and echo through the world for years to come – he, too, gratefully flying back to his nest.

Our chalet – called the Chalet de la Colline – turned out to be rather a large one which had only lately been completed. It seemed that the Englishman who had built it ran out of money, and the Workers' Travel Association took it over to run as a guest-house. Happily, none of the guests were due to arrive for some little while, and we had it to ourselves. There was a marvellous view up the valley, and the owner had left behind quite a good library, including *À la recherche du temps perdu*, which I settled down to read slowly and systematically. For Kitty, it was old territory. She was born at Château d'Oêx, the next place to Rossinière; at the Pension Rosat, still presided over by Madame Rosat, a stern, ageless lady. We went to pay our respects to her, and she remembered Mrs Dobbs well, saying of her, I thought with great acumen: '*Elle est très intellectuelle; elle voyage beaucoup.*' It just about summed her up. Most afternoons we walked a mile or so up the valley and then back. As the snow melted, the spring flowers, no less white, came out to take its place.

There are always ideal circumstances for reading any book, which should, perhaps, be indicated on the dust-jacket, along with particulars of the author and the subject. Rossinière was ideal for reading Proust, and whenever I think of Charlus or Swann or Odette or Albertine, the road up the valley to Château d'Oêx, and the flowers, and the cowbells sounding as the cattle were taken to the mountain pasture, come into my mind. I quite enjoyed the book, but not overwhelmingly; not at all as I did, for instance, Pascal and Constant and La Fontaine when I came to read them. The long maundering sentences, the prevailing flavour of snobbishness and perversity, of a sick mind at work, detracted from my enjoyment, even though I had to recognise the book's genius of a kind. Its great appeal to intelligentsia of all denominations, who have praised it inordinately, has been due, I suspect, to Proust's being yet another celebrant of a lost bourgeoisie. I should never be surprised to find a televised version of *À la recherche du temps perdu* enjoying as great and widespread a success as *The Forsyte Saga*, especially in the communist countries and Japan. The great literary quest of the twentieth century has been for writers with authentic *avant garde* credentials and strongly conservative, if not reactionary, predilections. Proust filled this role perfectly. So did Yeats and Pound, both of whom were overtly fascist in tendency; in Pound's case, in practice as well. Eliot, D. H. Lawrence, Hemingway, Aldous Huxley, too, and even Orwell in his odd way, came into this category. Most of the political heroes of our time have been of the Left, from Rosa Luxemburg to Che Guevara, and most of the literary ones of the Right. A two-way *Trahison des Clercs*, or double-Judas act.

Apart from Proust, my mind was endlessly preoccupied with thoughts of the Soviet régime. I felt furious about the whole experience, as though I had been personally cheated, and poured out my righteous indignation and hurt vanity in a series of articles as bitter and satirical as I knew how to make them. They probably struck most readers as being just angry. Clearly, I could not offer them to *The Guardian*, and so, going to the other extreme, I sent them to the old *Morning Post*, long since extinct, but in its day a reputable Tory newspaper of the extreme Right. The editor accepted five of them, rejecting two – the one about Red Imperialism, and another giving an account of how foreign journalists working in the USSR are induced to toe the Party Line. Subsequently, I tried this latter piece on *The Times*, where it was likewise rejected, even though at that time the paper had no correspondent in Moscow, and relied on the reports of a man named Urch in Riga. Anyone who had the curiosity to look up Urch's dispatches would find that they maintained a high level of accuracy and reliability; certainly by comparison with Duranty's, so prominently displayed in the columns of the *New York Times*. Again one marvels at the almost mystical importance attached to the location of a news-gatherer as distinct from the truthfulness of the news sent.

I was paid five guineas each for the five articles accepted by the *Morning Post*. It was not much, but in those days twenty-five guineas sufficed to keep us going in food for quite a while in Rossinière. In the Leftist legend of the thirties it is usually assumed that attacking the Soviet régime was made temptingly lucrative, whereas supporting it involved penury and perhaps martyrdom. For the most part, precisely the opposite was the case; most of the best-selling writers about the USSR were strongly favourable (for instance, Maurice Hindus, Dr Hewlett Johnson and the Webbs, whose *Soviet Communism: A New Civilisation?* had a very large sale, especially when, as Stalin got into his stride as the master-terrorist of the age, they dropped the question mark from the title – a vast and mercifully forgotten literature of Soviet adulation, all very profitable to its progenitors), whereas antagonistic works were difficult to get published and sure to be knocked or ignored. Even *Animal Farm*, one of the few undoubted works of genius of our time, was rejected by fourteen publishers on the ground that it was too hostile to the Soviet régime, before being accepted. One of the rejectors was T. S. Eliot on behalf of Faber & Faber.

The *Morning Post* articles attracted a certain amount of attention. Arthur Schlesinger told me, when he was working on his book, *The Age of Roosevelt*, that Henry Wallace used them as an argument against recognising the USSR when the matter was under consideration by the Roosevelt Administration. As he was Secretary of Agriculture and one of the President's inner circle of advisers at the time, he may even have had some effect. I was rather glad to be abroad and inaccessible when the articles appeared. Inevitably, they aroused the interest of organisations and individuals belonging to the wilder shores of international politics, such as ultra-royalist Russian exiles, and various brands of Ukrainian nationalists and separatists; curious societies and organisations with elaborate letter-heads dedicated to restoring lost cultures and recovering lost lands. I had no wish to get mixed up in such company, and kept on trying to explain, whenever an opportunity offered, that disliking the Soviet régime did not imply any particular liking for its predecessors or possible successors, or even a wish that the October Revolution had not happened.

It was the memory of my anxieties at this time which first drew me to George Orwell, who went through a similar experience as a result of the publication of his articles about his experiences during the Spanish Civil War, in which he exposed the monstrous hypocrisy and chicanery of

Communist policy in Catalonia. The articles were rejected out of hand by the *New Statesman*, and appeared finally in the *New English Weekly*, the rather obscure organ of the Social Credit Movement. When I got to know him, we often discussed how difficult it is, in an ideologically polarised society like ours, to take up any position without being automatically assumed to hold all the views and attitudes associated with it. Like voting the ticket in an American election, when by just pressing one button support is automatically accorded to a whole string of candidates for all sorts of offices. Thus to attack the Soviet or the Spanish Republican régime was automatically to support their Fascist or Nazi opponents; to expose the fatuities of the liberal mind, to commend the authoritarian one. Orwell's devastating exposure of the pursuit of power through revolution in *Animal Farm*, and of the maintenance of power for power's own sake in *1984*, was intended to show, with the desperate intensity of an utterly honest mind, that the world of the mid-twentieth century was moving towards a collectivised way of life, whose only truth would be slogans, whose only duty would be conformity and whose only morality would be power. Admittedly, the pioneer and first exemplar in this field was the USSR, but the trend, as was to become increasingly apparent, was universal. It was not by chance that he took the BBC as his model for the Ministry of Truth in *1984*; his picture of a continuing state of war whose aims and even location are largely unknown, has come to pass in Vietnam, and television has become Big Brother's provenance, if not his kingdom, just as he foresaw. All my own conclusions as a result of my time in the USSR pointed in exactly the same direction.

Soon the clients started arriving at the Chalet de la Colline, which was just as well; our money was again running out, and it was only when we had clients in residence that we could get any from the Workers' Travel Association – whose name, incidentally, soon became an embarrassment, and had to be used only as initials, proving once more that the more workers are cracked up and adulated in the abstract the less anyone wants to be categorised as a worker in practice. The clients, in any case, proved to be mostly school-teachers and accountants, with an occasional civil servant, though there was one authentic worker, a railwayman accompanied by his wife, of whom we all made a tremendous fuss to show how un-class conscious we were. As it happened, they were both as nice as could be, and managed with great ease to find congenial places to take a quiet glass of wine in the neighbourhood of Rossinière. Mrs

Dobbs also came to stay with us, engaging in some clandestine marketing of her paintings with the clients. Sometimes she accompanied me on my afternoon walk, talking all the way about such matters as whether there was a devil, and the prospects for all creation in due course becoming one. She had a way of shuffling and scraping her feet as she went along which produced a sandpaper effect by way of background to the rasp of her voice, thereby making the envisaged oneness of all somehow less alluring than might otherwise have been the case. One thought with relief of the aeons and aeons of time that must pass before this happy consummation would be realised.

We spent in all some three months in Rossinière, during which time I finished a book about my experiences in the USSR, later published as *Winter In Moscow*. As with the *Morning Post* articles, I wrote in a mood of anger, which I find rather absurd now; not so much because the anger was, in itself, unjustified, as because getting angry about human affairs is as ridiculous as losing one's temper when an air flight is delayed, or in a traffic jam. The only parts of the book I find tolerable are the humorous passages; laughter being a great prophylactic which disinfects anger as it does lechery and all other passions. When *Winter In Moscow* came out, it enjoyed a certain vogue among old Moscow hands like Chip Bohlen, Bill Stoneman and William Henry Chamberlin, who prided themselves on having a glossary of the real people behind my fictitious names. Cholerton said of it that it was the great anti-cant Bible of the USSR, which pleased me very much, but in actual fact it achieved nothing in the way of clearing up misconceptions and propaganda lies; people continued to regard as an open question whether there was forced labour in the USSR, and whether the confessions of the Old Bolsheviks to have worked for the British Secret Service, etc., etc., were genuine. Shaw's picture of Stalin as the Good Fabian, and Dr Hewlett Johnson's of him as building the Kingdom of Christ, continued to carry more conviction than mine of a bloodthirsty tyrant of unusual ferocity even by Russian standards. People, after all, believe lies, not because they are plausibly presented, but because they want to believe them. So, their credulity is unshakeable.

Sitting at my typewriter in the mornings, and tramping about the Canton de Vaud in the afternoons, I tried desperately hard to sort out my thoughts and emotions following the total reversal, in the light of what I had seen and understood in the USSR, of everything I had hitherto hoped for and believed. It was not just a disillusionment with the Russian Revolution as such; that, after all, was something that had happened, a historical event like any other, with causes and consequences which could be explored and evaluated. No more, for that matter, with the Soviet régime as such, which, with all its cruelties and privations, was a way of life like any other, endurable to the Russian people as being in their historical tradition. Anyway, an essentially *Russian* way of life rather than a Marxist one. Requiring, therefore, the move to Moscow from elegant Europeanised Petrograd-Leningrad – something that Dostoevsky, and Tolstoy, too, would have heartily endorsed. Requiring, also, for Red Czar a Georgian bandit like Stalin, not one of his Old Bolshevik colleagues like Trotsky or Bukharin or Zinoviev or Radek; mostly Jewish, 'rootless cosmopolitans', as they were later to be contemptuously dubbed when Stalin swung the Russians back to their traditional and habitual anti-semitism. These, Stalin decided (and he may well, from his own point of view, have been right), were better dead. And dead in the most humiliating way – beating their breasts, and abjectly apologising for doing things they couldn't possibly have done, being where they couldn't possibly have been, keeping assignations they couldn't possibly have kept.

All this likewise indubitably belonged to history, and would have to be historically assessed; like the Murder of the Innocents, or the Black Death, or the Battle of Paschendaele. But there was something else; a monumental death-wish, an immense destructive force loosed in the world which was going to sweep over everything and everyone, laying them flat; burning, killing, obliterating, until nothing was left. Those German agronomes in their green uniform suits with feathers in their hats – they had their part to play. So had the paunchy Brown-Shirts, and the matronly blonde maidens painting swastikas on the windows of Jewish shops. So had the credulous armies of the just, listening open-mouthed to Intourist patter, or seeking reassurance from a boozy sandalled Wicksteed. Wise old Shaw, high-minded old Barbusse, the venerable Webbs, Gide the pure in heart and Picasso the impure, down to poor little teachers, crazed clergymen and millionaires, drivelling dons and very special correspondents like Duranty, all resolved, come what might, to believe anything, however preposterous, to overlook anything, however villainous, to approve anything, however obscurantist and brutally authoritarian, in order to be able to preserve intact the confident expectation that one of the most thorough-going, ruthless and bloody tyrannies ever to exist on earth could be relied on to champion human freedom, the brotherhood of man, and all the other good liberal causes to which they had dedicated their lives. All resolved, in other words, to abolish themselves and their world, the rest of us with it. Nor have I from that time ever had the faintest expectation that, in earthly terms, anything could be salvaged; that any earthly battle could be won, or earthly solution found. It has all just been sleep-walking to the end of the night.

Index

Index

Aga Khan, the, 190
Agate, James, 185
Alwaye, 106f
Andrews, Rev. C. F., 189
Andreychin, 247
Aragon, Louis, 238
Armistice Day 1918, 70
Asquith, H. H., 88
Astor, Lady, 243
Augustine, St, 11
Ayerst, David, 268

Badoglio, Marshal, 194
Baldwin, Stanley, 134, 135, 192
Barbusse, Henri, 174, 250, 275
Barnes, Ralph, 234
Barnes, Dr W. E., 131f
Bashkertsef, Maria, 61
Beardsley, Aubrey, 78
Beaverbrook, Lord, 97, 157
Bellamy, Edward, 61
Benn, A. Wedgwood, 77
Berlin, 267-8
Beveridge, Sir William, 83
Bevin, Ernest, 76
Bhagavid Gita, the, 111, 127
Billington, Kevin, 51
Birkenhead, Lord, 221
Bismarck, Prince, 77
Blake, William, 19, 37, 56, 74, 150, 175
Bohlen, Chip, 274
Borodin, 235, 254
Brawne, Fanny, 92
Brecht, Bertold, 214, 253
Brooke, Rupert, 79
Bullett, Gerald, 187
Burton, Sir Richard, 124

Cantaloupe, Mlle, 85
Carlyle, Thomas, 60, 68, 72, 144
Carpenter, Edward, 44, 57
Carpenter-Garnier, Bishop, 117
Carswell, Catherine, 183
Chacko, K. C., 108
Chamberlain, Joseph, 146, 150
Chamberlain, Neville, 188, 240
Chamberlin, Sonia, 232, 240-2
Chamberlin, W. H., 203, 232f, 241, 245, 274
Chaplin, Charlie, 190
Chesterton, G. K., 13
Chekhov, Anton, 242, 252
Cholerton, A. T., 21, 228f, 240, 244, 246, 251, 261, 274
Christian Science Monitor, 232, 233, 241
Churchill, Winston, 134, 167
Clausewitz, Gen., 72
Clynes, J. R., 49
Coleridge, S. T., 60
Colony, The, 39, 41f
Comité des Forges, 68
Comfort, Dr, 230
Conquest, Robert, 261
Corke, Miss, 64f
Cotton, Mr, British Resident, 119-20
Courtney, Lord & Lady, 144
Cripps, Sir Stafford, 149, 208, 209
Cromwell, Oliver, 60
Crossman, R. H. S., 77
Croydon, 23f, 46, 50, 56, 68, 76
Crozier, W. P., 196-7, 199, 200f, 233, 268

Daily News, 13, 131
Daily Telegraph, 167, 198, 228

Dalton, Hugh, 49, 79
Dawson, Geoffrey, 97
de la Mare, Walter, 90
Dell, Robert, 189
Dickens, Charles, 25f, 72
Dickinson, Lowes, 25
Dmitrievna, Natalia, 228, 253
Dnieperstroi Dam, 245
Dobbs, Leonard, 85, 158
Dobbs, Mr, 88, 136, 139, 141, 143
Dobbs, Mrs, 89f, 135, 136-9, 141, 143, 144, 158, 269, 274
Dobrée, Bonamy, 154f
Donne, John, 141
Dora, 73f, 92
Dostoevsky, Feodor, 265-6, 275
Duranty, Walter, 254-6, 258, 263, 272, 275
Durrell, Lawrence, 164

Eden, Anthony (Lord Avon), 76, 233
Edward VII, 143
Ehrenburg, Ilya, 58, 207, 220
Ehrens, Russian censor, 223, 233, 246, 260, 261
Eisenstein, Sergei, 252
Eliot, T. S., 154, 155, 186, 236, 272
Ellis, Havelock, 143
Evening Standard, 170

Farouk, King, 164
First World War, 66f
Fischer, Louis, 246, 249-50, 255, 263
Fleurinski, 223
Forster, E. M., 154, 164
Forsyth, Matthew, 184
Francis of Assisi, St, 12, 18, 81
Frederick the Great, 60
Freud, Sigmund, 132
Fuad, King, 155

Gaitskell, Hugh, 77
Galsworthy, John, 120
Gandhi, Mahatma, 60, 109-11, 189f, 244, 247
George V, 190
Georgevna, Katerina, 251-2

Gide, André, 224, 275
Ginsberg, Allan, 102, 179
Gissing, George, 137
Goodman, Lord, 15
Gorki, Maxim, 236
GPU, *see* OGPU
Gregory, Maundy, 134
Grey, Earl, 67
Guardian, 20, 111, 112, 132, 144, 160ff, 269, 271
Guevara, Che, 111, 271

Hammond, J. L., 201
Harris, Mr & Mrs Duncan, 54f
Henderson, Arthur, 203
Herriot, Edouard, 244
Hetherington, Alistair, 200
Hindus, Maurice, 243, 272
Hitler, Adolf, 191, 240, 256, 259, 266, 275
Holland, Rev & Mrs W. H. S., 91, 105, 116f, 125
Hooper, Lester, 105, 115, 118, 125
Hopwood, Miss, 122, 125
Huntington, Constant, 185
Huxley, Aldous, 58, 187, 236
Huxley, Julian, 243

Ibsen, Henrik, 61
International Workers of the World, 247
Iszvestia, 220
Iyer, Sir C. P. Ramaswomy, 118

Jacob, Rev C. K., 93, 94, 97
Johnson, Amy, 207
Johnson, Dr Hewlett, 132, 149, 272, 274
Johnson, Dr Samuel, 25, 120, 176, 209
Jordan, Mr, 47

Kafka, 235
Kaiser, the, 69
Kalinin, 229, 248, 250
Kavafy, 164
Keats, John, 92

Kennedy, John F., 21
Kenyatta, Jomo, 100
Keynes, J. Maynard, 50, 79, 134
Khrushchev, Nikita, 174, 258
King, Martin Luther, 111
Kingsmill, Hugh, 85, 87
Kipling, Rudyard, 94, 135
Kirkwood, David, 193
Kitchener, F. M., Earl, 67
Kliasma, 222f
Knox, E. V., 82
Knox, Ronald, 82
Knox, Wilfred, 80, 82
Kraft-Ebbing, 143
Krokodil, 195, 248
Kropotkin, 60
Krupps, 68

Laski, Harold, 112, 149, 243
Laughton, Charles, 185
Lawrence, D. H., 44, 64, 65-6, 143, 176, 181, 183, 187, 236
Lawrence, T. E., 79
League of Nations, 71, 244
Leary, Dr Timothy, 59
Lee, (Lady) Jennie, 15
Lenin, 161, 206, 217, 230, 266
Lidiard, Miss, 39f
Litvinov, Maxim, 161, 189, 223
Lloyd George, David, 134, 143, 192
Lloyd, Lord, 155, 160, 192
Londonderry, Lady, 49, 195
Luciani, M., 230, 237, 239
Lunn, Sir Henry, 87-8, 141
Lunn's Tours, 85f
Lvovna, Klavdia, 220f, 223, 236, 251, 259

MacDonald, Ramsay, 49, 76, 92, 131, 148, 190, 192, 194f, 201
Macmillan, Harold, 248-9
McTaggart, Prof., 79
Madras Mail, 115
Maisky, 207
Malcolm X, 111
Malenkov, 208

Manchester Evening News, 166, 198, 201
Manchester Guardian, see Guardian
Marley, Lord, 230, 244
Martin, Kingsley, 112, 172, 173f
Martin, Olga, 173
Marx, Karl, 60, 132, 270
Mathai, Mr, 126-7
Maugham, Somerset, 119-20
Maxton, James, 193
Metropolitan-Vickers, 260f
Mihailovitch, Gen., 196
Milne, A. A., 163
Milne, Mrs, 84
Mirsky, D. N., 236f, 245
Molotov, 167, 208, 266
Monkhouse, Allan, 183, 260, 261
Monkhouse, Paddy, 170, 171, 197, 261
Montaigne, 124
Montreux, 269f
Moore, G. E., 127
Morgan, Charles, 184
Morning Post, 271-2
Morris, William, 61, 81
Mosley, Sir Oswald, 194
Muggeridge, Malcolm; passim; his souvenirs, 11; words his métier, 12; earliest writings, 13; early life, 16, 23f; early reading, 34; in Paris, 37; on prostitutes, 37; on free love, 38; visits The Colony, 40; contracts TB, 39; an unteachable child, 40; memories of Labour Party meetings, 47; elections, 52; on majority rule, 52; on BBC panels, 54; on the clergy, 55f; as cyclist, 57; on natural beauty, 58; on books, 59, 59-62; on Shakespeare, 59; on education, 62-64; in First World War, 66f; on Russian Revolution, 71f; in love with Dora, 73f; author of Three Flats, 158; Three Flats produced, 184; at Cambridge, 76f; on Public School system, 77f; on sycophancy, 76; friendship with Alec Vidler, 80; his agnosticism, 81; on death, 83f; brother Stanley, 83; works for

Muggeridge, Malcolm [*contd.*]
Lunn's Tours, 84f; friendships with Leonard Dobbs and Hugh Kingsmill, 85; teacher at Union Christian College, Travancore, 92f; on British Empire, 95f; on liner life, 97; on travel, 98-9; the reluctant sahib, 100-1; on examinations, 107; on education in India, 107f; on Indian nationalism, 109; meets Gandhi, 109-11; edits college magazine and produces college plays, 114; first journalism, 115; carrier of books, 124; ill at Alwaye, 125; with Vidler at Small Heath, 131; teacher in Birmingham, 132, 151; marriage to Kitty Dobbs, 140f; on marriage, 142; visits the Webbs, 145f, 205f; teacher in Egypt, 150f; at University of Cairo, 152f; birth of first son, 157-8; Egyptian politics, 159f; joins *Manchester Guardian*, 160; in Manchester, 165ff; on body antagonism, 175-6; book reviewing, 183-4; novelist, 186, 201, 225, 251; voyage to Russia, 210f; in Russia, 214ff; birth of second son, 260; leaves Russia, 265; goes to Montreux for W.T.A., 269; writes *Winter in Moscow*; in Second World War, 17

Muggeridge, Henry, father, 24f, 31-2, 33, 35f, 46f, 57f, 70f, 83-4, 92, 96, 115, 141, 184, 192, 194, 202, 203, 260

Muggeridge, Annie, mother, 31f, 46, 83-4, 115, 184, 240

Muggeridge (Mrs), Kitty, 11, 84, 88, 135, 138, 139, 140, 141f, 151f, 155, 157, 162, 163, 173, 176, 178, 180, 184, 186, 187, 200, 205ff, 210, 214, 219, 221, 225f, 231-2, 237, 239, 260, 269, 270, 273

Muggeridge, Stanley, 83

Murdoch, Iris, 35

Nahas Pasha, 160

Namier, Prof., 64, 127, 180

Nation, 50

Nehman, Russian censor, 223, 233, 263-4

Nehru, Pandit, 112

New Leader, 246

New Statesman, 13, 38, 50, 90, 112, 115, 154, 172, 174

New York Times, 254, 256, 258, 272

News Chronicle, 191, 228, 229, 230

Nineteenth Century and After, 191

Nixon, Richard M., 97

Northcliffe, Lord, 198

OGPU, 206, 213, 216, 220, 224, 234, 235, 246, 253, 261, 262

Orwell, George, 137, 175, 188, 235, 272-3

Osbourne, Lloyd, 186

Oumansky, 215, 217, 224, 233, 236, 244, 246, 248, 249, 250, 251, 254, 255, 257, 260, 263-4

Ovey, Sir Esmond, 253

Owen, Robert, 81

Patterson, Mr, 47

Pavlova, 97

Payne-Townshend, Charlotte (Mrs G. B. Shaw), 148

Peacock, Walter, 185

PEN Club, 138

Peron, Eva, 207

Pethick-Lawrence, Mr, 112

Picasso, 275

Playboy, 55

Podolski, Russian censor, 223, 228, 233, 255, 263

Potter, Richard, 139, 143, 145

Pravda, 216, 220, 228, 229

Prince Consort, the, 68

Prince of Wales, the, 79

Punch, 75, 163, 198

Pushkin, Alexander, 239

Quakers, 53f, 111

Quiller-Couch, Sir A., 79

Radek, 235, 275
Ransome, Arthur, 161f, 185
Ransome, Jenia, 162
Reed, John, 161
Rhondda, Lady, 185, 191
Roberts, Gen. (later F.M. Lord), 68
Roosevelt, Mrs Eleanor, 232
Roosevelt, Franklin D., 256
Rosat, Mme, 270
Rossinière, 269f
Rostov, 253, 256
Rousseau, J. J., 19, 34, 60
Ruskin, William, 60, 106, 111
Russell, Bertrand, 111, 148, 175, 187, 233
Russell Pasha, 153

Schlesinger, Arthur, 272
Schmidt, Herr, 221-2, 225, 227
Schopenhauer, 61, 72
Schweitzer, Albert, 111
Scott, C. P., 20, 132, 166, 167, 168, 174, 176, 189, 198f
Scott, E. T., 162, 166, 169, 177, 198f
Scott, John, 200, 201
Scrutton, Mr Justice, 191
Sedlac, Francis, 43f
Shaw, G. B., 50, 61, 72, 147, 184-5, 207, 243, 274, 275
Shaw, Nelly, 43, 45
Sheepscombe, 39-40
Silone, Ignazio, 20
Smuts, F.M. Jan, 97
Snow, Lord, 62, 188
Snowden, Philip, 49, 194f
Sokolnikov, 206, 208, 220
Sokolnikova, Mme, 207, 208, 220
Spence, Mrs, 199
Spencer, Herbert, 144
Spock, Dr, 12
Stage Society, 184
Stalin, Josef, 58, 138, 161, 217, 229, 234, 235, 240, 246, 255, 256, 258, 261, 262, 274, 275
Stanislavsky, 237, 252

Stead, W. T., 87
Stoneman, Bill, 274
Strachey, Lytton, 50, 79
Strang, William, 240
Straughan, Will, 40f, 62
Strong, Anna Louise, 254, 255
Swinburne, Algernon, 78

Tagore, Rabindranath, 232
Taine, H. A., 229, 258
Tass, 234
Taubkin, Dr, 225
Tawney, R. H., 61
Taylor, A. J. P., 180
Temple, Archbp. William, 56
Temps, Le, 230, 237
Thomas, J. H., 195f, 197
Time and Tide, 188, 191
Times, The, 97, 119, 132, 184, 188, 207, 256, 271
Times Literary Supplement, The, 64, 127, 155
Tolstoy, Leo, 34, 60, 111, 129, 266, 275
Tooth, Father, 79
Travancore, 104f
Trinity College, Kandy, 101, 102
Trivandrum, 118-20
Trotsky, Leon, 48, 149, 161, 254, 262, 275
Truman, Pres., 167

Union Christian College, 105f
Urch, Mr, 272

Varkey, Principal A. M., 126
Venketramen, Mr, 126-7
Vickers Co., 68
Vidal, Gore, 189
Vidler, Alec, 80, 131, 132
Voight, F. A., 190f, 257
Voroshilov, Marshal, 229
Vyshinsky, Andrey, 261

Wadsworth, A. P., 172
Wall Street Journal, 241
Wallace, Henry, 272

Webb, Beatrice and Sidney, 61, 72, 90, 137, 141, 143, 145f, 175, 195, 206f, 215, 272, 275
Wells, H. G., 38, 65, 138, 148, 234
Wesley, John, 54
Whitman, Walt, 44, 57, 60
Wicksteed, Mr, 214, 247, 275
Wilberforce, William, 81, 117
Wilde, Oscar, 86
Wilkinson, Louis and Nan, 86-7
Wilson, Harold, 21

Wilson, Woodrow, 71
Windmill Theatre, 57
Windsor, Duchess of, 207
Wittgenstein, 127
Wodehouse, P. G., 119, 163
Woolcott, Alexander, 242
Workers' Travel Association, 260, 270, 273

Zaglul Pasha, 160
Zaharov, Sir Basil, 68
Zeppelins, 69